ENVISIONING AFRICA

Racism and Imperialism in Conrad's *Heart of Darkness*

Peter Edgerly Firchow

THE UNIVERSITY PRESS OF KENTUCKY

Publication of this volume was made possible in part
by a grant from the National Endowment for the Humanities.

Scholarly publisher for the Commonwealth,
serving Bellarmine College, Berea College, Centre
College of Kentucky, Eastern Kentucky University,
The Filson Club Historical Society, Georgetown College,
Kentucky Historical Society, Kentucky State University,
Morehead State University, Murray State University,
Northern Kentucky University, Transylvania University,
University of Kentucky, University of Louisville,
and Western Kentucky University.

Editorial and Sales Offices: The University Press of Kentucky
663 South Limestone Street, Lexington, Kentucky 40508-4008

04 03 02 01 00   5 4 3 2 1

Frontispiece: Joseph Conrad at age twenty-six while vacationing in the then
Austrian province of Bohemia, seven years prior to voyaging to the Congo:
"Before the Congo I was just a mere animal." From Gérard Jean-Aubry,
Joseph Conrad: Life and Letters.

Library of Congress Cataloging-in-Publication Data

Firchow, Peter Edgerly, 1937-
    Envisioning Africa : racism and imperialism in Conrad's Heart of
darkness / Peter Edgerly Firchow.
    p.   cm.
    Includes bibliographical references and index.
    ISBN 0-8131-2128-0 (cloth : alk. paper)
    1. Conrad, Joseph, 1857-1924. Heart of darkness. 2. Conrad, Joseph,
1857-1924—Political and social views. 3. Political fiction, English—
History and criticism. 4. Imperialism in literature. 5. Africa—In literature. 6. Racism in literature. 7. Race in literature. I. Title.
PR6005.O4H47645   1999
823'.912—dc21   99-12673

In Memory of My Mother
Marta Loria Montenegro Firchow
"Life is real! Life is earnest!
And the grave is not its goal."

He was just a word for me. I did not see the man in the name any more than you do.
Joseph Conrad, *Heart of Darkness*

CONTENTS

Illustrations follow page 136

PREFACE

Except incidentally and by way of supporting my own argument, I have not in this book taken into explicit account the ample and varied critical history of Joseph Conrad's novel *Heart of Darkness*. I make no apologies for the omission because this task has already been admirably performed by Anthony Fothergill and Robert Burden. Nevertheless, though I have not systematically reviewed and summarized others' hypotheses and insights, I do wish to acknowledge the great help I have often received from them, even and especially when, after due consideration, I have reached quite different conclusions. As anyone engaged in the task of reevaluating *Heart of Darkness* after almost a century of intense and very diverse literary response must realize, the long journey up the immense and still growing river of print emerging from this novel is rather like Marlow's voyage up the Congo, often as productive of disorientation as it is of illumination. Like Marlow's too, it is a journey that in the end leads to a kind of heart of intellectual darkness, an aporial place where there are no final answers, filled though it is with echoing voices. Let me make clear, then, at the outset, that no final answers have been proposed here, for as Conrad knew so well, great literature (like life) asks questions that hint at answers rather than giving answers that preclude further questioning—and questing.

So much for what I have not done. On the more positive side, what I have attempted to do here is to place *Heart of Darkness* in a context that allows the controversial charges of its alleged racist and, to a lesser extent, imperialist bias to be examined in as objective a manner as possible. Establishing this context involves, among other things, attempting to discover what the words *racism* and *imperialism* mean—and meant—to Conrad, to his age, and to his contemporaneous and later critics, as well as to ourselves and to our very different world. Even more important, it involves keeping continuously in mind that *Heart of Darkness* is a work of art and not a sociological treatise, for it is only in relation to its aesthetic significance that we can establish what its real social and intellectual-historical meaning is. Our generation, all too given to confusing literature with sociology, must remember what an earlier generation might have benefitted from forgetting occasionally, namely that *Heart of Darkness* is, as R.C. Churchill put it, "perhaps the finest short novel in the language" (980).

An effective way of assessing the importance of the aesthetic dimension in *Heart of Darkness* is to ask ourselves whether the novel would have had the same impact on our thinking about racism and imperialism in Africa if Conrad had framed his ideas and impressions on these subjects in the form of a discursive essay or a documentary report. Such essays and reports were written and did have a profound impact at the time, notably Roger Casement's 1903 consular report detailing atrocities committed by Leopold II's agents in the Congo and E.D. Morel's *Red Rubber,* which dramatically exposed the ruthless abuse of African labor in the lucrative rubber trade. Both of these works were instrumental in bringing about the transfer of jurisdiction of the Congo in 1908 from Leopold's absolute rule to that of the relatively more humane, parliamentary Belgian government. This transfer led to the eventual cessation of the most comprehensive and brutal "system" of exploitation practiced in Africa at that time.

Even though Conrad's *Heart of Darkness* failed to have anything like the same kind of impact in practical terms, today it is still read and remembered whereas Casement's and Morel's works are forgotten. It is this crucial fact of the enduring aesthetic power of Conrad's novel that we must bear in mind when dealing with its other, more topical aspects, such as its supposed racism or imperialism. It is, after all, not primarily because of its concern with racism and imperialism but because of its great aesthetic power that it remains, a century after it was first published in 1899, one of the chief focal points of critical controversy and debate in the fields of literary theory and literary criticism, as well as in cultural anthropology. For if it is true, as the poet W.H. Auden once remarked, that "poetry makes nothing happen" (nothing, that is, in the so-called real worlds of politics and money), then it is also true, as Auden went on to say, that the poet (and only the poet) is able to "make a vineyard of the curse," is able to transform what was once an inner wasteland into a land of spiritual health, is able "in the deserts of the heart"—even in the harsh interior geography of the *Heart of Darkness*—to "let the healing fountain start."

I have called my book *Envisioning Africa*. Though the term *envisioning* used in this context may be surprising to some readers, it conveys, better than any other word I can think of, the fusion of simultaneously "seeing" things in reality and "seeing" them with the inward eye of the imagination. In this way it encapsulates the essentially double mission I have undertaken here, namely to do justice to the political and social significance of *Heart of Darkness* while at the same time doing justice to its aesthetic power. Such dual justice can only be rendered, I am convinced, in the form of a single, integrated justice; that is, the one task cannot be isolated from the other. They must be carried out together or not at all.

Envisioning also has a close connection with that method of analyzing literature which over the last thirty years has become familiar to students of literary theory and comparative literature as "imagology" or "image studies." Put simply, imagology is, as the name implies, the study of the ways in which national, ethnic, or racial images (stereotypes) are presented, transmitted, and perceived in literary contexts. Though this kind of study of literary texts has its roots in nineteenth-century positivism, its consciously theoretical underpinnings are relatively recent. The most notable exponent of the method is the Belgian comparatist Hugo Dyserinck, whose principal work, *Komparatistik: Eine Einführung* [Comparative Literature: An Introduction], has unfortunately not yet been translated into English.

To be sure, racial, national, and ethnic identity is not the only collective identity in which all of us participate, but for many of us living on the cusp of the twenty-first century it is, or has become, the most important such identity. Why this should be so is not entirely clear even to those who have made it their business to find out, usually formulating their (often less than wholly adequate) responses in a mixture of anthropological, sociological, and psychological jargon.[1] Although the rather primitive studies of national character that flourished in the late nineteenth and early twentieth centuries have by now largely vanished, supposedly more sophisticated ones employing techniques of ethno-psychology or social psychology, or both, are still being produced.[2] More common, however, and generally speaking intellectually more respectable, are studies focusing on national stereotypes rather than on national character, where the issue of a relation to a hypothesized social or biological reality is either avoided or explicitly denied. Menno Spiering, for example, insists bluntly on the "obvious" truth that "national identity is no ontological category, but a form of cultural production" (11).

Whatever side we take, the issues of national identity and national stereotyping are relevant and important to those of us who inhabit (either temporarily or more or less permanently) literary academia, grouped as we are in departments or faculties traditionally defined along strictly racial or national lines (e.g., English Literature, African American Studies, etc.). So, without presuming to provide a definitive answer to any of these overwhelming questions, we can see that canonical or would-be canonical literature, as well as the organized study of such literature in schools and universities, has played and continues to play a significant, if not always conscious, role in helping to shape and alter conceptions of racial, ethnic, and national identity (and, along with it, other types of collective identity). In other words, the presence of racial, national, or ethnic stereotypes in the literary products of high culture has helped to make us more aware of our own imagined collective national identities (or what is usually called our autoimage) as well as of the supposed national identities of other groups (or heteroimages).[3]

Nowadays this process is generally viewed negatively. That is, racial, ethnic, or national stereotypes—whether found in or outside of literary contexts—are invariably thought of as symptoms of prejudice or even of outright racism.[4] But even a cursory examination of actual literary texts reveals that racial, ethnic, or national outsiders have not always been presented unsympathetically. In fact, as Edith Hall has argued recently, there is a very old tradition of doing precisely the opposite, with "barbarian" characters in Greek tragedy, especially women—Hall cites Cassandra and Polyxena among others—being deliberately given "Hellenic" virtues in measures equaling or even exceeding those of comparable Greek characters, apparently in much the same way (and for similar reasons) that Tacitus endows his Germans in Germania with more than Roman courage and honor (211–12).[5] The intention here seems to be to establish a stereotype of "noble savagery" with which Greek or Roman "degeneracy" can be implicitly compared and censured. A further and more immediately relevant point is that national stereotypes, even when they involve depictions of rival and normally hated or despised nations or ethnic groups, need not necessarily be unfavorable. Nevertheless, they remain stereotypes.

This is all the more true, and more usual as well, when the stereotypes are supposedly reflections of one's own nationality. Then they tend to be almost uniformly favorable, though they are often accompanied by a kind of negative double. Among recent critics there even seems to be general agreement that positive or negative stereotypes almost never exist in isolation, so that, for example, in the foregoing example of positive "barbarian" stereotypes there is implicit a negative stereotype, which has been temporarily reversed for ironic effect. Such accompanying or implicit negative stereotypes are sometimes referred to as counteridentities, but more generally the concept of an interconnected positive/negative stereotype is subsumed under the general opposition of autoimage/heteroimage.[6] There are obvious links here to the currently popular psychosociological notion of the "Other," links that vividly suggest how different types of approaches to literature may in fact be pursuing quite similar ends.

The word *imagology* refers to the work on national images carried out by the so-called French school of comparative literature, ranging from Ferdinand Baldensperger in the early years of this century to Jean-Marie Carré and Marius-François Guyard in the forties and fifties, but it also implicitly evokes the once plentiful but now largely discredited *Bild* (German for image) studies dating from roughly the same period as Baldensperger's principal work.[7] Contemporary institutional imagology, however, has consciously and sometimes strenuously sought to distance itself from both of these strains of its ancestry, but especially the latter, chiefly because it views them as more or less deeply implicated in the very stereotypes they supposedly set out to examine. This is not to say, however, that all contemporary work along imagological lines is indebted to or even aware of Dyserinck's theoretical treatment of the subject. Edward Said's well-known *Orientalism,* for instance, appears to be wholly oblivious of any specifically imagological dimension but is nevertheless reckoned by some imagologists as a valid contribution to their discipline (Spiering 16).

For much of its early existence—from, say, the fifties into the early eighties—imagology languished under a debilitating critical cloud generated by the great comparatist René Wellek's spirited attack on the imagological practice of Carré and Guyard: he charged that it was wholly "extrinsic" to the study of literature. Dyserinck's initial theoretical efforts were primarily directed to dispelling that cloud, but even so it was not until the seventies and eighties, with the gradual demise of the New Criticism, that imagology managed to achieve a modicum of disciplinary respectability. Aside from Dyserinck's original home base at Aachen, there is now another imagological center at the University of Amsterdam, one that even publishes its own journal, *European Studies,* under the editorship of Joep Leerssen and others.

The idea of a national stereotype, it is important to remember, differs from that of national character in that the former makes no claim to anything more than a phenomenological reality. A stereotype, in other words, is simply a mental *image* that an ethnic or national group has of itself or of another equivalent group. There is a clear and generally acknowledged link between this conception of stereotypes and the idea of actual prejudice as practiced along racial or national lines; indeed, a strong element of imagological analysis is its conscious commitment to exposing the presence of such prejudice in literary contexts and of thereby enhancing mutual understanding among national and ethnic groups. This does not normally mean, however, that imagology represents an institutional effort to "cleanse" literature of national or ethnic stereotypes or to prevent their recurrence in future literary production; that is to say, on the whole there is no overt or programmatic ideological dimension to imagology. Its aim usually is the rather more modest and disinterested one of situating stereotypes in their appropriate historical context, without necessarily wagging one's raised index finger at supposedly offending authors.

Some imagological studies, to be sure, deviate considerably from the aforesaid norm. Edward Said's *Orientalism* makes no bones about its intention to expose a supposedly monolithic Western "false consciousness" about an "Orient" that is variously defined (or, more accurately, left undefined) as the Near East (primarily the Arabs) or the Near East plus India or the Near East plus all of Asia. Whatever else it may be, Said's book is certainly not a dispassionate examination of the supposedly concerted development by a group of influential orientalists, mostly travelers and scholars, of perverse Western images of Near Eastern or Asian populations; it is rather an attempt by an Arab-American partisan to trace the origins of an attitude that has shaped the political policy of Western states toward an area sometimes known as the Orient, along with an impassioned plea that this attitude be revised or abandoned. If imagology is in fact defined as the study of national stereotypes in literary contexts, it is difficult to see how the almost wholly political emphasis of *Orientalism* can be made to fit that definition. Stimulating, challenging, even on occasion outrageous—undoubtedly, it is all those things; but imagology? Probably not.[8]

In *Heart of Darkness* the stereotypical images are primarily those relating to Africa, both as a place and as a people—or, rather, several different places and different peoples, including a variety of distinct African ethnic groups (e.g., Nigerian and Guinean boatmen, Zanzibari soldiers, members of Congolese coastal and interior tribes, and East Africans from the Lake country). On the one hand, these images are collective in the sense that, despite a wide range of individual variation, there were shared areas of stereotypical response on the part of the Europeans who worked in or traveled through Central Africa during the closing years of the last century and who also bothered to record their impressions. Though I have relied in part on previous work by scholars such as Norman Sherry, Ian Watt, and Molly Mahood to get at this collective envisioning of Africa, I have supplemented their findings by working my own way through a large number of memoirs and biographies of Conrad's approximate contemporaries; for, oddly enough, there were very few works of fiction about the Congo in the 1890s. However, for reasons that probably have to do with the initially large proportion of non-Belgians in the employ of the Independent State of the Congo (1885–1908), its history is unusually rich in recollections and travelogues. As *The Cambridge History of Africa* notes, "the amount of publication by contemporaries is quite extraordinary, exceeding by far what was usual in other colonies" (Oliver and Sanderson 791).

This collective envisioning of Africa, however, provides only a supplementary context for the far more powerful and memorable envisioning by a particular artist who was writing at a particular moment in history and "seeing" what he saw through the lens of his own privately lived experience. But individual though Conrad was, he was also, as we all are, inescapably the product of his education and his time. In other words, though Conrad personally saw Africa and lived there for about six months in 1890, the Africa he described in *Heart of Darkness* must never be straightforwardly equated with what he actually saw and experienced there. It is something at once familiar and something quite different; it is a novel envisioning (and also a novel revisioning) of those experiences in the medium of fiction. And because Conrad was able to envision Africa so effectively, we share in that vision; we too have our part in envisioning and revisioning Africa.

I want to thank the University of Minnesota Graduate School and Office for Research for a small grant that allowed me to prepare the illustrations for publication, as well as Manfred Behler for allowing me to reprint in the preface parts of my essay "National Stereotypes in Literary Contexts," which first appeared in *L'imagine dell'altro e l'identità nazionale*. Special thanks go also to Sven Bäckman of the University of Lund in Sweden for inviting me, under the auspices of the Swedish

Fulbright Commission, to lecture on Conrad's *Heart of Darkness* in April 1996. At about the same time I also benefitted from the chance to discuss my ideas with lively audiences at the Universities of Växsjö, Sweden, and Greifswald, Germany. My able and committed students in the graduate seminar on Conrad's fiction at the University of Minnesota in the fall of 1996 provided me with a fresh sense of what Novalis meant when he said "my conviction gains infinitely the moment another soul will believe in it." (I also gained a new appreciation of the reasons why Conrad chose that visionary apothegm as the epigraph for *Lord Jim.*) Finally, I want to thank my wife, Evelyn, for being as always my shrewdest and, pending the reviews, my severest critic.

Introduction

Race, Ethnicity, Nationality, Empire

All is race; there is no other truth.
Benjamin Disraeli

Whatever happens we have got,
The Maxim gun and they have not.
Hilaire Belloc

"Your proposal delights me," Joseph Conrad wrote on the last day of 1898 to William Blackwood, the publisher of *Blackwood's,* who had asked Conrad a short time earlier to supply him with a suitable contribution for the one-thousandth issue of his magazine, scheduled to appear the following February. But delighted though he was, Conrad was not altogether sure whether the story he was working on so feverishly at the time was really the right thing for readers of that momentous millennial number of *Maga.* Not that he had any doubts about the quality of his workmanship; rather it was the subject of the story that seemed potentially troubling, because it dealt with "the criminality of inefficiency and pure selfishness when tackling the civilizing work in Africa" (Conrad, *Letters* 2:139–40).

Though at this stage Conrad had been working on the story for only about a month, he had already selected a title; it was to be called "The Heart of Darkness," but he hastened to reassure Blackwood that these ominous words did not mean that it would be "gloomy." It was the sort of story, rather, that probably would strike a familiar chord among readers of *Blackwood's,* for "the subject," Conrad went on to observe, "is of our time distinc[t]ly—though not topically treated." In other words, Conrad apparently thought of his story as resembling other stories that Blackwood and his readers would have encountered in the fiction, travelogues, and newspapers of the late nineties, though in its details not identifiable with any specific historical event. (This, along with the striking paucity of names for places and people, is probably what Conrad was referring to when he said that the story was not going to be "topically treated.") Comparing it with his earlier and only other story about Leopold's Congo, "An Outpost of Progress" (1897), Conrad emphasized that, though still telling a real story, "The Heart of Darkness" had a wider social and artistic scope. It was, as he put it, "less concentrated upon individuals." Presumably what he meant by making this last qualification was that his new story dealt generally or even symbolically with "the criminality of inefficiency" and not primarily with the fate of specific characters involved in such criminality, as the earlier story had done. In its final form, he told Blackwood, the new story would be less than twenty thousand words long (140).

Instead of a long short story, Conrad finally submitted to his publisher a short novel almost twice as long as his original estimate. But even despite the considerable increase in bulk and Conrad's sometime trepidation about its possible reception, "The Heart of Darkness" had no difficulty in meeting with William Blackwood's approval. In due course it was published in three installments, beginning with the one-thousandth anniversary issue of *Blackwood's* in February 1899. Nor was it greeted with adverse criticism on the part of the magazine's largely conservative and imperialistic readership, perhaps because (as later critics have maintained) this supposedly obtuse group did not altogether grasp Conrad's real intentions; alternatively, if we prefer to accept aesthetic reasons rather than political ones, it may have been received so well because the longer version of the story did after all "concentrate" on two of the most memorable, complex, and influential characters in modern British fiction, namely Marlow and Kurtz. For, uneventful and almost unremarked as their joint appearance was in the pages of *Blackwood's* a century ago, they have by now come to guard, like two ironic sentinels, the ominous ivory gates opening onto the largely gloomy heart of twentieth-century literature.

Not that this transformation took place rapidly. To be sure, it was not long before *Heart of Darkness*—as Conrad decided to call his story when he republished it in *Youth* (1902)—came to be recognized as the first and most incisive literary indictment of European imperialism in Africa. Even so it was not until sometime after the Second World War that the novel began slowly to turn into a "classic," that is, into an integral part of the canon of "required" texts that were and for the most part still are taught in introductory literary courses at colleges and universities throughout anglophone North America as well as, though to a much lesser extent, in Britain, the rest of Europe, and the Common-wealth states. The reasons for this are manifold; to cite only the most obvious ones, they have to do with (1) the phenomenal growth of so-called general education programs in the American university system and their need to identify and teach "great books"; (2) the vast popular-ity and respect enjoyed by Freud at this time, with the consequent criti-cal preference for works amenable to interpretation along Freudian lines; (3) the rise of the New Criticism and its programmatic fondness for densely symbolic, ironic, and ambiguous texts; and (4) the postwar boom in existentialist philosophy in Europe and the United States, which in-evitably generated sympathy for "authentic" sinner heroes like Kurtz. More recently and largely in connection with the massive onslaught of postcolonial, ideologically committed deconstruction of Western (and especially English) canonical literature, critical attention has focused chiefly on the novel's treatment of Africans and their exploitation by white imperial administrators.

Now, at the close of the twentieth century, for all of these as well as other, less intellectually respectable reasons (including its convenient brevity), *Heart of Darkness* occupies a unique place even among canoni-cal texts. Of what other literary work of equivalent antiquity can it be said that it is regularly discussed in the pages of the *New Yorker,* where two essays dealing with it have appeared during the last few years? De-spite (or more likely because of) being denounced as racist and imperial-ist by critics as distinguished as Chinua Achebe and Edward Said, *Heart of Darkness* has probably been the single most read and reprinted novel of high culture during the latter half of this century. As of this writing, it is readily available in a variety of paperback reprints as well as in at least two critical, casebook-format editions; it is the principal subject of at least three monographs in English (not counting this one) and two in Swedish (by Lagercrantz and Lindquist), as well as several separate col-lections of criticism.[1] It has become the chief, though not always the most amiable, meeting ground for opposing schools of thought among literary critics, cultural anthropologists, and historians dealing with the difficult and often tragic relations between Europeans and Africans at (and even since) the beginning of the twentieth century.

Because its alleged endorsement of racism has been the principal charge leveled against *Heart of Darkness* in the heated postcolonial critical debate of the last two decades—followed by the more attenuated charge of really supporting imperialism while seeming to subvert it—it seems advisable and even necessary to first clear the terminological ground before starting off on any discussion as to whether or how or to what degree *Heart of Darkness* is or is not racist and imperialist. This is all the more necessary and advisable because defining terms has not been the practice of all critics who have sought to come to grips with these profoundly controversial aspects of the story. Chinua Achebe, for example, simply assumes that his readers will understand what he means when he refers to *racism* both in the title and elsewhere in his justly celebrated essay "An Image of Africa: Racism in Joseph Conrad's *Heart of Darkness*" (1977), for otherwise he would surely have taken the trouble to tell them what he meant. But his meaning, and that of other critics of the novel, is by no means self-evident, either in terms of our time or in terms of Conrad's. It is after all important to know, as he along with virtually all other critics of Conrad's story apparently does not, that at the time Conrad was writing his novel, the word *racism* did not exist. The nonexistence of the word does not mean, of course, that the phenomenon itself did not exist; it unquestionably did. But it does mean that people then—even specialized and highly trained people in fields like sociology and anthropology—were accustomed to think very differently about the subject of race than we do at the end of the twentieth century. "We," for example—or the specialized and highly trained professional equivalents of the sociologists and anthropologists of a hundred years earlier—are convinced that such a phenomenon as race does not exist in any biologically valid sense. More on this later.

One reason the word did not exist when Conrad was writing his story is that thinking in terms of race ("race-thinking," as Hannah Arendt calls it in *The Origins of Totalitarianism*) was so widespread and so "normal" in developed countries like England during the late Victorian period that a word like *racism,* which suggests a negative view of thinking about race, was simply not needed and hence not thought of. The first word with these negative connotations is *racialism,* listed in the 1987 Supplement to the *Oxford English Dictionary* as occurring for the first time in 1907; it is defined as the "belief in the superiority of a particular race leading to prejudice and antagonism towards people of other races, esp. those in close proximity who may be felt as a threat to one's cultural and racial integrity or economic well-being."[2] (The first use of "racism" in this sense, according to the same source, does not occur in English until 1936, twelve years after Conrad's death.) Suggestively, the definition of *racialism* given by the *OED* Supplement—particularly the latter part of the definition—is obviously designed to fit encounters among differing racial groups in Western countries, such as Nazi Germany or

Fascist Italy, or the interracial conflicts in Britain in the post–World War II period (as the reference to "economic well-being" suggests), and in fact those are the sources of most of the supporting examples. This definition, however, would certainly not have satisfactorily described the "racist" attitudes toward Africans on the part of the very small group of Europeans in the Congo Free State during the 1880s and 1890s (including Conrad), since on the whole they neither felt their culture threatened nor (with a very few exceptions like Tippo Tib, who in any case was usually held to be Arab rather than African) believed that African rivals could seriously or negatively affect their economic status.

Significant, too, is that this definition implicitly (and explicitly in the example cited for 1938) accepts Jews as belonging to a distinct race.[3] Here we encounter one of the most important differences between the "race-thinking" of Conrad's time and that of most of the intervening period, including our own. This difference is profoundly significant, both in itself and for its relevance to any discussion of possible racism in *Heart of Darkness*. In the late nineteenth century, the word *race* was thought not to refer primarily, as the original *Oxford English Dictionary* (1884–1928) puts it, to "one of the great divisions of mankind, having certain physical peculiarities in common." That sense of the word was indeed one of the possibilities and was made clear by the last of the supporting examples: "Blumenbach proposed to establish five races: 1st, the Caucasian; 2cd, the Mongolian; 3rd, the Ethiopian; 4th, the American; 5th, the Malay." Nowadays, with various terminological modifications/modernizations, that is the generally accepted primary sense of the word *race*. But in the *OED* it ranks only fourth, preceded by the following earlier and evidently more important definitions: (a) "A limited group of persons descended from a common ancestor; a house, family, kindred"; (b) "A tribe, nation, or people, regarded as of common stock": and (c) "A group of several tribes or peoples, forming a distinct ethnical stock." The last of these meanings is especially relevant here, for in the supporting examples reference is made to a "great Hellen [Hellenic] race" and to the "whole German race." These last senses of the word *race* are no longer current; by now they have been wholly replaced by terms like *nation* and *ethnic group,* but for Conrad and his contemporaries they constituted the first and foremost accepted meaning of *race* when referring to another ethnic or national group.[4]

In this earlier sense of the word, Conrad is undoubtedly a "racialist," for his fiction deals from the very outset with the complex interrelations, confrontations, and conflicts between and among representatives (often explicitly seen as *representatives*) of various national and ethnic (in the old sense of *racial*) groups. In his first novel, *Almayer's Folly* (1895), for example, which is set in what today is Indonesia, there are several characters of Dutch or mixed Dutch-Malay ancestry, an Englishman, and a Chinese, as well as several Moslem and non-Moslem Malays. Other stories and novels feature prominently Malay, Arab, African (normally seen as belonging to various distinct tribal groups), English, Scottish, Irish, Dutch, German, French, Belgian, Swedish, Spanish, Italian, Polish, Russian, South American (both creole and indigenous), and North American characters. These figures are not described in an ethnically or nationally unbiased manner.[5] To any careful reader of Conrad's fiction, it must soon become clear that, with certain notable exceptions, Conrad is consistently less well disposed toward German, Russian, Dutch, Belgian, Arab, North American, or Irish characters than he is toward English, Scottish, Malay, or French ones. Such relative (though not always identical) rankings of ethnic collectives were not unusual at this time; the multicolored map that Marlow sees and comments on in *Heart of Darkness* provides a good example of one. In Arthur Conan Doyle's 1913 story "The Poison Belt," a more elaborate as well as ominous scale is worked out whereby the survival of the fittest is described in terms of which ethnic or racial groups are most likely to die of the effects of a mysterious poison; African and Australian aborigines were hypothetically expected to succumb first, Indians would precede Persians, and then would follow Slavs and Teutons, the southern French, and the French from the North.[6] On a more ironic note, Hilaire Belloc, who was of half-French and half-English parentage, put forward in "The Three Races" (1907) a poetic version of the commonly accepted "scientific" division of Europe into three distinct "racial" groupings, usually ranked in the following order: first, the Germanic or Nordic; second, the Celtic or Alpine; and last, the Iberian or Mediterranean:

I

Behold, my child, the Nordic Man
And be as like him as you can.
His legs are long; his mind is slow;
His hair is lank and made of tow.

II

And here we have the Alpine Race.
Oh! What a broad and foolish face!

His skin is of a dirty yellow.
He is a most unpleasant fellow.

III

The most degraded of them all
Mediterranean we call.
His hair is crisp, and even curls,
And he is saucy with the girls. (127)

As the popular examples of Doyle and Belloc suggest, Conrad was
by no means alone in thinking in stereotypical ways about other national or ethnic groups, though it should be noted that Conrad's fiction
tended in this respect to be subtler and more balanced than that of most
other writers of the period.[7] (For example, the vile German captain in
Lord Jim is more than offset by the saintly German merchant, Stein, in
the same novel.) Given the many years—half a lifetime, practically—
that Conrad had spent wandering the world in ships or being stranded
for weeks in remote places in the Pacific, often sharing close quarters
with people from a wide variety of national and ethnic backgrounds, it
is not surprising that he should seek to reflect this multinational,
multiethnic experience in his work. But although Conrad is clearly a
special case, much the same can be said of other, rather more sedentary
writers who were roughly his contemporaries: Henry James wrote novels that are populated with a congeries of American, British, French, and
Italian characters. The same is true of E.M. Forster, whose novels can
be, have been, and probably should be read as a series of attempts to
break down the absurdities of "race-thinking" (or "ethnic"-thinking)
among the British middle class during the early years of this century.
Also, viewed from a larger, sociocultural perspective, the phenomenon
of the influx of a wide variety of foreigners into English fiction during
this period is closely linked not only to the vast expansion of the Empire
(of which more later), but also to the beginnings of the tourist industry.
Thomas Cook and Son began its immensely successful international travel
business in the 1860s with tours to Switzerland and Italy and a decade
later had extended its reach to Palestine, Egypt, and points East. In *Lord
Jim* Conrad describes a scene in an unnamed Eastern port where a group
of tourists is alarmed by a sudden outburst of loud laughter on the part
of one of the main characters. Never before had so many people of middle-
class origins and middle-class prejudice traveled to such distant places
for pleasure or instruction.

Ironically, race-thinking reached a peak in Britain at precisely the moment when large groups of people involved in the military services, colonial administration, the merchant navy, and tourism were encountering other races and ethnic groups in real life for the first time. Their reactions, as documented in the fiction, journalism, travel books, and memoirs of the period, often reflect a hardening rather than an abatement of prejudice, but even when they did result in increased tolerance, it was almost invariably in the context of continued race-thinking. E.M. Forster, for example, depicts with profound sympathy the psychological and emotional conflicts between Germans and English in *Howards End* (1910) and between the English, the Hindus, and the Moslems in *A Passage to India* (1924), but he never abandons his conviction that there are and should continue to be various differing national groups and identities. Race-thinking could be good, as it was in Forster's case, or it could be bad, as in some of Kipling's writing, but it still remained race-thinking.

Recently, several notable literary theoreticians and critics have attempted to probe the subject of race, newly armed with the tools of postcolonial and poststructuralist doctrine. In so doing, they have inevitably been confronted with the problem of definition. Some of these scholars, like Henry Louis Gates, have resolved that problem by maintaining that, from a strictly scientific point of view, there is no such thing as race, since all the so-called races (Blumenbach's five) are cross-fertile and can therefore be said to belong only to a single racial category, namely the *human* race (4).[8] In Gates's view, it is the fact that colonialist Europeans "privileged writing" that allowed them to feel superior when they first encountered Africans who had not as yet developed a system of writing. Racism, so this argument runs, is therefore purely a product of social acculturation, having little or no basis in perceived physical differences. Gates's argument bears some resemblance to another put forward a few years later by David Mason, who suggests that European racism arose during the first great age of world exploration during the Renaissance as a way for Europeans to explain to themselves their apparently universal military superiority (i.e., the superiority of European military technology rather than, as with Gates, communications technology). Like Gates, Mason points out that there is no scientific support for the concept of race, but he differs by largely endorsing the continued use of the term by contemporary sociologists "because social actors treat it as real and organize their lives and exclusionary practices by reference to it" (6–8).

This is not, however, a view shared by another distinguished theoretician, Tzvetan Todorov. In his contribution to the same discussion,

Todorov defines *racism* as "the name given to a type of behavior which consists in the display of contempt or aggressiveness toward other people on account of physical differences (other than those of sex) between them and oneself" ("'Race'" 370). Here physical differences do matter, though it should be evident after a moment's reflection that, taken literally, this particular definition (Todorov proudly notes that it does not employ the word *race*) would include as *racist* attitudes of superiority by young people toward old, or healthy people toward the ill or handicapped, or even tall people toward short. Robert Ross's definition suffers from the same problem, though it is more carefully formulated: "By racism, we mean those systems of thought in which group characteristics of human beings, of a non-somatic nature, are considered to be fixed by principles of descent and in which, in general, physical attributes (other than those of sex) are the main sign by which characteristics are attributed. In addition, almost by definition, the systems of thought entailed in this require that there is a hierarchy of the various races, and that those people in the lower ranks of that hierarchy are seriously disadvantaged, at least if the proponents of racist thought are able to impose their will on the society in which they live" (Ross 1). In this respect the UNESCO definition of race, as found in the 1987 edition of the *OED,* is only slightly more satisfactory: it interprets *race* to mean "a division of man, the members of which, though individually varying, are characterized as a group by certain inherited physical features as having a common origin." Similarly, Philip Cummings's definition of *racism* in the *Encyclopedia of Philosophy* contends that it consists of the "doctrine that one group of men is morally or mentally superior to another and that this superiority arises out of inherited biological differences." Like Gates, but less emphatically, Cummings rejects the idea that, scientifically speaking, different races of humans exist (*Encyclopedia of Philosophy* 59–60). The UNESCO and Cummings definitions, however, share the defect of Todorov's in that they would apply almost equally to genetic differences like height or weight, though at least in Cummings's case this is not true of age; and both err in a way that Todorov does not by failing to exclude inherited sex difference from their definitions.

What makes these and similar definitions so confusing and ambiguous is that they seem desperately bent on avoiding the obvious issues that ever since Blumenbach (and even earlier) have been fundamental to defining supposed racial differences, namely skin color, eye color, facial features, hair color and texture, and skull shape. In this respect Conrad himself is evidently prepared to speak more clearly and directly, when, very near the beginning of *Heart of Darkness*, he has Marlow say that "'the conquest of the earth, which mostly means the taking it away from those who have a different complexion or slightly flatter noses than ourselves, is not a pretty thing when you look into it too much'" (*HD* 10). Although it is clear from what he says that Marlow does not approve of the manner in which the earth has been conquered, it is equally clear that for him *race*—a word that he, like Todorov, does not use—has something at least to do with coloration and facial features, as, for that matter, it also does for Belloc when he differentiates among the supposed three "races" of Europe.

What is important to note in connection with *Heart of Darkness* about all three of these definitions of *race* and *racism* is that none of them would find Conrad guilty of racism. For nowhere in the novel does Conrad or any of his narrators, personified or otherwise, claim superiority on the part of Europeans on the grounds of alleged genetic or biological difference. The derogatory comments made by Marlow about Africans, for example, do not pertain primarily to their physical appearance. If he does tend to find African faces grotesque, his judgment is purely aesthetic and has nothing to do with their intelligence or moral status. His other negative reactions have to do rather with what he believes is the behavior of Africans: their wild dancing, their cannibalism, their ritual human sacrifice, their misapprehension of modern European technology, their belief in sorcery and idols. All of these traits belong to the category of culture rather than to race or ethnicity, and they are therefore not racist in the sense suggested by Todorov, the UNESCO, or Cummings.

There are, however, other contemporary discussions of race and ethnic difference, largely put forward by sociologists rather than literary theoreticians, which are less problematic and therefore provide more specific help in determining the nature and possible extent of Conrad's racism. Notably, Zygmunt Bauman has established a useful tripartite gradation of reactions to the perception of difference between ourselves and the ethnic or racial "Other." He calls the first stage of such a reaction *heterophobia* and defines it as "a phenomenon of unease, anxiety, discomfort and a sense of loss of control commonly (and normally in the sense of sanely) experienced when confronted by the unknown" (Cohen 194). This description pretty accurately captures Marlow's response to the jungle and its inhabitants as he travels up the Congo River from the Central Station (Kinshasa) to the Inner Station (Stanley Falls). The second stage Bauman terms *contestant enmity*, which he defines as "a form of antagonism and hatred generated by the social practices of identity-seeking and boundary-drawing" (Cohen 194–95), a description that fits Marlow's attitude toward the Belgian agents in the Congo (with the exception of Kurtz) but is not relevant to his attitude toward the various African tribal groups he encounters. Finally, the last stage is outright *racism*, "which differs from contestant enmity by not admitting any possibility for a certain group of human beings to become part of the rational order. . . . Racism demands territorial exclusion or (in the case of the Holocaust Jews) extermination" (Cohen 195). Here again, Marlow explicitly admits the possibility of black Africans becoming "part of the rational order" (i.e., of world civilization) (see chapter 5), and it is only Kurtz who, in an apparent moment of madness, proposes to "exterminate all the brutes." There is no evidence that his proposal is endorsed by Marlow or by the Narrator or by Conrad himself; on the contrary, Marlow's shock when he encounters the scrawled postscript shows how far removed he himself is from similar thoughts.

It should be clear by now that it is formidably difficult to provide a satisfactory definition for either *race* or *racism*—of the former the 1987 *OED* Supplement remarks that it is "often used imprecisely; even among anthropologists there is no generally accepted classification or terminology," an observation that, if true, leads one to wonder what can possibly be meant by "imprecisely" here—but still it is possible to conclude that, whatever racism may be, there are certainly varying degrees of it; furthermore, even the least tinge of it can lead to fatal contamination.[9] In view of all this difficulty, it is perhaps simplest and best to adopt Frank Reeves's suggestion of separating *racism* into three distinct categories that correspond roughly to Bauman's: weak racism, medium racism, and strong racism. Weak racism, in this conception, is the belief that races (however defined, including ethnic and national groups) do exist and that they help to account for social phenomena. Medium racism is identical with weak racism, except that added to it is the belief that some races are superior and others are inferior. Strong racism goes beyond medium racism to prescribe a course of action based on alleged racial superiority, such as the suppression or elimination of other "races" (12–14). Applying Reeves's categories to *Heart of Darkness*, one is led to conclude that the novel is no more than weakly racist with respect to its attitude toward Africans, for it recognizes their difference from Europeans as a separate race but does not suggest an essential superiority to them (it does, however, imply a temporary cultural superiority). With regard to the Belgians, though, the story seems to endorse a medium racist attitude: the British characters in it, to wit Marlow and his audience aboard the *Nellie*, are consistently viewed as superior in intelligence, ability, and honesty to their purely Belgian equivalents. This comparison on Conrad's part seems to have been quite deliberate, since the position of the Director of Companies is roughly equivalent to that of the "great man" in his Brussels sanctuary; that of the Accountant in the Thames estuary corresponds to the Accountant at the Outer Station; and even the Lawyer is later evoked by the Mephistophelean Brickmaker. The essential superiority of the British is also suggested in characters who possess less-well-defined associations with Britain, such as the Russian who speaks English and reads British books or Kurtz, who had a partly English mother and was educated in Britain. How strongly Marlow at least, if not Conrad, feels contemptuous of Belgians is apparent from his resentment against all of those inhabitants of Brussels who are "hurrying through the streets to filch a little money from each other, to devour their infamous cookery, to gulp their unwholesome beer, to dream their insignificant and silly dreams" (*HD* 70).

That racism along with imperialism should be peculiarly a phenomenon of the nineteenth century has struck a number of thinkers as more than coincidental. Whether this was in fact the case remains a matter of debate, but even scholars who place the beginnings of both phenomena at a considerably earlier date usually insist that there is a close link between racism and imperialism.[10] Both Gates and Mason, for example, argue that European racism arose during the first great period of European global expansion in the late fifteenth century when Europeans first began to encounter and subjugate large numbers of non-Europeans. But the connection between writing, racism, and imperialism posited by Gates, or that between military conquest, racism, and imperialism posited by Mason, is not as deep and compelling as that pointed out by Hannah Arendt in her by now classic study, *The Origins of Totalitarianism* (1951). There, while speaking of the second great military expansion of European powers during the latter half of the nineteenth century, she observes that "the fact that racism is the main ideological weapon of imperialistic politics is so obvious that it seems as though many students prefer to avoid the beaten track of truism" (160). In her view, the history of the modern world since about 1850 must be viewed as a struggle between two dominant, opposing ideologies, namely "the ideology which interprets history as an economic struggle of classes" and the ideology "that interprets history as a natural fight of races" (159). (Ideology is defined here as the conviction of possessing knowledge of the universally valid but hitherto hidden laws of history.) Inevitably, so Arendt argues, nineteenth-century imperialism enthusiastically embraced the ideology of racism and thereby forged a crucial link in the tragic chain of events that led eventually to totalitarianism and genocide. It was not an inevitable combination, however. In isolation, either one of these forces might have been kept under control, and the subsequent course of history would have been much different, as well as a good deal happier. It was only their conjunction that led to disaster.

"It is highly probable," Arendt concludes, "that the thinking in terms of race would have disappeared in due time together with other irresponsible opinions of the nineteenth century, if the 'scramble for Africa' and the new era of imperialism had not exposed Western humanity to new and shocking experiences" (183). Whether this hypothesis is true, or even "highly probable," or merely the product of nostalgic wishful thinking on the part of an intellectual with a tendency (understandable among intellectuals) to overrate the importance of ideas in shaping the course of history, is impossible to say. As another and perhaps more hard-nosed intellectual, W.H. Auden, remarked of a later critical historical juncture for the West (the Spanish Civil War), "History may say 'Alas,' / But cannot help or pardon."

Arendt's argument, suggestive and even cogent as it is in some respects, is of course not the only possible or reasonable way to analyze the role played by imperialism at the close of the last century. Recently, however, her argument has been taken up with renewed vigor and with a specific emphasis on *Heart of Darkness* by Sven Lindqvist, who claims that the racist/imperialist scramble for Africa was the prelude to, and the model for, the horrific genocides of our century. Lindqvist's contention, along with its relevance for *Heart of Darkness*, is examined in detail in the concluding chapter of this book, but for the moment it is enough to note that the link between racism and imperialism is still accepted today by at least one serious scholar. This is not to say that imperialism and racism are viewed as *invariably* or *inevitably* linked. As we have seen, even for Arendt they were separable; and bad as imperialism on the whole turns out to be in her book, unlike racism it is not utterly unredeemed. Arendt distinguishes clearly, for example, between British imperialism, which in her view was inspired by a "legend," and other rival European imperialisms, which were rooted in ideologies. "And while the legend of the British Empire," she says, hedging only a little at the outset, "has little to do with the realities of British imperialism, it forced or deluded into its services the best sons of England. For legends attract [force? delude?] the very best in our times, just as ideologies attract the average, and the whispered tales of gruesome secret powers behind the scenes attract the very worst" (209). (The reference to the "worst" here may be an allusion to Kurtz.) Elsewhere in her book she makes Leopold II, king of Belgium and the absolute sovereign of the Congo Free State, "responsible for the blackest pages in the history of Africa" (185 n). By favorably contrasting British imperialism in this way with other European imperialisms (and especially with Leopold's), Arendt is putting forward a claim that closely resembles the one made by Marlow at the beginning of *Heart of Darkness* when he draws a distinction between the British Empire's redemption through the "unselfish belief in an idea" and all the remaining imperial powers, past and present, who merely engage in "robbery with violence, aggravated murder on a great scale, and men going at it blind" (*HD* 10).

Conrad himself does not use the word *imperialism* in *Heart of Darkness*, not even when Marlow glances at the map of Africa "marked with all the colours of a rainbow" (*HD* 13)—a political rainbow, which shone forth as the direct result of the most infamous imperialist scramble for territory and prestige in history. The closest he comes is the word *colonists,* which he uses by way of contrast with the word *conquerors* when referring to the Roman subjugation of Britain: "They were no *colonists,* their administration was merely a squeeze, and nothing more, I suspect. They were *conquerors,* and for that you want only brute force" (*HD* 10, my italics). Here "colonists" is clearly meant to be thought of favorably and "conquerors" unfavorably. Ironically, of course, the very word *colonist* is of Roman derivation, pointing directly to the fact that Britain was, as the relevant entry in the *OED* observes, divided into nine *coloniae,* of which London was one—"the biggest, and the greatest, town on earth," according to some of the first words in the novel (*HD* 7). It is difficult to tell here whether Conrad was himself aware of this irony, though his view of the Roman occupation of Britain is in some ways badly skewed (see chapter 4). Nevertheless, in general Avrom Fleishman is no doubt right when he observes that Conrad is anticipating the distinction made a few years later in J.A. Hobson's *Imperialism* (1902) "between 'colonialism,' or emigration to relatively unpopulated areas and the establishment of a culture attempting to reproduce that of the home country (e.g. Australia, New Zealand, Canada), and 'imperialism,' in which the settlers form a ruling caste among an overwhelmingly native population" (98). Hobson himself, who consciously avoids using the word in a negative sense, was skeptical about being able to determine the precise meaning of *imperialism* and any related terms. "A certain broad consistency in its relations to other kindred terms," he writes in the introductory chapter of his celebrated work, "is the nearest approach to definition which such a term as Imperialism admits. Nationalism, internationalism, colonialism, are equally elusive, equally shifty, and the changeful overlapping of all four demands the closest vigilance of students of modern politics" (3).[11]

The word *colonialism* is not listed in the original *OED*; and the 1987 Supplement, which does contain an entry for it, provides no definition that even remotely approximates Fleishman's or Hobson's. Instead, it defines the word as "now freq. used in the derogatory sense of an alleged policy of exploitation of backward or weak peoples by a large power." *Imperialism,* on the other hand, is defined in the original *OED* in quite different terms, as either (1) "an imperial system of government; the rule of an emperor, esp. when despotic or arbitrary"—a definition that, unlike the one for *colonialism,* omits any necessity for a foreign presence and focuses entirely on a "system of government," which, logically, cannot be "systematic" if it is at the same time also "arbitrary"; or (2) as "the principle or spirit of empire; advocacy of what are held to be imperial interests. In recent British politics, the principle or policy (1) of seeking, or at least not refusing, an extension of the British Empire in directions where trading interests and investments require the protection of the flag; and (2) of so uniting the different parts of the Empire having separate governments, as to secure that for certain purposes, such as warlike defence, internal commerce, copyright, and postal communication, they shall be practically a single state." The second of these two definitions consists practically by itself of a little essay in British propaganda, omitting all reference to subject peoples and describing the whole phenomenon not only in lofty abstractions but also entirely from the point of view of the rulers. In this respect it differs radically from the definition of *colonialism.* It also fails to account for at least one of the meanings cited among the supporting examples, where the *Daily Chronicle* is quoted as saying in 1898 (the year when Conrad began writing his story) that imperialism was "that odious system of bluster and swagger and might on which Lord Beaconsfield [Disraeli] and his colleagues bestowed the tawdry nickname of Imperialism." This, in fact, is a meaning that comes far closer to Conrad's description of imperialist activities in *Heart of Darkness* than does the official one provided by the *OED.*

More recently, in the entry "Imperialism/Nationalism" written by Seamus Deane for the well-known handbook *Critical Terms for Literary*

Study, Conrad is unambiguously described as revealing "the criminal nature of imperialism," though at the same time Deane cites and agrees with Edward Said's verdict that Conrad simultaneously "subverts *and* reproduces imperialism" (355–56). Deane also makes a distinction between imperialism and colonialism that differs profoundly from Conrad's or Hobson's. "As a system," Deane argues, "imperialism is distinct from colonialism by virtue of its more coherent organizational form and its more fully articulated characterization of itself as a missionary project to the world at large" (354). Imperialism, in other words, is nothing more than a coherently organized and ideologically committed colonialism. This is surely not a distinction that helps us understand Conrad's (or at least Marlow's) preference for colonists over conquerors, nor does it much clarify how Conrad might be reproducing imperialism's missionary project while at the same time subverting it. Rather, Conrad seems to be claiming that there are two kinds of imperialism: one is British and good; another is non-British and, to varying degrees, not good. Puzzling too is Deane's insistence that imperialism is, with the exception of the Japanese and Ottoman Empires, "a peculiarly Western form of domination," reaching back from the present day into the sixteenth century. He thus denies (unlike Conrad again) the relevance of the concept of imperialism to ancient empires such as the Roman, the Alexandrian, or even the Persian.[12] Perhaps this is because their "projects" were not missionary or, if they were missionary, then not to the "world at large" (the world was smaller then). Completely unexplained, however, is the omission (no pun intended) of empires with recognizable "missions" like those of China, which claimed to be the center of the civilized world; the India of the Moghuls, which was quite literally motivated by a mission of spreading Islam; and even the Aztec Empire, which was supremely confident that the gods were on its side. All of these empires extended into, and in some cases beyond, the sixteenth century. The fact that Deane fails to acknowledge them at all suggests that he is probably involved in some sort of missionary project of his own.

In conclusion, then, can we say that we have found an adequate terminology that can be used to determine whether Conrad or his narrators in *Heart of Darkness* are racist and imperialist? The answer, as so often in such situations, is both yes and no. Yes, if we can agree on a single definition that is both internally coherent and externally reflective of what we think are the facts. None of the previous definitions for either *racism* or *imperialism* satisfies those requirements, though some (like Reeves's) come closer than others. But even the least unsatisfactory definitions of *racism* are dependent on a prior, usually equally unsatis-factory, definition of *race* (except for Todorov's, which is not very satis-factory to begin with). The same is true, though to a lesser degree, of *imperialism,* as is evident in the case of Deane. At any rate, however, critics of *Heart of Darkness* should keep in mind that for Conrad all of these words (and where there were as yet no words, the corresponding concepts) did not convey the same meaning(s) to him as they do to us. As far as he was concerned, *race* included *ethnicity* and *nationality*; it was an inclusive word, with none or only a very few of the ominous connotations it was later to assume for a generation living after the Holocaust. And we should bear in mind as well that *imperialism* was not a universal bogeyman but could be both good and bad, depending on what nation was practicing it.

What else can a responsible person do when confronted with am-biguous and unsatisfactory answers like these to questions about a ma-jor canonical text of the late nineteenth century? Not a great deal, except to try to be as continuously aware and skeptical as possible of the many pitfalls of definition (and motivation) we face whenever such words are encountered. Though clarity of definition must be the starting point of all critical discussion, it will always be more a Weberian ideal to be striven for than something we can hope to meet with in practice. At a minimum, the critic must extend to the reader the elementary courtesy of identifying himself or herself and revealing the particular literary theo-retical flag she or he is flying under.

1

ENVISIONING AFRICA

True symbolism is where the particular represents the more general, not as a dream or a shadow, but as a living momentary revelation of the Inscrutable.

Goethe, *Maxims*

An historian of hearts is not an historian of emotions, yet he penetrates further, restrained as he may be, since his aim is to reach the very fount of laughter and tears.

Conrad, "A Familiar Preface"

Joseph Conrad's African experience was of relatively short duration. Not counting his somewhat muddled preparations in London and Brussels or the slow sea journey to and from the Congo Free State, it actually lasted a little less than six months, from mid-June to early December 1890.[1] Psychologically and emotionally it must have seemed a great deal longer, what with the disappointment of not being able to assume command of the small steamer that had been promised him by company officials back in Belgium; the increasing discomfort of illness; and the unavoidable necessity of having to associate uninterruptedly, often in a subordinate capacity, with people whose behavior and moral outlook he soon came to despise. It is perhaps partly for this reason that late in 1898, nearly ten years later, when he suddenly and unexpectedly stopped work on two other projects—the narratives that would eventually turn into *Lord Jim* and *The Rescue*—in order to describe his African experience in *Heart of Darkness*, he not only lengthened the experience by about a third to some eight months but even arranged to have it climax in a voyage to a distant, timeless past before the beginnings of chronology. Paradoxically, once there, his fictional alter ego Marlow encounters a man whose name (Kurtz) signifies brevity itself and whose memory, despite an acquaintance of no more than a few days, remains deep and indelible.

It is Marlow's search for this elusive figure—and the meaning of both search and figure—that forms the plot of *Heart of Darkness*, as well as the allegedly dark center of the tale that Marlow tells his friends aboard the yawl *Nellie* while awaiting the turn of the tide in the Thames estuary. That this search is also and inevitably a search for himself—even for *the* self—is something that the teller of the tale knows full well and that it does not take most readers long to grasp. It is a tale notoriously and heavily weighted with symbolism, for as Conrad once put it ironically in a letter to Elsie Hueffer—the wife of his sometime friend and collaborator, Ford Madox Ford—"What I distinctly admit is the fault of having made Kurtz too symbolic or rather symbolic at all" (*Letters* 3:211). Much later, in another letter to a different correspondent, Conrad explained what he had meant by "too symbolic": "A work of art is very seldom limited to one exclusive meaning and not necessarily tending to a definite conclusion. And this for the reason that the nearer it approaches art, the more it acquires a symbolic character" (*HD* 231). It is not coincidental, therefore, that the narrator of the frame story explains to his readers that Marlow's tales differ from those of other mariners in that, among other things, they consist of "inconclusive experiences." They differ in this respect because they belong to the realm of art, a realm where for Conrad there were no final answers but where it was nevertheless paradoxically necessary to keep looking for such answers.

One of the most important of these uncertain certainties, these questioning quests—both in the story itself and in the telling of that story—is what it means to be fully human. As the Dwarf remarks in the epigraph from Grimm's *Fairy Tales* that Conrad selected when he republished *Heart of Darkness* in book form, "'No; something human is dearer to me than the wealth of all the world.'" For Marlow the most immediate symbolic concretization of the answer to the urgent and profound question of what it means to be human is Kurtz, "the man in the name"—a man whose name suggests "shortness" to Marlow and who therefore in this sense at least is rather like a dwarf, though he strikes Marlow later as being nearly seven feet tall. Stripped to its essentials, Kurtz's story is also rather like a fairy tale about someone who gets lost in a dark forest and then falls victim to the black magic of powerful "sorcerers" whose spell can be broken only by a "pure," rescuing knight like Marlow. Significantly, the spell is, in fact, only dissipated once the riverboat has escaped the dark magical heart of the forest. Not until then does Kurtz, in a final moment of sudden self-illumination, realize the "horror" of what he has become. Only then is he permitted to die.[2]

Not surprisingly, what Marlow finds—or, rather, what *they* find, since there are two Marlows here, the younger actor and the older reflecter (and reflector)—is not a single answer but rather several answers, not all of them complementary or even uncontradictory. That is, he finds, as it were, several Kurtzes. It is these sometimes conflicting answers, these multifaceted Kurtzes, along with the sometimes conflicting Marlows who find those inconclusive answers (or fail to), that form the chief focal points of interest for this book. Inevitably those answers in turn provoke further questions to which yet more (tentative) answers are provided. That is, alas, how criticism—in this respect like Conrad's conception of fiction—works.

Heart of Darkness implies that a fair answer to such questions is possible only in a context where our supposedly distinctively "human" qualities are put to the severest possible test, preferably in conditions of great physical hardship and the most extreme isolation. For Conrad, here as virtually everywhere else in his fiction, it is axiomatic that the nature of human nature is discoverable only under duress. For him the study of the human psyche is and must always be psychopathology. To undertake such a study, the experimenter/explorer must therefore be prepared to subject herself or himself (or his or her fictional alter egos) to the most radical vivisection. That is why *Heart of Darkness* is set in a place that, along with the Arctic and Antarctic regions, was for Europeans in the mid-to-late nineteenth century the last of the great geographical unknowns.[3] The frantic search for the sources of the Nile was not occasioned merely by a scramble for loot and imperialistic prestige—it was that, of course—but at least for some of the best literary minds of the period, including Conrad's, it also represented more powerfully than anything else in their experience the quest for a "final" symbolic answer to the question of who we are. Thus, not only for Conrad but also for contemporaneous European writers as different as Gustave Flaubert and H. Rider Haggard, envisioning Africa in fiction became an analogue for the exploration of the hidden, dark regions of their inner selves. The visions they produced often—perhaps even invariably—turned into misconceptions and misrepresentations of Africa and Africans, as the Nigerian novelist and critic Chinua Achebe, among others, has powerfully argued.

Nonetheless, valid as this criticism may be from a (admittedly anachronistic) historical or sociological point of view, it needs to be remembered that, like Conrad, these writers were working in the medium of fiction, not in the supposedly more factual (or at least fact-oriented) medium of history or sociology. With the possible exception of a relatively small number of misguided and marginalized aesthetes, present-day readers are not likely to resort primarily to Conrad's story if they feel the need or desire to inform themselves about the condition of Africa either now or during the late nineteenth century; or, if they do refer to it for that purpose, then it is only to determine how Conrad's vision differs from their own by using *Heart of Darkness* as a stepping-stone to works of history or sociology or even criticism, such as Achebe's. It is in this sense that so much of the current critical reception of Conrad's story is misleading and even wrongheaded, producing further misconceptions rather than new perceptions. Conrad's main purpose in *Heart of Darkness* is to convey a *vision* of Africa rather than to provide a detailed description of its geography, socioeconomic conditions, and inhabitants; that *vision* must therefore be responded to primarily imaginatively and evaluated chiefly in aesthetic rather than sociological or ideological terms. Not that the latter are irrelevant: a *vision*, after all, is usually made up of elements that have some profoundly significant relation to reality. They help us, as the Russian Harlequin admiringly remarks of Kurtz, to "see things," including economic, social, and political things, even if only secondarily. Or, to quote the celebrated words of Conrad's own artistic manifesto, the preface to the *Nigger of the 'Narcissus,'* written not long before (1897): "My task which I am trying to achieve is, by the power of the written word, to make you hear, to make you feel—it is, before all, to make you *see*!" (147).

In reading Conrad's *Heart of Darkness*, then, we are not seeking to determine what the "real" Africa was like, assuming that such a determination is or was ever possible; instead, we want to know how (and why) Conrad *envisioned* Africa as he did, and what that *vision* meant to him and to his readers. It is, in other words Conrad's "image"—a word also used by Chinua Achebe—of Africa that is the object of discussion here, an image that, as the word itself suggests, was produced ultimately by Conrad's imagination. For some time already, such images (or literary stereotypes as they are more usually called) have been subjected to close literary analysis, though Achebe and other postcolonial critics of Conrad seem to have paid little attention to these precedents. But before taking up the question of how imagology (as the systematic study of literary stereotypes is called) specifically relates to *Heart of Darkness*, it needs to be stressed that in the final analysis we can expect to find answers to our questions about *Heart of Darkness*—including questions about its expression of racism or imperialism—only in the geography of Conrad's imagination and in the experiences that helped to shape it.

The most important of those experiences was the half-year or so that Conrad spent in Leopold II's *L'Etat Indépendant du Congo* or "Congo Free State," as English-speakers, following Stanley's example, tended to call it. Crucial as this experience was, however, it was not the only constituent element in establishing Conrad's imaginary Africa. Among other important differences between Conrad's actual experience and his rendering of that experience in *Heart of Darkness* is the striking figure of Kurtz. That the climax of the story should be situated in this emaciated would-be demigod with a head as white and shiny as ivory itself is almost, as Conrad put it, "too symbolical." In this respect the plot of *Heart of Darkness* seems nearly as improbable as that of H. Rider Haggard's novel *She*, which culminates in the heart of Africa with the discovery of an ageless white female god. The racial (and even racist) aspects of both of these mysterious figures are integral to our understanding of both Conrad's and Haggard's fictions, though in the former case at least we must always bear in mind the ironic as well as the symbolic dimensions of his "envisioning." That the object of Marlow's obsessive quest in *Heart of Darkness* should be a white man has struck Achebe, and no doubt many other contemporary readers, as trivial and even offensive. After all, sub-Saharan Africa is and was populated chiefly by black Africans. Again, valid as this criticism is from the point of view of population statistics, it is not valid from the point of view of the imagination of a European artist like Conrad. Aside from the wisdom of writing about what one knows—that is, in Conrad's case, chiefly Europeans and how they perceive and relate to non-Europeans—rather than about what one does not know (again in Conrad's case, Africans and their perceptions or conceptions of Europeans), finding a *white* man (or, quite literally, a *blank*) at the center of what was then generally envisioned as the center of the *dark* continent was and continues to be one of the most devastating ironies of the story.

That is not to say that Conrad's actual experience of Africa and Africans did not contribute powerfully to the creation—to the *envisioning*—of this story. The fact that Conrad lived for a time in the Congo—and nearly died there—gives *Heart of Darkness* an authenticity that undoubtedly has contributed to its enduring power and appeal. It also complicates matters. Is Marlow merely a mouthpiece for Conrad? A convenient mannikin on which or whom to hang his own experience(s)? Or is he a "persona"—a real though possibly simplified aspect of Conrad's own personality from which the author nevertheless remains (or remains partially) distanced? Or perhaps a mere mask to hide behind? And why bother to have a Marlow at all? Why not tell the story from an omniscient point of view or from that of an only vaguely realized or "dramatized" narrator?[4] Again, the answers to these questions are and will be to some degree inconclusive, yet they must be asked, for on them depends the larger answer to who "we" are, and what our essential identity is. And they must be asked primarily in a way that recognizes the status of *Heart of Darkness* as primarily an aesthetic construct, as a work of the imagination.

In "An Image of Africa: Racism in Conrad's *Heart of Darkness*," Chinua Achebe explicitly examines, as his title makes clear, the *image* of (black, sub-Saharan) Africa that Conrad depicts in his novel. In Achebe's view that image is almost entirely negative, a portrait of a dark, irrational, timeless place populated by a dehumanized race of savages who lack language and who are hungry for human flesh. It is this image of Africa that he believes *Heart of Darkness* has perpetuated among several generations of readers, though he emphatically does not claim that it is uniquely the product of Conrad's individual imagination. On the contrary, the extraordinary power it has exercised and continues to exercise on its primarily Eurocentric audience resides in its confirmation of an already existing image or stereotype of Africa as the "Other," as the imagined (and imaginary) composite of all those things that white Eurocentrics most fear and abominate, especially in themselves—of the "horror," in short. This image of Africa "was and is," so Achebe tells us, "the dominant image of Africa in the Western imagination and Conrad merely brought the peculiar gifts of his own mind to bear on it" (*HD* 261). Whether we agree with this assertion or not, it is clear that Achebe does not mean to imply that Conrad was actually attempting in *Heart of Darkness* to portray Africa as it *really* was or still is; rather, he was *really* portraying Africa as it existed in his mind, and, more generally, as it existed (and still exists) in the modern European collective imagination. In this sense *Heart of Darkness* is not *really* about Africa at all; it is *really* about the deepest psychic fears in Conrad's and his readers' psyches.

But if we grant the validity of Achebe's assertion, then it cannot also be true that in *Heart of Darkness* Conrad is merely showing a "preposterous and perverse arrogance in thus reducing Africa to the role of props to the break-up of one petty European mind"—that is, Kurtz's mind (Achebe, *HD* 257). There is a basic contradiction here, for either imagined Africa is of supreme importance to the European mind as an obsessive "Other," or else it is merely a chance setting for a novel by a literarily gifted Anglo-Pole who happened to portray in passing a place of little or no significance to the European imagination as a whole. But if the latter, then it would seem hardly worthwhile to waste one's time and ink on so unimportant a phenomenon. The fact is that *Heart of Darkness* does loom very large, not just in the Western imagination (whatever that may be) but also in Chinua Achebe's imagination, so that for good or ill (mostly the latter, of course, in Achebe's view), *Heart of Darkness* is and will no doubt remain one of the most profoundly significant landmarks in the long and mostly melancholy history of conceptions and misconceptions between Europeans and Africans.

Given the fact that Achebe explicitly professes to be dealing in his essay with the European "image" of Africa, it is odd that he never goes much beyond generalizing about the "Western imagination" and its supposedly stereotypical view of Africa. It is as if this "deep" psychological revulsion against Africa on the part of the West is something that can be assumed by all of us without further proof or investigation beyond the blundering remarks of a white passerby whom Achebe happens to meet in an Amherst parking lot, a naive letter he receives from a young student in Yonkers, a reference that he makes to an unnamed essay written by the historian Hugh Trevor Roper, an equally undocumented quotation from the celebrated physician and musicologist Albert Schweitzer, and an ignorant article that he runs across in the *Christian Science Monitor* that fails to distinguish clearly between dialects and languages in Africa.[5] The reader is then asked to accept this random and ill-assorted collection of anecdotes as a convincing portrait of how the Western mind envisions Africa.

Perhaps even more astonishing than Achebe's miscellaneous evidence is that critics—among them at least one of the most distinguished of American critics, Gerald Graff—have not challenged Achebe about it, insisting at least that he provide a few more examples of a less eclectic nature (Graff 27–28). (It should be noted, though, that other aspects of Achebe's argument have been strongly challenged.)[6] This is not to say that Achebe is necessarily wrong; it is simply to observe that he has not proved that he is right. What is more, given Achebe's explicit interest in images and in the operations of the imagination, it would have been useful and certainly more persuasive if Achebe had taken the trouble to analyze some of the more notable prior examples of Western literary images of Africa. One wonders especially what he might then have made of Kurtz's companion and apparent mistress, the regal Black Amazon figure who is obviously, though Achebe does not admit it, the only character in the novel who is depicted in a wholly sympathetic way. In strictly historical terms, this character no doubt owes a good deal to the use of an elite female army unit in the Kingdom of Dahomey—much in the news in 1897 when the British launched a devastating attack against Benin—but this fact does not account for the Black Amazon's essential nobility or her apparently tragic romantic involvement with Kurtz.[7] It is her *image* rather than her "reality" that matters here, for it is an image that deeply affects our whole understanding of the nature of Africa. It is her image that in fact adds a radically different, supplementary meaning to the word "heart" when used in connection with Africa (in terms of her manifest *courage*, for example, or her deep and passionate commitment to Kurtz). Had Achebe examined this striking figure more carefully, he might have seen that in describing this relationship Conrad was alluding intertextually to Virgil's Dido and Aeneas. Once the intertextual connection is recognized, it also becomes clear that in portraying Kurtz's life with the Black Amazon in the heart of Africa, Conrad is not merely providing a "backdrop" for the breakup of a trivial Western psyche. The intertext here, after all, is the *Aeneid*, one of the chief archetypal narratives in the Western literary tradition and certainly one that has massively shaped the Western literary tradition and, along with it, its imagination, not least with respect to the ways in which the West has traditionally envisioned Africa. Like Kurtz, Aeneas becomes entangled with an African queen and her people, both of whom he later abandons. Like Kurtz again, Aeneas acts reluctantly and against his own emotional inclinations because he fears that if he fails to do so he will be untrue to himself as well as to his "higher" duty to the gods and to his mission vis-à-vis his own culture. Not that the resemblances are precise or wholly consistent (part of the intertextual relation is surely ironic)—but even so there is a sense in which it is true that Aeneas, like Kurtz, has caught a glimpse of the "horror" of yielding to a supposedly "soft and sinful" option rather than adhering to the straight and narrow path of "virtue."[8]

If reading *Heart of Darkness* and the *Aeneid* intertextually in this way has any validity, if indeed it offers a specific and demonstrable insight into Conrad's image of Africa, then it follows that, whatever else one may say about it, his image of Africa is not "quite simply" the result of an inveterate desire in "Western psychology" to set Africa up as a foil to Europe or as "a place of negations" versus "a state of grace" (*HD* 251–52). A contrast *is* clearly drawn between Europe and Africa in both the *Aeneid* and *Heart of Darkness*, of that there can be no doubt; to that extent Achebe is undoubtedly right, but it is by no means a simple and straightforward contrast, with all the positives on one side and all the negatives on the other. Paradoxically, in part because of the controversy stirred up by Achebe's attack, *Heart of Darkness* has come to be recognized by more and more critics as fundamentally and essentially very much of a *mixed* thing, a tale full of ambiguities and unresolved contradictions. Its indictment of imperialism, for example, is scathing, but only of a certain kind of imperialism; it mocks the sham policies elaborated in a despicable European Whited Sepulchre that are shabbily administered by hypocritical "Pilgrims" in the Congo, but at the same time it espouses the virtues of "real work" that is carried out by the British elsewhere in Africa. It shows overwhelming pity for the oppressed Africans in the so-called Grove of Death, but it also finds the antics of the African fireman as comic as "a dog in a parody of breeches" (*HD* 38). It simultaneously denies and upholds the ideals for which the Europeans claim to have to come to Africa, for their torch is one that both sheds light and burns villages. It is horrified by the atrocities committed by Kurtz but at the same time explicitly affirms that he was a "remarkable" man. Not that this deeply mixed quality of the story is aesthetically or even ethically to be censured, for it is precisely because of these contradictions and ambiguities that it remains vital and relevant and true.[9]

This essentially ambiguous or "mixed" quality of Conrad's tale becomes even clearer if we take another suggestive intertext into account, namely Goethe's *Faust,* again one of the archetypal stories in the Western literary tradition. Kurtz, like Faust, is a "universal" man, immensely gifted in various ways, as artist, writer, publicist, explorer, administrator. Like Faust too, he has gone beyond the conventions of his society to dabble (and more than dabble) in forbidden knowledge. And like Faust again, Kurtz is deeply torn between the power and pleasure that such new knowledge conveys and the pangs of guilty conscience at the crimes he has committed in the process of gaining that knowledge, thereby forfeiting his "soul." Suggestively, the contrast between these two Fausts— the "good" and the "bad"—is drawn symbolically in much the same way in both *Faust* and *Heart of Darkness*. That is, by means of contrasting two radically different types of women: the innocent and trusting German Gretchen, whom Faust betrays and abandons (the Intended of Conrad's story), and the splendid and foreign Helen, beautiful and sexually sophisticated (Conrad's Black Amazon). Again the two texts are not to be read in terms of straightforward equivalence—Kurtz's abandonment of the Intended, for example, is figurative rather than actual, as in Faust's case; but the parallels are nevertheless striking. This is true especially of the vision of the "horror" that descends on Kurtz at the climactic point of his existence, a vision that Marlow interprets paradoxically as both a sign of Kurtz's profound degradation and a hope of his possible salvation. For like Kurtz, Faust was a "remarkable man," someone who "struggled" (*HD* 67) and failed spectacularly; who wrought destruction upon the humble and innocent while claiming to pursue a higher civilizing mission (notably in the Baucis and Philemon episode); but also someone who nevertheless is saved because of the intensity of his quest for an "idea" beyond himself. In the end Kurtz's harsh *moral* condemnation of himself is, as in Faust's case, what saves him. Comparing his own possible last words and what might have been his own verdict on himself had he followed Kurtz into the abyss—"a word of careless contempt," he thinks, is what he would probably have uttered—Marlow concludes that he much prefers Kurtz's moral passion to his own habitual, self-deprecating cynicism: "Better his cry—much better. It was an affirmation, a moral victory paid for by innumerable defeats, by abominable terrors, by abominable satisfactions. *But it was a victory*" (*HD* 70, my italics). Despite everything, then, Kurtz is, so it would appear, saved, and we must envision him, as Goethe does in the case of Faust, dwelling among the angels.[10]

Conrad's retelling of the Faust story in *Heart of Darkness* is, of course, also encrusted with ironies. One of the chief ironies is that it is told by Marlow, whose closest equivalent in Goethe's verse play is Faust's *famulus*, Wagner, a humble and somewhat obtuse personage. Not that Marlow is dull-witted or in any way ridiculous—after all, he is British rather than Belgian or even German—but he does function, as critics have often noted, as a kind of alternative to Kurtz. If nothing else, his determination to find Kurtz in the "heart of darkness," his taking Kurtz's side against that of the Pilgrims, his falling ill and nearly dying after Kurtz's demise: all these suggest that Marlow is to be viewed as an apprentice or "junior" Kurtz/Faust—a kind of younger brother, as it were. But when viewed from such a perspective, the Faust story of course becomes radically skewed. For one thing, it becomes funny.[11] Not "funny," perhaps, in the sense of provoking us to uproarious laughter, but definitely comic in the sense of what has come to be called "black humor." For Conrad this is what comedy was inevitably like in any case. "It is very difficult to be wholly joyous or wholly sad on this earth," Conrad wrote with apparent regret toward the end of his life in the preface to *A Personal Record*. "The comic, when it is human, soon takes upon itself a face of pain" (xviii). He had not felt much differently about it as a young man. Writing to his "aunt" back in Belgium while stopping in the

Canary Islands en route to the Congo, Conrad expressed grave doubts about his own future, implying that, as far as he was concerned, there might not be a great deal of it. "And, consequently," he wondered, "why be sad about it? A little illusion, many dreams, a rare flash of happiness followed by disillusionment, a little anger and much suffering, and then the end. Peace! That is the programme, and we must see this tragi-comedy to the end" (*Letters* 1:51). Life, as depicted in Conrad's fiction, may not always be nasty, brutal, or even short, but it certainly has a marked tendency to be informed by a grim and cruel comedy whose values and choice of victims are not easily comprehended. What is easily grasped, however, is that this comedy almost always involves taking an "absurd" stand that is characterized by a curious mixture of skepticism and idealism. Symbolic of that comedy is the perpetual smile on the shrunken lips of the severed head that Marlow sees just before he meets Kurtz for the first time; it is a face of pain, which nonetheless wears a kind of smile, or to be more accurate, a horrible grin.

All of this may come as a surprise to many readers of Conrad, who would probably agree with H.G. Wells that Conrad possessed no sense of humor whatever. "'One could always baffle Conrad,'" Wells patronizingly maintained, "'by saying "humour" [as an explanation for apparently odd behavior on the part of English people]. It was one of our damned English tricks he had never learnt to tackle'" (qtd. in Baines 234). One wonders in this connection just how perceptive Wells himself was in grasping the subtle dimensions of Conrad's sense of the comic, for there are unquestionably humorous elements in *Heart of Darkness*. Some of his thumbnail sketches of character are almost Dickensian. This is striking in the case of the old doctor in Brussels who takes Marlow's pulse, wants to measure his head "in the interests of science," and inquires if there is any history of madness in his family. Here, surely, is a satirical edge that cuts in a variety of directions: against a pseudoscience in Europe that will later find its equivalent among the sorcerers in the heart of Africa; against the madness of the whole imperial enterprise in Africa, as confirmed later when Marlow watches a French cruiser firing pointlessly and without apparent effect into the vast African coastline, or when he observes an analogous "objectless blasting" of a hillside at the Outer Station; and, finally, against Marlow himself, who despite having received a clear warning that what he is about to do is utterly mad, resolves to go forward anyway. Similarly, the Accountant at the Outer Station, whom Marlow at first mistakes for a "vision," got up as he is in "a high, starched collar, white cuffs, a light alpaca jacket, snowy trousers, a clean necktie, and varnished boots. No hat. Hair parted, brushed, oiled, under a green-lined parasol held in a big white hand" (*HD* 21). This "hairdresser's dummy"—for, like most of the Belgians in the story, he is dehumanized—is clearly intended to be perceived as a comic figure, despite (or even because of) the "respect" he elicits from Marlow. He foreshadows another peculiarly attired but more significant figure who, in a very different way, is also meticulous about his appearance, and for whom Marlow also evinces a modicum of esteem. This is the so-called Russian Harlequin, whose explicit linkage with the Harlequin tradition unmistakably signals that he is meant to be thought of at least partly in comic terms. At once amazingly innocent and profoundly shrewd, he is a kind of wonderful mixture between Parsifal and Papageno, able to diagnose quite precisely the degree of danger emanating from Kurtz's moods but at the same time utterly deceived by his imposing airs. The phrase he repeats about Kurtz—that "he enlarged my mind"— turns out to be grimly humorous in the context of the shrunken skulls that his despotic friend has set up on poles in front of his house. And in a way that affects the whole tone of the story, the Harlequin's symbolic attire makes one see the characters and events as if suddenly altered by a twist of the narratorial kaleidoscope: for his very person implies that we live, as Yeats was later to phrase it memorably, "where motley is worn." "We" (or some of us at any rate) live in a *casual* comedy that makes no sense and leads nowhere, in a kind of happenstance world inhabited by a comic opera chorus of sham Pilgrims, along with a Mephistophelean Brickmaker who makes no bricks and whose diabolic schemings yield not souls but a few wretched privileges like candles to help light up a vast heart of darkness. Likewise casually comic are the Manager, who is able to live because he has no entrails, and his grotesque uncle who, like a malevolent Sancho Panza, comes riding into camp on a donkey.[12] They too live in a world where motley is worn and where, to allude again to Yeats, they spend their time fumbling in greasy tills and adding prayer to shivering prayer. Only Kurtz and Marlow seem more or less exempt from this comic horror, though the former is surely funny for the overwhelming, Cecil-Rhodesian extent of his egotism, and the latter for his "fantastic vanity" in hoping not to be considered less appetizing by his cannibal crew than the other whites on board his little steamer (*HD* 43).

In its deliberate mixture of the comic with the tragic, of the farcical with the profoundly serious, *Heart of Darkness* is very much a modern work of art, as T.S. Eliot clearly recognized when he first thought of choosing a phrase from the novel ("Mistah Kurtz—he dead.") as an epigraph for *The Waste Land* but rejected that idea and used the phrase instead for the grimly humorous "The Hollow Men." Certainly H.L. Mencken recognized the marvelous way in which Conrad combines the comic and the tragic, the farcical and the sublime, in this story. "Here we have all imaginable hopes," he concluded after rereading the novel in 1922, "reduced to one common denominator of folly and failure, and here we have a play of humor that is infinitely mordant and searching. . . . The farce mounts by slow stages to dizzy and breath-taking heights. One hears harsh roars of cosmic laughter, vast splutterings of transcendental mirth, echoing and reëchoing down the black corridors of empty space" (519).

Successfully combining apparently disparate elements in this way, *Heart of Darkness* turns out to be very much of a "mixed" thing. And by refusing to accommodate its vision to a single point of view (the story is told by two narrators, neither of whom attempts to suppress the voice of the other, or even the voices of the other characters); by insisting on combining a mode of presentation that is at once intensely realistic and profoundly symbolic (as in the infamous Grove of Death, for example); by infusing virtually everything with an apparently corrosive irony that at the same time allows the sham gold to be separated from the real (Marlow himself, perhaps Kurtz); by fusing comedy with tragedy—by all of these means it reveals that it is intent on portraying not a single, chemically pure truth but one that is whole, reflecting the often contradictory and sometimes incomprehensible world we live in. It is this power of unifying opposites, of making the reader *see* reality and symbol simultaneously, that makes us certain of the heart's affections as well as the profound truth of the imagination.

2

A MERE ANIMAL IN THE CONGO

What makes mankind tragic is not that they are victims of nature, it is
that they are conscious of it. To be part of the animal kingdom under
the condition of this earth is very well—but as soon as you know of
your slavery the pain, the anger, the strife—the tragedy begins.
                                Joseph Conrad to R.B. Cunninghame Graham

The impact of the African experience on Conrad, both as man and as
writer, was, it seems fair to say, out of all proportion to its length. Speaking about it to his oldest and most trusted literary confidant, Edward
Garnett, Conrad once said categorically, "[B]efore the Congo I was just
a mere animal"[1] (Jean-Aubry, *Life* 1:141). This is almost certainly an
exaggeration, but even discounting a little for Conrad's alleged penchant
for "adjectival insistence" (so-called by F.R. Leavis), what he says is
pretty direct and unambiguous, made only more urgent by a single mono-
syllabic modifier. Garnett glosses it, a little too insistently I think, to
mean that for Conrad "the sinister voice of the Congo with its murmuring undertone of human fatuity, baseness and greed had swept away the
generous illusions of his youth, and had left him gazing into the heart of
an immense darkness" (8). In somewhat simpler words, Garnett believes
that after emerging from the Congo Conrad had ceased to be an idealist.
The experience had been an essentially negative one that permanently
killed off a formerly naive and youthful self, leaving behind the hard-
bitten, middle-aged ironist whose outlook was permanently affected by
having once caught a glimpse of the existential horror.

   According to Conrad's first biographer, Gérard Jean-Aubry, also a
personal friend, what Conrad really meant by saying that he had been
an animal before going to the Congo was that "during the first fifteen
years of his seafaring career he had lived as though hardly aware of his
own existence, without ever reflecting on the reasons of his own or other
people's activity." He had been so busy living, it seems, that he had found

no time for thinking. It was only because he fell seriously ill in the Congo and therefore even after his return to Europe was forced to remain more or less bedridden for several additional months, that he began to withdraw into himself and to reflect on "those memories with which his life, though he was only thirty-three, was already extraordinarily full, and to try to estimate their value both from the human and the literary point of view" (*Life* 1:141–42). Fundamentally, then, it was not any profound psychological or even spiritual experience in or of the Congo that had altered Conrad, as Garnett believed. Instead it was a purely physical matter, an accident of illness that had compelled a man essentially of unthinking action to transform himself into one of self-conscious contemplation—to become, in short, an artist. Conrad, it seems, needed illness to be born into awareness; without it, he would have remained, as it were, a kind of Anglo-Polish, sea-going version of a Hans Castorp who had never bothered to ascend the magic mountain.

Jean-Aubry is of course aware that there are certain inherent obstacles to this line of argument, notably the fact that Conrad had already started writing some time before he ventured into the Congo. As Conrad himself recounts it in *A Personal Record*, he almost lost the partially completed manuscript of *Almayer's Folly* when the canoe he was in narrowly avoided tipping over on the way back down the Congo River while attempting to negotiate "a specially awkward turn of the Congo between Kinchassa and Leopoldsville"[2] (*Record* 14). Nevertheless, Jean-Aubry remains adamant. The writing that was a mere sideline for the physically fit Captain Korzeniowski became an absolute necessity for the physically frail Joseph Conrad. It was in this sense only that the Congo did away with the animal in Conrad—the animal, that is, of his physical well-being.

Although it would be unwise to simply disregard these interpretations of the significance of Conrad's Congo experience put forward by two friends who were intimately acquainted not only with the work but also with the man, there does seem to be something curiously obtuse about both. Surely, to say that one has ceased to be an animal is to say something that does not, on the one hand, simply refer to the state of one's physical health or, on the other, merely imply that one has lost one's youthful illusions. Whatever else it may be—and both Garnett and Jean-Aubry are right, I think, in attempting to look beneath the verbal surface, to try, as it were, to find the man beneath the words—ceasing to be an animal suggests something positive, a kind of moral improvement. It also, especially in the context of contemporaneous stereotypical associations with the Congo (associations supposedly themselves reinforced by Conrad's novel) is very much a paradoxical statement. After all, in the West the Congo was usually thought of as an "animalistic" place, not only in the sense of harboring multitudes of strange and exotic animals but also in the sense of being populated by "savages" and "primitives" whose way of life struck many westerners as resembling that of animals. According to Nancy Stepan, nineteenth-century scientific textbooks habitually compared Africans to apes; and even more serious scientists, such as T.H. Huxley, who denied that Africans represented the so-called "missing link" between apes and humans, tended to use animal imagery when writing about them (Brantlinger, "Victorians" 201, 184). As Chinua Achebe puts it ironically, *Heart of Darkness* is set in "a place where man's vaunted intelligence and refinement are finally mocked by triumphant bestiality"[3] (*HD* 252). In contending that it was the experience of the Congo that made him stop being an animal, then, Conrad was putting forward a notion that at least on the surface must have seemed unconventional and even contradictory, at least to himself.[4]

There is something else here too. To stop being an animal and to become some other being—that is, some supposedly superior being—is an idea that inevitably evoked at the turn of the century, as it still does today, Darwinian and Spencerian ideas of evolution and progress. These ideas have often and usefully been brought to bear on the interpretation of *Heart of Darkness* by modern critics,[5] but so far as I know they have not been applied to Conrad's own psychological experience of the Congo in order to help explain how a sometime "animal" named Korzeniowski was able to evolve into a full-blown "human" named Conrad. If one does apply this body of thought in such a way, though, one can begin to see the "man" as well as the "animal" in the name; that is, one can begin to see how Conrad conceived of his African experience—and its envisioning and revisioning in *Heart of Darkness*—as one that resembles the celebrated Darwinian Ernst Haeckel's "biogenetic law." This law (nowadays, by the way, largely discredited) posits that "ontogenesis is a brief and rapid recapitulation of phylogenesis" or, in other words, that the development of the individual organism repeats in microcosm the whole development of the species of which it is a part (*Encyclopedia of Philosophy* 399). From Conrad's perspective and extended from biology to culture, this would have meant that his individual experience in and of the Congo matched the general cultural experience of humanity as it moved from "animal" to "human" existence.[6]

All of this, of course, still does not quite explain what being an "animal" signified for Conrad either personally or in the larger and more public context of late-nineteenth-century sociobiology. These questions are not easy to answer, though some attempt must be made to answer them if one is to have any real hope of getting at the heart of *Heart of Darkness* and at Conrad's own sense of the meaning of his African experience. There is, fortunately, a little further help available, help that comes, in fact, directly from the horse's mouth. Writing in late December 1903 to Roger Casement, an old acquaintance whom he had first met in Matadi (the Outer Station of *Heart of Darkness*) many years before, Conrad points out to him how extraordinary it is that the same "conscience of Europe" that had succeeded in suppressing slavery seventy years earlier still tolerated it in the Congo Free State. "And yet nowadays," he goes on to say,

> if I were to overwork my horse so as to destroy its happiness of physical wellbeing, I should be hauled before a magistrate. It seems to me that the black man—say, of Upoto [on the Congo River]—is deserving of as much humanitarian regard as any animal since he has nerves, feels pain, can be made physically miserable.[7] But as a matter of fact his happiness and misery are much more complex than the misery or happiness of animals and deserving of greater regard. He shares with us the consciousness of the universe in which we live—no small burden. Barbarism per se is no crime deserving of a heavy visitation.[8] (*Letters* 3:96)

Among other things, what emerges from this letter is a confirmation of Garnett's and Jean-Aubry's belief that for the Conrad who had once been an "animal" himself, the word *animal* was not entirely or inevitably negative in its connotations. Here animal happiness is unambiguously defined as "physical well-being." Furthermore, it is also crystal clear that Conrad explicitly affirms the humanity of black Africans, defining that humanity as the shared burden of "consciousness of the universe," so that in this instance at least we do not find him celebrating, as Achebe accuses him of doing in *Heart of Darkness*, "the dehumanization of Africa and Africans" (*HD* 257). What being burdened with the consciousness of the universe actually and specifically means is, however, not quite so clear. A few more insistent adjectives would have been helpful here. Nonetheless, it seems safe to say that Conrad's choice of words suggests something religious, even mystical. It may be that he is alluding to the biblical Logos and therefore to the consciousness of God— and of being like unto God. He is certainly being very "modern" here, for the universe he describes is like that of the existentialists, demanding rational behavior but at the same time preventing us from exercising it consistently. In any case, Conrad's conception of human consciousness is certainly "much more complex" than mere physical well-being and, though it may include happiness, one of the primary terms of its definition, *burden*, suggests that it is also negative.

It is particularly ironic that, of all the novelists who wrote at the turn of the nineteenth into the twentieth century, Conrad should now be censured for alleged insensitivity to the plight of non-Western people. How odd this is may be seen from the fact that, when he first began to publish in 1895, Conrad felt he needed to protect himself against attacks for writing "'decivilized'" tales about "strange people and prowls [of "animals" apparently] in far-off countries, under the shade of palms, in the unsheltered glare of sunbeaten beaches, amongst honest cannibals and the more sophisticated pioneers of our glorious virtues." Life in those distant places, Conrad protested, did not consist simply of "a yell and a war dance," nor were all problems there to be resolved simply "in the barrel of a revolver or on the point of an assegai." People living in those distant places were not different in any way that really mattered, for, as he affirmed explicitly, "there is a bond between us and that humanity so far away," a humanity consisting of real men and women, not of the popular stereotypes of contemporaneous adventure fiction. Such penny-dreadful phantoms Conrad was content to leave to others; as for himself, he meant to "sympathize with common mortals, no matter where they live; in houses or in tents, in the streets under a fog, or in the forests behind the dark line of dismal mangroves that fringe the vast solitude of the sea. For their land—like ours—lies under the inscrutable eyes of the Most High. Their hearts—like ours—must endure the load of the gifts from Heaven: the curse of facts and the blessing of illusions, the bitterness of our wisdom and the deceptive consolation of our folly" (*Almayer's* ix–x). Here again, as in the letter to Casement, life is described in terms of a *burden*—an ironic load of gifts from Heaven—that all humans are fated to bear, a *burden* that, however, is also a *bond* that unites us all. This is the familiar *condition humaine*—one that for Conrad was explicitly a condition much the same whether humanity happened to reside in Africa, Asia, or Europe.

What light does all this shed on Conrad's transition from animal to human during or after his stay in the Congo? I think it suggests that it was somehow because of his experience in Africa that Conrad became fully aware (or at least thought he did) for the first time of the significance of the "universe in which we live"; that is, he became aware of the complexity of existence in a context where he was put to what must have seemed to him the most extreme physical and spiritual test. *Heart of Darkness* is an attempt to render that context and that test in an imaginative retelling. Even so, Conrad's crucial realization that he had changed in some profound manner is not to be equated simply, in the way Garnett did, with the loss of youthful idealism; it is rather a simultaneous retention of that idealism along with the adoption of a new, self-conscious point of view regarding the (comic as well as tragic) pretensions and dimensions of such idealism. Put in this way and viewed from this perspective, it is the story of how the "animal" Marlow who lived and worked in the Congo came to be the "human" Marlow who tells the former's story while aboard the *Nellie* at the mouth of the Thames. Not that the one wholly excludes the other, though the strong associations with Buddhism that attach to the older, narrating Marlow seem to suggest a movement away from the things of the body toward those of the spirit. The younger, "active" Marlow, on the other hand, is viewed as having been unduly impulsive (in rushing to the Congo, for example) and as sometimes so involved in his actions, so *unconscious* of his surroundings, that it takes him minutes or even longer before he even realizes what is happening. Ian Watt has famously found a name for this kind of momentary lack of awareness in Marlow; he calls it "delayed decoding" and ascribes it primarily to Conrad's impressionist technique (*Conrad* 175–79). But it has at least as important a substantive function, I think, as it does a technical one, namely to provide insight into the younger Marlow's character, thereby revealing his "animalistic" unawareness of the "universe we live in."[9]

As so often with Conrad, it is difficult to be certain what key words mean. Whatever else may or may not be true, though, it is probably safe to say that Conrad had once thought of himself as having been (and perhaps had in fact been) a "mere" or "perfect" animal; but he had also, at one and the same time, remained quite human—human enough at any rate to pass the test for Ordinary Master in the British Merchant Marine Service not long before turning thirty. To spell it out as plainly as possible, by saying he had been an animal Conrad did not, of course, mean that before going to the Congo he had been in the habit of running about on all fours. Being an "animal" was his figurative, metaphoric way of expressing his former lack of full consciousness. In this sense, one might add, most humans are animals in their youth, and some of them probably never fully graduate into "humanity." Humanity and animality are therefore not mutually exclusive. This is an equation that holds true also for the world depicted in *Heart of Darkness*.

It is in this metaphoric and specifically *human* sense of the word "animal," then—the sense in which Conrad had applied the word to himself—that we are to evaluate the various "animals" of *Heart of Darkness*. To begin with, it is important to realize that they belong to various categories. They are not confined, as almost certainly the majority of Conrad's initial, predominantly white audience must have assumed— and as readers as perceptive as Achebe still do—to Africans.[10] Along with Conrad himself—the Conrad of the Congo—and his alter ego Marlow, they definitely include virtually all of the whites in Africa, even and especially Kurtz. Indeed, in one of the most dramatic scenes of the novel Marlow sets out to "hunt" down and waylay a Kurtz who is crawling away from the river like an animal "on all-fours," apparently in a last-ditch attempt to resume his sometime leading role in mysterious totemistic rites. As he confronts Kurtz in the darkness, Marlow glances backward and sees a nearby fire where "a black figure stood up, strode on long black legs, waving long black arms across the glow. It had horns— antelope horns, I think—on its head. Some sorcerer, some witch-man, no doubt; it looked fiend-like enough" (*HD* 64). Here Kurtz's animalism is unmistakably linked with diabolism, though not, I think, in an entirely negative way; for, despite his antelope horns, the African Sorcerer is shown in an upright human position, whereas the European Kurtz is on all fours, like an animal.

In his critical remarks on this passage, Chinua Achebe neglects to take into account the symbolic contrast between the human African and the animal Kurtz implicit here; he points to it instead as an instance of what he feels is Conrad's psychotic fixation on blackness and obsession with "niggers." In fact, however, he quotes only a fragment of a sentence from the original description: "'A black figure stood up, strode on long black legs, waving long black arms. . . .'" Of this partial sentence he remarks with apparent justification that it is "as though we might expect a black figure striding on black legs to wave white arms! But so unrelenting is Conrad's obsession" (*HD* 258). What Achebe fails to note here—apparently deliberately, since he omits the crucial last three words of the sentence: "across the glow"—is that Conrad's emphatic focus on the blackness of the figure refers not primarily to its racial origins but rather (1) to its being silhouetted in the surrounding darkness against the fire and (2) to the Sorcerer's "black arts," which are apparently elements of the "unspeakable rites" to which Kurtz is addicted. Further corroboration of Conrad's linkage of black with night rather than with race is provided by Marlow's description of the appearance of the three fetishmen on the following day as he prepares to steam off downriver: "In front of the first rank along the river three men plastered with bright red earth from head to foot strutted to and fro restlessly. When we came abreast again they faced the river, stamped their feet, nodded their horned heads, swayed their scarlet bodies" (*HD* 66). A little further down the same page they are even described as "the three red chaps." Their ceremonial dancing and horned headgear make the identification with the "sorcerer" whom Marlow had seen the previous evening complete, but now Marlow is as insistent about their redness as he previously had been about their blackness, a fact that Achebe neglects to observe or, at any rate, to comment on.[11] As for Conrad's "niggers," it is true that both Marlow and to a lesser degree Conrad himself go out of their way to use this derogatory term. Ian Watt's claim that "in those days . . . such terms as 'nigger' were not regarded as offensive" is not really supported by the evidence ("Critics" 7). On the contrary, the entry "nigger" in the *OED*—an entry composed at approximately the time *Heart of Darkness* was published—defines it as "a negro (colloq. and usu. contemptuous)." Gilbert Murray, writing in 1900, refers to the word *nigger* as being obsolete except in South Africa, where it is "still used very much in the old [pejorative] sense. Naturally" (121 n). In the earlier context of *Conrad in the Nineteenth Century*, however, Watt treats this issue rather differently. Without referring specifically to the word *nigger,* he admits that "Conrad habitually uses the derogatory racial terms which were general in the political and evolutionary thought of his time. This might pose a serious problem if *Heart of Darkness* were essentially concerned with the colonial and racial issue in general. But it is not." According to Watt, Conrad's more limited intention is merely to show that "imperial or colonial experience is bad for the whites" (*Conrad* 159); Conrad's interest in how it affects nonwhites is therefore, by implication, secondary. R.B. Cunninghame Graham's famous antiracist and anti-imperialist essay, "Bloody Niggers," unambiguously makes clear that for most British conservatives at the turn of the century *nigger* was a term of contempt applied generally to "all those of almost any race whose skins are darker than our own, and whose ideas of faith, of matrimony, banking, and therapeutics differ from those held by the dwellers of the meridian of Primrose Hill." However, "in consideration of the 'nigger' races which God sent into the world for whites (and chiefly Englishmen) to rule, 'niggers' of Africa occupy first place" (66). That Conrad was aware of this derogatory sense of the word is evident not only from his close friendship with Cunninghame Graham but also from his remark to Ford Madox Ford about how the French showed less prejudice in their colonizing activities because "they had none of the spirit of Mr. Kipling's 'You Bloody-niggerisms' about them" (F.M. Ford 259). In nevertheless using the word himself—in one instance even in the title of a novel—Conrad (and Marlow) is (are) undoubtedly reflecting the racist usage of the Merchant Navy, where Conrad had first learned to speak colloquial English. As a nonnative speaker of English, Conrad may have been attempting to convey in this way what he perhaps thought was a "natively" English impression. Indeed, his need to filter his experience through a persona like Marlow reflects an uncertainty on his part that his audience would "identify" with a narrator who was foreign. *Foreigner,* after all, as George Orwell was later to point out, always meant "dirty foreigner" in the years before the Great War.[12]

What is unmistakable about the scene describing Kurtz's crawling back to the Sorcerer's fire, however, is that Kurtz—or some part of Kurtz, anyway—has here deliberately and freely chosen to become an "animal." This is not the case with the last of a group of dying Africans whom Marlow encounters earlier in the story in the grim "grove of death." In an image that prefigures Kurtz's later attempt at escape, Marlow watches "horror-struck [as] one of these creatures rose to his hands and knees and went off *on all-fours* towards the river to drink. He lapped out of his hand, then sat up in the sunlight crossing his shins in front of him, and after a time let his woolly head fall on his breastbone" (*HD* 21, my italics). Unlike the dying Kurtz, this dying African has been forced against his will to abandon the upright position that affirms his humanity. He has been thrust into "animality" by a system of organized and quite literal brutality.

This brutality is everywhere apparent in the Congo, but it reaches a kind of climax in the so-called Eldorado Exploring Expedition, which arrives one day suddenly and rather absurdly, mounted on donkeys, at the Central Station.[13] Its leader is the Manager's uncle, who resembles a fat butcher, exhibits a pig-like cunning, and "during the time his gang infested the station spoke to no one but his nephew" (*HD* 33). The Uncle is also given to grunting (*HD* 35), which, along with his porcine appearance, certainly further suggests his bestiality. (In other contexts, however, as we shall see, grunting can have favorable connotations.) "Infestation," moreover, suggests something even less appealing than the pigs and asses with which he and his group are closely identified. Not surprisingly, therefore, when much later Marlow receives news that all the donkeys had died, he comments sardonically that he knows nothing "as to the fate of the less valuable animals"[14] (*HD* 35). By comparison, most of the Africans strike him as infinitely preferable. Not that he romanticizes them. Avrom Fleishman is, I think, right in arguing that Conrad does not idealize the native at the expense of the colonizer, though in some important respects this is both more and less true of Conrad's Pacific stories and novels than it is of *Heart of Darkness* (82). Certainly there are not any "noble savages" here of the sort that populate the Zulu novels of H. Rider Haggard. But neither is there any close interracial friendship between equals that would correspond to that of Jim and Dain Waris or Stein and the Rajah, in *Lord Jim*.[15]

I do not think Lionel Trilling accurately describes Marlow's (or Conrad's) response either, when he argues that "it is one of the great points of Conrad's story that Marlow speaks of the primitive life of the jungle not as being noble or charming or even free but as being base and sordid—and for that reason compelling; he himself feels quite overtly its dreadful attraction" (20). It is certainly true that Marlow powerfully feels this attraction himself, though it is not quite true that he thinks of it exclusively as being "base and sordid." The attempt to define the precise nature of the attraction is something I take up later, but for the moment it needs to be said that for Marlow (and probably also for Conrad) there exists, on occasion at least, real *nobility* in the "savage." This is most apparent in the famous "restraint" that the cannibal crew aboard Marlow's riverboat exercises in not devouring Marlow and his white companions, even though they are desperately hungry and vastly outnumber the whites. But it is evident also in less dramatic and more conventional ways, as in the fact that, despite the heavy odor of death that surrounds most blacks and whites in this story, the Africans (and only the Africans) are able nevertheless at times to exhibit a powerfully appealing vitality.

The most vital—the *best*—Africans are those who fit most naturally into their environment and who, to use Marlow's word for them, embody the greatest "reality." The least vital people are those who have abandoned, especially when they have done so voluntarily, their original environment or "place" in order to assist in invading that of others—though the cannibals and Kurtz's Lake tribe are notable exceptions to this rule. Such people lack reality and are, on the whole, mere "shams."[16] To this latter category belong not only virtually all of the whites (in

Europe as well as Africa) but also most of the Africans at the Outer Station, especially those in the Grove of Death, as well as such detribalized Africans as the Helmsman and the Manager's "boy." To the former category, on the other hand, belongs notably the black crew that Marlow encounters briefly on one of his stops along the African coast while en route to the Congo. His description of this group is of crucial importance:

> The idleness of a passenger, my isolation amongst all these men with whom I had no point of contact, the oily and languid sea, the uniform sombreness of the coast, seemed to keep me away from the truth of things within the toil of a mournful and senseless delusion. The voice of the surf heard now and then was a positive pleasure, *like the speech of a brother*. It was something natural, that had its reason, that had a meaning. Now and then a boat from the shore gave one a momentary contact with reality. It was paddled by black fellows. You could see from afar the white of their eyeballs glistening. They shouted, sang; their bodies streamed with perspiration; they had faces like grotesque masks—these chaps; but they had bone, muscle, *a wild vitality*, an intense energy of movement that was *as natural and true as the surf along their coast*. They wanted no excuse for being there. They were a great comfort to look at. (*HD* 17, my italics)

Chinua Achebe, who quotes this passage (with the significant omission of the first three sentences) in his well-known essay "An Image of Africa: Racism in Conrad's *Heart of Darkness,*" implies patronizingly that it functions as a "nice little vignette" and "as an example of things in their place" (*HD* 254).[17] Further examples of the same sort of "things" include the cannibals and Kurtz's black female warrior companion, whom Achebe calls the "Amazon" and who, in his view, "has obviously been some kind of mistress to Mr. Kurtz."[18] What particularly offends Achebe in Conrad's rendering of all of these people is his refusal to grant them speech. "It is clearly not part of Conrad's purpose," Achebe remarks, "to confer language on the 'rudimentary souls' of Africa. In place of speech they made 'a violent babble of uncouth sounds.' They 'exchanged short grunting phrases' even among themselves." As for the two minimal instances when Africans are permitted to speak intelligibly in English, these constitute, in Achebe's view, even more insidious insults, for Conrad's sole purpose in allowing them to talk is to let "the European glimpse the unspeakable craving in their hearts" (presumably cannibalism) (*HD* 256–58).

Before trying to come to grips with these charges, I would like to return to Conrad's earlier description of the black coastal crew and paraphrase the passage in a manner that highlights significant points of contact with Achebe's critique. It opens with Marlow briefly sketching a context for his own increasing sense of unreality. As a professional seaman traveling as a passenger on a foreign ship, he is now both literally and figuratively at sea, with no job on board and, apparently, no connection with the other seamen. Further, as an Englishman (and possibly also as an intellectual), he is utterly out of touch with the other passengers; and as a "romantic" person whose mood swings are strongly affected by the climate and his natural surroundings (here both are dull and uniform), he has difficulty in orienting himself emotionally and spiritually. In consequence, Marlow finds himself able to communicate effectively only with the voice of the surf; or, rather, he finds that the surf is the only voice that speaks effectively to him. He recognizes that voice as specifically resembling a brother's, a voice explicitly conveying a meaning. When he then sees a boat manned by a group of skillful and energetic paddlers, they strike him as being simultaneously grotesque, vital, and real. He immediately associates them—presumably chiefly because of the sounds they make—with the surf. They are, to repeat his words, "as natural and true as the surf along their coast" (*HD* 17).

It is hard to understand how this passage could have been meant by Conrad to be patronizing or offensive to Africans. It is true that the faces of the men strike Marlow as resembling "grotesque masks"—Conrad's appreciation, or rather lack of adequate aesthetic appreciation, of African masks is a particularly sore point with Achebe—but this is the only possibly negative element in the whole description. Achebe claims that it was because he was "blinkered . . . with xenophobia" that Conrad failed to take cognizance of the artistic achievements of the Fang people, who lived just north of the Congo and who are "without a doubt among the world's greatest masters of the sculptured form." Achebe goes on to observe that the modern discovery of African art by Europeans "marked the beginning of cubism and the infusion of new life into European art, which had completely run out of strength" (*HD* 260). Conrad's knowledge of the Fang was probably restricted to what Burton says of them in *Two Trips to Gorilla Land and the Cataracts of the Congo*, namely that they practiced ritual cannibalism and that they were well advised to avoid contact with whites (1:212, 226). Moreover, whatever our views on the subject of the debt of modernist art to African sculpture may be, it does seem a little unfair of Achebe to censure Conrad for not appreciating the latter's significance at a time (1899) when only the most advanced European painters and sculptors were beginning to be aware of it themselves. And if we are to believe such a knowledgeable commentator as Marianna Torgovnick, avant-garde artists like Manet and Picasso "used blacks and African masks in connection with debased sexuality, especially the depiction of prostitution and brothel life" (99). This hardly sounds like an invigorating infusion of unprejudiced aesthetic appreciation. Moreover, as Michael North points out, late in life both Picasso and Gertrude Stein strongly disclaimed ever having been influenced by African sculpture. North disagrees with this disclaimer, but he nevertheless argues that the European modernists were "unable to escape the contradictions of European colonialism; that is, their use of African motifs and masks was not merely aesthetic but was closely linked to perpetuating negative stereotypes of Africans" (59–60, 76). That Conrad himself apparently considered African masks grotesque is further suggested by his (or rather, his narrator's) unmistakably racist description of James Wait's face as "the mysterious, the repulsive mask of a nigger's soul" (*Nigger* 11). Finally, David Denby observes in connection with Achebe's negative comments about Conrad's failure to take the artistic achievements of the Fang people into account that "Conrad certainly did not offer 'Heart of Darkness' as 'a picture of the peoples of the Congo' [a phrase quoted from Achebe], any more than Achebe's 'Things Fall Apart,' set in a Nigerian village, purports to be a rounded picture of the British overlords" (127).[19]

It is not that Conrad fails to realize that African artifacts do have an aesthetic dimension, no matter how grotesque Marlow may consider them. Significantly, the Mephistophelean Brickmaker at the Central Station collects African artifacts as objets d'art and hangs them alongside a painting by Kurtz. In any event, there can be no doubt that the men on the boat do possess a language (they shout) and that they are shown to use that language in an artistic manner (they sing). Their aim in doing so, presumably, is twofold: to establish a rhythm that will coordinate their paddling and to attract the attention of the ship's passengers, so as to sell them food or souvenirs, or both. (Most likely these boatmen are Krumen, who specialized in ferrying passengers and cargo at ports along the West African coast.) Whatever their purpose and actual intelligibility, however, the sounds they make undoubtedly possess meaning for Marlow, a great deal more meaning certainly than do the sounds produced, for example, by his fellow passengers. They are the sounds, too, of the surf, the sounds of a vital natural world that are unambiguously defined as those of a brother.[20]

One reason, very likely, why they are fraternal is that they are the sounds of the sea, a form of natural speech with which the seafaring

Marlow has been long familiar. That is probably also why the African coastal boatmen are viewed, even if only indirectly, as brothers: they share, along with Marlow and his friends aboard the *Nellie*, the "bond" of the sea. To recognize the existence of such a bond, however, is not by any means to suggest that Marlow himself equates these black canoers with his London friends, or that he is about to take them aside, like the garrulous ancient mariner he is, and compel them to listen to another of his "inconclusive tales." Achebe, I think, is quite right in arguing that Marlow esteems the boatmen primarily because they are so very much at home in the waters along *their* own coast; it is this very fact that for Conrad confirms their reality. Nevertheless, for whatever reason and however momentarily, it is undeniable that they are perceived as resembling brothers, a point that Achebe fails to take into consideration when he accuses Conrad of being a "bloody racist."[21] Conrad, I agree, *is* by some of today's standards in some ways and on some occasions a racist, though I do not agree that he ever is a "bloody" one.[22] In terms of his treatment of black Africans in this story, he is at worst a "weak" racist in Reeves's terminology. This is an issue that I treat in more detail later, but for the moment it needs to be said that Conrad's supposed "bloodiness" is, as here, mostly a function of Achebe's skewing the available evidence. When, for example, he neglects to quote the first three sentences of the passage just discussed, it is obvious that its significance must be radically altered. The crucial links between the sound of the surf, the voices of the boatmen, the nonverbal communication of meaning, and the voice of a brother, are all broken.

In terms of Achebe's argument, the reference to Africans as brothers is particularly important, because in his view Africa in general—but primarily sub-Saharan Africa, I think—is for Europeans the "Other" rather than the brother.[23] "Quite simply it is the desire," he says, generalizing in a way that comes dangerously close to being much more than weakly racist itself (again in Reeves's sense), "one might indeed say the need—in Western psychology to set Africa up as a foil to Europe, as a place of negations at once remote and vaguely familiar, in comparison with which Europe's own state of spiritual grace will be manifest" (*HD* 251–52).[24] Aside from the fact that Europe, at least that part of Europe represented in Conrad's story by the "whited sepulchre" of Brussels, is hardly set up as a place of salvation or even as an attractive alternative to the Congo, there are, as Achebe is fully aware, several instances in which a kinship between Africans and Europeans is clearly suggested. Even the inverse symmetrical structure of the narrative evokes this connection, with the frame story set in the estuary of the Thames, where Marlow and his friends await the turning of the tide so as to continue their outward-bound voyage, and the principal narrative set on the Congo River, where Marlow endures a variety of longer delays in order to complete his inward-bound voyage.[25]

According to Achebe, however, the unmistakably corresponding settings on the two rivers are designed to reveal difference rather than similarity. The Congo River, Achebe tells us, is for Conrad "the very antithesis of the Thames." In fact, Achebe goes so far as to suggest that Conrad's intention is to portray the one as "good" and the other as "bad." When Marlow explicitly announces that "this" (meaning the Thames) has also been "one of the dark places of the earth," Achebe interprets that assertion as expressing Conrad's worry about some "lurking hint of kinship, of common ancestry" between Europeans and Africans. In Conrad's view the Thames, so Achebe maintains, has "conquered its darkness, of course, and is now in daylight and at peace." Aside from the fact that just as Conrad began to write *Heart of Darkness*, Britain and France had narrowly avoided going to war over the Fashoda Incident and that as he finished it, the Boer War was about to begin—in other words, whatever peace "the Thames" possessed at this moment in history was extremely precarious—it is simply not true to say that the river is "in daylight" at the beginning of Conrad's narrative. It is not true either factually or symbolically. "The air was dark above Gravesend," the narrator of the frame story informs us quite specifically about his surroundings in the second paragraph of the novel, "and farther back still seemed condensed into a mournful gloom brooding motionless over the biggest, and the greatest, town on earth" (*HD* 7). Whatever else can be said about this description, there can be no doubt that there is not a lot of daylight here. Moreover, what little light there is does not seem to hold out promise for greater illumination in the future. It is a land and skyscape more reminiscent of Hardy than of Conrad, laden as it is with ominous personifications of supernatural forces and conveying unmistakably the dark and characteristically apocalyptic mood of fin de siècle pessimism.

That Conrad wants his readers to see the resemblance rather than the difference between the Thames and Congo Rivers is evident too when he has Marlow ask his friends to imagine how they would feel if "a lot of mysterious niggers armed with all kinds of fearful weapons suddenly took to travelling on the road between Deal and Gravesend catching the yokels right and left to carry heavy loads for them." Here the implied comparison is between the portage linking Matadi and Kinshasa and a similar but hypothetical one connecting Deal and Gravesend (*HD* 23), the latter being the harbor closest to the site where the *Nellie* is temporarily anchored. This comparison can be understood only as suggesting similarity rather than difference. To be sure, Achebe is right in the sense that it was difference rather than similarity that was usually stressed in other discussions of the Congo River. So, for instance, in *La Civilisation et les grands fleuves historiques* (1889), Léon Metchnikoff describes the Congo River as the river that "above all has remained up to the present day the river of barbarism," comparing it with that other great African river, the Nile, which in his view is "incontestably one of the principal creators of those glorious civilizations which have shone forth brilliantly over the Western world for the last 6000 or 8000 years" (200, my translation).

It is odd also that, despite his insistence that for the European the African is invariably the embodiment of the "Other" rather than the brother, Achebe is nevertheless fond of quoting that "extraordinary missionary" Albert Schweitzer's remark about the African being "indeed my brother but my junior brother"[26] (*HD* 257). According to Achebe this odious comparison is part and parcel of the kind of "liberalism" that in the early years of the century touched all the best minds of Europe and America, including Conrad's. Hence the "bleeding heart sentiments" of Marlow uttered about the so-called Grove of Death on the outskirts of the Outer Station, where he is horrified to find large numbers of weak and starving Africans waiting to die. This kind of liberalism, in Achebe's view, is reprehensible chiefly because it manages "to sidestep the ultimate question of equality between white people and black people" (*HD* 256). This conclusion, even if we disregard what seems a patently unjust dismissal of the sincerity of Marlow's (and I think also Conrad's) compassion for these victims of imperialism, seems an odd one to draw. Odd, if for no other reason than that Schweitzer so obviously does *not* "sidestep" the issue of equality between the races. For Schweitzer it is self-evident that he and his fellow whites represent the older brother who has the power as well as the responsibility to tell the younger brother what to do. Whatever steps Schweitzer may be taking here, he is definitely not stepping aside into ambiguity. Whites, in Schweitzer's view, are not equal to but superior to blacks.

Schweitzer's sense of patronizing (rather than fraternizing) superiority emerges even more unambiguously if one restores the original context for Achebe's quotation:

A word in conclusion about the relations between the whites and the blacks. What must be the general character of the intercourse between them? Am I to treat the black man as my equal or as my inferior? I must show him that I can respect the dignity of human personality in every one, and this attitude in me he must be able to see for himself; but the essential thing is that there shall be a real feeling of brotherliness. How far this is to find complete expression in the saying and doing of daily life must be settled by circumstances. *The negro is a child*, and with children nothing can be done without the use of authority. We must, therefore, so arrange the circumstances of daily life that *my natural authority* can find expression. With regard to the negroes, then, I have coined the formula: "I am your brother, it is true, but your elder brother."[27] (130–31, my italics)

In expressing this view Schweitzer was in no way unusual; after all, his fellow Europeans thought well enough of him and of his views to award him the Nobel Peace Prize. Undoubtedly, in expressing what today strikes us as an odious comparison, Schweitzer was merely reflecting the standard scientific outlook of most Europeans of his generation and of the generation preceding his. Charles Darwin, for example, while strongly opposing slavery, believed in the superiority of the white race to other so-called racial groups. So did other eminent biologists, such as Alfred Wallace and T.H. Huxley, though the latter felt that blacks (and women) should be treated with added consideration precisely because of their supposed inferiority (Bannister 184–86). For Patrick Brantlinger, the whole climate of positivistic scientific thought engendered by Darwin and his disciples was racist: "Darwinism lent scientific status to the view that there were higher and lower races, progressive and non-progressive ones, and that the lower races ought to be governed by—or even completely supplanted by—civilized, progressive races like the British" ("Victorians" 187). In the entry "Negro" in the standard reference work of the time, the eleventh edition of the *Encyclopedia Britannica*, it is unambiguously stated that "mentally the negro is inferior to the white" as well as to the yellow races. Even though this supposed inferiority is said to be "exaggerated," and it is even admitted that "it is not fair to judge of his mental capacity by tests taken directly from the environment of the white man," the conclusion is still that "the mental constitution of the negro is very similar to that of a child." That Conrad shared some or even many of these views about blacks is possible, though up to now no convincing evidence has been adduced to prove it. At the same time it must be remembered to his credit that he consistently mocked notions of white superiority in his fiction, in both its Pacific and its African settings. Where Conrad *was* demonstrably racist (in the older, more inclusive sense of the word *race*) is in his belief in the superiority or inferiority of the European "races" or nations in relation to each other—not that this is something Conrad himself admitted to openly. Writing to Kazimierz Waliszewski in December 1903, Conrad protested that in *Heart of Darkness* he was not seeking to depict the "inferiority of races": "It's the *difference* between the races that I wanted to point out" (*Letters* 3:94).

Conrad's national/ethnic prejudice was, however, not a static, unchanging thing, even with regard to his adopted homeland. Though in his early fiction the English as a national group are almost always depicted as superior to their European as well as non-European rivals and opponents, hints of a more critical view eventually surface. So, for example, the Liverpool crew of the *Judea* in "Youth" are prepared to risk their lives and do their duty in a way that only an English crew could. "It was something in them," Marlow tells us, "something inborn and subtle and everlasting. I don't say positively that the crew of a French or German merchantman wouldn't have done it, but I doubt whether it would have been done in the same way. There was a completeness in it, something solid like a principle, and masterful like an instinct—a disclosure of something secret—of that hidden something, that gift of good or evil that makes racial difference, that shapes the fate of nations" (*Youth* 28). However, only a few years later, Conrad's narrator in *Nostromo* feels free to venture the following generalization about the supposed national characters of Latins and Nordics: "There is always something childish in the rapacity of the passionate, clear-minded, Southern races, wanting in the misty idealism of the Northerners, who at the smallest encouragement dream of nothing less than the conquest of the earth" (278).

Even if Conrad explicitly and, on the whole, disingenuously denied advocating racism in a European context, Achebe is nonetheless right in suggesting that his "liberalism would not take him quite as far as Schweitzer's, though. He would not use the word *brother*, however qualified; the farthest he would go was kinship" (*HD* 257). To be sure, *brother* was not a word that fell easily from Conrad's lips in other contexts either. In fact, Conrad, who was an only child, seems to have had little use for "brotherhood" of almost any sort. Writing to his friend Cunninghame Graham in February 1899 (at the very time he was finishing *Heart of Darkness*), Conrad dismissed the ideal of "international fraternity" in the following summary terms: "There is already as much fraternity as there can be—and thats [*sic*] very little and that very little is no good. What does fraternity mean. Abnegation—self-sacrifice means something.

Fraternity means nothing unless the Cain-Abel business. Thats [*sic*] your true fraternity" (*Letters* 2:159). It is clear, however, that Conrad is here attacking a conception of brotherhood that derives from the French Revolution and that had been adapted to socialist propaganda; in the same letter he affirms, apparently without sensing any evident contradiction, his need to "keep my thinking inviolate as a final act of fidelity to a lost cause," that is, presumably to the cause of Polish nationalism. Brotherhood, though not so named, is here apparently confined, so far as Conrad is concerned, to fellow Poles.

There is, to be sure, the exception about the boatmen already noted, whose fraternal nature Conrad acknowledges at least indirectly; and Achebe himself seems to imply that Conrad wants us to see a kind of symbolic junior-senior relation between the Rivers Congo and Thames when he ironically excludes the former from having achieved the superior "River Emeritus" status of the latter (*HD* 252). But even if for Conrad whites and blacks are not brothers, they are unquestionably related. And kinship, no matter how remote, remains kinship—it is not the utterly abjured and unrelated "Other." At one critical point in *Heart of Darkness*, however, kinship almost vanishes altogether before being once again decisively affirmed. This occurs in a passage that Achebe quotes at great length—though still not, I think, at sufficient length to represent Conrad's (or Marlow's) position accurately and fairly—after which he concludes summarily that "herein lies the meaning of *Heart of Darkness* and the fascination it holds over the Western mind," namely in Marlow's observation that "'what thrilled you was just the thought of their humanity—like yours. . . . Ugly'" (*HD* 254).[28]

I do not propose to quote the entire passage here myself, since it is one of the most familiar in the whole book and is often quoted or referred to by critics of *Heart of Darkness*. Marianna Torgovnik, for example uses a large chunk of it to preface her chapter on Conrad in *Gone Primitive* (141). I want to make it clear as I omit reproducing the offending passage, however, that I do not deny that it contains several unmistakably racist aspersions on Marlow's and perhaps also Conrad's part regarding the behavior of blacks living along the shores of the Congo River upstream from the Central Station. (The racist views expressed here belong to the "medium" category on Reeves's scale and are phrased in such a way as to make their subsequent denial more dramatic.) To summarize briefly, the occasion is Marlow's sense of moving back in time—remote, primeval time—as he guides his little steamer slowly toward Kurtz and the supposed heart of darkness. What he sees and hears en route strikes him at first as no more than "a black and incomprehensible frenzy." He is initially unable to understand the utterance and gestures of the supposedly "prehistoric man" he encounters, because he thinks that he and his companions "were too far and could not remember, because we were travelling in the night of the first ages, of those ages that are gone leaving hardly a sign—and no memories." Tempted suddenly to dismiss these apparently mad creatures on the shore as "inhuman," Marlow stops himself in midsentence and explicitly affirms their humanity as well as their "remote kinship" with him. "Ugly" as their shouting, leaping, spinning, and making of horrid faces still seem to him, he now recognizes, even if only reluctantly, that there is a meaning in such activities, a meaning that he now must confess to being able to comprehend himself.[29]

This is where Achebe stops quoting the passage. Since, however, it continues on without a break for several more sentences in a direction rather different from the one implied by Achebe, I will herewith provide the missing parts. "And why not?" Marlow inquires a little defensively about his newfound ability to understand what seemed to him only a moment earlier an incomprehensible frenzy.

> The mind of man is capable of anything—because everything is in it, all the past as well as all the future. What was there after all? Joy, fear, sorrow, devotion, valour, rage—who can tell?—but truth—*truth stripped of its cloak of time.* Let the fool gape and shudder—the man knows and can look on without a wink. *But he must at least be as much of a man as these on the shore.* He must meet that truth with his own true stuff—with his own inborn strength. Principles? Principles won't do. Acquisitions, clothes, pretty rags—rags that would fly off at the first good shake. No. You want a deliberate belief. An appeal to me in this fiendish row—is there? Very well, I hear, I admit, but I have a voice too, and for good or evil mine is the speech that cannot be silenced. Of course, a fool, what with sheer fright and fine sentiments, is always safe. Who's that grunting? (*HD* 38, my italics)

Without forgetting for a moment Marlow's racist observations at earlier points in this passage (the section quoted by Achebe in his essay), it must be clear, I think, to any fair-minded reader that Marlow takes most if not all of these back in the sentences that follow (that is, the sentences just quoted here but omitted by Achebe). Particularly important is Marlow's rejection of his previously expressed belief that in traveling backward in time he was encountering people living at a stage of cultural and perhaps even biological development so much earlier than his own that he, as a modern European, could not "remember" being like them. This was because there was no historical record of their mode of existence to help him remember and hardly any other surviving "sign" to show what they had been like (almost certainly an allusion to the relative paucity of archeological evidence).[30]

What Marlow is referring to here is, I think, the contemporaneous anthropological theory that posited, as Peter Bowler observes, that "each society followed an independent line of evolution, but all were moving in parallel along the same scale of development. Some had advanced further than others, and the lowest societies thus exhibited exact equivalents of the stages through which the more advanced had passed in the distant past"[31] (37). This theory has close connections with nineteenth-century historicism, and in its general outlines it was endorsed by all of the leading ethnological and anthropological thinkers of the late nineteenth century, including such eminent figures as Edward B. Tylor and Sir Henry Maine. In *Psyche's Task* (1913), the great cultural anthropologist Sir James Frazer even puts the idea in a context that evokes Haeckel's biogenetic law: "For by comparison with civilized man the savage represents an arrested or rather retarded stage of social development. And an examination of his customs and beliefs accordingly supplies the same sort of evidence of the evolution of the human mind that an examination of the human embryo supplies of the evolution of the human body" (Bowler 37). (Achebe satirizes a version of this theory in the person of the colonial government official at the close of *Things Fall Apart*.)

Even within this general consensus, however, there were significant deviations. As Ernst Cassirer points out in *The Myth of the State* (1946), Tylor's conception of primitive society was limited strictly to its social aspects; in other words, though in his view it was perfectly appropriate to speak of such a thing as a "primitive culture," it was quite wrong to speak of a "primitive mind." Cassirer states unambiguously, "According to Tylor, there is no essential difference between the savage's mind and the mind of the civilized man" (9). In this respect the argument of Tylor's *Primitive Culture* (1871) closely resembles and anticipates, as we shall see, the conception of Stone Age man that Marlow arrives at after some delayed decoding, as he travels up the Congo to find Kurtz. The opposing point of view, that there *is* a difference between the so-called primitive and the civilized mind, was most forcefully argued by the great French cultural anthropologist Lucien Lévy-Bruhl in *How Natives Think* (1910): again in Cassirer's words, "it is vain to seek for a common measure between primitive mentality and our own" because the former is "not a logical, but a 'pre-logical' or mystic mind." According to Lévy-

Bruhl, this difference in mentality is evident especially in corresponding differences in language structure, characterized in the case of primitive languages by their lack of logic (13). This is a position that Cassirer, along with virtually all subsequent thinkers on the subject, finds completely untenable, as exemplified by Edward Sapir's observation that "when it comes to linguistic form, Plato walks with the Macedonian swineherd, Confucius with the head-hunting savage of Assam" (qtd. in Pinker 27). By way of extenuation, however, it should be noted that late in life Lévy-Bruhl modified his position by proposing that "mystic" and "logical" mentalities were not mutually exclusive but coexisted in differing proportions among so-called primitive and civilized peoples. "Let me expressly correct what I believed to be true in 1910," he writes: "there is no primitive mentality which is distinct from the other. . . . There is mystical mentality more marked and more easily observed among primitives than in our own society, but present everywhere in the human mind" (xvii).

From Achebe's point of view, of course, these distinctions are mere variations in prejudice, for whether we accept Tylor's or Lévy-Bruhl's argument, we are still confronted here, now dressed in scientific garb, with none other than Schweitzer's notorious junior brother, not quite grown up as yet in the way that his European older brother supposedly is, though at least he now has some real hopes of doing so in the dim evolutionary future.[32] For most of these anthropologists, however, the degree of kinship they were prepared to acknowledge was not that of a brother but rather of a distant forefather, possibly an uncle many times removed. Nor was the kind of life that these remote, immature ancestors of modern European humanity were supposed to have experienced, ever imagined as particularly noble or pretty. On the contrary, it was, to repeat Marlow's word, "ugly." Bowler recounts, for example, how in *Prehistoric Times* (1865), the distinguished British anthropologist Sir John Lubbock "spared no effort to paint a depressing picture of savage—and hence of prehistoric—life. Modern primitives were dirty, they had little religion, few morals, and no respect for women or the aged. Yet our own ancestors had lived like that for untold millennia as they gradually mounted the scale of social progress" (80–81). This way of thinking about so-called primitive and prehistoric societies continued well into the twentieth century, even decades after Conrad had published *Heart of Darkness*. In fact, by a curious irony of intellectual history, it was only through the writing and teaching of another Pole—the great social anthropologist Bronislaw Malinowski—that a radically different, culturally relativistic outlook came to dominate Western anthropological thought. In Malinowski's new ethnography, for the first time distinctions between "civilized" and "savage" people became meaningless[33] (Rossetti 486).

How deliberately self-ironic and culturally relativistic Marlow is in this supposedly ultraracist passage becomes indisputably clear once we are aware that he—or rather, Conrad—is closely following a passage in *Through the Dark Continent* where Stanley pauses to give his impressions of Uhombo village, located somewhere between the Ugandan lake country and the upriver cataracts of the Congo. "I saw before me," Stanley writes, "over a hundred beings of the most degraded type it is possible to conceive, and though I knew quite well that some thousands of years ago the beginning of this wretched humanity and myself were one and the same, a sneaking disinclination to believe it possessed me strongly." Conversing with the village chief, whom he addresses according to local custom as "Brother," he is struck by a face that "is like an ugly and extravagant mask, clumsily manufactured from some strange, dark brown material." He is even more repelled by the appearance of the other inhabitants of the village, for, "as I looked at the array of faces, I could only comment to myself—ugly—uglier—ugliest." However, after going on to comment unfavorably on their attire and odor, Stanley suddenly notices that "there is a loud interchange of comments upon the white's appearance, a manifestation of broad interest to know whence I came, whither I am going, and what is my business. And no sooner are the questions asked than they are replied to by long-drawn ejaculations of 'Wa-a-a-antu!' ('Men') 'Eha-a, and these are men!'"

It now dawns on Stanley that the villagers have been responding to his manner and appearance much as he has to theirs: "Now imagine this! While we whites are loftily disputing among ourselves as to whether the beings before us are human, here were these creatures actually expressing strong doubts as to whether we whites are men!" Like Conrad, Stanley is able to see the situation from the point of view of the "other" side and to confront the basic question that haunted much of the latter (post-Darwinian) half of the nineteenth century: namely, just what is it that constitutes our humanity? Stanley did not have to wait long for an answer. It is an answer deeply rooted in the human heart, which for him is neither dark nor blank (or white) but universal. As he stands watching the villagers, one of his own men is suddenly injured by a falling pole: "And all at once there went up from the women a genuine and unaffected cry of pity, and their faces expressed so lively a sense of tender sympathy with the wounded man, that my heart, keener than my eyes, saw through the disguise of filth, nakedness, and ochre, the human heart beating for another's suffering, and I then recognized and hailed them as indeed my own poor and degraded sisters" (*Dark Continent* 2:57–60). Though these sisters are apparently still not quite up to his level—they remain, after all, "degraded" and possibly even "junior"—Stanley recognizes his profound kinship with them (and with their "brothers" too) and manages to "see" in them the compassion (or charity or agape) that is essential to all humanity, hidden though it may be by a "cloak" of different customs, language, and time. Like Marlow, though in a more traditionally Christian way, he "sees" more deeply because he does not rely exclusively on his eyes. Instead, he uses his heart as a more trustworthy guide to ultimate truths, and the cry of pity that moves him is much like the cry of sorrow that Marlow is able to interpret correctly because he too has learned to listen more with his heart than with his ears.

It is significant, I think, that Marlow first accepts and then rejects cultural evolutionism, that is, the theory of a gradual, progressive human development as reflected in the best scientific thinking of the late nineteenth century.[34] Not that (here at least) Conrad anticipates Malinowski by adopting a modern theory of cultural relativism, although it is true that one of his most characteristic fictional strategies is based on cultural relativism (without, of course, using this term). Essentially, the device involves a reversal of roles, as when Marlow's audience is invited to imagine what would happen if "a lot of mysterious niggers armed with all kinds of fearful weapons suddenly took to travelling on the road between Deal and Gravesend catching the yokels right and left to carry heavy loads for them" (*HD* 23). Similarly, in the novel *The Inheritors*—on which Conrad was collaborating with Ford Madox Hueffer not long after completing *Heart of Darkness*— a woman from a superior species inhabiting the fourth dimension explains to the narrator that after being conquered "we should be treated as we ourselves treat the inferior races. There would be no fighting, no killing; we—our whole social system—would break as a beam snaps, because we were worm-eaten with altruism and ethics" (13).[35] Jacques Berthoud argues that the real significance of Marlow's Congo experience is that it "brings home to him the relativity of his own culture; not only are European concepts, such as 'waging war' or 'dispensing justice,' incomprehensible to the native inhabitants; but the very foreignness of the new environment renders such ideas unreal to those allegedly in possession of them" (Berthoud, "Conrad" 57). In this respect, at least, Achebe and Conrad would seem to agree. "'There is no story that is not true,'" says one of the characters in *Things Fall Apart*. "'The world has no end, and what is good among one people is an abomination with others'" (Achebe, *Things* 130). How influential Conrad's example remains is evident from Conor Cruise O'Brien's horrified reaction to Belgian atrocities in Katanga: he asks his readers to speculate on how they would react to the presence of African bandits in Hertfordshire (O'Brien 237).

Essentially, however, Conrad is no cultural relativist. His outlook in the main reflects an older, more traditional view of a universal, stable human nature, one that encompasses all the possible basic human traits and emotions—"joy, fear, sorrow" and so on. Time is not—or is no longer—the force that reveals or even creates human development, for there is no such thing as development in anything other than a superficial sense. Time is now recognized as being merely a "cloak" that, once removed, will reveal an essential truth hidden beneath. And what is this truth? Most importantly, it is a *naked* truth. It is the *essential* truth, only visible when everything belonging to the surface (such as civilization) has been removed. This may seem shocking to "fools" who seek refuge in the "principles" and "pretty rags" of so-called civilization (as the Russian Harlequin apparently does?), but it is only when the man on the boat—along with the other men on that other boat, the *Nellie*—faces the man on shore on equal terms, as a kind of "brother" stripped physically and spiritually naked, that he can *understand* who he himself is and whether or not he has the "true stuff" in him. If he does possess that "stuff," if he has the necessary courage, as Marlow apparently did, then and only then will he find a voice—and a speech to go with that voice— that "for good or evil . . . cannot be silenced." His voice and his speech will then be added to the frenzied speech of the man on shore. That speech too is one that, for good and evil, cannot be silenced, if for no other reason than that it too forms an essential component of Marlow's own language and of the story he tells.[36]

A voice and a speech to go with that voice—these are clearly very important to Marlow. They are also essential to *Heart of Darkness* itself, for it is only through Marlow's voice that his friends are able to hear the tale that makes up most of that story. His voice and his words cannot be silenced, for if they are, there is no story. Voice and speech are the aesthetic Logos without which there is nothing. But this does not mean that Marlow is intent on silencing other voices. Even without dragging in the shade of Bakhtin, it is evident that there are numerous competing and sometimes contradictory voices in *Heart of Darkness*, including those of the unnamed narrator of the frame story.[37] *Voice* as such is in fact a recurrent theme of the story, particularly in connection with Kurtz. On a more general level, it is also something of a thematic obsession in Conrad's work of this period, as, for example, in the gradual identification of speaker with voice in the two quite different contexts of James Wait in *The Nigger of the 'Narcissus'* and Stein in *Lord Jim*. What Conrad seems to be implying by emphasizing an invisible (and even disembodied) voice over a visible, incarnate speaker is that the existence of a solitary voice forces auditors to rely entirely on their ability to envision or imagine the "reality" behind that voice, just as readers are compelled do as they reconstitute that voice in their minds, doing so paradoxically by means of the words they see on the page with their eyes. Even Marlow's group of privileged listeners is forced into an analogous situation, after the surrounding darkness engulfs them and allows them access only to Marlow's voice. Significantly, Marlow himself "sees" Kurtz for the first time in the darkness, as he overhears the conversation of the Manager and his uncle. What we hear seems ultimately more constitutive of our sense of reality than what we see.

As is indicated in the passage where Marlow admits to understanding the meaning of what the voices on shore howl and utter, an actual lexical and grammatical knowledge of the language of others is not a prerequisite to comprehending their meaning. In "An Outpost of Progress"—written not long before *Heart of Darkness*— Conrad mocks his Belgian "protagonists'" inability to understand the "different kind of gibberish" spoken by the leader of a group of what they realize too late are slave traders. Conrad's irony exposes their supposed superiority as consisting of real inferiority (*Unrest* 97). In *Heart of Darkness*, however, despite his sometimes admittedly offensive descriptions of African languages, Marlow never reveals this kind of ignorant "superiority." On the contrary, when he hears the three painted fetishmen uttering their magical incantations as he prepares to steam downriver with the dying Kurtz on board, he is able to distinguish clearly between their specialized religious words and "ordinary" human language. "They shouted periodically together," he says of them, "strings of amazing words that resembled no sounds of human language" (*HD* 66). Marlow, in other words, may not be able to understand literally what it is they are saying—how could he or why should he, after all, given the short time he has spent in the Congo?—but he understands perfectly the significance of their speech. As a matter of historical fact, all the notable British explorers from Mungo Park on down made serious efforts to learn the languages of the places and people they were planning to visit (Park 5). Both Livingstone and Glave remark how their English got rusty for want of practice, and Stanley concludes *Through the Dark Continent* (1878) with a long appendix providing "Simple Rules for Pronouncing African Words" (2:376–96). Similarly, Hermann von Wissmann's *Im Innern Afrikas* devotes a part of its extensive appendix to a grammar and lexical comparison of the languages of the Baluba, Bakuba, and Batua (Wissmann, *Innern* 444–49). Kurtz, though he has spent only about a year in the Inner Station, speaks the language of the Lake tribe fluently, as his long conversation with the Amazon makes clear.[38]

That is why, I think, Achebe's criticism of Marlow (and Conrad) for supposedly refusing to grant language to the Africans in this story is really beside the point. Marlow does understand what they mean even if he does not understand what they say. Although he has not been in the Congo long enough to learn to speak any of the African languages, he understands, for example, more fully than any one else (black or white) on board the riverboat what the significance is of the cries they all hear as they approach Kurtz on the final leg of their journey. The others think Marlow mad as he lectures them about it, but he turns out to be right in having recognized in these cries, violent as they are, "an irresistible impression of sorrow. The glimpse of the steamboat had for some reason filled those savages with unrestrained grief. The danger, if any, I expounded, was from our proximity to a great human passion let loose. Even extreme grief may ultimately vent itself in violence—but more generally takes the form of apathy" (*HD* 44). Here again the basis of Marlow's analysis is his conviction that there is a universally valid human psychology, one that holds as true in the heart of darkness as it does in a dimly illuminated Brussels drawing room.

By now it should be apparent that in charging Marlow and Conrad with intentionally denying language to Africans—of making them communicate among themselves either by means of "'a violent babble of uncouth sounds'" or "'incomprehensible grunts'" (*HD* 255)—Chinua Achebe is, if not wrong, at any rate profoundly misleading. The "violent babble" exists as "babble" not primarily for its own sake, but in order rather to convey to Marlow's Western listeners the impression of incoherence that these sounds made on his untrained Western ear.[39] As for the "violent" part, that is something Marlow understands, as we have seen, full well, and in his view only "fools" would or could misunderstand otherwise. The grunts seem a different matter, for they apparently suggest that the beings who make them are subhuman, like pigs. The

careless reader may indeed come away with such an impression. However, as anyone who bothers to look back a few paragraphs will note,
Marlow concludes the long passage in which he recognizes his kinship
with the "man of frenzy" by inquiring, "Who's that grunting?" This
question clearly refers to one of the listeners aboard the *Nellie* and not
to anyone within the actual tale. Nor is it the first time the possibility of
a grunt has been raised as a means of communication among Marlow
and his friends. Immediately after Marlow opens his tale by announcing
that the Thames has also been one of the dark places of the earth, the
unnamed narrator assesses his own and his fellow listeners' response by
remarking that "no one took the trouble to grunt even" (*HD* 9). Marlow
himself utters a grunt after finishing his description of the map of Africa
hanging in the company's offices in Brussels[40] (*HD* 14).

Grunts, it is clear, are at least as frequent and meaningful among
Marlow's friends as they are among the Congo cannibals.[41] (At another
point in the narrative, Marlow complains about one of his friends sigh-
ing "in this beastly way" [*HD* 48]). In both contexts these sounds are
clearly (if, admittedly, paradoxically) intended to be read as positive;
that is, they are characteristic verbal signs made by men of action who
are not accustomed to waste words. The grunt of Marlow's unnamed
listener is interpreted by Marlow as a kind of reality check, ironically
questioning the sincerity of his (Marlow's) "fine sentiments" since these
were not followed up by his going "ashore for a howl and a dance"
himself (*HD* 38). In the case of the cannibals, the grunts are not an
isolated "vignette," as Achebe suggests, but part of an extended comparison between their response to the prospect of sudden attack and
that of Marlow's white companions. The comparison turns out to be
entirely to the detriment of the latter group. After pointing out that the
cannibals are at an equal disadvantage with the whites, belonging as
they do to a distant tribe and being just as much strangers to this part of
the river as they are, Marlow notes that the cannibals' faces are "essentially quiet," while at the same time revealing an "alert, naturally interested expression." The frightened whites, on the other hand, aside from
being "greatly discomposed," had "a curious look of being painfully
shocked by such an outrageous row" (*HD* 42). To be shocked in such a
context, as we should realize by now, is an obvious sign of being a "fool."
No wonder, then, that Marlow's Belgian companions can only stammer
and wonder in vain "what is the meaning" or else stand about like stooges,
gaping "open-mouthed for a full minute." To make the contrast even
more vivid, one of the rattled whites is described as "a little fat man with

sandy hair and red whiskers, who wore side-spring boots, and pink pyjamas tucked into his socks." This ludicrous figure is contrasted with the austere figure of the headman of the cannibal crew, "a young broad-chested black, severely draped in dark-blue fringed cloths, with fierce nostrils and his hair all done up artfully in oily ringlets" (*HD* 41–42).

It is from the latter person that Marlow receives the advice that they should launch an attack. "'Catch 'im,' he snapped with a bloodshot widening of his eyes and a flash of sharp teeth—'catch 'im. Give 'im to us.' 'To you, eh?' I asked; 'what would you do with them?' 'Eat 'im!' he said curtly, and leaning his elbow on the rail looked out into the fog in a dignified and profoundly pensive attitude" (*HD* 42). Among the least important things that could (and should) be said about this exchange is, I think, Achebe's comment that it serves "Conrad's purpose of letting the European glimpse the unspeakable craving hearts" of Africans (*HD* 255–56). What really does seem remarkable about it, in the context of possible linguistic understanding or misunderstanding, is that Marlow and the cannibal headman are able to talk perfectly intelligibly in (more or less pidgin) English to each other. That this must be assumed to be a quite ordinary, daily occurrence is suggested by Marlow's earlier having gone forward (to the cannibals) and "ordered the chain to be hauled up short" (*HD* 41). There is no doubt that the cannibals understand Marlow's orders, for he overhears their "short grunting phrases" while they are engaged in the strenuous physical effort of hauling up the chain. That is why it is so puzzling that Achebe should be outraged at Marlow's (or Conrad's) making the cannibals exchange their "short grunting phrases" even, as he says pointedly, among themselves. What is so surprising about this? After all, it seems only natural that they should speak their own language among themselves. It would be a great deal more peculiar if they spoke pidgin English to each other, as Germans are notoriously made to do in older American war films, usually uttering a series of guttural sounds, interspersed with occasional *Heil Hitlers* and *Achtungs*. To be sure, it seems insulting that the language of the cannibals should strike Marlow as consisting of "short grunting phrases," but even if grunts were not viewed in Marlow's vocabulary more often than not as positive phenomena, as already mentioned, the grunts would still refer only to Marlow's own impression of the language, not to the language itself. Besides, when the cannibals do speak to Marlow, they speak English—or at least the headman does. All this is perfectly normal and as it should be.

There is a final grunt we need to consider before passing on to other matters. This is a grunt belonging to Carlier, one of the two pathetic Belgian "protagonists" of Conrad's only other story set in the Congo, "An Outpost of Progress" (1897). Thinking to outsmart their foreman, a shrewd, articulate, and unprincipled African named Makola, Carlier and his companion Kayerts are themselves duped in a transaction involving an exchange of ivory for slaves. In effect, they suddenly find themselves forced either to forfeit the ivory or else admit to the odium of having engaged in slave trade. Being the out-of-place, out-and-out shams they are, they feebly try to avoid the issue by obfuscating it with words. "'We can't touch it [the ivory], of course,' said Kayerts. 'Of course not,' assented Carlier. 'Slavery is an awful thing,' stammered out Kayerts in an unsteady voice. 'Frightful—the sufferings,' grunted Carlier with conviction" (*Unrest* 105).

This grunt by Carlier, unlike most of the other grunts we have encountered so far, is not a good grunt.[42] It is a grunt of false assertion, a hypocritical grunt. Its hypocrisy is masked, however, as the narrator of the story informs us, even from themselves. That such a thing should be possible is entirely the result of language itself, for it is by means of language that we separate abstract idea from concrete feeling; or, to be more precise, it is by this means that we can simulate feelings that may have no real existence within ourselves. "They believed their words," the anonymous narrator observes of the stammered and grunted exchange between Carlier and Kayerts. "Everybody shows a respectful deference to certain sounds that he and his fellows can make. But about feelings people really know nothing. We talk with indignation or enthusiasm; we talk about oppression, cruelty, crime, devotion, self-sacrifice, virtue, and we know nothing real beyond the words. Nobody knows what suffering or sacrifice mean—except, perhaps, the victims of the mysterious purpose of these illusions" (*Unrest* 105–6). Here are meanings, as it were, that lie too deep for mere words.[43]

In part, what the narrator is saying is similar to what Marlow tells his listeners aboard the *Nellie* about the necessity of looking for the "true stuff," for "a deliberate belief" beneath the "principles . . . acquisitions, clothes, pretty rags" that we use to hide ourselves from ourselves. Language is also one of those "acquisitions," perhaps the most insidious acquisition of all, but also one of the most necessary and even triumphant. It is insidious when it hides, as in the case of Kayerts and Carlier, what is inside them (or what is not); it is triumphant when it expresses one's "own inborn strength," as it apparently does in Marlow's case. Then it finds a voice and a speech to express that strength. It is to this double function of language—to hide and to reveal, to lie and to tell the truth—that one needs to attend continually in reading Conrad. It is certainly something that Marlow takes the greatest care to do, himself; and that is why he is able to "understand" others—black as well as white others—as well as himself, in a way that no other character in the story does.

If, then, it is language that is traditionally said to distinguish humans from animals, Conrad's remark about having been a mere animal before going to the Congo may be further interpreted to mean that only those who are fully conscious of their linguistic status and power are to be considered fully human. Only the artist, in other words, is able to accomplish what the rest of humanity dimly strives to become. But to accept such a view would be, as we have seen, to go utterly against the conclusions that both Marlow and Conrad have drawn about the nature of language in *Heart of Darkness* and in "An Outpost of Progress." The final lesson that they, along with Carlier and Kayerts, learn in the heart of Africa, or do not learn as the case may be—and it is a lesson that we also do or do not learn at our peril along with them—is that language belongs to the surface of the human psyche, but meaning is of the depths. Language can and often does deceive, whereas meaning does not, though one must have the "true stuff" to grasp what that meaning is. It is the fundamental difference between the spirit and the letter, the soul and the body. Hence, if Conrad is a racist, it is in this "weak" or surface sense only. In the end, both the man on the ship and the man on the shore are men, no more and no less. Though their languages may be different and even mutually incomprehensible, their meanings are identical. It is at this deeper level that their kinship is successfully expressed—at the level of their common humanity—so that although their words may be denied, and indeed often are, their voices remain forever indistinguishable and inextinguishable.

3

ENVISIONING KURTZ

Ivory introduces into the country at present an abnormal state of things. Upon this one article is set so enormous a premium that none other among African products secures the slightest general attention. . . . In addition to this, of half the real woes which now exist in Africa ivory is at the bottom.

Henry Drummond, *Tropical Africa*

Conrad's *The heart of darkness* [*sic*] paints a portrait that only partially corresponds to the change in behavior and personality structure that affected lonely agents, and in the interior almost all of them were lonely. His picture is overdrawn.

Jan Vansina, "King Leopold's Congo, 1886–1908"

In the "Author's Note" that he wrote in 1917 on the occasion of the republication of *Youth* in the edition of his collected works, Conrad remarks of *Heart of Darkness* that, like "Youth," it is a story based on "experience too; but it is experience pushed a little (and only very little) beyond the actual facts of the case for the perfectly legitimate, I believe, purpose of bringing it home to the minds and bosoms of the readers" (*HD* 4). In the years since Conrad wrote these words, a great deal of effort has been expended by critics and biographers in attempting to gauge the precise nature and degree of actual personal "experience" in the story. (If the spirit of Conrad is somewhere gazing down on these efforts, I think he too must be impressed by their awful extent and efficiency.) According to Norman Sherry, who has led the way here, Conrad was not being quite ingenuous when he claimed to have "pushed" his own experience only a "very little" beyond the "actual facts." After having dug long and deep in contemporaneous publications and records (including those of the Belgian Company, which originally employed Conrad), Sherry has been able to point out numerous significant deviations both from Conrad's own biographical experience and from the larger historical context[1] (*Western* 9–136).

Not that Sherry means to wag a finger at Conrad, even though he does occasionally use the word *distortion* (in quotation marks) for the changes Conrad makes. Essentially, Sherry justifies those changes, that "distortion," by arguing that Conrad's "perception of the 'inner truth' of his material—not of his personal experience but what that experience had allowed him to perceive . . . enforced upon him all the further steps in the moulding of his own material" (*Western* 342). Aside from numerous relatively minor changes, these "further steps" were two in number: first, Conrad made the Congo, especially upstream of Kinshasa, a great deal more isolated than it was at the time he had gone there in the summer of 1890. Also, the river itself was not a snake lying in wait and surrounded by a primeval jungle, as he describes it in the story, but was already at this time a fairly well-traveled waterway, with several trading stations along the way and with numerous riverboats steaming upstream and downstream at the very moment Conrad was making the journey himself. Most strikingly, perhaps, Kurtz's lonely, ruined trading post at the Inner Station bears no realistic relation to the thriving commercial settlement that had been recently reestablished at Stanley Falls.[2]

Writing in 1895, Robert Brown notes that "on stretches where ferocious cannibals tried to intercept Mr. Stanley's party for culinary purposes, thirty-five steamers puff so familiarly as scarcely to arouse the interest of the *blasé* barbarians." According to Brown's statistics, five years after Conrad's stay in the Congo there were approximately one thousand Europeans living in the Congo, about half of them Belgian nationals. Moreover, the armed forces of the Congo Free State consisted of approximately four thousand native soldiers, "divided into eight companies, under eighty European officers, who drill these troops in four camps of instruction" (182–83). According to H.M. Stanley, in 1892 (two years after Conrad left Africa) there were more than thirty steamers on the Congo River, along with forty steel boats, plying the river between numerous company and missionary stations ("Slavery" 623). Anyone relying solely on the evidence of *Heart of Darkness* would be led to believe that there were only three company stations of any consequence along the whole length of the Congo at the time the story takes place. It should be noted, however, that even as late as 1895 one of Stanley's former associates, Alfred Parminter, observed that "the Congo government had not established any administration beyond the river banks and that 'the country is, as it was in 1884, one dense, swampy forest, absolutely unknown to Europeans'" (Cookey 40).

The second major change Conrad undertook, according to Sherry, was to revise his own experience in the Congo, one that in fact had been pretty much of a muddle and had consisted mostly of a succession of frustrations and disappointed hopes. In the fiction Marlow, by contrast, is provided with a coherent "story" in which he assumes an active and even prominent role, leading ultimately to "an illuminating point of climax" for him, if not always for his audience.[3] Moreover, as Sherry goes on to argue, Marlow "is given the legacy of Conrad's hard-gained insight—he is skeptical from the first. Brussels is 'sepulchral' . . . Conrad is taking revenge upon his own gullibility, and at the same time making his hero a man not easily gulled by the heroics of colonisation" (*Western* 345–46).

Impressive as Sherry's work is in establishing the "actual facts" behind *Heart of Darkness*, it has not been accepted without protest. This is especially true of Zdzislaw Najder, who objects to Sherry's claim that in 1890 the Congo River upstream of Kinshasa was no longer isolated in the way described in *Heart of Darkness*. In Najder's view Sherry fails to take into adequate consideration the immensity of the Congo River in this particular segment of its course, stretching as it often does to a width of over ten miles, so that even if six small steamboats can be proved to have passed the *Roi des Belges* when Conrad was on board, there is no proof that Conrad saw any of them and even some likelihood that he would not have seen them. Najder also faults Sherry for naively accepting as valid evidence the contemporaneous reports about the Congo that were published in *Mouvement Géographique*, a Brussels journal that had a vested interest in making the Congo Free State appear more "civilized" and less isolated than it actually was (*Joseph Conrad* 134).

Though Najder is probably right in objecting to the reliability of some of Sherry's data—and therefore to the conclusions based on that data—there can be little doubt that Conrad deliberately made the Congo out to be not only more isolated but also more chaotic and poorly managed than it actually was. As another, more recent biographer of Conrad, John Batchelor, points out, Sherry's case is supported further by the fact that before publishing the novel Conrad cut three paragraphs near the beginning of the original manuscript describing Marlow's arrival at the unnamed capital of the Congo Free State (Boma), where he finds, among other things, some (admittedly shabby) government buildings, a hotel and a steam tramway.[4] "By cutting down all the detail," Batchelor concludes, "he [Conrad] plays down evidence of 'civilization,' and I think we can take it that a similar editing of his recollection has taken place throughout the novella. The impact of the European is to be seen exclusively as mindless cruelty" (88). In other words, Conrad wanted to make quite sure that his indictment of (Belgian) imperialism was not attenuated by any possibly mitigating circumstances, such as evidence of actual rational and constructive activity.[5]

Taking note of all of these alterations to his own experience in *Heart of Darkness* is important in allowing us to ascertain more exactly what it was that Conrad meant to bring home, as his 1917 "Author's Note" put it, "to the minds and bosoms of the readers." This is especially the case with one highly significant change not yet mentioned, namely the addition of a character who appears to have had an only minimal basis in the reality of Conrad's African experience. This, of course, is Kurtz. Although it has long been known that the *Roi des Belges* picked up at Stanley Falls a gravely ill company agent named Georges Antoine Klein, who was a French national and who died on the voyage back; and although it has also been known that in the manuscript version, the first few references to Kurtz were originally to Klein, there is no evidence that, beyond the purely external circumstances of his death and his analogous German name (Klein means "small" in German), Klein's life or character bore any meaningful resemblance to the life and character ascribed by Marlow to Kurtz.[6] Norman Sherry devotes a whole chapter of his book to demonstrating why the innocuous Klein has (perhaps fortunately for him) no claim to be mistaken for Kurtz. Sherry devotes another chapter to proving that, instead, "at least in part the inspiration for Kurtz" was Klein's immediate superior, the highly enterprising Belgian military officer Arthur Hodister. According to Sherry, Hodister was well known as a man of considerable ability and integrity; he was responsible for some intrepid exploring, collected a large quantity of ivory, did some writing for newspapers in Belgium, and had influential friends in Europe. Though Conrad probably never met Hodister personally, Sherry is convinced that he must have heard of him from various sources, much as Marlow hears of Kurtz in the story.

Sherry's identification of Hodister is highly speculative, not only in terms of what Conrad "must" have known about him (and how), but with regard to Hodister himself. Among other things, Sherry hypothesizes a possible rivalry between Hodister and Alexandre Delcommune (the original model for the Manager's uncle), as well as a dislike for him on the part of the latter's brother, Camille Delcommune (the Manager

himself). So far as any actual evidence is concerned, all of these speculations are without foundation.[7] Most damaging of all, Sherry fails to acknowledge fully the radical differences between the ways in which
Hodister and Kurtz met their deaths, and therefore he fails to take into
account the profoundly differing implications of those deaths. In the
case of Hodister, he died, according to the report from the London *Times*
reprinted by Sherry, at the hands of treacherous Arab slave traders while
attempting to negotiate an armistice. Upon the failure of the negotiations, Hodister and his two white companions were taken prisoner, tor-
tured, and decapitated. Their heads were stuck on poles and their bodies
were eaten. Of all this Sherry observes, with remarkable understatement,
that "Hodister's fate was not precisely that of Kurtz." He then goes on
to confuse the issue further by proposing grandly that "it might be said
of both men that their faith in their ability to command the 'exotic immensity' of the Congo jungle led to their being destroyed by that same
Immensity—by its inhabitants in the case of Hodister and its primitive
customs in the case of Kurtz" (*Western* 110–11).

Just what Sherry means by Kurtz's having been destroyed by "primitive customs" is puzzling, since one of the few points of similarity between Kurtz and Klein is the fact that both unmistakably died of tropical
fever (probably malaria), the most common cause of death among whites
in nineteenth-century Central Africa. Ironically, Kurtz is a man of violence who dies (though not peacefully) in bed. Hodister, on the other
hand—at least if one is to believe contemporaneous news reports, which
is all we, or Sherry for that matter, have to go on—was a military man
who met a violent death while trying to make peace. If, therefore, Conrad
did indeed take him even "in part" as a model for Kurtz, it could only
have been in order to denigrate the activities of the agents of Leopold II
by a nasty species of character assassination. If so, this would fall squarely
under the rubric of what Batchelor sees as Conrad's plan to show how
all Europeans (with the notable exception of Marlow) are propagators
of "mindless cruelty." It is, I confess, an explanation that strikes me not
only as unlikely in itself but also as utterly uncharacteristic of Conrad's
generally responsible use of biographical and historical material. This is
not an explanation, I should hasten to add, proposed by Sherry himself,
who, in the final analysis, provides no explanation at all as to why Conrad
might have chosen so unlikely a model as Hodister for Kurtz.[8]

It may not be surprising, therefore, that Hodister has not been widely
accepted as "the" original for Kurtz. Of recent biographers only Roger
Tennant (80) and Jeffrey Meyers (*Conrad* 104) follow Sherry's lead here.

But if not Hodister, then who? The answer unfortunately is—multitudes. Starting off, as Sherry does, with Klein and Hodister, Ian Watt adds a series of further possibilities, most of them already suggested by earlier critics: Emin Pasha (born Eduard Schnitzer in Germany), whom Stanley attempted to relieve in 1887 and who was killed by Arabs in 1892; the Englishman Edmund Barttelot, in charge of Stanley's rear guard during the Emin Pasha Relief Expedition and killed in a skirmish (favored by Jerry Allen); Charles Henry Stokes, an Irish ivory trader summarily hanged by a Belgian officer, Lothaire, in 1895; Carl Peters, the notoriously cruel German explorer of East Africa (proposed by Hannah Arendt); the French captain Paul Voulet, who imitated Peters's example in Senegal; and last, but certainly not least, the infamous/famous Anglo-American explorer who more than any other single figure helped establish the Western stereotype of "darkest Africa" (a stereotype echoed by Conrad's title)[9] and who served as Leopold II's principal agent in the early stages of Congo exploration and exploitation, Henry Morgan Stanley. Of Stanley, Watt remarks that he is "probably of central importance, though not so much as a basis for the character of Kurtz as for the moral atmosphere in which he was created" (*Conrad* 142–45).[10]

None of these models quite fits Kurtz, some because they were, so far as we know, simply taking part in officially sponsored military-commercial expeditions or else too "selfless" in their devotion to the cause of antislavery (Hodister as well as Barttelot and the others); or because they were more victims of Arab atrocities than perpetrators of individual acts of aggression themselves (Hodister, Barttelot, and the others again); or because they were too private and obscure in their work (Klein and Stokes); or, finally, because they were too prominent and successful (Emin Pasha, Peters, and especially Stanley). None of them appears to have committed anything like the brutal "raiding" of villages, using warrior tribes as the means, that Kurtz does in *Heart of Darkness*. This is a "system" that in fact was notoriously a specialty of the Arabs, notably of Tippo Tib, whose headquarters were at Stanley Falls (the Inner Station).[11] From all this it seems most reasonable or, at any rate, least problematic to conclude, as Najder does, that "the model for Kurtz was supplied on the one hand by literary and philosophical tradition, on the other by the behavior of a great many Europeans in Africa. In the end, as a character with his own specific life history, Kurtz is the author's own creation" (*Joseph Conrad* 526).

That Conrad meant Kurtz to be thought of more as a representative or, as he remarked himself, a *symbolic* character rather than as the fictional rendering of a particular individual also seems evident from the general way in which Kurtz conforms to the description of company officials in the Congo provided by Robert Brown in 1895. After suggesting that those officials who were stationed on the lower reaches of the Congo were, generally speaking, law-abiding, he adds that in the case of those "working" along the upper reaches (the location of Kurtz's Inner Station), "where the natives are more savage, and infinitely more difficult to deal with, martial law is entrusted to young officials, poorly paid, often of slender ability, not always of the best character, and invariably beyond the checks afforded by the presence of those whose example and authority might restrain the exercise of petty despotism. The natives have been treated as if they were slaves, and otherwise irritated in a manner little calculated to endear the white man and the white man's ways" (183). Kurtz, in other words, should probably be thought of as a deliberately fictional character who shares traits with a wide variety of Europeans who worked or traveled in the vicinity of Stanley Falls in the 1880s and 1890s rather than as the embodiment of a specifically identifiable historical personage.

This view has the additional merit that it is partly confirmed by a letter written by Conrad in December 1903, in which he says that he "took great care to give Kurtz a cosmopolitan origin," presumably so as not to have him be too closely identified with any particular European power (in the context of the letter this seems to refer to Germany rather than Belgium). This intention is confirmed by the text, where it is made clear that Kurtz was partly educated in England and that his mother was half-English and his father half-French. Though his actual nationality is never mentioned, his close links with Brussels and the "Intended" suggest he must be Belgian. His name also hints at a German connection. On the basis of his explicitly cosmopolitan origins, Kurtz has often been viewed by critics as the incarnation of European (not merely Belgian) imperialism in Africa. Although this may be true, it also needs to be stressed that Leopold's Congo Free State was (until about 1890 at any rate) unique in its essentially *internationalist* constitution as well as in its employment of agents and military personnel from all European nations, especially Great Britain, Scandinavia, and Italy.[12] The first two governors of the Congo Free State were in fact Englishmen: Henry Stanley and Francis de Winton. From this perspective, it is not important who Kurtz's specific real-life original(s) might have been, for he is to be understood primarily as an overtly symbolic figure, as Conrad himself noted, though (as ever) with a certain degree of irony.

Nevertheless, in the same letter Conrad also reverts to the idea that his writing is always solidly based on personal experience. "I take my characters where I find them," he asserts bluntly (*Letters* 3:94). And in a letter to his French translator about a year and half earlier, he describes *Heart of Darkness* as "a wild story of a journalist who becomes manager of a station in the interior and makes himself worshipped by a tribe of savages" (*HD* 209). The identification in this unguarded summary of a specific profession is partly supported by references in the story to Kurtz's journalistic activity. Shortly before his death Kurtz tells Marlow that he "had been writing for the papers and meant to do so again" (*HD* 68); and later still, although Marlow openly confesses to being at a loss as to what Kurtz's actual profession was (or even if he had a profession), the two that do occur to him emphasize journalism, along with painting: "I had taken him for a painter who wrote for the papers, or else for a journalist who could paint" (*HD* 71). There is no single person Conrad had met in the Congo who exactly fits that description, yet there are several well-known figures closely associated with the Congo during the late nineteenth century who seem vaguely appropriate. H.H. Johnston, E.J. Glave, and H.M. Stanley all wrote for the papers and, to judge from the evidence of their books, the first two at least were competent in drawing.[13] None of them ever went "native," however, or had to be rescued from their supposedly worst desires. Even so, it may be that Conrad wanted his readers to think of such contemporary figures in connection with Kurtz, though not necessarily to go so far as to identify him with any particular individual.[14] What this suggestion also proves is that, though he does not say so, Conrad's "experience" is not just autobiographical but extends to the vicarious experience of his reading, so that Kurtz's origins are to be sought not only in the Congo but also in books, especially books with which Conrad had been familiar since childhood.

What seems quite apparent at the end of this largely fruitless search for a real, historical Kurtz is that there is none, not at least in the sense of satisfying all the main elements of his character and experience as described in *Heart of Darkness*. That, of course, does not mean that the search should not or will not continue. Critics seem almost as mesmerized by Kurtz as Marlow is—or as the Russian Harlequin is. Michael Levenson is surely right in bringing in Max Weber's terminology to help define Kurtz as an archetypally charismatic figure, not only in terms of his hypnotic power over some of the other characters in the story but also in terms of his enduring fascination for many of its readers (396–

401). He remains, as Conrad no doubt wanted him to remain, ultimately mysterious because obscured by contradiction and ambiguity. Rather like Wait in *The Nigger of the 'Narcissus,'* whom he also resembles in other ways, Kurtz seems to retain a magical grip on life, moribund though he is.[15] And perhaps it is finally because we encounter such difficulty in finding a local habitation and a historical name for him, that Marlow himself at first (and Conrad behind Marlow) finds it so hard to "see" Kurtz. It takes time in Conrad's world for a truly fictional character to come to life.

There are other important aspects of Conrad's narrative that are also unclear or, historically speaking, out of focus. For just as Conrad cannot be pinned down about an original for Kurtz, and studiously avoids place names—never mentioning Belgium or Brussels by name, or even the Congo or Africa itself—so the date when the story takes place is purposely left vague. Critics have nevertheless naturally tended to assume that the frame narrative is set in the "present" (1899) and the main narrative in 1890, when Conrad himself was in Africa. Ian Watt, for example, has Marlow blow the steam-whistle of his river-boat in 1890 without even bothering to provide any reasons for choosing that particular date (*Conrad* 141). This date may, of course, actually be the "right" one, but, though it *is* clear from the existence of the older narrating Marlow that a considerable number of years must have elapsed since the younger Marlow encountered Kurtz at the Inner Station, it is not clear that this number necessarily adds up exactly to nine. It could have been as many as fifteen (especially after Conrad's excision of the Boma passage for book publication) or perhaps as little as five. In favor of the former number(s) is Conrad's focus on the importance of the ivory trade, which would have been a signal to the attentive reader that the time of the main narrative must have been relatively remote, for by the mid-nineties the chief export from the Congo had become rubber rather than ivory. Perhaps the most logical year would be 1888, when, according to R.W. Beachey, both Belgians and Arabs began to steal ivory rather than to barter for it. It was also during that year that serious conflicts between Belgians and Arabs over ivory began to develop in the area of Stanley Falls (278). The total omission by Conrad of any reference to the brutal methods used by the Belgians generally (not just by Kurtz) to enforce rubber collection is odd, since by 1899 the general public in Britain was gradually becoming aware through newspaper reports of Belgian atrocities in the Congo as well as of the economic motives behind them. For Conrad's artistic purposes, however, ivory was clearly preferable, in terms of the *white* oppression in the *dark* continent, to the mostly colorless and, literarily and symbolically speaking, quite uninteresting rubber. In favor of the briefer period of about five years is the circumstance that Conrad apparently takes the so-called Arab Wars for granted when describing the drastic "methods" used by Kurtz to obtain his ivory. And even if Conrad did not expect his readers to make this connection, he himself clearly did when, for example, he alludes in the story to the tribal revolts during the last years of the century by using the word *rebels*. Patrick Brantlinger quite rightly, I think, emphasizes the influence on *Heart of Darkness* of the reading Conrad did after his return from the Congo, both of books, such as Sidney Hinde's *Fall of the Congo Arabs* (1897), and of newspaper reports in the *Times*. There is, for example, an almost unmistakable reference to the so-called Stokes affair of 1895 (when an isolated Irish trader was summarily hanged by a Belgian officer) in the conversation between the manager of the Central Station and his porcine uncle overheard by Marlow: "'No one, as far as I know, unless a species of wandering trader—a pestilential fellow snapping ivory from the natives.' Who was it they were talking about now? I gathered in snatches that this was some man supposed to be in Kurtz's district, and of whom the Manager did not approve. 'We will not be free from unfair competition till one of these fellows is hanged for an example,' he said. 'Certainly,' grunted the other; 'get him hanged! Why not? Anything—anything can be done in this country" (*HD* 34). What Brantlinger does not make sufficiently clear, however, when he observes that the "Arab rivals of the Belgians are conspicuous in the story only by their absence," is that in terms of physical appearance if not religion or class, the Arabs were often identical with the people whom, like the Belgians, they were oppressing (*Rule* 263). For Conrad, the fact that in the wars that some of the Congolese tribes waged against the Belgians, they were led by Islamic leaders of Central or East African ethnicity would perhaps not have been an important consideration.

It is only through Marlow's eyes that we are able to "see" Kurtz at all, which is why we do not see Kurtz until Marlow first sees him. This is true on a quite literal level. Initially Kurtz is only a name. Marlow *hears* of Kurtz from various people long before he ever manages to see him. The closer he gets to seeing him, the more knowledgeable about him his informants become, but they further complicate the issue not only by the greater or lesser extent of their knowledge (and the differences and contradictions within that accumulating body of knowledge) but also by what we succeed in learning (through Marlow again) about their own characters and their dispositions toward Kurtz. So Marlow's first informant, the Chief Accountant at the Outer Station, is obviously an admirer of Kurtz, predicting that Marlow will eventually meet that "first-class agent," that "very remarkable person" when he reaches the heart of the real ivory country from which Kurtz is sending back "as much ivory as all the others put together" (*HD* 22). Though Marlow provides us with a vividly drawn sketch of the Accountant's character and appearance, his function in the story, so far as Marlow is concerned, is limited to his connection with Kurtz. "I wouldn't have mentioned the fellow to you at all," he tells his friends aboard the *Nellie*, "only it was from his lips that I first heard the name of the man who is so indissolubly connected with the memories of that time" (*HD* 21). Nevertheless, once Marlow *has* mentioned him and made us see him—with a mixture of irony, contempt, and respect—as a "hairdresser's dummy," we necessarily adjust our response to Kurtz in line with our response to the Accountant. Is Kurtz primarily remarkable to the professionally interested Accountant because of the amount of ivory he sends back? Because he has shown that he is capable of doing "real work" in circumstances in which no other white man has managed to do so? Is Kurtz therefore also remarkable in the ambiguous way the "hairdresser's dummy" is remarkable? Does the Accountant's careful attention to his own appearance and to the accuracy of his books, along with his complete inattention to the welfare of the human beings around him, black or white, augur a similar attitude in Kurtz? More questions of a similar but even more complex sort arise when Marlow goes on to interview others about Kurtz or overhear them speak about him, as he does not only in the cases of the Manager and his uncle, but also with the Mephistophelean Brickmaker; the Russian Harlequin; and, most ambiguously of all, Kurtz's bereaved fiancée.

Inevitably this increasing multitude of interlocking questions is extraordinarily difficult to answer; and their degree of difficulty is raised to an even higher power when we realize that any answers we may arrive at, before they can be validated, must be filtered through our understanding/evaluation of Marlow's own character and reliability. It is as if we were trapped in a house of mirrors, with Kurtz's image revealed to us through a succession of variously distorted reflections and all of these reflections reflected once again by a kind of huge master-mirror (Marlow) that takes up most of the house itself. To be sure, we are also helpfully provided with what looks like a minimally "unreflected" peephole into that house of mirrors, namely the opening section of the story, which is narrated by an unnamed friend of Marlow's. We seem to be permitted, in other words, to "see" Marlow through the presumably objective medium of a trustworthy observer and not just another distorting mirror. Or perhaps not?

There is something else here too, something intended to intrigue our minds as readers, if not always our bosoms. That is, the questions raised by the Accountant's remarks about Kurtz (or, for that matter, the remarks of the other characters about Kurtz) apparently do not present the same degree of difficulty or complexity to Marlow's auditors aboard the *Nellie* as they do to us or even to the young "active" Marlow himself (as opposed to the older "inactive" teller of the story). That is because, as Marlow points out, "'Of course you fellows see more than I could then. You see me, whom you know'"(*HD* 30). That this statement is meant to be taken with at least a pinch of irony, though not perhaps by Marlow himself, is indicated by the immediately following sentence informing us that "it had become so pitch dark that we listeners could hardly see one another." Nonetheless, it is true that Marlow's listening friends do "know" him in a way that we as mere readers cannot; hence they are in a much better position to correlate his words to what they know of his character and so arrive at a "correct" interpretation. To some extent, this may also be the reason why the narrator of the frame story takes the trouble to warn us that for Marlow-the-story-teller "the meaning of an episode was not inside like a kernel but outside."[16] That is, for him (and so presumably for us too) the meaning should not be looked for in the message but in the medium, in the way in which the story is told—a distinction rather like the earlier one between words and meaning. It would appear, then, that by providing us with this clue the narrator is trying to help us find our way around the intricacies of Conrad's house of mirrors. We certainly need all the help we can get.

Kurtz, of course, does himself eventually put in a brief personal appearance, though even then it is mediated via Marlow's eyes and ears. For most of the story Kurtz is, as we have seen, doubly mediated, first through Marlow and then, successively, through at least one additional character. Part of the reason (and surely part of the effect) of this procedure is to keep raising the level of suspense in the reader's mind, and possibly also in his or her bosom—this delaying strategy also explains why *Heart of Darkness* is sometimes called a detective story, though in my view its structure resembles more the procedure of gathering evidence characteristic of a trial lawyer.[17] Another reason may be that Conrad wishes to build up Kurtz's personality for us entirely out of the reactions of others who encounter him, so as to convey in this way more naturally and persuasively its extraordinary power and attraction—much as Conrad's friend John Galsworthy was later to attempt to do with Irene Forsyte in *The Man of Property* (1906). Certainly the intensity of the emotional response shown by Kurtz's Lake tribe (and especially by the Black Amazon) at the prospect of his imminent departure is impressive not only in itself but as testimony to the emotional power that Kurtz wields over them. To a greater or lesser degree this also holds true of the reactions of the other characters, and particularly of Marlow himself, who, despite strong and justified reservations, finally proclaims Kurtz to have been a "remarkable man." And we readers must believe him, for why would he have expended his breath, and the time of his friends, in recounting his story if Kurtz had been unremarkable? And surely we readers and critics agree, for how else to explain the *immensity* of the critical literature that has grown up around this story and to which this study makes yet a further contribution?

Kurtz's effect on Marlow's imagination is gradual but inexorable. Nevertheless, even though Marlow keeps hearing about him, he has difficulty *seeing* him. Standing at the edge of the great river, and aware of the vastness of the surrounding forest as it lies revealed in the moonlight, Marlow is struck by the stark contrast between his own smallness and its bigness. He wonders what there might be in the depths of that forest. "I could see a little ivory coming out from there," he says, "and I had heard Mr. Kurtz was in there. I had heard enough about it too—God knows! Yet somehow it didn't bring any image with it—no more than if I had been told an angel or a fiend was in there" (*HD* 29). Marlow is obviously intrigued by Kurtz, but much of that interest at this stage is primarily attributable to his dislike of those who oppose him and plot against him. The enemy of my enemy, as it were, is my friend. It is this dislike of Kurtz's detractors rather than any positive attachment to Kurtz himself that also leads to what he claims to have been his first lie, not a real lie actually but more a lie by default, when he allows the Brickmaker to deceive himself into believing that he (Marlow) supposedly has influential friends in the company headquarters in Europe (which, of course, he has).[18] Marlow tells his friends aboard the *Nellie* that he lied in order to help "that Kurtz whom at the time I did not see—you understand. He was just a word for me. I did not see the man in the name any more than you do" (*HD* 29).

This is an odd but, partly for that reason, remarkable and even memorable phrase—"the man in the name." Just how one is supposed to go about looking for a man in a name is never made clear. The name in this case is "Kurtz," which in German, as Marlow later explicitly points out, means "short." When he finally does get to see him at the Inner Station, it turns out that "the name was as true as everything else in his life—and death. He looked at least seven feet long" (*HD* 59). So it does not appear that the name itself provides much help in getting at the nature of the man, unless one wants to argue trivially that it promises his life will be short or that somehow the "cur" in Kurtz is meant to suggest his essentially animal nature and thereby allude proleptically to the famous episode in *Lord Jim* where Jim mistakenly thinks Marlow has referred to him as a cur.[19] Less fancifully, it may be that we are meant to think primarily of "name" in the extended sense of "reputation," so that Marlow's inability to see the man in the name would refer primarily to his inability to envision what sort of man it is that has been able to gain so formidable a reputation. Here, however, "man" cannot refer merely to Kurtz's actual "image" or to his physical appearance (since Marlow could easily have asked someone about that), but to something more spiritual, something that might provide a key to his character, especially to its moral fiber (or about whether he is an "angel" or a "fiend," as Marlow speculates).[20]

In a more metaphysical sense, the "name" might also be thought of as equivalent to the merely physical "accidents" of a person, whereas the "man" is the essence, the "quiddity"—again a distinction similar to the one between the superficiality of language and the depth of meaning. That we are intended to allow our thoughts to stray at least some distance into such philosophical byways is suggested by the manner in which Marlow, after coining his enigmatic phrase, suddenly turns on his auditors, inquiring aggressively if they "see him? Do you see the story? Do you see anything?" (*HD* 30). On the basis of these unanswered questions Marlow goes on to lament the difficulty—indeed the impossibility—of communicating to another person "the dream-sensation" when one is relating a dream, or the "life-sensation" when, as here, one is giving an account of a particular epoch of one's existence. What all this seems to suggest is an existential solipsism ("We live, as we dream—alone"); in other words, the only man within any name whom we can ever have any hope of "seeing" is the man we are ourselves. Yet it seems—for why else does Marlow continue to tell his story?—that we must continue to make the attempt to do so, an attempt that in the final analysis is the search for *the* man in *the* name; that is, a quest for an Everyman, for the basis of what makes us essentially human, for what is hidden beneath the purely nominal surface of language.

Marlow does not have to wait long to catch a glimpse of Kurtz. Lying half-asleep on the deck of his beached steamboat, he chances to overhear the Manager and his uncle discussing Kurtz. He learns that the Manager's authority was bypassed when Kurtz had been sent directly to the Inner Station; that within a year he had dismissed his single white assistant as incompetent but had quickly followed that up by sending out large quantities of high-quality ivory that he had originally intended to accompany downriver himself. He had started out on a journey to take it downriver, in fact; on the way, however, he had suddenly turned back, leaving the ivory in the care of a trusted English half-caste clerk. Uncle and nephew are nonplussed by this sudden reversal, but Marlow reacts very differently. "As for me," Marlow says when he overhears this anecdote about Kurtz, "I seemed to see Kurtz for the first time. It was a distinct glimpse: the dugout, four paddling savages, and the lone white man turning his back suddenly on the headquarters, on relief, on thoughts of home perhaps, setting his face towards the depths of the wilderness, towards his empty and desolate station. I did not know the motive. Perhaps he was just simply a fine fellow who stuck to his work for its own sake" (*HD* 34).

In this first vision of Kurtz, Marlow sees him not as angel or fiend, but as hero. Marlow is now able to "see" him for the first time, because he is suddenly able to fit him into an established and familiar mould—that of the heroic explorer. For Conrad—and for Marlow too, at least insofar as Marlow reflects Conrad's psyche here—this was precisely how he had always imagined Africa. Looking back late in life at the kind of "world of mentality and imagination" he had first entered as a young boy, Conrad recalled that it was figures like Bruce, Speke, and Burton "and not the characters of famous fiction who were my first friends" (*Last Essays* 22). In some cases, Conrad goes on to say, an automatic association soon arose between a particular explorer and a particular part of the world. Gifted already as a young boy with an eidetic imagination, Conrad *saw* (and continued to *see* even as an old man) actual images of his heroes.[21] When he thought of the Western Sudan, for example, there arose inevitably the "vision of a young, emaciated fair-haired man, clad simply in a tattered shirt and worn-out breeches, gasping painfully for breath and lying on the ground in the shade of an enormous African tree (species unknown), while from a neighboring village of grass huts a charitable black-skinned woman is approaching him with a calabash full of pure cold water, a simple draught [of] which, according to himself, seems to have effected a miraculous cure."[22] This emaciated young man is Mungo Park, the first of a long line of chiefly British explorers of the interior of sub-Saharan Africa. Similarly, Conrad describes David Livingstone as "the most venerated perhaps of all the objects of my early geographical enthusiasm." As with the Western Sudan, so with Central Africa—the words automatically "bring before my eyes an old man with a rugged, kind face and a clipped, grey moustache, pacing wearily at the head of a few black followers along the reed-fringed lakes towards the dark native hut on the Congo head-waters in which he died, clinging in his very last hour to his heart's unappeased desire for the sources of the Nile" (*Last Essays* 23–24).

It is not, I think, unreasonable to surmise that it is this vivid image of a dying but still indomitable Livingstone, accompanied only by a few faithful black followers, who, after having refused Stanley's offer to take him home, still stubbornly pursues his dream—that it is this very image that can be traced, even if only faintly, beneath the heroic image of a similarly solitary and fearless Kurtz that Marlow sees for the first time at the Central Station. It is not, of course, the last or the only image of him that Marlow will glimpse. There will be other images, radically different ones, but it is important to bear in mind that Marlow's first "sight" of Kurtz has been of heroic dimensions. It is against this first vision that the subsequent ones must be measured; and the intensity of Marlow's later reaction against Kurtz is a direct function of the intensity of his initial admiration for him. It is in this sense and for this reason, I think, that Norman Sherry is profoundly mistaken in suggesting that Conrad has altered Marlow so as not to reflect the naïveté of his own youthful experience of the Congo—the experience, in other words, of Conrad the "animal"—providing him supposedly with "the legacy of [his own] hardgained insight—he is skeptical from the first" (*Western* 346). That simply cannot be true, for if it were, Marlow would never have been able to "see" Kurtz initially in the heroic garb of a Livingstone. The only skeptical element in this first vision of the young Marlow is the veiled irony of the older Marlow's concluding remark about the possibility of Kurtz's being a "fine fellow" devoted to his work, a faint hint that prepares us for the younger Marlow's subsequent disillusion.[23]

Though Kurtz personally puts in only brief and mostly shadowy appearances in the novel, he is nevertheless the second most important character in it. He is also a character who, like Marlow, undergoes development, even if it is only development of a very peculiar sort. That development is due partly to the progressive and at times varying responses to him of the minor characters, but chiefly it is the result of the successively different ways in which Marlow "envisions" him. It is the circumstance of this development, in fact, that also partly accounts for the variegated, multifaceted, and even contradictory aspects of Kurtz's personality, for they represent successive, altering, and sometimes alternating "visions" of Kurtz's identity. This "developing" nature of Kurtz also helps to explain why Kurtz can appear to be not only heroic but also a sham, "hollow," and even evil—an apparent contradiction that Albert Guerard sees as the aesthetic flaw at the heart of *Heart of Darkness*[24] (37).

The second time in the narrative that Marlow sees Kurtz, it is in the flesh, though before that happens his imagination has already transformed Kurtz from a visual to an auditory phenomenon. Under the mistaken impression that the attacking tribe has probably killed Kurtz, Marlow suddenly realizes that all along he has been looking forward to a *talk* with Kurtz. "I made the strange discovery," he says, "that I had never imagined him as doing, you know, but as discoursing. I didn't say to myself, 'Now I will never see him,' or 'Now I will never shake him by the hand,' but 'Now I will never hear him.' The man presented himself as a voice." Just why Marlow should shift in this way from "seeing" Kurtz to "hearing" him, and even deny that such a shift has taken place, is not explained, but it is perhaps due to his apparently frustrated hopes of *hearing* from Kurtz about what he thinks must have been his heroic adventures as an explorer. It is also partly attributable, I think, to a growing suspicion during the voyage upriver that Kurtz is less of a heroic explorer and more of an amoral or even immoral entrepreneur. "Hadn't I been told," he says by way of what seems intended as an explanation of his new attitude, "in all the tones of jealousy and admiration that he had collected, bartered, swindled, or stolen more ivory than all the other agents together?' (*HD* 48). Note how the unethical nature of Kurtz's mode of acquisition is made progressive, reflecting the stages of Marlow's own progressive disillusionment.

Some considerable part of the transformation from the visual to the auditory manner of imagining Kurtz, however, is the result of the narrator Marlow's anachronistic introduction of information about Kurtz that the young Marlow only gains later. It is the Russian, whom at this stage in the narrative Marlow has not yet met, who first informs him of the supposedly great powers of verbal expression possessed by Kurtz; yet even so, immediately after the attack, Marlow is already discoursing ironically about the manifold gifts of this "gifted creature" and proposing that the one gift that "stood out pre-eminently, that carried with it a sense of real presence, was his ability to talk, his words—the gift of expression" (*HD* 48). Just what Conrad's ultimate point is in collapsing chronology in a way that focuses attention on Marlow's shift from eye to ear is not easy to fathom, but it may be in order to suggest to his readers that Marlow himself has relied too exclusively on his ears—that is, he has relied excessively on the testimony of others in shaping his visual (ethical) *image* of Kurtz. Here again we encounter a distinction between what we see ("reality" and "meaning") and what we hear ("sham" and "words"). Marlow himself, as we realize with a sinking feeling, also becomes in the course of the story progressively less of an image for his friends and more of a voice. And Marlow too seems to be more "gifted" with the great and ambiguous gift of expression than with any other "gift." If Marlow therefore is to be identified with Conrad, then Conrad too is posing a question here about the ultimate purpose—or, rather, purposelessness—of language and narration.[25]

In what has become for most readers the most memorable scene of *Heart of Darkness*, Marlow manages to recombine the faculties of sight and hearing so as to perceive Kurtz fully for what seems to be the first and last time. Entering his cabin one evening, Marlow witnesses a change coming over Kurtz's face such as "I have never seen and hope never to see again. Oh, I wasn't touched. I was fascinated. It was as though a veil had been rent. I saw on that ivory face the expression of sombre pride, of ruthless power, of craven terror—of an intense and hopeless despair. Did he live his life again in every detail of desire, temptation, and surrender during that supreme moment of complete knowledge? He cried in a whisper at some image, at some vision—he cried out twice, a cry that was no more than a breath: 'The horror! The horror!'" (*HD* 68).[26] No booming voice here and no grand eloquence, just a momentary vision in candlelight and a barely heard cry, but the veil has been torn and Marlow has at last gained full insight into the man in the name. So, for that matter, has Kurtz, for the "image," the "vision," that he sees in the brief moment before his death is the very same image that Marlow has seen all along, the vision of the essential self, the "naked man" stripped of all pretty rags and illusory names of self-deception, the image of Kurtz himself.[27]

But climactic and apparently final as this scene is, Marlow still has not "seen" the last of Kurtz. For a year later, as he is about to enter the house of Kurtz's grieving fiancée—the portentously unnamed "Intended"—hoping to rid himself at last of "all that remained of him with me" and thereby consign those remains to the "oblivion which is the last word of our common fate" (*HD* 71), he suddenly has once again "a vision of him on the stretcher opening his mouth voraciously as if to devour all the earth with all its mankind. He lived then before me, he lived as much as he had ever lived." And as Marlow waits in the drawing room for the Intended to receive him, he hears again "the whispered cry, 'The horror! The horror!'"(*HD* 72) Nor is even this the last vision Marlow will have of a Kurtz whose image stubbornly refuses to go away. As Marlow speaks with the Intended about Kurtz and as she tells him of her memories and her grief, he suddenly has a new vision of the two of them together: "I saw her and him in the same instant of time—his death and her sorrow—I saw her sorrow in the very moment of his death." And as if unable to get over his astonishment at the novelty and intense reality of this vision himself, he repeats. "Do you understand? I saw them together—I heard them together" (*HD* 73).

It is therefore with a sort of grim humor that Marlow responds to the Intended's emphatic remark that neither she nor anyone else will ever see Kurtz again: "Never see him! I saw him clearly enough then. I shall see this eloquent phantom as long as I live" (*HD* 75). The man in the name whom the young Marlow had once been unable to envision has now become for the old Marlow the ghost in the mind whom it is impossible to exorcise. As Marlow tells his friends, he has kept faith with Kurtz beyond the grave sufficiently to give him indisputably the right to lay the ghost of his memory, if he chose to do so: "But then, you see, I can't choose. He won't be forgotten" (*HD* 51). Marlow is haunted by Kurtz, not in any crude ghost-story way, but by the eidetic images of him that have come to inhabit his mind. In the end the man in the name survives as a man in Marlow; he has been, in fact, transformed into an integral part of Marlow himself, just as he has, though one hopes with rather less horrific tenacity, in all of us who have heard his voice and seen his image.[28]

4

IMPERIAL SHAM AND REALITY
IN THE CONGO

Hoo, Hoo, Hoo.
Listen to the yell of Leopold's ghost
Burning in hell for his hand-maimed host.
                    Vachel Lindsay, "The Congo: A Study of the Negro Race"

The King acted for Africa! What was the center of Africa before 1876?
A vast region, mysterious, inaccessible, backward; the fertile terrain of
customs which were still barbarous and abominable; the reign of ignorance and poverty; a land of all sorts of horrors; the hunting ground of
the slaving hordes.
                    P.A. Roeykens, "Leopold—Patriot and Philanthropist"

Though *Heart of Darkness* has been and continues to be subjected to
the minutest critical examination and cross-examination, so far as I know
no critic has ever noted Marlow's insistence on distinguishing between
two Kurtzes, an "original" one and a "sham." He does this twice. The
first instance occurs in the context of defining Kurtz's origins—hence,
evidently, one of the indicated meanings of the word *original*. In this
passage, Marlow ironically refers first, using the third person singular
neuter pronoun, to Kurtz as "the initiated wraith from the back of Nowhere" (the source apparently of the sham Kurtz) that "could speak
English to me" (*HD* 50). Then Marlow suddenly rehumanizes Kurtz by
using the third person singular masculine pronoun, announcing that "the
original Kurtz had been educated partly in England and—as he was good
enough to say himself—his sympathies were in the right place" (my italics). The second occasion for making the distinction takes place as Marlow
listens to Kurtz's voice discoursing at length about itself as the steamboat makes its way back from the Inner Station. "Oh, he struggled, he
struggled," Marlow says of him.

The wastes of his weary brain were haunted by shadowy images now—

images of wealth and fame revolving obsequiously around his unextinguishable gift of noble and lofty expression. My Intended, my station, my career, my ideas—these were the subjects for the occasional utterances of elevated sentiments. The shade of the *original* Kurtz frequented the bedside of the hollow sham whose fate it was to be buried presently in the mould of primeval earth. But both the diabolic love and the unearthly hate of the mysteries it had penetrated fought for the possession of that soul satiated with primitive emotions, avid of lying fame, of sham distinction, of all the appearances of success and power. (*HD* 67, my italics)

Just who is this "original" Kurtz? (There is evidently no need to ask who the "sham" Kurtz is.) In the first passage he is the young Kurtz who was partly educated in England and therefore managed to get his sympathies located "in the right place." This would seem to suggest that the original Kurtz was not only ethnically part British but also politically pro-British (there was in fact a strong British contingent in the employ of the Congo Free State, from Stanley on down); that he accepted and practiced the characteristic British virtues as exemplified by Marlow and his friends aboard the *Nellie*; and that, in short, he was "one of us." The second use of "original" with reference to Kurtz is more ambiguous and difficult to define. Certainly, however, the emphatic contrast of the *original* with the *sham* Kurtz suggests that the former is not a sham but something like the "original" as defined by the earlier use of the word. But still it remains unclear in what sense this original Kurtz frequents the bedside of the sham Kurtz. Are we to take this to mean that Kurtz's egomaniacal monologue is occasionally interrupted by periods of sanity and modesty? If so, there certainly is not much evidence in the text for such behavior, unless we are to interpret his incessant "struggles" as indications of the survival of his better half. And what about the "it" in the final sentence? Does "it" refer to the original Kurtz or to the hollow sham? Or somehow to both? What is the significance in this connection of the curious transposition of adjectives in the phrases "diabolic love" and "unearthly hate"? Does the latter apply to the original Kurtz and the former to the sham? Or again to both? Is there a further suggestion here that the two have become so inextricably entangled that they can no longer be separated?[1]

Whatever the answers to these questions, it seems clear that in Marlow's view there had once been a "real" Kurtz, one who may in fact have been as heroic as he had "originally" envisioned him. What happened to this original Kurtz that he should have become a sham, or at least become a quasi-sham or at times a sham? For it is clear that somehow and to some degree the original Kurtz survives in the sham, that there is still a man in the name. One answer to this question, a simple one but not necessarily for that reason wrong, is that because of a fatal flaw (presumably hubris) the original Kurtz ceased to act and to think in a gentlemanly manner and became an immoral brute who decapitated people, possibly ate parts of their bodies, certainly stuck their heads on poles, stole large quantities of ivory by main force, and took to participating in "unspeakable rites." This is something that, as Marlow intimates, might not have happened had Kurtz remained "in his place," that is, if he had not ventured alone into the heart of darkness, where like Conrad himself he "had no business" to be, and where there were no external societal restraints to control his rampant ego.[2] Inevitably, he was therefore forced to rely entirely on whatever inner resources of restraint he possessed, because when one finds oneself, as Kurtz did, in "solitude without a policeman," then "you must fall back upon your own innate strength, upon your own capacity for faithfulness" (*HD* 49-50). However, Kurtz's inner strength, rather like Jim's in the very different circumstances of the *Patna*, turned out to be not "good enough," though this is a fact that seems to have eluded his consciousness until the final moments of life.

The "original" and the "sham" Kurtz, as we have seen, are not always easily identifiable, respectively, with the "real" and the "false" one, or even perhaps with the "good" and the "bad." A striking example of this confusion is the infamous scribbled gloss about exterminating "all the brutes" at the close of Kurtz's essay on the suppression of "savage" customs in Africa. This pious document is clearly the product of the original Kurtz, the bearer of the imperial torch, whereas the note represents equally clearly an afterthought by the sham, or the ruthless maverick entrepreneur. But which in fact is more sincere or "real"? For Marlow there seems little doubt. The report is a sham, a well-meaning sham perhaps, but vague and without practical use. The brief scrawled retraction, on the other hand, strikes him as being "luminous and terrifying like a flash of lightning in a serene sky" (*HD* 51). Horrible as it is, it seems to emerge from a far more fundamental and genuine part of Kurtz's being than do the verbose, lofty, and altruistic sentiments. That is perhaps why Conrad himself, writing to Cunninghame Graham at just about the same time as he penned Kurtz's gruesome exhortation, expressed sympathy for the "extreme anarchists" and their "'hope for general extermination.'" The words that follow this devastating remark are almost like a psychological elaboration of Kurtz's own genocidal mania: "Very well, it is justifiable and, moreover, it is plain. One compromises with words. There's no end to it. It's like a forest where no one knows the way. One is lost even as one is calling out 'I am saved!'" (*Letters* 2:160). For Kurtz too there is no more compromise with words once he has entered the forest and gotten lost in its darkness; there is only the terrifying clarity of the most brutal kind of action.

Not that this is by any means the final word of Marlow (or Conrad) on Kurtz. As has often been pointed out, Kurtz's lack of restraint is contrasted vividly and apparently paradoxically with the immense and to Marlow inexplicable restraint exercised by the cannibal crew in not taking advantage of what seems like a good opportunity to overwhelm the physically weaker and much less numerous whites on board, thereby providing an opportunity to satisfy the hunger from which they have been suffering for weeks.[3] Marlow finally ascribes their restraint to "some kind of primitive honour" (*HD* 43), but what he misses in making the comparison is that the cannibal crew possesses a great advantage over Kurtz; that is, they form a group that is strongly bonded by a common origin and tradition, whereas Kurtz has long been, except for occasional visits by the Russian, the only member of his ethnic "tribe" for hundreds of miles around.[4]

Kurtz's situation is archetypal in Conrad's fiction, especially in the fiction dating from about the time he wrote *Heart of Darkness*: the typical protagonist, often an exile, finds himself far from home and his own kind; he is then tempted, by excessive pride and by actual or imagined superior ability, into believing that he is morally above the conventions of his own society and therefore justified in doing just about anything he pleases, including the exploitation of supposed inferiors. With various modifications, this is the situation of Almayer in *Almayer's Folly*, of Willems in the later parts of *Outcast of the Islands*, of Jim aboard the *Patna*—though paradoxically not in Patusan—in *Lord Jim*, and, transposed into a quasi-farcical mode, of Kayerts after killing Carlier in "An Outpost of Progress." In each case except the last, the protagonist has some older, paternal figure who helps guide him from a distance, representing a link to the old values: Tom Lingard for Almayer and Willems, Marlow and Stein for Jim, and the "gang of virtue" back in Europe for Kurtz. All four also have correspondingly immoral or amoral enemies: the Arabs for Almayer, the Pirates and Almayer for Willems, the German Captain and Gentleman Brown for Jim, the Manager and his uncle for Kurtz. Finally, each one also has a faithful and noble woman who loves him: Nina in Almayer's case, Aissa in Willems's, Jewel in Jim's, and the African Princess as well as, from a distance, the Intended in Kurtz's.

This repeated pattern is so striking that it is hard to avoid seeing in it a kind of compulsive fictional mirror for Conrad's own psyche, one in which Conrad consciously or half-consciously saw reflected (and distorted) his own situation as an exile from Poland, forced, without anyone of his own kind nearby to help him in moments of crisis, to fall back entirely on his own inner resources, able to count only on the distant and intermittent guidance of his uncle and guardian Tadeusz Bobrowski, as well as occasional assistance from his young, beautiful, and gifted "aunt," Marguerite Paradowska. Here, in the variously awful fates of these four projections of his imagination, he could see what would be his own lot unless he managed to hold on to the solid support of the values that had been instilled in him during childhood. However, even without insisting on any such autobiographical psychological links, it seems clear that for Conrad all four of these characters represent studies in what later anthropologists would come to call "detribalization."[5] That is, all four have for greater or lesser periods of time and for different reasons, both willingly and unwillingly (in the various cases) become separated from the tribal/national center from which they draw their moral strength. Although they may attempt to adapt—never with more than partial success—to the customs and ethic of another tribe, their failure to achieve integration is always due to an abiding sense that the culture of their new tribe is inferior to that of their old one.

That Conrad means us to understand that Kurtz's moral downfall is due to a process of detribalization (he, of course, does not use the word) is apparent from the way in which Kurtz is linked in Marlow's mind with the only other person who dies on board the riverboat, the African Helmsman. Like Kurtz, the Helmsman is inordinately impressed with his own talents—"he thought all the world of himself" (HD 45)—when he is in the company of others, but is utterly unable to carry out his responsibilities when he is not. He belongs to a distant coastal tribe and was "educated by my poor predecessor," the late Danish captain Fresleven, the violent manner of whose death strikingly anticipates the Helmsman's and is likewise the result of an inability to cope adequately when finding himself "out of place." The immediate cause of the Helmsman's getting himself killed is his opening of the shutter in the pilot-house to allow him to fire a rifle at the attackers on shore. So far as we know, he is the only African to do so, joining thereby the Belgian Pilgrims below who have been emptying their rifles in an equally foolish and ineffectual manner (attempting, as it were, to "exterminate all the brutes"). On the Helmsman's part this is a symbolic act of detribalization. Fittingly, therefore, for having adopted the worst customs of his new tribe, Conrad sentences him to death.

The connection of the Helmsman with Kurtz is first made explicit when Marlow suddenly thinks of Kurtz as he tosses a shoe soaked with the Helmsman's blood overboard. But there are other, less explicit and more important connections, including the fact that in his last moments of life the Helmsman apparently attempts to communicate with Marlow and then "frowns heavily, as though in response to some sign we could not see, some whisper we could not hear" (*HD* 47). Like Kurtz, the Helmsman seems to have a vision—of the horror?—just as he dies; and like Kurtz, his image is thenceforward indelibly inscribed in Marlow's memory: "And the intimate profundity of that look he gave me when he received his hurt remains to this day in my memory—like a claim of distant kinship affirmed in a supreme moment" (*HD* 51). The very words "supreme moment" are harbingers of that other "supreme moment"— Kurtz's death and vision of "the horror"—which are described a few pages later. So too with the less distant "kinship" that he feels for Kurtz, which impels/compels him to narrate his story.

Aside from Marlow himself, who is often viewed by critics as a kind of double for Kurtz—for if he were not, how could he manage to understand him so well?—there is at least one other figure in the story whose situation is meant to be compared with Kurtz's and thereby help explain him. (Conrad's fiction often proceeds by means of demonstrating how different types of characters react to similar environments or challenges, as in the cases of Brierly, Gentleman Brown, and Jim in *Lord Jim*.) This is the "decent young citizen in a toga" whom the older, narrating Marlow imagines coming to "savage" Britain in the wake of Roman imperial expansion. Significantly, this figure is preceded by another, a sometime "commander of a fine—what d'ye call 'em—trireme" in the Mediterranean who is unexpectedly transferred north to take charge of a much smaller riverboat, which has been ordered to move supplies up the Thames into a wilderness where they "must have been dying like flies." Of this nameless person, Marlow observes that he "did it very well too, no doubt, and without thinking much about it either, except afterwards to brag of what he had gone through in his time, perhaps" (*HD* 10). It is difficult not to associate this capable seaman with those two other equally capable seadogs, Charlie Marlow and Joseph Conrad, both of whom also relinquished real or imaginary commands of larger ocean-going craft to serve on small steamers plying the Congo River.[6] Like the Roman captain, Marlow does not devote much thought to what he is doing at the time; he is completely preoccupied with the mundane details of keeping the boat afloat (being in this respect rather like Conrad's "animal"), satisfied that "there was surface-truth enough in these things to save a wiser man" (*HD* 38). Only much later does he get around to attempting to discover the wider significance of his experience and to "brag" about it to his friends aboard the *Nellie*.[7]

The "decent young chap in a toga," on the other hand, resembles Kurtz by having come out into the darkness in order to "mend his fortunes." Like Kurtz too, once he reaches "some inland post," he begins to feel the "utter savagery" of his surroundings, and though he does not understand that "mysterious life of the wilderness" and even detests it, he also yields to its fascination: "Imagine the growing regrets, the longing to escape, the powerless disgust, the surrender—the hate" (*HD* 10). The very phrasing used here to describe the process of the young Roman's gradual moral deterioration anticipates Marlow's description of Kurtz's mind just before he dies: "Did he live his life again in every detail of desire, temptation, and surrender during that supreme moment of complete knowledge?" (*HD* 68). This "surrender," this loss of self-restraint, is something that Conrad himself feared and abominated, evidently because he too felt its powerful attraction. Commenting on this "horror" in the very different context of the allegedly excessive "dryness" (irony presumably) of his fiction, Conrad observes that he would certainly like to possess a magic wand with which to elicit at will the tears and laughter of his readers instead of whatever response it is that irony evokes. But there is a price to be paid for such a gift. For "to be a great magician," Conrad goes on to say,

> one must surrender oneself to occult and irresponsible powers, either outside or within one's breast. We have all heard of simple men selling their souls for love or power to some grotesque devil. The most ordinary intelligence can perceive without much reflection that anything of the sort is bound to be a fool's bargain. I don't lay claim to particular wisdom because of my dislike and distrust of such transactions. It may be my sea training acting upon a natural disposition to keep good hold on the one thing really mine, but the fact is that *I have a positive horror of losing even for one moving moment that full possession of myself which is the first condition of good service.*[8] (*Record* xix, my italics)

Though it is clear that Conrad (and perhaps Marlow too) expects his audience to use the very brief, hypothesized account of the experiences of the Roman commander and the Roman citizen to provide a rough framework for the much longer and vastly more complex account of Marlow's and Kurtz's experiences, it is not immediately clear what that framework is supposed to be. Certainly the moral decline of the Roman citizen, though regrettable, is viewed dispassionately. Perhaps it is simply because he never takes on real fictional flesh—because he has no name and therefore cannot become a "man"—that Conrad and Marlow do not make much of a fuss over him. He is after all doubly or even triply fictional. There is, to be sure, a very latinic "fascination of the abomination" about him, as befits a young chap in a toga, but there is no "horror," no epiphanic moment of sudden self-recognition. Moreover, the Roman's "surrender" seems purely passive, a kind of yielding to a "soft" option, whereas, whatever Kurtz's surrender may be conceived of as having been, it certainly was not that.[9] Kurtz becomes the chief, even the "god," of his newly chosen people, whereas the Roman citizen seems simply to vanish into an ill-defined morass of self-disgust and self-hatred. Even—or particularly—at his worst Kurtz keeps sending out vast quantities of high-quality ivory; even—or particularly—at his worst Kurtz remains "efficient." His work, if not the moral impulse behind it, remains "real." Not so, apparently, the formerly decent young chap in a toga. Though we are never provided with any details of the abominable things that so fascinated him, and though it is certainly within the realm of possibility that he has abandoned his toga and started painting himself blue, still, given his weakness and passivity, it is hard to think of him as having turned on the screws so as to extract more taxes or as having raided villages in order to secure additional slave labor. Nor, for that matter, is there any indication that the degenerate citizen and the upright captain have met or share any contact beyond a shadowy coexistence in the same paragraph.

Marlow's response to Kurtz is radically different, so different in fact that one is led to wonder what it is in Kurtz's moral deterioration that makes it so much worse (and so much more worth telling) than the Roman's—Kurtz is in fact the abomination that brings about Marlow's fascination. If one cares to pursue this line of inquiry a little further, some additional and even more important differences quickly emerge that distinguish Kurtz from the Roman. The first is that the latter lives "in the midst of the incomprehensible which is also detestable" (*HD* 10), whereas Kurtz understands full well the precise nature of the new cultural environment that he inhabits. When Marlow blocks his return on all fours to the fire and the Sorcerer's incantations, asking Kurtz if he knows what he is doing, the latter replies, "Perfectly" (*HD* 64). And when, on the following day, the boat pulls away from the shore and the Black Amazon and her followers break out into a "roaring chorus of articulated, rapid, breathless utterance," Marlow asks him again if he understands all this, and he replies with almost equal succinctness, "Do I not?" (*HD* 66). Kurtz's intelligence, as Marlow discovers to his surprise, has remained "perfectly clear;" it is his soul that "was mad" (*HD* 65). The Roman, on the contrary, is merely disgusted with himself and displays no signs whatever of any grand, diabolic intensity. He resembles Kayerts more than he does Kurtz.

The other aspect of Kurtz that makes him so different from the decent Roman citizen is that Kurtz—both the original and the sham—is truly "remarkable." The "original" Kurtz, as Marlow discovers from interviewing or overhearing several of the former's friends, enemies, and associates in the course of the story (as well as Kurtz himself), was a great deal more than a merely "decent" citizen. He was a man who showed unusual ability in a variety of endeavors—journalism, the arts, politics—someone who possessed the capacity to touch "decent" people as various as the Russian and the Intended to the depths of their being. Nor has the sham Kurtz lost any of his "original" charismatic power, as is evident in the reaction of the Black Princess and of Marlow himself. It is in fact the very loftiness of Kurtz's *original* status that makes Marlow (and eventually Kurtz himself) feel all the more intensely the distance that he has "fallen," just as Lucifer's descent into hell is more horrific and terrifying (and more worth narrating) than that of a minor bureaucratic mischief-maker like, say, the Manager.[10]

The most important difference between Kurtz and the decent Roman, however, lies not in their individual character and genius or lack thereof; it resides, rather, in the moral nature of the larger collective enterprises of which they are both parts. The Roman commander goes out into the heart of darkness only because he has, as it were, been commanded to do so; the decent Roman citizen goes purely in order to make money. Thus, whatever moral qualities may or may not redeem them as individuals, the larger cultural entity of the Roman Empire, which they both serve, stands condemned as nothing more than "just robbery with violence, aggravated murder on a great scale, and men going at it blind— as is very proper for those who tackle a darkness"[11] (*HD* 10). In this sense the Roman commander's quiet competence ultimately functions only to make the robbery greater and the murder more frequent, whereas, paradoxically, the sometime decent Roman's moral decline may actually diminish both. Collectively, their only justification is their greed; their "system" of exploitation consists simply of "brute force," which, as Marlow notes, is nothing to boast of because it is merely a function of their opponent's weakness. It belongs, as the adjective "brute" indicates, to the "animal" realm, which Conrad had himself once inhabited and which, in this context at any rate, possesses no positive moral dimension.

Marlow and his friends aboard the *Nellie*, however, claim to belong to a cultural entity that, though undoubtedly also participating in "the conquest of the earth," does so competently and with "an idea at the back of it, not a sentimental pretence but an idea; and an unselfish belief in the idea—something you can set up, and bow down before, and offer a sacrifice to" (*HD* 10). In contrast to the Roman Empire, which was merely a "squeeze," their own British Empire is allegedly saved by its "efficiency—a devotion to efficiency." What is more, it differs further from the Roman Empire in that it is an empire of "colonists" and not simply of "administrators." Just how India, say, might have been fairly described as part of a "colonial" rather than an "administrative" empire or just what Marlow (or Conrad, for that matter) means by "efficiency" is never explained, though the latter quality is probably to be equated with the "real work" that, in his view, is being carried out in that "vast amount of red" that he sees displayed on the map of Africa when he visits the company offices in Brussels.[12]

Altogether Marlow's description of what Roman Britain was supposed to have been like seems, once one begins to look at it a little more closely, eccentric and even downright wrongheaded. His bald assertion, for example, that the Romans "were no colonists" but mere administrators is at the very best a half truth. As virtually all nineteenth-century historians were agreed (and subsequent ones too, for that matter), the Romans settled or "colonized" (and in the process thoroughly "Romanized") that part of Britain that was eventually to become the "heart" of England, namely the southern and eastern parts. In fact, as Conrad and Marlow must have been fully aware themselves, the "biggest, and the greatest, town on earth," whose "mournful gloom" the occupants of the *Nellie* view in the distance near the beginning of the story, was originally a Roman foundation bearing a name that had been first conferred on it by Romans. Certainly the cities, roads, forts, villas, temples, and walls that the Romans built over the course of four centuries in and for their British province were not merely the means of fostering some purely administrative "squeeze." And though the Romans were undoubtedly "conquerors" to begin with, it is simply false to assert that they ruled Britain by "brute force." Nor is there much evidence that they were ever in the habit of grabbing whatever they could "for the sake of what was to be got," or that they were given to committing "robbery with violence, aggravated murder on a great scale." Neither, so far as anthropological studies are to be relied on, did the primarily Celtic population of pre-Roman Britain "have a different complexion or slightly flatter noses" than the Romans did themselves. In fact, when the Romans finally withdrew their last remaining garrisons from Britain in the fifth century, that action was greeted by the abandoned provincials with an intensity of sorrow and regret that, more than anything else in the story, evokes the sorrow of Kurtz's followers as they watch his departure.

In this context it is perhaps useful to quote briefly from what might justifiably be considered a "consensus" view about Roman Britain at the turn of the nineteenth into the twentieth century, namely the treatment given the subject in the classic eleventh edition of the *Encyclopedia Britannica*:

> In the lands looking on to the Thames estuary (Kent, Essex, Middlesex) [which is, let us remember, where Conrad's story opens], the process [of Romanization] had begun before the Roman conquest. It was continued after that event, and in two ways. To some extent it was definitely encouraged by the Roman government, which here, as elsewhere, founded towns peopled with Roman citizens—generally discharged legionaries—and endowed them with franchise and constitution like those of the Italian municipalities. It developed still more by its own automatic growth. The coherent civilization of the Romans was accepted by the Britons, as it was by the Gauls, with something like enthusiasm. Encouraged perhaps by sympathetic Romans, spurred on still more by their instincts, and led no doubt by their nobles, they began to speak Latin, to use the material resources of Roman civilized life, and in time to consider themselves not the unwilling subjects of a foreign empire, but the British members of the Roman state.

Furthermore, as the foregoing account makes clear and as Conrad, himself an avid reader of history and geography, must also have considered obvious, the Roman Empire's imperialist activity had never been confined to Britain. In fact, at the height of its power, the Roman Empire—by virtue of its soldiers, to be sure, but also by virtue of its laws, its roads, its settlements, and its "administrators"—had succeeded in linking the greatest part of western and southern Europe, along with all of northern Africa, together into a single coherent civilization. Indeed, insofar as "Europe" still has a meaning today as a unified culture, this is largely due to the enduring impact of Roman imperial expansion and civilization. Even during the late nineteenth century, when, after the astonishing military successes of Bismarck's Prussia, it had suddenly become fashionable for many English people to prefer their supposed Germanic or Teutonic origins to their Celtic and Roman ones, it was utterly unheard of for historians to claim that the Roman conquest of Britain had been a deplorable event that should never have happened. It seems highly unlikely that Marlow's little audience of well-established ex-seagoing administrators aboard the *Nellie* would ever have agreed with such an assessment.[13] Not surprisingly, therefore, not even the anti-Roman and anti-imperialist Marlow presumes to make such a claim, at least overtly, though a linkage of the Roman Empire with Leopold's very different enterprise in the Congo (or even, much more indirectly, with British imperial expansion in other parts of Africa and in Asia) is unmistakably suggested by the reference to the general exploitation of people with non-Caucasian complexions and facial contours. Marlow himself seems to insist on this point, though just what his purpose might be in doing so remains unclear. Perhaps it is simply to show that human nature, along with imperialist human beings, has not changed a great deal since that "other day," which dawned some nineteen hundred years earlier; or perhaps it is meant primarily to suggest that Marlow has learned in the Congolese school of hard knocks to look past the facade of every imperialist sham at the shameful reality lurking beneath. Perhaps. What is certain, however, is that Marlow's comparison must have made British readers of (or "listeners" to) his story—even, paradoxically, those of the ultraconservative, Empire-touting *Maga*—sympathize and even identify with the oppressed African population of the Congo, since the latter were being maltreated by Belgian "administrators" in much the same way that their own ancestors supposedly had been by the Romans.

Marlow's (and apparently Conrad's) insistence that the kind of imperialism practiced by the Romans in Britain and the Belgians in the Congo is identical renders unlikely Andrea White's hypothesis that Conrad is expressing in *Heart of Darkness* a nostalgia for an earlier and supposedly more humane imperialism ("Conrad" 183). Conrad's views on the nature and even the desirability of imperialist "squeezes" were not consistent, however. In *Lord Jim*, for example, Marlow exalts the combination of courage and greed that led the Dutch and English pepper traders to the Malaysian Archipelago in the early seventeenth century:

Where wouldn't they go for pepper! For a bag of pepper they would cut each other's throats without hesitation, and would forswear their souls, of which they were so careful otherwise: the bizarre obstinacy of that desire made them defy death in a thousand shapes—the unknown seas, the loathsome and strange diseases; wounds, captivity, hunger, pestilence, and despair. It made them great! By heavens! it made them heroic; and it made them pathetic too in their craving for trade with the inflexible death levying its toll on young and old. It seems impossible that mere greed could hold men to such a steadfastness of purpose, to such a blind persistence in endeavor and sacrifice. And indeed those who adventured their persons and lives risked all they had for a slender reward. They left their bones to lie bleaching on distant shores, so that wealth might flow to the living at home. To us, their less tried successors, they appear magnified, not as agents of trade, but as instruments of a recorded destiny. . . . (137)

Significantly, the heroism of these Kurtzian predecessors was, as Marlow presents it, something completely self-contained. They might have cut each other's throats, but they did not cut anyone else's; they might have left their bones to bleach on distant shores, but other people's bones were left conspicuously undisturbed. Ultimately, so it appears, they were not even agents of some down-to-earth trading company but rather representatives of divine providence. The early imperialist adventurers, in this flattering conception, were *blind* to the very light that their self-immolating torches were supposedly shedding on the darkness.

If the readers of *Maga* could thus simultaneously savor the joys of being victims and masters of empire, they could also take comfort in Marlow's implicit suggestion that, since the decline and fall of the Roman Empire had been caused by its "inefficiency" and its purely administrative, squeezeful nature, the British Empire might very well be exempt from a similar fate. After all, unlike the Roman entrepreneurial squeeze, it was a "purely" colonizing venture. Such consolation was especially needful at a time when comparisons with Rome and the passing of other earlier empires were becoming increasingly frequent and ominous—a mood of apocalyptic, fin de siècle pessimism that is captured in contemporaneous works as different as H.G. Wells's *Time Machine* and Rudyard Kipling's "Recessional." In fact, not long after the *Maga* publication of "The Heart of Darkness," the unspoken (if not the unspeakable) fears of supporters of British imperialism seemed suddenly confirmed by the initial disasters of the Boer War in the autumn of 1899. Now even the stiffest of upper lips began to twitch noticeably. No doubt it was precisely because of this feeling of inner uncertainty and insecurity that an immense wave of rabid jingoism swept through much of the English population, producing a frenzy of yelling and cursing (especially in the press) not altogether unlike that described by Marlow on his voyage up the Congo. It even overwhelmed the otherwise utterly meek and mild-mannered poet Algernon Charles Swinburne and impelled him to give vent to his impotent rage in the following effusion:

Vile foes like wolves set free
Whose war is waged where none may fight or flee,
With women and with weaklings. Speech and song
Lack utterance now for lo[a]thing. Scarce we hear
Foul tongues that blacken God's honoured name
With prayers turned curses . . .
To scourge these dogs agape with jaws of flame. (qtd. in Angell 105)

Had Conrad's novel appeared in *Maga* at this momentous time, it is likely that its unmistakably anti-imperialist message would have met with little sympathy or even tolerance. By the end of the Boer War in 1902, however, public sentiment had already shifted sufficiently in the opposite direction that when the story first appeared in book form, it succeeded quite unintentionally in expressing a sense of disillusionment and cynicism, one that was also abetted by the growing outrage against Belgian atrocities in the Congo. By this time even an ardent old imperialist like the earl of Cromer could admit to himself in *Ancient and Modern Imperialism* (1910) that "nations wax and wane" and that the "far distant" day might yet arrive when the British would be "handing over the torch of progress and civilization in India to those whom we have ourselves civilized." However, lest any hasty expectations should be aroused, Cromer made it clear that such a transfer would have to be delayed "until human nature entirely changes, and until racial and religious passions disappear from the face of the earth." Any "relinquishment of that torch" prior to the arrival of that happy day, Cromer warned, "would almost certainly lead to its extinction" (127). Torches, apparently, have to be treated with great care, for they are liable to go out quickly in hands that are not as careful and experienced as the British.

All this talk of British imperial "torches" and "sacred fires" can, has, and no doubt also should be seen as possibly ironic on Conrad's part. Nevertheless, on balance Conrad actually does seem to have intended his readers to respond to these symbols positively as sources of light rather than merely of smoke. Certainly irony and admiration for empire were compatible, as is evident in the case of another celebrated contemporaneous ironist, A.E. Housman, who, while impugning God, exempts the British Empire from criticism in *A Shropshire Lad* (1896).

The opening poem of that collection, "1887"—the year when Victoria (now also empress of India) celebrated her diamond jubilee—refers to the bonfires as beacons burning to "heaven," commemorating fallen army comrades who "shared the work with God" in Asia and beside the Nile (11). It should also be noted in this connection that, in terms of economic hard facts, the British Empire never profited commercially from its tropical and subtropical possessions (with the exception of India). Even hostile critics, notably J.A. Hobson, did not dispute this curious economic fact but searched instead for answers to the question as to why Britain was prepared to "embark on such unsound business" (qtd. in Stokes 292). This does not mean, of course, that individual fortunes were not made out of imperial ventures (or adventures) that represented losses to the nation as a whole.

If, however, Marlow's analysis of Roman imperial rule in Britain is far-fetched on closer investigation, what he says and implies about Belgian imperial rule in the Congo is amply verified by the evidence. Belgian rule is purely "administrative," without any redeeming "colonial" component whatever; and though in theory there is supposed to be lawful trading with, and employment of, the Africans, so far as the evidence of Marlow's eyewitness account shows, these consist chiefly of providing the cannibal crew with apparently useless lengths of brass wire, shooting carriers along the roads, uprooting large numbers of people from their homes and either compelling them to perform seemingly pointless tasks in chain gangs or else consigning them to slow deaths by disease or starvation, or, finally—as in the case of Kurtz—raiding their villages and looting their ivory. It is therefore, I think, to the collective Belgian enterprise in the Congo, and not just to Kurtz's individual acts of depredation, that Marlow is referring when he tells the Manager that there is "no method at all" here (*HD* 61). Like his Romans (and like the symbolic, blindfolded figure in Kurtz's painting), they are all stumbling along helplessly in the dark.

Unlike Marlow's version of the Roman Empire, however, Leopold II's imperialistic Congo Free State did have an explicit "idea" behind it, being in fact the only new African state created during the period of the "scramble for Africa" to possess an internationally ratified mission to foster free trade, abolish slavery, and, in general, "educate" the African population. In 1890—the year when Conrad himself traveled to the Congo—the Anti-Slavery Conference in Brussels specifically authorized the Congo Free State to undertake a so-called antislavery war against the "Arabs" in the interior of the country, an opportunity that, in the view of at least one British observer, was "soon seized upon as an excuse for the further extension of the Congo State four years afterwards" (Brown 183). (This part of the Congo Free State was located near the great interior lakes of Central Africa—hence, presumably, Kurtz's link with the "Lake tribe" who become his special followers.) Kurtz's closely written seventeen-page report to the International Society for the Suppression of Savage Customs is obviously inspired by this officially sanctioned mandate. By the time Marlow gets to see it, he himself has evidently grown disillusioned with Leopold's Congo in general and with Kurtz in particular, so that this treatise is dismissed by him with corrosive irony as a vague, high-sounding collection of magical but ultimately meaningless phrases producing the impression of "an exotic Immensity ruled by an August Benevolence" (HD 50). In the interval Marlow had apparently been reading reports of Leopold's systematic atrocities in the Times, the Spectator, and, as we shall see later, very likely also in the Century Magazine. That is no doubt why the older Marlow almost explicitly equates Kurtz, the highly gifted exponent of the hocus-pocus of white "progress," with those red-painted sorcerers who, as he is about to depart, periodically shout "strings of amazing words that resembled no sounds of human language" (HD 66). In both cases—not only the white but also the black (or red) magic—these utterances are clear manifestations of pure "sham" rather than of shamanism; they are words issuing straight from the maw of the devil of folly and consist entirely of vox et praeterea nihil. But Marlow himself had apparently once accepted just about all of these ideas, for otherwise why should he have been so dismayed by the reality he encountered in the Grove of Death or by the chaotic mismanagement and petty plotting at the Outer and Central Stations?[14] And even after those initial experiences of disillusionment, he clearly continued to carry forward the bulk of his baggage of imperial idealism, so far as Kurtz is concerned, at least up the point of his encounter with the Russian, for he allows himself to be identified as a fellow member of the "gang of virtue" to which the "original" Kurtz had belonged.[15]

Marlow's eventual condemnation of Belgian exploitation of the Congo is clearly, if at first only symbolically, foreshadowed (he even uses the word) in the initial impressions he receives of the effects of "progress" at the Outer Station.[16] These consist, to begin with, of a graveyard of rusting equipment and disused (and misused) machinery, with a boiler "wallowing in the grass" and an upside-down railway car looking "as dead at [sic] the carcass of some animal." Not only are the machines wantonly abused in this environment of "rapacious and pitiless folly," but the human beings fare even worse, moved about randomly as they are in chain gangs or abandoned like rubbish beside a "vast, artificial hole somebody had been digging on the slope, the purpose of which I found impossible to divine" (*HD* 19-20). Mysterious though the specific role of this hole may be in furthering the sham "work" that is supposedly being carried out in the Congo Free State, its symbolic function is crystal clear; it is the mass grave that has been dug by Belgian "administrators" in which to bury their moribund black "helpers," people whom they have maltreated even more than they have their machines and their animals. The machines that do not work and the people who cannot— here, at the edge of the ironically named Congo Free State and still quite distant from the dark heart he is traveling toward, Marlow is confronted with the grim detritus of an imperial method that consists, as he later comes to realize, of "no method at all."

In this profoundly negative description Conrad is reflecting, perhaps quite consciously, a wider British view about Leopold's Congo that was beginning to emerge during the mid-nineties, partly as a result of the Stokes affair. As Jules Marchal notes, starting in late 1895 the *Times* published several interviews, both with missionaries as well as with a former agent, Alfred Parminter (a friend of E.J. Glave's), that clearly indicated that all was not well in Congoland (2:58–62). In an editorial entitled "The Black Question," published in the *Spectator* on October 19, 1895, the claim was made that "the Government of the Congo Free State is a new instance of what Mr. Gladstone once styled 'the negation of God erected into a system.'" After quoting unnamed "white witnesses of good character" to the effect that Congolese soldiers were bringing to their superior officers "'baskets of human hands, often including those of children,'" the editorial went on to acknowledge that Britain "helped to create what is, we fear, a most oppressive Government, and we are responsible up to the limit of our power of prevention for these oppressions" ("Black" 512–13). At the end of May 1896, another editorial appeared in the *Spectator* under the heading "The Congo State and the English Government." It was occasioned by the publication in the *United Service Magazine* of a report on "The Congo State: A Revelation," written by Capt. Philip H.B. Salusbury who, along with 170 other British officers, had volunteered in 1894 for service in King Leopold's army, the *Force Publique*. Of his experience there Salusbury wrote, among other things, that "the boasted work of civilisation is murder, rapine, plunder and cruelty in the most awful degree ever reached; the pretended enfran-

chisement of slaves is the introduction and maintenance of slavery under barbarous conditions, unequalled in the history of plantations, or of
the Southern States of America." And, further, in words that almost
anticipate Conrad's: "Of any conduct approaching in degree of horror
the daily barbarity I saw committed, no history known to me bears
record." After quoting these passages and pointing out that the "King of
the Belgians is responsible and we can only hope that up to now he is
ignorant of the kind of things that are done there," the editorial concluded with the hope that "when Parliament meets next week we shall
have some information as to what steps the Government are taking to
ensure that, whatever else the Congo authorities may think fit to do,
they shall not cheat and murder British subjects nor insult a British representative" ("Congo" 766–67). With respect to *Heart of Darkness,* what
is remarkable about these editorials and Salusbury's report is that they
seem to prove that public outrage in Britain against what was happening
in the Congo originated, not only among missionary circles or even mili-
tant reformers like Fox Bourne, but also in the very heart of British
imperialism, the Liberal Unionist press and the Army. This fact also shows
that Conrad's chiefly imperialist-sympathizing readers in *Blackwood's
Magazine* would not have been likely to interpret his harsh critique of
Belgian behavior in the Congo as in any way applicable to British activities in other parts of Africa.[17]

One of the dying blacks in particular symbolizes Marlow's horrified
sense—and behind him, Conrad's—of the results of the Leopoldian policy
of pitiless greed and folly. Among the diseased and starving figures lying
about "confusedly in the greenish gloom"—much like the machinery
Marlow had nearly stumbled over—he suddenly glimpses "a face near
my hand. The black bones reclined at full length with one shoulder against
the tree, and slowly the eyelids rose and the sunken eyes looked up at
me, enormous and vacant, a kind of blind, white flicker in the depths of
the orbs which died out slowly." Unnerved and somewhat unsure as to
what he should do, Marlow offers the dying man a ship's biscuit that he
finds in his pocket. It is a gesture that seems intended to suggest not so
much his genuine (and not, as Achebe implies, "sham") humanitarian-
ism as his utter helplessness in the face of such incomprehensible and
innocent suffering. At a loss to do or say anything else, he suddenly
notices how the virtually motionless and lifeless man "had tied a bit of
white worsted round his neck." It puzzles Marlow and sets him to wondering: "Why? Where did he get it. Was it a badge—an ornament—a
charm—a propitiatory act? Was there any idea at all connected with it.

It looked startling round his black neck, this bit of white thread from beyond the seas" (*HD* 20–21).

Like the artificial hole whose purpose Marlow had found impossible to ascertain a moment earlier, this mysterious white cloth around the neck of the dying man performs a symbolic function whose meaning must be unmistakably clear to all of Conrad's readers (though surprisingly few have actually commented on it) and perhaps even to Marlow's auditors aboard the *Nellie*.[18] It is the "badge"—or symbol—of the crimes that the invading whites have committed on his person. And not only on his person but on his mind as well, for as Marlow observes with apparently unwitting irony, they have succeeded in duping him into tying a noose around his own neck, deceiving him with the promise of Western clothing that supposedly represents progress and civilization but in reality confers only suffering and death. The blindness of his eyes, along with the emphatic whiteness of their orbs, reinforces not only his own inability to grasp what has been done to him but also connects his wretched fate with the symbolic pattern of blindness—of failing to *see* the essential truth, except in moments of "horror" like Kurtz's or, as in this instance, Marlow's—that runs like a "white thread" through the whole narrative.

Like the dying black man on the hillside, the young Marlow remains blind for most of the story to the full implications of what he has physically witnessed but has not morally grasped. However, even the older, disillusioned Marlow who narrates the story of Kurtz never grows so cynical that he rejects the idea of a civilizing mission altogether; he simply restricts it to the British. In other words, it is not the idea itself that is flawed; it is the execution of that idea at the hands of non-British people. Despite its official mission and Kurtz's seventeen-page idealistic treatise, there is no "idea at all connected with" Belgian imperialism, but there surely is with British imperialism. By implication, therefore, if the British had assumed control of the Congo—as, for example, Stanley had originally hoped they would—instead of Leopold II, there would have been "real work" carried out here too, not the mere sham appearance of work.

Writing to H.H. Johnston in 1883, Stanley had urged him not to allow the Congo to fall under Portuguese control: "Would you rob the natural birthright of the millions of Englishmen yet to issue, seeking homes similar to those which their forefathers built in America and the Indies?" (qtd. in Anstey 251). Conrad's preference for British imperialism would not have occasioned any surprise, for distinguishing between "good" British and "bad" non-British imperialism was fairly common among contemporaneous British writers, even including members of the Congo Reform Movement such as Morel and Fox Bourne. Kidd puts the difference on a "scientific" basis by arguing that the "Continental Powers of Western Europe" display an "old style" imperial attitude in the tropical regions, whereas Britain and the United States pursue a "policy, slowly and painfully learnt after a century of larger experience" according to which territory is held "as a trust to civilization" (58). Also the entry "empire" in the classic eleventh edition of the *Encyclopedia Britannica* claims that British imperialism is "closely allied to federalism," which, "making for a single whole, is very different from that Bonapartist imperialism, which means autocracy; for its essence is free co-ordination, and the self-government of each co-ordinated part." Writing specifically of the Belgians in the Congo in 1895, Robert Brown remarks that they are "entirely inexperienced, lacking the traditions in dealing with savage races that have, in different ways, been the secret of British and French success as the expanders of empire, and only too ready to ape bad models, the majority of the Congo officials have proved sadly unfitted as pioneers of civilisation" (182). Conrad himself contends in an 1898 review of Hugh Clifford's *Studies in Brown Humanity* that "of all the nations conquering distant territories in the name of the most excellent intentions [e.g., like Kurtz's], England alone sends out men who, with such a transparent sincerity of feeling, can speak, as Mr. Clifford does, of the place of toil and exile as 'the land which is very dear to me, where the best years of my life have been spent'—and where (I would stake my right hand on it) his name is pronounced with respect and affection by those brown men about whom he writes" (*Notes* 58–59). Even a contemporary critic like Daniel Vangroenweghe, who condemns all imperialist practice in Africa without exception, concludes that the atrocities committed in the name of Leopold II were nevertheless unique: ". . . never, so far as is known at any rate, did the attempt to make a profit overseas either by a State or by a Head of State lead to acts of cruelty as monstrous as those recorded in Leopold II's Congo, carried out by agents totally under the control of the King" (Vangroenweghe 22; my translation).

Marlow reflects Conrad's views when he agrees with his friend, the narrator of the frame story, that "light came out of this river [the Thames] since" the time of the Roman conquest and he hopes, knowing all the while the hope is vain, that this light may last for as long as "this old earth keeps rolling" (*HD* 9). The precise nature of this "light" is further defined by his friend as one that the "great [British] knights-errant of the sea," regardless of whether they were "hunters for gold or pursuers of fame," had borne with them along with "the sword, and often the torch, messengers of the might within the land, bearers of a spark from the sacred fire" (*HD* 8). These heroic and chivalric figures are also identical, I think, with those chiefly British explorers of whom Conrad observes at the very close of his late essay "Geography and Some Explorers" that they "went forth each according to his lights and with varied motives, laudable or sinful, but each bearing in his breast a spark of the sacred fire" (*Last Essays* 31).

A "sacred fire" is presumably in its origins Greek rather than Roman, the product of a supposedly colonizing rather than conquering imperial people. Being sacred, it is also something before which one can, and probably should, "bow down and offer a sacrifice to." In fact, it is just this readiness to bow down and sacrifice that apparently characterizes "genuine" British imperialism and helps to distinguish it from the "sham" Belgian variety. The ironically named Pilgrims bow down before money and worldly power; the only fire they are aware of is the one that demolishes their storehouse at the Central Station. Even Kurtz, once he betrays his "original" allegiance to his mission, can only get others to bow down and sacrifice to his own person; he has substituted a physical self and an arbitrary ego for an abstract idea. No longer possessing a guiding belief outside and above himself to bow down to, he is now, having become pure ego, utterly lost. For it is not enough to have an "idea," such as the idea of efficiency; there must also be "*devotion* to efficiency." It is not enough to have an "idea," but there must also be an "unselfish *belief* in the idea" (*HD* 10, my italics). For unless *idea* is bonded to *faith*, or to use one of Conrad's favorite words, to *fidelity*, the idea is worse than useless, leading as it does to pretense and sham. In this sense, Leopold's Congo Free State is even more reprehensible than Marlow's version of the Roman Empire, for the latter at least had the courage to be brutally honest in carrying out its "squeeze." The Roman Empire, whatever else may be said against it (or is in fact said against it by Marlow), appears at any rate in his view to have worshiped "the devil of violence, the devil of greed, and the devil of hot desire" (*HD* 19)—dangerous devils, to be sure, but never mere shams. Leopold's empire, on the other hand, has bowed down before "a flabby, pretending weak-eyed devil of a rapacious and pitiless folly," a sham devil with whose profoundly "insidious" nature Marlow is destined to become more intimately acquainted only "several months later and a thousand miles farther" upstream (*HD* 20).[19]

Critics of Conrad's story have sometimes taken Marlow's opening remarks in *Heart of Darkness* about the need for something to "bow down before, and offer a sacrifice to" as confirming Conrad's ironic intention to reveal Marlow's complicity (and that of Western imperialism generally) with the sacrifices depicted in the Grove of Death or in the severed heads surrounding Kurtz's residence at the Inner Station. Although it would clearly be unwise ever to underestimate Conrad's capacity for irony, it would, I think, be utterly foolish to jump to the conclusion that everything in Conrad's work must be contaminated with irony. Conrad *does* have a code of values, though admittedly it is not a very long one. If he did not have one—and if he did not and could not expect his readers to share (or at least understand) that code—his irony would be quite meaningless. One of the nonironized ethical constants in Conrad's work is the admiration expressed by sympathetic characters, such as Marlow himself or even the narrator, for other characters who are prepared to risk (or "sacrifice") their lives for what they believe in. This admiration extends even to figures like Gentleman Brown who are otherwise depicted as evil. It certainly extends to admirable characters like Dain in *Almayer's Folly* or the Black Amazon in this story.

In this connection Jim's "sacrifice" represents an interesting and complex example of how a European's commitment to a non-European community is to be evaluated. When Marlow sends his package of documents to the "privileged man" toward the end of *Lord Jim*, he does so with the clear intention of making the latter question his previous judgement that Jim's life in Patusan was a waste because ""giving your life up to them" (*them* meaning all of mankind with skins brown, yellow, or black in colour) "was like selling your soul to a brute."" In the opinion of the "privileged man"—who may also be identical with the narrator of the frame story—sacrificing one's life to such people was "only endurable and enduring when based on a firm conviction in the truth of ideas racially our own, in whose name are established the order, the morality of an ethical progress. 'We want its strength at our backs,' you had said. 'We want a belief in its necessity and its justice, to make a worthy and conscious sacrifice of our lives.'"(201).

For the Privileged Man, in other words, only a culturally or ethnically (or "racially") grounded ethic can provide a credible rationale for risking one's own life in the attempt to benefit the lives of those not belonging to one's own group. Jim, like Kurtz, by separating himself off from his own "tribe" and devoting his life to the people of Patusan, will never achieve a meaningful sacrifice. His "detribalization," though deliberate and beneficial, nevertheless isolates him and puts him "out of place." Marlow, though, despite his assertion that he will "affirm nothing" about the moral significance of Jim's life and death in Patusan, clearly thinks otherwise about it, for why else should he have submitted his "evidence" to the Privileged Man for final adjudication? Indeed, he explicitly raises the "question" as to whether Jim had not in the end "confessed to a faith mightier than the laws of order and progress." Just what that greater faith might be is not made clear, but whatever it is, its moral claim is in Marlow's view superior to the culturally relativistic one put forward by the Privileged Man. There is even an unmistakable hint that Jim's sacrifice is comparable to that of Christ, a "Lord" who died for all mankind and not merely for the subgroup into which he happened to have been born or to which he attached himself in later life (*Lord Jim* 201).

That Conrad identified Belgian imperialism with rapacious hypocrisy and unmitigated folly emerges, if anything, even more clearly from his only other African story, "An Outpost of Progress," composed in 1896. Ironically, in view of the later and better known story about the brilliant and versatile Kurtz, Conrad's two principal Belgian characters in this story, the comically thin and stupid Carlier and the comically corpulent and stupid Kayerts, are duped like "children" (*Unrest* 89) by their far shrewder and more unprincipled African clerk, Makola. Though themselves without any redeeming gifts of mind or character, they begin to "think better of themselves" after reading in some old papers an article that might have been penned by the "original" Kurtz himself while still plying his journalistic trade back home in the Whited Sepulchre. This particular article treats "in high-flown language . . . of the rights and duties of civilization, of the sacredness of the civilizing work," and it also extols "the merits of those who went about bringing light, and faith and commerce to the dark places of the earth" (94). When, without their knowledge or even suspicion, Makola one night exchanges their intoxicated servants and employees for several tusks of prime-quality ivory, they are at first reluctant to accept the benefits of what they soon come to realize has hardly been a "progressive" bit of good imperial business but rather a very old-fashioned piece of shabby *slave* trade. Eventually, however, the "two pioneers of trade and progress" hypocritically justify their complicity to themselves, thereby acting in complete accordance with the teachings of the imperial devil of rapacious folly.

As is the way with this particular devil, folly leads to further folly, and Kayerts shoots the unarmed Carlier dead under the erroneous assumption that his own life is being threatened. He then lets himself be half-persuaded by the scheming Makola that Carlier had "died of fever," and he even goes so far as to persuade himself that "the fellow dead there had been a noxious beast anyway" and that "one death could not possibly make any difference; couldn't have any importance, at least to a thinking creature" (*Unrest* 115). When, however, his quasi-Nietzschean supermanic thoughts and his ensuing all-too-human slumbers are interrupted by the sudden arrival of the company steamer, Kayerts realizes that the bullet in Carlier's still-unburied body will hardly convince others of his supposed death by natural causes. He then promptly proceeds to hang himself. By the time he is discovered, he is already dead, but nonetheless, "irreverently, he was putting out a swollen tongue at his Managing Director," the understandably astonished chief executive administrator of "the Great Civilizing Company" himself[20] (116–17).

As is evident from even the foregoing rather sketchy summary, "An Outpost of Progress" (which might more accurately but less ironically have been entitled "An Outpost of Folly") represents a treatment, though in a more direct narrative mode and in a more grimly comic mood, of some of the same themes, characters, and situations that are more fully and subtly developed in *Heart of Darkness*. But though it is admittedly a cruder and more obvious story than its successor, "An Outpost of Progress" is also for that reason extraordinarily useful in letting us gain glimpses of what Conrad's "original" intentions might have been. So, for example, once one has read the description of the blowing of the steamer's whistle near the close of "An Outpost of Progress," one's sense of the analogous scene in *Heart of Darkness* where Marlow blows the steamer's whistle is inevitably altered for the worse. For one thing, even though Marlow's decision to sound the whistle is judged to be morally right because it saves the people on shore from being shot at by the insanely enraged Pilgrims, the presence of the steamer itself (and of its screaming voice) is—as the earlier story makes clear—ultimately unjustified because it is "out of place." The steamer, after all, is a *machine*, an emblem of that European, technological "progress" of which Kayerts, Carlier, Kurtz, and even Marlow are the local representatives and agents. What Kayerts hears at first as inhuman shrieks, he soon—after allowing his somewhat befuddled intelligence to engage in a little "delayed decoding"—identifies as the impatient whistles of an approaching steamer. He then goes on to realize what the implications of this signal are for him and proceeds to act accordingly without further delay. What Kayerts never manages to understand amid all his befuddled decoding, however, and what therefore the intruding narrator must explicitly and with obvious irony inform us of, is that "[p]rogress was calling to Kayerts from the river. Progress and civilization and all the virtues. Society was calling to its accomplished child to come, to be taken care of, to be instructed, to be judged, to be condemned; it called him to return to that rubbish heap from which he had wandered away, so that justice could be done" (*Unrest*, 116).

That "rubbish heap" is Brussels, is Belgium, is Europe—and wherever these go on their variegated imperial and civilizing missions, they take along their "rubbish" and then they leave it behind to pollute the as yet unspoiled environment and its not altogether innocent inhabitants. In this particular case the "rubbish" consists of Kayerts and Carlier. And why are they "rubbish"? Why are they, as the narrator puts it so unambiguously, "two perfectly insignificant and incapable individuals"? (*Unrest* 89). Quite simply, because they have never managed to become completely human. They are, as the narrator again informs us, machines, utterly unfitted even for grappling with everyday, material problems, not to mention the inevitable complex interaction with "pure unmitigated savagery, with primitive nature and primitive man," which brings "sudden and profound trouble into the heart" and "tries the civilized nerves of the foolish and the wise alike" (89). Since Kayerts and Carlier certainly do not belong to the category of the wise, their foolish and ironically civilized "nerves" do not allow them to realize that the "pure, unmitigated savagery" that they encounter in Africa is chiefly located within their own breasts.

Progress is a machine that sometimes takes the form of a steamer, and its usual emissaries are evidently little, mechanical men like Kayerts and Carlier. They are mechanical because the society that produces them needs and wants them to be mechanical. Hence, it has forbidden them to engage in any and "all independent thought, all initiative, all departure from routine . . . under pain of death. They could only live on condition of being machines" (*Unrest* 91). Once Kayerts, under the pressure of circumstances, begins to deviate from his mechanical routine by killing Carlier, "society" promptly imposes the death penalty on him, the actual execution of which, however, like the man with the symbolic noose whom Marlow encounters in the Grove of Death, he forestalls by carry-

ing out on himself. At an even deeper level of (symbolic) irony, the ultimately Christian ideals that are espoused by this society—and which are
mechanically mouthed by Kayerts and Carlier—are the immediate cause
of Kayerts's death. For it is on a large cross, marking the grave of an
"original" Kurtz-like predecessor, which has more recently been straight-
ened and weight-tested by Carlier, that Kayerts is made to hang himself.
On some blasphemous level—blasphemous at least for a Catholic like
Conrad—the final "outpost" of progress depicted in this story is this
specifically Christian post, emblematic of the "sacred" fire and "decorated" with a corpse in much the same way as Kurtz's "outposts" are
with decaying heads.

The fact that, when spoken aloud, Kayerts's name evokes that of
Kurtz is probably not altogether coincidental. Indeed, the relation between Kayerts and Carlier is a little reminiscent of that between Kurtz
and the Russian Harlequin. Like Kurtz, Kayerts is the "Chief"; and like
Carlier, the Russian has good reason to fear for his life. The differences,
of course, are at least as striking as the similarities. Kurtz is truly a chief,
not a mere sham like Kayerts. The rites he participates in may be diabolical, but they do not pay homage to a flabby devil of rapacious folly.
Both Kurtz and the Russian are extraordinary people, devoted each in
his own eccentric or perverse (or both) way to a Carlylean "gospel" of
work; and they are unquestionably capable of dealing with their "dark"
environment in innovative and imaginative ways that distinguish them
utterly from the mechanical reactions of those two pathetic Pilgrims of
Progress in the earlier story. If Kurtz fails, his failure is at least on a
grand scale, so grand that Marlow can even credibly argue that in the
end it has turned into a "victory," even a "moral victory" (*HD* 70).
Whatever he is at the moment of death, he is not a "sham," though like
Kayerts and Carlier he has, in part at least, fallen victim to the Belgian
sham god of rapacious folly.[21]

The fact that the Russian reminds Marlow of a harlequin does not
necessarily diminish his stature; it merely transposes it into a partially
comic mode. That the Russian functions as a "double" for Kurtz and for
Marlow himself is apparent from his self-effacing devotion to and intimate identification with Kurtz, both of which mirror Marlow's own,
admittedly somewhat more skeptical, interest in and fidelity to Kurtz.
That he is intended to be viewed ironically—to some extent at least—is
apparent from the manner in which his repeated remark about Kurtz's
having "enlarged my mind" (*HD* 53, 63) contrasts markedly with the
people whose minds Kurtz has forcibly shrunk and prominently displayed

on a number of poles in front of his house. His carefully patched, parti-colored costume also suggests that there is method in his folly—that he is deliberately playing the fool in order to avoid being "exterminated" himself. In this way, rather like the traditional Harlequin of the Panto-mime, he can accomplish his work while remaining "invisible" (with his clothing functioning literally as camouflage). That his motley clothing also evokes the map of Africa as seen by Marlow in the company offices in Brussels is something critics have often noted and attributed without much debate to Conrad's supposedly anti-imperialist intentions in the story. Jeremy Hawthorn even goes so far as to suggest that the cartridges in the Harlequin's red pocket and "Towson's Inquiry" in his blue pocket not only evoke the colors of the Union Jack but also represent the mar-riage of firepower and seapower characteristic of British imperialism (194). If this is indeed the case, one is left wondering why Conrad took such pains to be so covert in his anti-British sentiments as to resort to concealing them quite literally in the pockets of a Russian. Furthermore, what is also never adequately addressed in all of this alleged political and sartorial allegory is why the Harlequin should be a Russian at all, when traditionally the Harlequin has been either of Italian or French origin. There is no record of Conrad's ever having met Russians while in the Congo, nor did Russians figure largely (or even at all) as employees of the company.[22] A Russian named Bohndorff, however, did visit Stanley Falls in 1886, as a member of an Austrian geographical mission led by Oscar Baumann and Oscar Lenz (Ceulemans 71); and there is also a possibility that Conrad may have known Wilhelm Junker's *Travels in Africa, 1882–86*, which was translated into English in 1892. Though of German origin, Junker was actually a Russian subject. The last stages of his African explorations especially are reminiscent of Conrad's depic-tion of the Russian's naïveté. Like the Russian, Junker seems to have wandered quite alone and unharmed for four years through the densest and most dangerous parts of the Lake country before heading for the coast in 1888 in order to avoid being captured by the Mahdists (McLynn 117–18). Another reason is perhaps to be found in that Kurtz (like Junker) bears a German name, for as Conrad was later to point out in a discus-sion of the relationship between Germany and Russia, "Germany has been the evil counsellor of Russia on all the questions of her Polish prob-lem" (*Notes* 95). That Conrad had Germany very much in mind when developing the character of Kurtz emerges from a 1903 letter in which, while discussing the German threat to Britain, he says that he "took great care to give Kurtz a cosmopolitan origin" (*Letters* 3:94).

If the Russian Harlequin, then, is a species of wise fool or *faux naif*, this is certainly not the case with Kurtz, not even with the "sham" Kurtz and definitely not with the "original" one. With his great talents and partly British educational and ethnic background, the "original" Kurtz seems to have been, in fact, eminently fitted to be a bearer of the so-called sacred fire. Hearing about him from various more or less reliable sources, Marlow finally catches a glimpse of him in the apparent guise of a knight-errant, as he "sees" him suddenly turning his back on comfort and company to face further hardship upriver. In fact, however, the man whom Marlow "sees" here is no longer the original Kurtz but already the sham, anticipating a later solitary return, not with four paddlers but on all fours, and not impelled by a spark of the sacred fire but rather drawn to an infernal fire lit by diabolical sorcerers preparing midnight dances and "unspeakable rites" to worship the "godlike" Kurtz. Nevertheless, though in the final analysis Marlow may no longer be sure who the man *in* the name was, he knows for certain that he has met a man *with* a name, sometimes a sham but also someone real, someone who had possessed, as he concludes, a *remarkable* identity. Even more than Marlow himself, Kurtz has *faced* the man on the shore, "with his own true stuff—with his own inborn strength"(*HD* 38). That his truth and his strength were neither true nor strong enough to withstand those of the man on the shore makes Kurtz's story tragic, but it does not make it foolish or petty like the stories of his fellow Belgians in the heart of Africa.

5

UNSPEAKABLE RITES AND SPEAKABLE RIGHTS

The functional anthropologist (and only for him do I feel responsibility), studies the white savage side by side with the coloured.
                                                        Bronislaw Malinowski

Savages are but shades of ourselves.
                                                        Ovid

With the obvious exception of Kurtz, not a single one of the Congo Belgians in Conrad's novel is anything more than a stereotype. Even the Accountant at the Outer Station, the only male Belgian character other than Kurtz who can be said to possess any sort of redeeming qualities, is a caricature, an absurd "hairdresser's dummy" who walks about with oiled hair and a green-lined parasol. For the rest, they consist either of ridiculous "Pilgrims" dressed variously in pink pyjamas, a papier maché Mephistophelean Brickmaker who makes no bricks,[1] and a Manager without entrails who is visited by an Uncle who looks like a "butcher in a poor neighborhood" (*HD* 32). The Belgians in Belgium do not fare much better. They are either described as speechless zombies inhabiting a Whited Sepulchre, as in the case of the two women guarding the entrance of the company's main office; or they are like "the great man himself," a "pale plumpness" measuring a mere five feet six inches and murmuring vague platitudes about the excellence of Marlow's French; or else a downright lunatic like the cranium-measuring company Doctor who himself evidently suspects all his outgoing patients of being mad and whose only parting advice to them is to "keep calm" (*HD* 14–15)— a phrase ironically echoed later in the Manager's criticism of Kurtz, when he faults him for failing to act "cautiously, cautiously" (*HD* 61).[2] Even the "Intended," Kurtz's fiancée, pure and unsullied though her fidelity undoubtedly is, partakes of both the deathliness of her fellow citizens (she is an "eloquent phantom" and a "tragic and familiar Shade" [*HD*

75]) and of their madness. When he first catches sight of her, Marlow is seized by a sudden panic "as though I had blundered into a place of cruel and absurd mysteries" (*HD* 73). She too has her assigned role in the performance of the notorious and mysterious "unspeakable rites."

As for Kurtz, who seems to be the exception to this general rule of bestialized, anonymous, and dehumanized Belgians, it is important to remember that Kurtz is not a "pure" Belgian. His variegated national origins of course help to make him the central symbolic figure of the story—a kind of imperialist European Everyman—but they also distinguish him ethnically from the rest of his (less ambiguously) Belgian compatriots. Nevertheless, Kurtz shares with these other Belgians their chief stereotypical traits of morbidity and madness, qualities that he can be said to possess in even greater measure than anyone else in the story, given his ghoulish and egomaniacal nature. Paradoxically, however, this excess tends to make him resemble his compatriots less rather than more. In going beyond the stereotypical limits in the intensity of his ambition and the depth of his emotion, he shows that he is able to respond to the complexity of his environment at a level that no white person in his surroundings matches and no one other than Marlow and (perhaps) the Russian Harlequin is able to comprehend. That is why, despite all his manifold reservations and ironies about Kurtz, Marlow finally and explicitly affirms that he was "a remarkable man" (*HD* 69). Lilies that fester may smell far worse than weeds, but for all their malodorousness the fact remains that they were, once, lilies.

If therefore Achebe is right in maintaining that Conrad calls "the very humanity of black people into question" in *Heart of Darkness* (*HD* 259), then that accusation does not hold entirely true for Kurtz, or at least it does not for the greater part of the story. For Kurtz, despite his evident inhumanity to individual blacks (the "rebels," for example) and despite the notorious genocidal gloss added to his report to the International Society for the Suppression of Savage Customs, has become one with the blacks with whom he lives, especially with the "wild and gorgeous" Black Amazon, whose fierce vitality stands in marked contrast to the languid morbidity of his white fiancée back in Brussels.[3] Even though he has been at the Inner Station only for a little more than a year, Kurtz speaks the language of his adopted people fluently, is actively involved in their rituals and raiding parties, and feels himself connected to them through powerful, almost unbreakable emotional bonds. They clearly return his feelings in equal measure, filled as they are with a deep and abiding sorrow at his imminent departure.

It is because of this undeniable solidarity between Kurtz and "his" people in the heart of Africa that Frances Singh has even gone so far as to claim that Kurtz's wish to "exterminate the brutes" refers not, as everyone has hitherto believed, to the Africans, but instead to his fellow European colonizers. In other words, it would appear that through his experience of "going native," Kurtz has been transformed into a fervid, precocious anti-imperialist. "What Kurtz developed in the jungle, there-fore," Singh argues, "was not an 'unlawful soul,' but historical foresight" (277). Though I confess that this idea strikes me as extremely unlikely, it does certainly indicate that Kurtz's supposed position as a symbolic repre-sentative of the evils of Western imperialism is by no means self-evident to all observers who, like Achebe, come from parts of the globe that were once ruled from London. Indeed, to support Singh's hypothesis, there is even the testimony of one English veteran of the *Force Publique,* Capt. Philip H.B. Salusbury who, after expressing his "horror" at the "daily barbarity committed by these youthful Neros" in the employ of the Congo State, went on to "rejoice" at the numerous Belgian agents being "killed by exasperated natives year after year," thanking God "for having at least removed another with whom to compare Satan were to do a grave injustice—to the latter" (Salusbury, "Revelation" 323).

So too with the notorious skulls that Marlow sees "ornamenting" Kurtz's decrepit dwelling and which he at first mistakes for wooden knobs. In a passage in which corrosive irony is laced with sardonic humor, Marlow describes how, looking through a telescope, he discovers that

> these round knobs were not ornamental but symbolic; they were expressive and puzzling, striking and disturbing—food for thought and also for vul-tures if there had been any looking down from the sky; but at all events for such ants as were industrious enough to ascend the pole. . . . I had expected to see a knob of wood there, you know. I returned deliberately to the first [head] I had seen—and there it was black, dried, sunken, with closed eye-lids—a head that seemed to sleep at the top of that pole, and with the shrunken dry lips showing a narrow white line of the teeth, was smiling too, smiling continuously at some endless and jocose dream of that eternal slumber.[4] (*HD* 57)

This horrific vision, according to C.P. Sarvan, has impressed the novelist Ngugi Wa Thiong as "the most powerful indictment of colonialism. No African writer . . . ha[s] created so ironic, apt, and powerful an image: ironic when one considers that Kurtz and many others like him had come to 'civilize' the non-European world; apt when one recalls what they really did" (285).

Certainly, despite the fact that the older Marlow disclaims feeling any "surprise" on the part of his former younger self at being confronted with this view, it is clear that he was in fact overwhelmed by it. And who would not have been? In its own way this place of active killing is as grim and forbidding as the Grove of passive Death that Marlow had encountered earlier. It is also, as Marlow reminds us explicitly, "symbolic." Moreover, though Conrad would probably not have been aware of it, it is strikingly realistic, for as John Batchelor points out, a scant half-dozen years after Conrad left the Congo, "a Captain Rom, station commander of Stanley Falls—the equivalent of Kurtz's inner station—did in reality use the heads of twenty-one 'rebels' as a decorative border for the flower-bed in front of his house" (85). E.J. Glave, who visited Stanley Falls in 1895 and actually met Captain Rom, describes the same scene in more detail: "Recently the state post on the Lomami lost two men killed and eaten by the natives; many women and children were taken, and twenty-one heads were brought to the falls, and have been used by Captain Rom as a decoration round a flower-bed in front of the house!" ("Cruelty" 1/97, 706).[5]

Hideous, symbolic, and even real as all this is, this scene must nevertheless also be viewed and interpreted from the perspective of traditional Central African tribal customs. For in terms of the Congo at the close of the nineteenth century, what Kurtz did (and Rom after him) was entirely within the bounds of privilege accorded to tribal chiefs. Indeed, Norman Sherry recounts that having his head put on a long pole "and placed beside that of M. Noblesse in front of the Palace of Nserera, the chief of the tribe" is what actually happened to the very person whom Sherry identifies as Conrad's model for Kurtz, namely the Belgian officer Arthur Hodister. Sherry then goes on to quote a passage from a Belgian missionary that rivals Conrad's in grisliness: "The outpost is surrounded by fifty-two human heads planted on the ends of poles; for the most part they still retain the skin on which the hair had been growing, as well as scraps of flesh. It is ignoble—and to suggest that whites are supposed to live there! This outpost belongs to Mounié-Mohara. It's a real den of bandits" (Western 117–18, my translation).

Fifty-two skulls is an unusually large number for a chief to have put on display, but what matters here is not so much the numbers as the tribal institution that validated those numbers. According to Emil Torday, skulls could be valuable commodities in strictly symbolic ways even to venerable and quite nonviolent chiefs. One of these chiefs, Mapanda, possessed a "museum of skulls" consisting not only of "the crania of enemies and slaves who had been eaten in the village, but also crania sent as tribute by the neighbouring villages, who have to transmit to him in recognition of his overlordship the skulls of all enemies whom they kill in war." Later, he encounters and interviews another, younger chief who has at his back "a number of upright sticks with a human skull on the top of each"[6] (69, 229). Achebe himself acknowledges the ritual function of human skulls in the Nigerian tradition when, in *Things Fall Apart*, he describes how his protagonist Okonkwo returned from battle with five human heads, from one of which he continued to drink on ceremonial occasions (*Things* 14).[7]

What, then, is the significance of the skulls Marlow sees encircling Kurtz's outpost? Are they to be understood in the context of contemporaneous Congolese tribal tradition, a tradition within which the display of severed heads would have been viewed as a perhaps cruel but nonetheless valid "symbolic" expression of a chief's power? Or are they to be viewed, as Ngugi Wa Thiong—along with virtually all other critics of the story—views them, namely as gruesome manifestations not only of Kurtz's own private genocidal impulses, but also of the genocidal nature of the Western imperial power that had, whether it foresaw the possibility of such horrific consequences or not, sent him to the heart of Africa to do its bidding? On the one hand, I think, the answer to this question depends on whether we ask it of Marlow or of Conrad. If we ask it of the former, it seems clear that his horrified response is very much that of Ngugi Wa Thiong and most other readers of the story. If, however, we ask it of Conrad, then we must take into consideration the distinct probability that he knew that this sort of grisly display was part of an accepted tribal warrior tradition, like the taking of scalps among certain American Indian tribes; and that, if this is so, by not communicating that awareness to his reader, he was either intending to make Kurtz (and Belgian and possibly European imperialism generally) look bad in comparison with the Africans, thus confirming Batchelor's theory of Conrad's radically anti-imperialist intentions in the story; or else he was implying that Kurtz had identified with the morally repugnant (to him as well as to Marlow) African tribal rituals.[8]

If the latter is the case, then it follows that the Central Africans who traditionally ate human flesh, whether ritually or not; who practiced ceremonial human sacrifice; and who displayed human skulls as symbols of their leaders' power over life and death, were indeed "evil." For then it must be true that, as Patrick Brantlinger puts it, Conrad "paints Kurtz and Africa with the same tarbrush. His version of evil—the form taken by Kurtz's satanic behavior—is going native. Evil, in short, *is* African in Conrad's story; if it is also European, that is because some number of white men in the heart of Africa behave like Africans" (*Rule* 262). In Brantlinger's view, of course, none of these allegations is true: cannibalism is something Conrad "probably" never encountered while in Africa and, somewhat contradictorily, it was also something practiced by the adherents of both Arabs and Belgians.[9] Moreover, the cutting off of hands was a practice unknown in the Congo before it was supposedly introduced there by the Belgians—the conclusive evidence cited for this assertion, again of a somewhat contradictory nature, is that Conrad had never heard of it while he was in the Congo; and as for any "unspeakable rites" involving human sacrifice, Brantlinger simply takes no cognizance of them. Finally, on the basis of a single remark by Sir Harry Johnston, he ventures to make the sweeping generalization that a "great many Kurtz-like Europeans went native in Africa and elsewhere and often practiced genocide as a hobby" (*Rule* 268).[10]

If Brantlinger is right about all of these allegations, then it must be acknowledged that Conrad was not only a racist but a bloody—or, in Reeves's terms, "strong"—racist who deliberately vilified black Africans by means of his "stress on cannibalism, his identification of African customs with violence, lust, and madness, his metaphors of bestiality, death, and darkness, his suggestion that traveling in Africa is like traveling backward in time to primeval, infantile, but also hellish stages of existence" (*Rule* 262). Sweeping though they are, for most of these charges Brantlinger's evidence is either scanty or, in some instances, nonexistent. There is, for example, no evidence that Conrad identifies African customs with "lust"; there are no scenes of sexual license anywhere in the story, and even Kurtz's relation with the Black Amazon is kept so vague that a hostile critic like Achebe is limited to claiming that she has "obviously been *some kind of* mistress to Kurtz" (*HD* 255, my italics). Also, if there is lustfulness anywhere in this relationship, it must be primarily on Kurtz's side, since presumably it was he who made her his some kind of mistress (if, in fact, he did) rather than the other way around. As for Conrad's insistence on the alleged "madness" of African customs, there are no mad (in the sense of insane) Africans in the story. Madness is entirely confined to the whites, both in Africa (Kurtz, the French cruiser) and in Belgium (the Doctor). Violence, to be sure, Conrad does associate with Africa, but it is both black violence and white violence; and, in terms of quantity at any rate, there is rather more of the latter than of the former. The "bestiality," too, is very much a two-sided affair, as we have already seen, with Conrad himself admitting that "before the Congo, I was a mere animal." The notion that the trip upriver is also a journey backward in time is explicitly qualified by Marlow to the point of actual denial; and whatever racist overtones the description of the journey admittedly has, they are not so rabid that one would insist on using the adjective *hellish* for them. Finally, if indeed there is evil in the heart of Africa, then there is also evil in the heart of Belgium, for unlike the dark heart of Africa the Whited Sepulchre is populated, except of course for the Intended, entirely with ghouls—and even she is a "Shade." A "heart," even if dark, is after all still preferable to a tomb.

There is, however, a more important issue that needs to be raised in connection with Brantlinger's claims about Conrad's supposed racism in this story. Like many other critics whose intentions are manifestly good, he minimizes any aspect of African life and society that does not conform to current Western ideas of appropriate moral conduct. So, despite ample evidence to the contrary, he either denies the existence of cannibalism in the Congo or suggests that it was practiced "by both sides," a profoundly misleading remark since it implies that whites participated in cannibalism, a claim that none of the evidence Brantlinger cites supports. Moreover, whether real or not, according to Brantlinger Conrad "probably" did not witness any cannibalism while in the Congo, so that his treatment of it must be strictly imaginary; oddly enough, however, the same criterion does not apply to what Conrad saw or did not see of Belgian behavior in the Congo. The fragmentary journal that Conrad kept while in the Congo is not particularly critical of Belgian administration, nor does it give instances of widespread or even occasional atrocities committed by Belgians against Africans (the dead carrier he finds lying along the road is only *suspected* of having been shot by a white official; the evidence Conrad cites is at best circumstantial). According to Molly Mahood, whom Brantlinger refers to elsewhere with approval, "it is hard to find evidence that in 1890 Conrad witnessed much brutality and oppression [on the part of the Belgian agents], though plenty of slovenliness and incompetence offended his seaman's eye" (6). H. Grattan Guiness, who visited the Congo at just about the same time as Conrad was preparing to leave it, later noted that except for some ill treatment of the carriers on the way to Matadi, he observed nothing that seemed worthy of complaint. It was only several years later, at the end of 1895, that he became concerned when the first reports of Congo atrocities began to reach London (17).

Although Brantlinger does not specifically deal with the "violence" associated with the dances of fetishmen at the Inner Station, he forestalls possible negative reactions by suggesting that "Kurtz's Intended is perhaps the greatest fetishist of all, idolizing her image of her fiancé" (*Rule* 262).[11] The subject of human sacrifice is never raised. So far as Brantlinger is concerned, cruelty and torture are monopolies of the whites in Africa. Forced labor and slavery are practiced only by Belgians and to a lesser extent by their rivals, the Arabs; there is no hint that the taking and holding of slaves was a well-established custom among certain tribes in the Congo. Saying all this of course does not in the least exonerate the cruel and unjust policies and practices of Leopold's rule, though it needs to be remembered (as it rarely is by critics of this novel) that the worst offenses occurred several years *after* Conrad had left the Congo. Undoubtedly in the closing years of the nineteenth century the Africans in the Congo were largely victims of Leopold's vicious "administration," which for the first time in their history had introduced oppression on a vast and systematic scale. But it must not be forgotten that, despite its at times admittedly ("weak" to "medium") racist tone, Conrad's story was the very first and only important English work, either fictional or documentary, to point out just how brutal it was, doing so several years before Casement and Morel followed it up with their more detailed but certainly not more powerful indictments.

But brutal as Leopold and his representatives were, they did not introduce cannibalism, human sacrifice, shamanism, or tribal dances into the Congo. These were already well-established traditional practices, deeply rooted in Central African society. From our more "enlightened" Western point of view, recognizing the existence of such practices is apparently so repugnant to some critics and cultural historians that denial, as in the case of Brantlinger, is the only possible response. (The same is true of Abdul JanMohamed, who finds Conrad's "depiction of the intimated cannibalism . . . tasteless and probably groundless"; he also unaccountably identifies the Black Amazon as a "dark, satanic woman" [90].) In this respect, Conrad seems to be both more honest and less racist. He recognizes that different societies have different mores and customs and that they do not lose honor or value in his eyes if they fail to conform to his own Western European catalog of permitted behavior.[12] That is why he does not censure the cannibals on board his steamer for being what they are; on the contrary, they are shown, as virtually all modern critics of the story agree, to be *morally* superior to the Belgians. The fact that he does censure Kurtz for attempting to play the god to his tribe, or for participating in "unspeakable rites," is a very different matter; Kurtz after all belongs to a different tribe, to Marlow's own tribe, one that has different customs—*different* but not necessarily in an absolute sense better. In Marlow's culturally relativistic view, the Africans have a *right* to their rites, whatever they may be. Kurtz, however, who is "out of place"—or detribalized—does not.

Significantly, these "unspeakable rites" have vexed critics almost as much as Kurtz's notorious last words. Nearly fifty years ago F.R. Leavis noted petulantly that Conrad, by practicing "an adjectival and worse than supererogatory insistence on 'unspeakable rites'" attempted to "make a virtue out of not knowing what he means" (179–80).[13] However, if one is prepared to exercise a little patience with Conrad's insistent adjectives, as well as practicing a modicum of tolerance with respect to his apparently recalcitrant adverbs, verbs, pronouns, and nouns, it may be possible to arrive at fairly specific conclusions about what those rites were. Conrad, *pace* the no doubt unquiet ghost of Leavis, knew very well what he meant. Nor is this by any means a trivial question, for on the answer we give hinges an important part of our understanding of Kurtz's final experience of the "horror."

Marlow refers to the unspecified "rites" for the first time just after mentioning Kurtz's grand, and also grandiloquent, treatise addressed to the International Society for the Suppression of Savage Customs.[14] Clearly this treatise and the mysterious "rites" are somehow connected, and not only, I think, in Marlow's own mind. "Seventeen pages of close writing," Marlow observes, examining the evidence judiciously in his lawyer-like manner. "He had found time for it. But this must have been before his—let us say—nerves went wrong and caused him to preside at certain midnight dances ending with unspeakable rites, which—as far as I reluctantly gathered from what I had heard at various times—were offered up to him—do you understand—to Mr. Kurtz himself" (*HD* 50). In other words, the subject of unspeakable rites has actually been raised repeatedly in Marlow's presence, and most likely also by a number of different people, not just by the Russian Harlequin. If then the rites are unspeakable, they are, oddly enough, at the same time very speakable, too. They are unspeakable, apparently, only in the sense that the older, narrating Marlow refuses to speak of them, whereas the younger, acting Marlow was, by his own admission, willing to speak of them, even if only "reluctantly." The rites have become unmentionable in public—even among a group of intimate male friends, like those aboard the *Nellie*—probably (at least in part) because they are too close to the "horror."

What emerges unmistakably from Marlow's remarks, however, is that the "unspeakable rites"—whatever else they may have been—were of a religious nature, with Kurtz himself functioning as the deity for whom the rites were performed. ("Rites" are essentially religious in nature, as is confirmed by the *OED*, which defines them primarily as "a formal procedure or act in a religious or other solemn observance.") That there is a direct link between the unspeakable rites and Kurtz's treatise—and that in retrospect Marlow realizes that there is such a connection—is apparent from what the latter says about the treatise only a moment later: "The opening paragraph, however, in the light of later information, strikes me now as ominous. He began with the argument that we whites, from the point of development we had arrived at, 'must necessarily appear to them [savages] [*sic*] in the nature of supernatural beings—we approach them with the might as of a deity,' and so on, and so on" (*HD* 50). Here the connection becomes virtually explicit. Arriving in Africa, burdened with a heavy baggage of cultural evolutionary thought (as indicated by the notion of "point of development"), Kurtz had tricked his followers into thinking him gifted with superhuman powers. Initially he seems to have done so in order to further his supposedly noble purpose of "suppressing savage customs," but the actual experience of divinity apparently went to his head, and thereafter he engaged in the "unspeakable rites" for purely egotistical reasons. From all this it seems clear that Kurtz (the "original" Kurtz anyway) was a cultural evolutionist who believed that in traveling upriver he was in fact going back in time and that time was not, as Marlow realizes, a mere "cloak" but an essential factor separating "developed" from "undeveloped" peoples.

The irony of Kurtz's transformation is, of course, unmistakable. An idealist, whose avowed aim has been to exterminate "savage" customs, promptly succumbs to those customs (or "rites") himself; a philanthrope who has traveled to the heart of Africa in order to promulgate the message of universal brotherhood winds up exhorting his readers to "exterminate all the brutes." The extent of Kurtz's divinity becomes evident—again ironically—in the episode that follows almost immediately upon Marlow's reflections regarding the "unspeakable rites." This is the scene where he confronts a Kurtz who has been crawling, like a beast, on all fours toward some "midnight dances." Apparently Kurtz has been trying to get himself worshiped again amid a celebration of further unspeakable rites. Certainly there is a fire, with a "sorcerer" moving rhythmically about it, perhaps in the expectation of welcoming the return of the beast-god Kurtz. Indeed, the implication is very strong that the whole scene is meant to be read in the light (admittedly, the rather murky light) of Marlow's preceding reflections regarding the "unspeakable rites." Marlow, who suddenly becomes aware of the dangerous situation he finds himself in, manages through "a flash of inspiration" to speak the right words so as to break what he decides must be a "spell," presumably one connected with the Sorcerer, whom he sees only a short distance away. The words Marlow speaks to Kurtz are "'You will be lost . . . utterly lost'" (HD 65). As it turns out, they are clearly the "right thing," though whether they break the spell or merely put it temporarily in abeyance remains for the moment uncertain. In any case, the spell, Marlow decides, is ultimately one that has been emitted, as it were environmentally, by a personified "wilderness that seemed to draw him to its pitiless breast by the awakening of forgotten and brutal instincts, by the memory of gratified and monstrous passions. This alone, I was convinced, had driven him out to the edge of the forest, to the bush, towards the gleam of fires, the throb of drums, the drone of weird incantations; this alone had beguiled his unlawful soul beyond the bounds of permitted aspirations" (HD 65). Having exceeded those bounds, having, as Marlow so vividly puts it, "kicked himself loose of the earth," Kurtz is now completely "alone." He is as alone, and as "utterly lost," as another illustrious predecessor had once found himself after exceeding "the bounds of permitted aspirations" by convincing himself that he was like unto God.[15]

That Kurtz should be (or should have been) "alone" while remaining very much in the company of the Black Amazon and his African followers is, on the face of it, rather odd. How can he be "alone" when he is so obviously surrounded by a multitude of enthusiastic and admiring people? Or are we to interpret Marlow's remarks in a "strong" racist way to mean that in his view the presence of Africans is irrelevant, that when a white man leaves the company of his kind and of his color he is "alone"? This is, after all, what the particular adjective "alone" seems to insist on meaning here, and it is almost certainly how Chinua Achebe would have read it. Nevertheless it is not, I think, what Marlow means when he uses it. What he really means is that Kurtz, being now "out of place" in the heart of Africa as the Africans are not, has also overstepped "permitted" boundaries as they have not overstepped them and by definition—not belonging to his cultural "place"—cannot do. The "permission," after all, to attempt to realize certain "aspirations," or not to do so, is "given" not by any particular individual but by a moral code, a culturally determined ethos. Put in anthropological terms, Kurtz has been detribalized, or more accurately, he has detribalized himself by participating in rites that are not "permitted" by his Belgian or, more generally, by his European tribe. They are rites, in other words, to which he has no right. It is in this sense that he is now "alone." He no longer adheres to the code of the culture from which he springs, but even so he does not accept, other than opportunistically, the cultural code of the people whom he rules and among whom he lives (and by whom he is accepted). He has fallen, as it were, into the vacant, amoral space between the European and the African tribes, because he belongs to both and yet to neither.

Exceeding permitted, or morally and socially sanctioned, limits is the "crime" that Marlow convicts Kurtz of, though for the Africans the identical rites are "permitted" and therefore constitute no "crime."[16] "Barbarism per se," Conrad wrote to Roger Casement in late 1903, "is no crime deserving of a heavy visitation"[17] (*Letters* 3:96); and as Marlow remarks when he compares the "subtle *horrors* [my italics]" of Kurtz's rule with the "pure, uncomplicated savagery" of those whom Kurtz rules, the latter have "a right to exist—obviously—in the sunshine" (*HD* 58). In this specific instance Marlow shows himself to be very much a cultural relativist; but here he is able to practice cultural relativism without contradiction because the rites, in spite of what he says of their unspeakableness, do not affect his conception of the nature of human nature. They have a *right* to their rites. The fact that an action is permitted by one tribe in one place but not by another in the same place has nothing to do with what human beings essentially are or can potentially become in different places. It does, however, have everything to do with not being able to maintain one's own tribal conditioning under radically changed cultural circumstances. Marlow, after all, belongs to Kurtz's own tribe (as well as to a specific subgroup within that tribe, the "gang of virtue"), so that he knows full well what is permitted to Kurtz, and to himself, and what is not.

Though Marlow does not specify in so many words just how Kurtz exceeded those limits, it should by now be fairly clear that, by attempting to become more than human, Kurtz has succeeded only in being less than human. Here again we are confronted with the central question of the book: what is it that makes human beings human? Just as during the period of his "ascendancy," Kurtz had been accustomed to force visiting chiefs to literally "crawl" (*HD* 58) on the ground when they came to see him, so now Kurtz himself is obliged to crawl just as servilely in order to reach the site of his former triumphs. As to the precise nature of the "unspeakable rites," Hunt Hawkins is, I think, right in identifying these with ceremonial human sacrifice, something that Stephen Reid had already suggested in 1963 in the context of a discussion of the relevance of Frazer's *Golden Bough* to *Heart of Darkness* (Hawkins, "Critique" 295). Though Reid's hypothesis about the Russian Harlequin's having been selected by the Black Amazon as a successor to the "dying-god" Kurtz seems unlikely and is unsupported by textual evidence, the explanation of the sacrificial rites themselves as being essentially religious in nature seems valid, especially since that is what Marlow himself indicates they are[18] (Reid 45). In this connection, it needs also to be recalled that, according to the historical record, human sacrifice was regularly practiced on ceremonial occasions in the Congo until at least the close of the nineteenth century.[19] For example, Hunt Hawkins quotes the African American journalist George Williams—who visited the Congo at the time Conrad was working there—writing in an open letter to King Leopold, that "cruelties of the most astounding character are practiced by the natives, such as burying slaves alive in the grave of a dead chief" (Hawkins, "Racism" 166). According to the entry for the Congo Free State in the eleventh edition of the *Encyclopedia Britannica*, "elaborate funeral rites, often accompanied by human sacrifice, play a most important part in native life." E.J. Glave, who had already completed a stay of six years in the Congo by the time Conrad arrived there, describes in grisly detail the mass executions he witnessed on the occasion of a chief's death. He also provides a powerful account of one of the ways in which victims were sacrificed, an account that is worth summarizing briefly if only to indicate what Marlow might have said of the unspeakable rites if he had felt free to speak openly of them.

Glave describes the ritual, unlike Marlow's "midnight dances," as beginning early in the morning with the beating of drums and the gathering of the villagers. The latter then begin to dance and sing, accompanied by war horns, exerting themselves violently and trying to outdo each other in the vigor of their dancing. At noon large jars of palm wine are distributed and a "general bout of intoxication" ensues. The intended victim is then carried into the center of the village, where his head is fastened to a ring tied to a tensed, bent-over pole a few feet away. He is immediately surrounded by dancers who mimic his expressions of pain until finally the executioner arrives, at which point silence descends on the whole village. This figure, as depicted by Glave (also in an accompanying sketch), bears an uncanny resemblance to Marlow's Sorcerer, especially in terms of his emphatic blackness, though of course here the figure is seen in daylight. "The executioner," writes Glave, "wears a cap composed of black cocks' feathers; his face and neck are blackened with charcoal, except the eyes, the lids of which are painted with white chalk. The hands and arms to the elbow, and feet and legs to the knee, are also blackened." After first dancing wildly around the victim, the executioner then pretends to strike at him with his sword; finally, after marking a line on the victim's neck with chalk, he decapitates him, thereby bringing "to a climax the frenzy of the natives; some of them savagely puncture the quivering trunk with their spears, others hack at it with their knives, while the remainder engage in a ghastly struggle for the possession of the head, which has been jerked into the air by the released tension of the sapling." After the conclusion of this struggle, the dancing and singing resume while another victim is prepared for the same fate. "Sometimes," Glave concludes, "as many as twenty slaves will be killed in one day. The dancing and general drunken uproar are continued until midnight when once more absolute silence ensues, in utter contrast to the hideous tumult of the day." Powerless on this particular occasion to do anything to stop the carrying out of these rites of human sacrifice, Glave vowed to prevent any future occurrences, at least in the limited area over which he had control (*Savage* 122-26).

Glave's account of the rites he witnessed differs in some respects from Marlow's vague hints about the "unspeakable rites," as well as from the brief depiction of the "sorcerer" whom Kurtz is crawling toward. The only really significant difference, however, is that the rites are usually performed *after* the death of a chief, a fact that also affects Reid's Frazerian "dying-god" interpretation.[20] The other differences are relatively minor, such as the circumstance that in Glave's case the rites were carried out primarily in daylight, whereas in Marlow's they are apparently conducted only at night. It may be that Conrad simply was not fully aware of how and when these ceremonies of human sacrifice were usually conducted, though he did once tell Arthur Symons quite explicitly that he had witnessed "all those sacreligious rites" (qtd. in Hawkins, "Racism" 166). Some of the less important differences may also point to Marlow's (and/or Conrad's) adding details that would make the rites both more familiar and more "magical" to Western listeners or readers. That would also explain why the executioner becomes a sorcerer and why rites that were generally conducted in broad daylight have to be rescheduled for the midnight, or witching, hour. Naturally, from the point of view of dramatic effect, mysterious and unspeakable rites are best performed in the dark; and of course it is only right and fitting that this should be the case if we remember that they take place in the so-called heart of darkness.[21]

Even taking all these differences into account, it is more than probable that Marlow's "unspeakable rites" involve human sacrifice and that this is the real reason why they are "unspeakable." The only alternative that critics have proposed with any frequency or conviction, namely that the rites are primarily cannibalistic, seems less likely, though cannibalism may play, as Reid has suggested, a subordinate role in the more comprehensive ritual of human sacrifice. Bernard Meyer, who is probably the most explicit advocate of identifying Marlow's "unspeakable rites" with cannibalism, bases his conclusion largely on the presence of the human skulls surrounding Kurtz's residence. But just how the mere fact of their existence succeeds in removing for Meyer "any doubts that above all else this is a tale of cannibalism" is not explained (168). In any case there is no logical or necessary connection between the skulls and cannibalism; nor, for that matter, is there one between the skulls and ritual human sacrifice. Different as they are, the two are nonetheless connected in that they reveal dramatically Kurtz's power and cruelty. The skulls, of course, are by no means "unspeakable," for the older Marlow speaks of them in some detail, and even goes out of his way to claim that he was not surprised to see them. Nor for that matter is cannibalism "unspeakable," as far the younger or even the older Marlow is concerned. After all, the majority of the former's crew consists of cannibals, and he makes no attempt to find euphemisms for what he thinks is their preferred diet; on the contrary, what they do is so very "speakable" that Marlow even makes jokes about it. Not that this means that Marlow approves of the mounting of skulls on poles or the eating of human flesh. It is clear that he does not approve, but it is also clear that his approval or disapproval of these specific issues is something that is not directly linked to Kurtz's participation in any supposedly unspeakable rites.

Recently, two critics have put forward yet another possible way of accounting for the unspeakability of the rites. The first represents part of a feminist project to reinterpret *Heart of Darkness*, whereas the second is more or less a derivative of a Freud-inspired theory put forward several decades ago (and subsequently repudiated) by Frederick Crews. The first hypothesis is self-confessedly "speculative" but is nonetheless advanced with vigor and confidence. "What, then has Kurtz done?" asks Marianna Torgovnick in *Gone Primitive*. He has, she says, "corrupted the idea of work and carried it to the extreme of enslavement." He has "allowed himself to be worshipped by his African followers." He has lost restraint. "But," Torgovnick goes on to say, "Kurtz has done more, a 'more' that remains less specified than his corruption of imperial policy." What, we wonder, might this mysterious and less specified "more" be? It is, quite simply, that Kurtz has had sex with the Black Amazon, thereby committing miscegenation and challenging "a boundary highly charged in the West, the boundary of race" (146–47). Torgovnick does not imply that Kurtz and his alleged mistress did anything unseemly, such as participating in orgies or performing the sexual act as a "rite" in public. In fact, in the context of her discussion of the "more" that Kurtz did, Torgovnick does not even refer specifically to the phrase "unspeakable rites," though there can be no doubt that she means us somehow to include it in our thoughts. Just why she would want to avoid it so assiduously, however, is an interesting question in itself, the answer to which seems to be that the story itself provides no justification whatever for viewing the relationship between Kurtz and the Black Amazon as involving any rites, unspeakable or otherwise.[22]

Hence, interesting as Torgovnick's hypothesis is, it remains unconvincing. Torgovnick must be given high marks for being one of the few critics to recognize that the Black Amazon belongs to the tribal aristocracy, but her claim that she is not be viewed as "high-minded" in the way that Kurtz's Belgian fiancée is (or is said to be), is not corroborated by the evidence of the story. On the contrary, the Black Amazon's courage and her fidelity—the latter being the primary virtue in Conrad's ethical code—are of the highest order. When the boat leaves the Inner Station, bearing the dying Kurtz with it, the Pilgrims get their guns ready to celebrate their departure with their own version of human sacrifice, "exterminating," as it were, "all the brutes" on shore. To prevent this from happening Marlow repeatedly blows the steam whistle, causing the closely packed mass of about a thousand people to break up in panic. Even the three sorcerers who a moment earlier had been strutting bravely and uttering their mysterious incantations suddenly drop, as if shot dead, to the ground. Not so with the Black Amazon. "Only the barbarous and superb woman," Marlow notes with evident admiration, "did not so much as flinch and stretched tragically her bare arms after us over the sombre and glittering river" (HD 66–67).[23]

This is supposed to be the woman who, in Torgovnick's view, is not "high-minded" and who is "presented as all body and inchoate emotion" (147). Such an accusation is, to put it bluntly, absurd, for if anyone in the whole story is noble ("high-minded") and fearless, or powerfully motivated by a sharply focused and indomitable will, then it is the Black Amazon. As for miscegenation being "simply not within the ken of the narrative; it is a 'love which dare not speak its name'" (147), this charge is almost equally absurd. As anyone familiar with Conrad's work must know, miscegenatious relationships are close to the center of his early fiction, with the nonwhite (or mixed) women invariably shown to be morally superior (in both courage and fidelity, as well as intelligence) to their real or potential white lovers, as in the cases of Nina in *Almayer's Folly,* Aissa in *Outcast of the Islands,* and even Jewel in *Lord Jim.* Though it is true that Conrad never openly depicts a sexual act taking place between the races, neither does he do so for couples belonging to the same race. Indeed, given the Victorian taboos regarding the depiction of sexual activity by anyone at all, regardless of race, religion, or national origin, he would have been mad to do so. And he certainly would (and could) not have expected to get his work published in respectable magazines or by respectable publishing houses.[24]

As for the second novel interpretation of the "unspeakable rites," Reynold Humphries's long essay "Restraint, Cannibalism and the 'Unspeakable Rites' in *Heart of Darkness*" (1990), here too an essentially sexual reading is put forward. Not that Humphries denies the fundamental correctness of the party of the cannibalists—their point of view strikes him, he says, as a "perfectly justifiable position to adopt"—but he nevertheless wishes to find an interpretation that is "more complete and coherent" (59). As for the idea that the rites might involve human sacrifice, Humphries takes no account whatever of this possibility, not even to dismiss it. What is of utmost importance as far as he is concerned is the presumed fact that "the word 'unspeakable' is the locus of the unconscious in the text" and that the critic's task is therefore "to decide what the rites might refer to and, more to the point, *for whom,* as their existence is uncertain" (60). Their existence is "uncertain" apparently because they are never described and because Marlow (and we) know of them only by hearsay. Moreover, "eye-witness reports are notoriously unreliable, especially when something as redolent with fantasy as sexuality is concerned" (61). Oddly enough, however, reports from the unconscious do not appear to be subject to the same risks of unreliable transmission.

Though Humphries announces his intention not to elongate an already overextended Kurtz on a Procrustean psychoanalytical couch, most of his essay is in fact devoted to an application of the Freudian concepts of anality and orality to *Heart of Darkness,* with special attention being paid to Kurtz's relevant orifices. It is true, however, that Humphries's initial hypothesis—that the rites are to be identified with homosexual acts (sodomy mostly)—is arrived at largely without Freud's assistance. Instead, Humphries relies chiefly on the Russian Harlequin's testimony regarding his conversations about love with Kurtz. He particularly cites the following passage: "'We talked of everything,' he said quite transported at the recollection. 'I forgot there was such a thing as sleep. The night did not seem to last an hour. Everything! Everything. . . . Of love too.' 'Ah, he talked to you of love!' I said much amused. 'It isn't what you think,' he cried almost passionately. 'It was in general. He made me see things—things'" (*HD* 55; Humphries, "Restraint" 62–63).

Humphries analyzes this passage in the light of Marlow's conscious and unconscious thoughts, including "his own sexual fantasies about things African." Though Humphries prefaces his remarks by saying that "we have no idea what Marlow thinks," he nevertheless blithely goes on to propose that "consciously, Marlow is thinking of love in general, but unconsciously of love in particular." From this assertion it then follows that the Russian picks up on Marlow's "unconscious" and "particular" meaning and is thereby led to betray "a homosexual attachment to Kurtz." He then goes even further to betray himself still more overtly "by wanting to kiss Marlow when the latter returns the seamanship manual to him." However, he manages to restrain himself in time, since "male bonding must not be seen to veer towards the feminine, given the latter's 'unspeakable' implications" ("Restraint" 63). Miscegenation, so it would appear, is not the only love whose name Conrad does not dare to speak, though he apparently has no qualms about dropping obscure hints all over the place. Nevertheless, it remains unclear just how the Russian's allegedly homosexual proclivities, certainly unrequited in Marlow's case and possibly also in Kurtz's, are supposed to have had a ritual dimension. As far as Humphries is concerned, homosexuality may be defined as a rite in and of itself.

Not that homosexuality by any means exhausts the ample and sometimes oddly variegated significance of the "unspeakable rites." As with Frederick Crews before him (56), Humphries goes on to identify the rites, both culturally and psychically, with "the desire for union with the mother and the concomitant, and necessary, taboo of incest" ("Restraint" 72). Again, it is left unexplained—as it was by Crews—just how or why such an incestuous union could or should be described as a "rite," even when, as it were, it is broadly and metaphorically construed. In some ill-defined way that is supposedly connected with Kurtz's obsessive orality, these rites are also, according to Humphries, related to capitalism, since

Kurtz's "need to swallow everything" is "a metaphor for the imperialist desire to possess, to incorporate economically in order that nothing be left over. . . . Capitalism cannot tolerate leftovers, as only when everything is incorporated into the one economic system can this system then present itself as *natural*, thus denying its aggressive aspects" (Humphries, 72).

We have traveled a long way, it seems, and mostly upriver, with Humphries as our guide, through the vast blank spaces of the mother's body and onward into the all-consuming maw of a monstrous Capitalism, a journey that has grown not only unspeakable but very nearly incomprehensible too. It is not only Capitalism, one is forced to conclude, but also Humphries himself who is unable to tolerate leftovers, for whatever may be true of the former, there can be no doubt that the latter confronts readers of Conrad's story with the demand that they be prepared to swallow everything that he places on the critical table. In this respect at least, Humphries, if not Conrad, has allowed orality—and presumably, after an appropriate interval, anality—to, as it were, simultaneously swallow and expel everything. Paradoxically, however, by now, nearly a century after Conrad first conceived the tale that would prove so nourishing to subsequent generations of readers and critics, such an immense quantity and variety of interpretive fare have been loaded onto it that the tale itself is in danger of disappearing from sight, buried beneath an unceasing and apparently ever-increasing mass of commentary. Given, then, the distinct possibility—even the probability—that Conrad's text will one day become unreadable and even invisible, it may be that the mystery of Conrad's unspeakable rites will also be transformed into a mess of unspeakable "writes"—the result of criticism pursuing its essentially cannibalistic rituals of devouring "primary" texts in order to transform them internally—and eternally—into "secondary" ones.

6

E.J. GLAVE, CAPTAIN ROM, AND THE MAKING OF *HEART OF DARKNESS*

What can I do? I MUST get ivory. I have no law or regulation book. I am the only law and only God in Katanga.

E.D. Morel, *Red Rubber*

Under the pressure of physical suffering, the intellect sees wrongly, the heart deceives itself, the unguided soul strays into an abyss.

Joseph Conrad

Recently Edward James Glave has been mentioned by Sven Lindqvist in connection with *Heart of Darkness* as an "old Congo hand" who was in a position to know what atrocities were being committed during the mid-1890s in the Congo Free State. As evidence, Lindqvist quotes at some length from the last essay Glave wrote for the *Century Magazine* not long before his death of tropical fever in Matadi (Conrad's Outer Station) on May 12, 1895. Lindqvist's quotations are meant to show how Glave, even though he supposedly had relatively little contact with Africans, finally came to realize that the Belgian "system" of economic exploitation in the Congo was cruel and even genocidal. Nonetheless, Glave, who was (according to Lindqvist) writing under pressure from fellow whites shortly before he died, remained unwilling to condemn the brutal actions of the Congo State's agents as fully as they deserved. Instead, he merely proposed that "'their commercial transactions need[ed] remedying,'" an unduly "mild" judgment that, Lindqvist concludes, is identical with the one "made on Kurtz in *Heart of Darkness*; his trading methods were unsound and had to be abandoned" (23).

A few pages later Lindqvist returns to Glave's essay and cites another passage describing how the sometime Arab "method" of collecting ivory by pillage and murder was continued by the Belgians at Stanley Falls long after the departure of Tippo Tib and also how the station chief, Captain Rom, decorated a flower bed in front of his house with twenty-one heads that had been cut off during a reprisal raid against a nearby native village. Lindqvist also cites a brief account of Rom's brutal action that was published in the *Saturday Review* on December 17, 1898, arguing that if Conrad failed to read about Rom in Glave's essay when it was published the year before, he certainly must have seen the subsequent report about him in the *Saturday Review*. It was, after all, on precisely the next day that he began work on *Heart of Darkness*, and one of the most dramatic scenes in that novel, as Lindqvist goes on to point out, is a vivid description of half a dozen heads mounted on poles standing in front of Kurtz's residence at the Inner Station (29).

Even more recently, Adam Hochschild has argued in the pages of the *New Yorker* (April 14, 1997) that "almost all of Conrad's many biographers" have overlooked "several likely models for the novel's central figure, who is one of the twentieth century's most notorious literary villains—Mr. Kurtz" (40). One of the most likely of these likely models, he maintains, is Captain Léon Rom, whom Conrad "almost certainly had in mind" while writing *Heart of Darkness*. Without referring to Glave by name (he figures only as an anonymous "British explorer"), Hochschild quotes the infamous passage from Glave's last *Century* essay about the twenty-one heads, acknowledging, however, Lindqvist's priority here. He notes approvingly the latter's point that "even if Conrad missed the *Century* article, the London *Saturday Review*, a magazine that he admired and read faithfully, picked up the story of Rom and his twenty-one severed heads in its issue of December 17, 1898" (43). Hochschild also suggests that Rom's *Le Nègre du Congo* (1899), which, however, apparently contains no reference to the twenty-one skulls, is "an odd little book— jaunty, arrogant, and sweepingly superficial," composed in a voice that "we might imagine Mr. Kurtz to be writing about savage customs that need to be suppressed" (44). Naturally, given the date of publication of Rom's book, there can be no question that Conrad read it before completing *Heart of Darkness*.

It is tempting to accept Lindqvist's and Hochschild's arguments at face value, but unfortunately a few nagging doubts remain. To begin with, as far as Conrad's possible or "likely" knowledge of Rom is concerned, neither critic takes into account that Glave was publishing his report in an American periodical, the *Century Magazine*, whose readership in Britain may or may not have included Conrad at this time. As for the reference to Rom in the *Saturday Review,* there is no actual evidence that Conrad saw it and no recognition of the fact that he might easily not have, since Rom's "story," as retold by the *Saturday Review*, runs to only a couple of sentences mixed in with two paragraphs of editorial commentary on the economic situation of the Congo Free State; and even those two paragraphs are buried among a mass of other miscellaneous topical information. Also it is not quite so clear as Lindqvist makes out that Conrad did actually begin work on *Heart of Darkness* precisely on December 18, 1898, the day after he had supposedly read about Rom in the *Saturday Review*. In fact, the first unambiguous reference to "The Heart of Darkness" occurs in Conrad's correspondence on December 31, and the first ambiguous one on December 13, presumably several days before he would have seen the relevant issue of the *Saturday Review* (*Letters* 2:139, 129). It is perhaps with these doubts in mind that Zdzislaw Najder chooses a date somewhere "around December 15" as a kind of compromise guess (*Joseph Conrad* 249). Problematic too is the circumstance that Conrad had already written about his experience in Africa, though not by any means as vividly or as autobiographically, much earlier in "An Outpost of Progress" in July 1896. Apparently he did not need to be prodded by newspaper accounts to revert artistically to his unhappy time in the Congo.

Furthermore, Lindqvist's and Hochschild's occasionally casual treatment of the available evidence, as well as their readiness to engage in airy speculation, do not make one feel confident in their judgment. Not only is Hochschild guilty of extreme reductionism in making Kurtz out to be a "notorious literary villain," but, added to Lindqvist's penchant for finding certainty where only possibility and plausibility exist, he also has a way of exaggerating the originality of his findings. Thus, though it is true that virtually all biographers of Conrad have ignored Rom's relevance to the *Heart of Darkness* (the notable exception is John Batchelor), none omits reference to the fact that by the early years of the twentieth century the Congo Free State was being condemned internationally for the terrible atrocities committed against Africans in its name and by its agents. What is more, though Conrad's biographers may have been negligent, Conrad's critics have known and written about Rom's skulls for at least the last twenty years, that is, ever since Molly Mahood first mentioned them in *Colonial Encounter* in 1977 (13). Presumably one of these critics is in fact the immediate source of Lindqvist's awareness of the relevance of Rom to *Heart of Darkness*, as well as Hochschild's mediate one. In Glave's original text, the single short paragraph describing Rom's atrocity reads as follows:

The State soldiers are constantly stealing, and sometimes the natives are so persecuted that they resent this by killing and eating their tormentors. Recently the State post on the Lomami lost two men killed and eaten by the natives. Arabs were sent to punish the natives; many women and children were taken, and twenty-one heads were brought to the falls, and have been used by Captain Rom as a decoration round a flower-bed in front of his house! ("Cruelty" 706)

As for Batchelor's brief discussion of Rom's relevance to *Heart of Darkness*, his source is not Mahood but John Lester's 1982 note arguing that Captain Rom should be considered another possible model for Kurtz (Batchelor 85). Lester in turn cites an unnamed American missionary, writing in 1896, who is quoted by Peter Forbath, *The River Congo* (1977), to the effect that "'[w]ar has been waged all through the district and thousands of people have been killed and twenty-one heads were brought back to Stanley Falls, and have been used by Captain Rom (the station commander) as a decoration around a flower-bed in front of his house'" (374). On the basis of this information, Lester then goes on to speculate that, although there is no actual evidence that Conrad knew about Rom or his severed heads, "it would surely be a huge coincidence if he was unaware that, six years after his own visit, heads had indeed stood in the place where those of Kurtz were said to have been" (112).[1] Like Hochschild, however, Lester fails to observe that it would have been even odder if Conrad had known, for vast as Conrad's intuitive powers undoubtedly were, even Lester cannot explain how Conrad could have gained access to the unnamed American missionary's information.[2] Lester seems unaware that at this time the sole public account of Rom's activities was Glave's *Century* essay, so that if Conrad did in fact know of Rom, his ultimate source could only have been Glave. Moreover, to judge by the almost identical wording of the last part of the American missionary's report, it is directly indebted to Glave's account and may have been copied from it. Be that as it may, the problem remains that Glave's essay was written for an American rather than for a British journal, a circumstance that even Molly Mahood does not take into account; neither, for that matter, does Patrick Brantlinger, who also quotes the passage (*Rule* 261).[3]

There is some evidence not cited by either Lindqvist or Hochschild, however, that might incline one to believe that Conrad had read Glave or at least heard about him. To begin with, though *Century Magazine* was published in New York, its title page indicates that it was also distributed in Britain during the relevant period by either T. Fisher Unwin or Macmillan. Conrad read a story published in the issue that appeared earlier during the same year as Glave's essay "Cruelty in the Congo Free State." That was Stephen Crane's "A Man and Some Others," published in *Century Magazine* in February 1897, a tale for which Conrad expressed immense admiration (*Letters* 1:415) and which may have led him to look at subsequent issues of the journal. If he did, Rom's name may also have struck a familiar cord in Conrad's memory, for from March to October 1890 Rom was station chief at Léopoldville, raising the possibility that Conrad may have made his acquaintance in early August or late September when he himself was staying in nearby Kinshasa (*BCB* 2:822–23).[4]

As for Glave, although there certainly is no direct evidence that Conrad knew anything about him, there is a certain amount of circumstantial evidence that he did. Most of this evidence derives from Glave's book *In Savage Africa, Or Six Years of Adventure in Congo-Land,* which was first published in New York in 1892 and then republished the following year in London with the first four words of the original title omitted. Given Conrad's professed love for reading explorer literature generally, as well as his particular interest in works relating to Central Africa, it is certainly within the realm of possibility that Conrad may have read the book. In this autobiographical work (parts of which had appeared earlier in a variety of American journals), Glave describes his life and travels in the Congo Free State from 1883 to 1889. During the first three years he was employed by the Congo Free State, and during the last three by the Sanford Exploring Expedition (a trading company), control over which was assumed by the Congo State in December 1888 under the new name of "Societé Anonyme Belge" ("Compagnie" 413). The book is prefaced by a brief endorsement written by his sometime mentor and friend, Henry Morgan Stanley, and contains numerous illustrations, many of them produced by Glave himself. Like Kurtz, Glave not only had influential friends in high places, but he also sketched well and wrote well.

The often suggestive parallels with Conrad's story, however, do not merely apply to Kurtz but also—and perhaps even more strikingly—to Marlow and even Conrad himself. There is, for example, Glave's recollection of how, as a boy, he was fascinated with the blank spaces in the center of the map of Africa:

> But I remember that, even at school, Africa had a peculiar fascination for me. A great map of the "Dark Continent" hung on the walls of my class-room; the tentative way in which the geographers of that day had

marked down localities in almost unknown equatorial regions seemed to me delightful and mysterious.

There were rivers with great estuaries, which were traced on the chart for a few miles into the interior and then dribbled away in lines of hesitating dots; lakes with one border firmly inked in and the other left in vaguest outline; mountain ranges to whose very name was appended a doubtful query; and territories of whose extent and characteristics, ignorance was openly confessed by vast unnamed blank spaces. (*Savage* 16)

In his autobiography, *A Personal Record,* Conrad recalls that in 1868, "when nine years old or thereabouts [actually more like eleven], . . . while looking at a map of Africa of the time and putting my finger on the blank space then representing the unsolved mystery of that continent, I said to myself with absolute assurance and an amazing audacity which are no longer in my character now: 'When I grow up I shall go *there*'" (13). And, of course, in *Heart of Darkness* itself, Marlow, looking at a map of Africa in a London shop-window, remembers how "as a little chap I had a passion for maps."

I would look for hours at South America, or Africa, or Australia and lose myself in all the glories of exploration. At that time there were many blank spaces on the earth and when I saw one that looked particularly inviting on a map (but they all look that) I would put my finger on it and say: When I grow up I will go there. The North Pole was one of these places I remember. Well, I haven't been there yet and I shall not try now. The glamour's off. Other places were scattered about the Equator and in every sort of latitude all over the two hemispheres. I have been in some of them and . . . well, we won't talk about that. But there was one yet—the biggest—the most blank, so to speak—that I had a hankering after.

True, by this time it was not a blank space any more. It had got filled since my boyhood with rivers and lakes and names. It had ceased to be a blank space of delightful mystery—a white patch for a boy to dream gloriously over. (*HD* 11–12)

That Conrad had the corresponding passage in the novel in mind when he wrote about his boyhood fascination for Africa in *A Personal Record* is apparent from the close resemblance in some of the wording of the two passages. That he may also have had Glave in mind when he wrote both (but especially the former) is suggested not only by the generally similar contents of all three passages but also by specific words, such as *blank* and *mystery*, that are featured prominently in all of them. Also, Marlow's remark that by the time he was grown up the blank spaces had become filled with "rivers and lakes and names" may be echoing Glave's observation that his map in school contained rivers that "dribbled away in lines of hesitating dots," lakes with only one clearly designated shoreline, and mountain ranges lacking names. Significantly, the sequence of "rivers," "lakes," and "names" is identical in the two passages.[5] In this connection, we should remember that Conrad's memory sometimes had a way of (perhaps unconsciously) confusing what he had actually lived through with what he had merely read. The scene lifted from Mungo Park's *Travels* that he had once told Edward Garnett about as something he had experienced himself and meant to include in *Heart of Darkness* is a case in point.

In isolation, then, though this bit of evidence concerning a shared interest in African maps may not be particularly persuasive, when it is added to other possible borrowings from Glave, the case becomes less easy to dismiss. Thus, it may be more than coincidental that both Glave and Marlow, immediately after referring to their fascination with maps in childhood, pass on to their obsession with securing some kind of employment that would allow them entry into the heart of Africa. Reflecting that "members must frequently be wanted, and sometimes at a moment's notice, to join some perilous enterprise," Glave begins by "laying siege" to the "Association Internationale Africaine" in Brussels and bombards them with letters. He eventually is hired, concluding somewhat wryly that the main reason for his success may have been his persistence: "I really believe that rather than submit to the incessant worry of receiving and answering my pestering communications he [Leopold's close adviser, Colonel Strauch] had given me the appointment" (*Savage* 18). Unlike Glave or, for that matter, Conrad himself, Marlow gets his appointment "very quick," but only after he had also "worried them" in vain for an extended period of time. In the end, giving up hope of getting a job on his own merits, he resorts, as Conrad did, too, to pulling strings— that is, to using his aunt's connections with influential people in the unnamed trading company. This strategy is admittedly different from Glave's, but there is a distinct similarity in that Marlow, like Glave, thinks of applying for a job in the first place only after reasoning that a big trading company must need employees: "Dash it all, I thought to myself, they can't trade without using some kind of craft on that lot of fresh water—steamboats! Why shouldn't I try to get charge of one" (*HD* 12).[6]

Once in Africa, both Marlow and Glave—but not Conrad—are intimately involved in the difficult and time-consuming task of getting a steamboat afloat at the Kinshasa (or Central) Station. In Glave's case this also meant arranging to have the disassembled vessel transported overland by carriers and then reassembled and riveted together: "All the machinery was made in sections as light as possible, and the hull composed of small plates to be rivetted together when it reached its destination. The charge of this construction was also one of my duties, in which I was greatly aided by Mr. W. J. Davy, who was to rebuild the boat, and officiate as engineer when she was afloat on the waters of the Upper Congo" (Glave, *Savage* 170–71).[7] Once the ship—the *Florida*, which coincidentally, Conrad was promised the command of (Jean-Aubry, *Life* 1:139-40)—was launched, Glave used it on a mission to explore the commercial potential of "the little known regions of the far interior." Steaming up the muddy waters of the Lulungu River, he forestalled any attempt at aggression on the part of potentially hostile natives by sounding "a blast on the harmony whistle [that] would quiet their loud talk into whispered words of fear" (*Savage* 189). Glave describes in greater detail the powerful effect of the steam whistle during a subsequent voyage up the Ruki River:

> We had a harmony whistle on board which alarmed them [the natives] a great deal. Just before leaving their beach, on continuing my voyage, I called my men together by blowing the whistle. The poor natives of Nkolé, superstitious, as all savages are, thought it was some angry spirit who was kept by me to terrify people, and who gave vent to his feelings in this way. The natives on the beach beat a hasty retreat at this unusual sound, and those who were in canoes lost all presence of mind. Some jumped into the river; and we steamed away leaving in our wake a mass of upturned canoes and struggling figures, while on shore the beach was deserted, and from behind every tree black faces grinned in safety at their less fortunate friends in the water. (*Savage* 236)[8]

On the Lulungu River Glave encountered vast native slave markets, with as many as five hundred slaves offered for sale in a single village. These captives were transported up the Oubangi River, he notes, where they were exchanged for ivory. Glave then goes on to remark that there the "natives who are confirmed cannibals buy their slaves solely for food. Having purchased slaves, they feed them on ripe bananas, fish, and oil, and when they get them into good condition they kill them. Hundreds of the Balolo slaves are taken into the river and disposed of in this way each month. A great many other slaves are sold to the large villages on the Congo, to supply victims for the execution ceremonies" (*Savage* 191-92). Proceeding upward along the Malinga River, Glave reached an abandoned village consisting of seven "old, dilapidated habitations, built on piles, with a floor just above the water's edge. Placed on sticks in front of them were several whitening skulls. What a tale of suffering these grim and hideous trophies told!" (194). Undaunted, Glave continued upriver to the village of Baulu, where he bought "in one afternoon and through the night four thousand pounds of elephant tusks at an average of two cents per pound" (198). In other villages he managed to strike even better bargains, for "many of the people have no idea of its [ivory's] value at all. I remember I purchased one tusk weighing seventy-five pounds for beads and shells of the value of one dollar" (200). On this expedition, several of Glave's crew were Balolo cannibals, for whose work Glave had nothing but praise. Indeed, prior to leaving on this mission of exploration and trade, Glave had spent several months almost alone at the Equator Station, the only other outsider being a Zanzibari soldier. Nevertheless, though the surrounding natives "could easily have overcome me and pillaged my post," they never showed the least sign of hostility. "I felt just as secure among them," Glave concludes, "as I do in London and New York" (203).

As anyone familiar with *Heart of Darkness* will acknowledge, there are several points of close resemblance between Glave's account of his voyage up the Lulungu and Malinga Rivers and Marlow's description of the voyage up the Congo River to the Inner Station (Stanley Falls). The most striking of these shared elements are the extended voyage upriver into a hitherto relatively unknown region aboard a small steamer partly manned by a cannibal crew, the surprise expressed by both Marlow and Glave that they felt completely safe even though outnumbered by supposed "savages," the claim that food cannibalism was a common practice in remote areas of the Congo State, the stop at a settlement displaying several skulls mounted on poles at its entrance, the use of the steam whistle to intimidate villagers, the interpretation of Western technology (here the whistle, in *Heart of Darkness* the steam boiler) from the natives' point of view as embodying powerful spirits, and the accumulation of great quantities of high-quality ivory by a "first class agent."

One might add to this list Glave's rather unusual experience (like Kurtz's) of having been in sole charge of a station at Lukolela for more than a year, during which time he was only rarely in touch with other whites. At first he was overcome "by a feeling of momentary sadness and depression . . . as, returning to my hut, I realized my complete isolation," but gradually he became engrossed in the task of setting up the station and getting to know the people and language of the local Babangi tribe. His account of how the Babangi patiently taught him their language is especially memorable, revealing not only Glave's intelligence

Joseph Conrad at age thirty-nine, six years after his return from the Congo, now "humanized." From Gérard Jean-Aubry, *Joseph Conrad: Life and Letters.*

A map of Africa in 1898, shortly before Conrad began writing *Heart of Darkness,* showing the results of the infamous scramble for colonial territory among the European nations. From the *Fortnightly Review* (November 1898).

Banana, shown here about 1888, was the first port of call for most ships arriving from Europe. From Hermann von Wissmann, *My Second Journey through Equatorial Africa.*

Boma, pictured about 1886, was the capital of the Congo State, a place described as a "comedy of light at the door of darkness" in a passage later deleted by Conrad from the original manuscript (*HD* 18). From P. Möller, *Tre År i Kongo* (1887).

Matadi in 1895, Conrad's Outer Station, where, aside from the Accountant's shabby office, "everything else in the Station was in a muddle—heads, things, buildings. Caravans. Strings of dusty niggers with splay feet arrived and departed; a stream of manufactured goods, rubbishy cottons, beads, and brass-wire se[n]t into the depths of darkness, and in return came a precious trickle of ivory" (*HD* 21). From *Century Magazine* 54 (May-October 1897).

Work on the railway in 1895 linking Matadi (Conrad's Outer Station) and Stanley Pool (the Central Station). "I came upon a boiler wallowing in the grass, then found a path leading up the hill. It turned aside for the boulders, and also for an undersized railway truck lying there on its back with its wheels in the air. One was off. The thing looked as dead as the carcass of some animal. I came upon more pieces of decaying machinery, a stack of rusty rails. . . . They were building a railway" (*HD* 19). From *Century Magazine* 54 (May-October 1897).

"Next day I left that station at last, with a caravan of sixty men, for a two-hundred-mile tramp" (*HD* 23). Note the Congo State flag carried by the lead porter. From P. Möller, *Tre År i Kongo*.

"They wandered here and there with their absurd long staves in their hands like a lot of faithless pilgrims bewitched inside a rotten fence" (*HD* 26). From Camille Coquilhat, *Sur le Haut-Congo*.

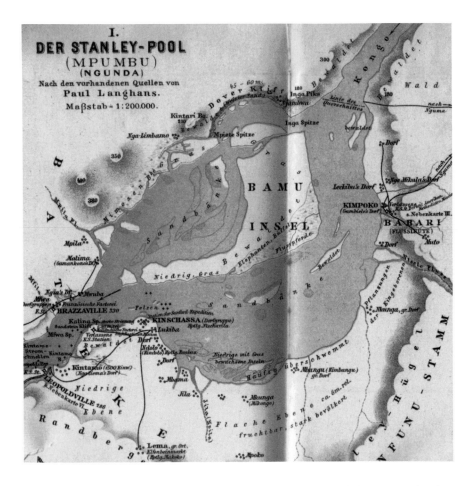

Map of Stanley Pool, circa 1887. From *Mittheilungen der k.k. geographischen Gesellschaft.*

Stanley Pool as seen from Léopoldville, near Kinshasa (Conrad's Central Station). "On the fifteenth day I came in sight of the big river again, and hobbled into the Central Station. It was on a backwater surrounded by scrub and forest, with a pretty border of smelly mud on one side, and on the three others enclosed by a crazy fence of rushes" (*HD* 24). From *Mittheilungen der k.k. geographischen Gesellschaft.*

The *Stanley*, one of several steam-powered boats on the upper reaches of the Congo River, circa 1888. From Camille Coquilhat, *Sur le Haut-Congo.*

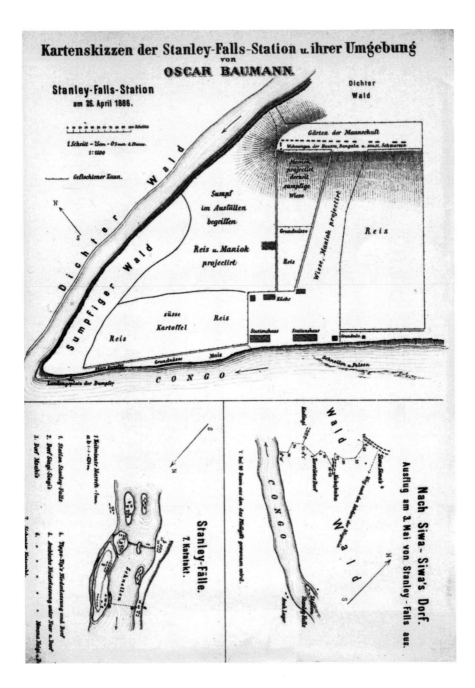

Map of the old Stanley Falls Station (Conrad's Inner Station) in 1886. From *Mittheilungen der k.k. geographischen Gesellschaft.*

"A fusillade burst out under my feet. The pilgrims had opened with their Winchesters and were simply squirting lead into that bush. . . . I stood in the doorway, peering, and the arrows came in swarms. They might have been poisoned, but they looked as though they wouldn't kill a cat" (*HD* 4, 6). Men ashore versus men aboard on the Congo River, circa 1888. From E. J. Glave, *In Savage Africa.*

The new Stanley Falls Station as Conrad saw it in 1890. "Through my glasses I saw the slope of a hill interspersed with rare trees and perfectly free from undergrowth. A long decaying building on the summit was half buried in the high grass; the large holes in the peaked roof gaped black from afar; the jungle and the woods made a background" (*HD* 52). From *Scribner's Magazine* (February 1890).

Arab and Matamatamba ivory and slave raiders meeting with Congo State officials at the old Stanley Falls Station around 1886. From P. Möller, *Tre År i
Kongo*.

"Ivory! I should think so. Heaps of it, stacks of it. The old mud shanty was
bursting with it. You would think there was not a single tusk left either above
or below the ground in the whole country. 'Mostly fossil,' the Manager had
remarked disparagingly. It was no more fossil than I am, but they call it fossil
when it is dug up" (*HD* 49). Ivory tusks on display at the Arab settlement near
the new Stanley Falls Station in 1890, not long before Conrad stopped there for
a week. From *Scribner's Magazine* (February 1890).

Congo State Officials dining at the old Stanley Falls Station in 1886. From P. Möller, *Tre År i Kongo.*

The new Stanley Falls Station in 1895 at the time when Capt Léon Rom was station chief. From *Century Magazine* 54 (May-October 1897).

Walter Deane was chief of the old Stanley Falls Station at the time of its destruction by the Arabs in 1886. An Englishman, Deane precipitated the attack by refusing to relinquish an African woman who was claimed as a slave by one of the neighboring Arabs. From Camille Coquilhat, *Sur le Haut-Congo*.

"This must have been before his—let us say—nerves went wrong and caused him to preside at certain midnight dances ending with unspeakable rites, which—as far as I reluctantly gathered from what I heard at various times—were offered up to him—do you understand?—to Mr. Kurtz himself" (*HD* 50). From *Harper's Weekly* (January 11, 1890).

"I pulled the string of the whistle, and I did this because I saw the pilgrims on deck getting out their rifles with an air of anticipating a jolly lark. At the sudden screech there was a movement of abject terror through that wedged mass of bodies. 'Don't! don't you frighten them away,' cried some one on deck disconsolately. I pulled the string time after time. They broke and ran, they leaped, they crouched, they swerved, they dodged the flying terror of the sound" (*HD* 66). From Hermann von Wissmann, *My Second Journey Through Equatorial Africa*.

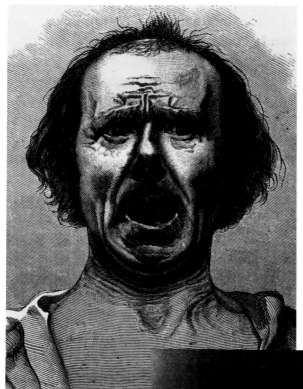

"He cried in a whisper at some image, at some vision—he cried out twice, a cry that was no more than a breath: 'The horror! The horror!'" (*HD* 68). The expression of "horror" as depicted in Charles Darwins's *The Expression of the Emotions in Men and Animals.*

The English explorer E.J. Glave, one of many possible originals for Kurtz (and Marlow). From *Century Magazine* 50 (May-October 1895).

KING OF THE BELGIANS.

The president of the Congo State, Leopold II of Belgium and I of the Congo.
From *Review of Reviews* (May 1890).

"Been some talk of late of trouble in Belgium. No trace of it in Bruges, where the people throng the streets to see the KING come and go, welcoming and speeding HIS MAJESTY with hearty cheer." When Conrad republished *Heart of Darkness* in book form in 1902, his depiction of Leopold's "trouble" clearly differed radically from the general view provided in the British press. From *Punch* (July 2, 1902).

and assiduity but also his sense of the ridiculous figure he was cutting in the eyes of his teachers (*Savage* 46; 49). As Charles Liebrechts, who knew him well, remarks of Glave, he was able to respond correctly in difficult situations because "his knowledge of the indigenous people was so profound (he spoke Bayanzi especially like a native)" (153).[9]

A strong link between Glave and the "original Kurtz" (as well as with the "gang of virtue") is also the former's emphasis throughout his book on the need to find an effective means of ridding the Congo of slavery, a theme that is also central to the *Century* essays. (And, like Kurtz, Glave bears a name that may be of German origin.) A more tenuous possible link with the "sham" Kurtz is that Glave may have had at least one native mistress. In late May 1887, James Jameson, who was part of Stanley's Emin Pasha Relief Expedition, met Glave at the Equator Station on the Congo, noting that he was now employed by the Sanford Exploring Expedition, having left the service of the Congo State "like many more, as rats leave a sinking ship." In the immediately following sentence, Jameson goes on to observe how "one of the chief occupations of the Belgian officers at the different stations is to civilize the country by adding to the population specimens of half-breeds, as they are all more or less married to native women" (50). That Jameson restricts his remarks to Belgians may of course mean that he wished to exclude Glave from the practice, though this seems a little improbable.

To be sure, the differences between Glave and Kurtz are at least as great as the similarities. Though Glave was close to his African companions and workers, often to the point of identifying strongly with their interests (Lindqvist, it must be said here, is dead wrong about Glave's allegedly limited contact with Africans), he certainly never "went native" or participated in "unspeakable rites" in any capacity other than that of horrified observer. Also, Glave never lost his faith, as Kurtz did, in the idealistic "civilizing mission" of whites in the Congo. Though he remained convinced that Africans needed to be disciplined as part of the process of "educating" them, he was very much against unduly harsh treatment, especially of women and children. Further, though it is true that like Kurtz, Glave toward the end of his life grew disillusioned with the possible success of the antislavery movement in the Congo, he never repudiated the rightness of the cause, only the honorableness of the agents who were carrying it out. In this respect he is worlds apart from Kurtz. He differs radically, too, in that his "treatise" on the abolition of the slave trade and the civilizing mission of European nations in Africa was composed *after* he had spent six years in the Congo State, whereas Kurtz wrote his at the beginning of his stay there. If, then, at the close of his book on Africa, Glave uses the word that has become identified with Kurtz, it is definitely not for the same reasons. Glave's "horror" arises from what he has seen others do, rather than what he has done himself. "It should always be remembered," he writes, using language that in places seems to echo that of Kurtz's treatise, "that the *suppression* of slavery in Africa does not mean merely striking the fetters from the limbs of the slave; its end is not only the substitution of paid forced labor, but also the relief of enslaved *humanity* throughout all these regions from a life of *unspeakable horror*" (*Savage* 243, my italics). Glave, it is clear, never doubted the humanity of the Africans he met or felt that they lacked the "right stuff." He credits the Zanzibaris who accompanied Stanley with enabling him to carry out his exploits, and as for himself, he has "sincere admiration for the brave young Ba-Nkundu with whom I have fought side by side against overwhelming odds of hostile cannibals. Such plucky and devoted fellows as Bongo Nsanda and Bienelo are a credit *to any nation*" (245, my italics).

Glave's gradual disillusionment with Leopold's Congo State is more in line with Marlow's loss of confidence in Kurtz (and in the sincerity of Belgian ideals generally) than it is with Kurtz's dramatic and sudden loss of faith in his "civilizing" mission. Whereas in the last chapter of *In Savage Africa* Glave attacks only the "system" of pillage, murder, and enslavement practiced by Tippo Tib and his Zanzibari Arabs, by the midpoint of his journey across Africa five years later he began to suspect that the "system" now practiced by Leopold's agents in the upper reaches of the Congo might not be a whit better. Glave's understanding of the real situation, like Marlow's, was subject to considerable "delayed decoding." Thus, on August 13, 1894, not long after having reached Congo State territory, Glave writes in his diary that "the Belgians are undoubtedly the friends of the natives, and no nationality is displaying such zeal in removing the lawless influences of the land. The Belgian policy is liberal and thoroughly anti-slavery. Within the last few years they have done wonders." Nevertheless, despite this expression of confidence in an apparently flawless record, Glave could not quite make out why, "incomprehensibly, Africans are leaving Belgian territory for the British" ("Heart of Africa" 927). At another station a couple of months later, he had the distinct impression that "the released natives are [not] very happy with the Belgians; there is too much stick for the slightest offense." By early December he began hearing unconfirmed rumors of slave raiding on the part of a white officer at the Kabambarré Station, but when he actually got there he was favorably impressed by the station chief, Lieutenant Hambrusin. To be sure, Glave was a little taken aback when Hambrusin had an African soldier hanged for murder, apparently only one of several such hangings occurring recently. On December 23 Glave rationalizes such brutality by arguing that when Hambrusin "took over the Station the men here were in a rebellious state, ill-treating the natives, robbing, and even killing. Hambrusin executed a few, and the natives, seeing that they would have justice from the whites, remained friendly."[10] On Christmas Day, Glave's feelings are even more charitable: "I must not forget the kindness of the Belgians. Everywhere they have rendered me kindly aid and saved me all sorts of bother and expense. Their hospitality has been unbounded. Nobody, however, has pleased me so much as Hambrusin" ("New Conditions" 907–11). The one "blemish" in all this apparent harmony was the brutal and uncontrolled treatment too often meted out by Congo State soldiers to their "prisoners." Glave expresses hope, however, that such behavior will soon change for the better now that Hambrusin has received additional staff to help enforce discipline among his soldiers.

A month later, at the Riba-Riba Station, Glave was rapidly growing less hopeful. Not only was he disgusted by the cruel ill-treatment of women "prisoners," who were flogged and chicotted mercilessly for "desertion" (!), but he also began to realize that, although the Congo State was perhaps doing the Africans a "kindness" by requiring them to repay its "civilizing" work by making them give of their labor, it was definitely not doing them a kindness by adopting the "policy of the Arabs" and treating the natives "with the utmost severity." As he moved closer to Stanley Falls, he grew ever more alarmed at the arbitrary and cruel behavior of state officials. At Wabundu Station, just upstream from the Falls, he was horrified to learn that two days before he arrived, the acting chief officer, Laschet, had in a fit of rage hanged two Sierra Leone soldiers without trial, despite the fact that they were both British subjects. By the time he reached the Falls themselves, he was no longer able to escape the horrifying reality that was staring him in the face: the Congo State was not only employing the same brutal "means as in days gone by, when Tippo Tib was one of the masters of the situation"—that is, it was not only raiding villages, killing or enslaving the inhabitants, and holding them ransom for ivory—but it had also "established a monopoly by driving out the Arab and Wangwana competitors" ("Cruelty" 702-6). Symbolic of this drastic change in Congo State policy were the twenty-one heads decorating the flower-beds in front of Captain Rom's residence.

As he traveled farther down the Congo, repeating Marlow's journey in reverse, he steamed past stations he had not so long ago helped found and direct himself. Now he saw the full extent of the horrifying effects of the "fiendish policy" employed by the state to collect as much rubber as possible: "hundreds of slaves, mere children, all taken in unholy wars against the natives," along with "thousands of people . . . killed and homes destroyed." That was definitely not how it used to be in the "old, humane days," Glave now reflects wistfully, "when we white men had no force at all. This forced [rubber] commerce is depopulating the country" ("Cruelty" 699–707). Some of the other Europeans he met were equally horrified. Stopping in Kinshasa in mid-March to collect his mail, he heard everywhere "the same news of the doings of the Congo Free State—rubber and murder, slavery in its worst form." Though there was distinct evidence of progress and prosperity, and communications and transport especially had improved markedly since his last stay in the Congo six years earlier, Glave could not help feeling that these benefits did not outweigh the great evil caused by the Congo State's abominable way of carrying on the rubber trade. "The wretched rubber business should be stopped," he concluded; "this would remove the great evil. It is the enforced commerce that breeds all the trouble." Three weeks later, seeing the dead body of a carrier on the trail—something Conrad had also witnessed and recorded in his diary a few years earlier—Glave could no longer suppress his feelings of indignation: "These posts ought to give some care to the porters; the heartless disregard for life is abominable. Two days ago a native applied to me for medicine and food; he was ill and starving. The same day I met a poor liberated slave, emaciated, with nothing to eat. I gave him food, but could not understand his language, as he was a poor wretch stolen from a far-away home. Native life is considered of no value by the Belgians" ("Cruelty" 708–13). It should not be difficult to recognize in this outburst of moral outrage—and in this gesture of helpless humanity—a rather similar reaction described by Marlow as he copes with the mute request of a dying African in the "Grove of Death" at the Outer Station (Matadi).

Without altogether grasping the significance of what he saw in the Congo during the latter part of 1894 and the early part of 1895, Glave was witnessing a massive social and economic transformation brought about by two factors, not unrelated: (1) the final defeat in 1894 of the so-called Congo or Zanzibari Arabs centered in Stanley Falls and (2) the deliberate shift in commercial policy by the Congo State from ivory to rubber. Neither of these changes had yet taken place at the time Glave left the Congo in 1889, and they were just beginning to happen when Conrad left there in late 1890. Although the 1892–94 war with the Arabs had begun almost accidentally and against the express wishes of Leopold and his advisers—they had preferred to wait until the armed forces of the Congo State would be stronger—its rapid and successful prosecution by the young Francis-Henri Dhanis (later elevated to a baronetcy for his services) permanently removed a dangerous rival from the field. Now at last it was possible to fully exploit the commercial possibilities of the Upper Congo region without having to make use of Arab or native African intermediaries—or even, for that matter, of any of the non-state-owned European trading companies. For, already by 1891, in complete violation of the original Berlin agreement of 1885, Leopold had proclaimed his exclusive right to exploit vast portions of the Upper Congo as a "domaine privé," where, as it were, no poaching by others would be allowed. Despite protests from the trading companies (especially the Dutch), leading to a few relatively minor concessions, Leopold succeeded in establishing his new claim (Stengers, "Leopold's" 318–19). In December 1892 he followed it up by secretly instituting a system of commission payments to state agents, so that now "the necessary labor and food was by compulsory work in lieu of taxes. Before that date, services had to be paid for and obtained through the co-operation of neighboring local chiefs" (Morel, *History* 59 n; Vansina, "King" 335–39).[11] The result was a "system" of serfdom similar to the feudal one that had prevailed in Europe during the darkest period of the Middle Ages. In Harry Johnston's view, it was this system of payment by commission that lay "at the bottom of so much of the early Congo troubles," since it "urged reckless, conscienceless men to abuse the power of their guns and soldiers in raiding the country, in imposing all sorts of taxes, fines and contributions on native villagers or native chiefs, in declaring to be the exclusive property of the State all ivory and, later, all the produce of the forests outside the circle of native habitations" (*Grenfell* 448). The administrative foundations of this infamous "Leopoldian system" of exploitation of forced labor had in fact been laid as early as March 1890, with Camille Coquilhat being the person primarily responsible for its initial formulation. The three main points of this secret "system" were: the exclusion of all commercial competitors from areas not yet opened up; the establishment of additional military outposts to facilitate taxation and rubber collection; and the payment of bonuses to officials of the Congo State. None of these "principles," however, became fully operational until the end of 1892, and none of course were made public in the British press until 1895 at the earliest (Vangroenweghe 85–86).

Leopold was by this time in desperate financial straits. Despite a large loan from the Belgian government in 1890, his Congo State was eating up his private fortune at an alarming rate. As Samuel Nelson points out, by 1890 "receipts were only 1.2 million Belgian francs while expenditures were 4.5 million francs. Most of the deficits fell upon Leopold, who had not anticipated running a colony would be so costly. It is estimated that the king spent nearly thirty million francs on the Congo between 1876 and 1890, rapidly depleting his own resources" (83). The income from ivory on which Leopold had hitherto depended reached a peak of about five million francs in 1890, at which level it then stagnated and even declined, as the world price for ivory fell (Gann and Duignan 117; Nelson 55). Financial salvation, however, was now actually just around the corner, though that corner was a totally unexpected one. Leopold's particular salvation—and eventual damnation—came in the form of rubber. Rubber grew wild in fairly large quantities, but it was not evenly distributed and required harvesters to traverse much terrain to find the vines. It was therefore an extremely labor-intensive commodity. Preoccupied as the Congo State was with establishing its territorial claims, along with first avoiding and then fighting a war with the Arabs during the first decade of its existence, rubber was largely neglected in favor of ivory. As Jan Vansina points out, not until "1889 did the State begin an active campaign to collect rubber" (Vansina, *Tio* 427 n). Only gradually and, as it were, accidentally—as with the Arab War—did Leopold realize what immense profits might be realized from collecting and exporting rubber (Stengers, "Leopold's" 319). In 1894 the directors of the *Societé Anonyme Belge* reached the momentous decision to focus their resources primarily on rubber collection rather than ivory, and two years later 43 percent of all revenue produced by the Congo Free State derived from trade in this commodity. By 1900 the percentage had shot up to 80 percent, with the result that for "nearly two decades (1892–1910), the political economy of the Congo Free State was inextricably linked to the trade in rubber." From the midnineties onward "the rubber trade dominated all aspects of colonial life in the Free State"—and especially, one might add, virtually all aspects of colonial death too. The Congo Free State had become a "green hell" (Nelson 64, 81–83, 222 n. 4).

Financially speaking, the turnaround year for Leopold was 1895, when he had to resort for the last time to the Belgian government for a loan to help forestall bankruptcy. By the beginning of the new century, the Congo Free State was making a profit, even an immense profit—the only Central African colony ever to do so. Leopold used the income first to restock his own fortune and then to subsidize construction of large public buildings and monuments in Belgium (Stengers, "Leopold's" 319–20). It was all due to rubber, and to the terrible "system" devised by state administrators to collect it. The worst period of abuse was from 1896 to 1902, when, as Harry Johnston put it, "the misery and blood-shed inflicted on the negroes rivalled, perhaps exceeded, that which took place elsewhere under the Arabs" (*Grenfell* 459). Naturally, the rest of the world could not be kept entirely in the dark about what was happen-ing in the Congo. Aside from Glave, reports of atrocities began to leak out via the missionaries. The first of these revelations did not reach Brit-ain until the end of 1895, however, with the arrival in London of Rev. J.B. Murphy of the American Baptist Mission (Guiness 17). By 1896 matters had reached a point where Sir Charles Dilke raised questions about Congo atrocities in Parliament and proposed reconvening the powers that had sanctioned the establishment of the Congo Free State some ten years earlier in Berlin. But the idea did not appeal to the British government. Nevertheless, Murphy's testimony and that of a Swedish missionary, Sjoblöm, as well as "the published diary of Glave" were the impetus that led to protest meetings of H.R. Fox Bourne's Aboriginal Protection Society and the eventual formation of the Congo Reform Movement under the direction of E.D. Morel (Morel, *King* ix; Morel, *Red Rubber* 8–9, 46). In due course, protected though he was from un-pleasantness by a host of court flatterers, King Leopold began to receive news of atrocities being committed in his Congo domain. The allegedly astonished Leopold claimed to be determined to put an end to such a blot on his reputation. "'We are condemned by civilized opinion,' he wrote in September 1896. 'If there are abuses in the Congo, we must make them stop'" (Stengers, "Leopold's" 321). But, mighty and cunning though he was, in this respect his sovereignty was severely limited; the abuses—and the reports of them—began to multiply at an alarming rate. It was not long before he was forced to abandon the role of the royal bearer of light to a distant realm plunged in darkness. By 1904, except for a few die-hard supporters in Belgium, Leopold had come to be iden-tified throughout the world as the veritable Prince of Darkness.[12]

What does all this historical background prove in terms of Glave and Conrad? It proves once and for all that neither Glave nor Conrad was or could have been aware of the events that were to take place in the

Congo several years after they had left it. In Glave's case, it is clear that he became aware of the horrifying changes only on his return to the Congo at a time when the "system" was beginning to take full shape in 1894 and 1895. Even Roger Casement's 1903 Report and the diary on which it was based confirm the immense difference that the rubber trade had made in the Congo in the last years of the century, for throughout both works Casement continually refers, either explicitly or implicitly, to an earlier, happier time when the villages were not deserted and the people were not maltreated and killed by Leopold's agents. To be sure, Casement's suspicions about what might be happening in the Congo certainly predate his official report by several years. Conrad was similarly uninformed, though his realization of what was really happening probably did not occur until much later—possibly in 1897 after reading Glave's last *Century* essay and, arguably, perhaps not until after completing *Heart of Darkness*. Significantly, morally disgusting as Kayerts and Carlier are in "An Outpost of Progress" (which Conrad finished in July 1896), neither character is ever accused of committing atrocities, and their single act of slave trading is not deliberate. Even Kurtz himself, who does commit atrocities—displaying for instance the severed heads of various "rebels"—is only shown to advocate genocide, not to practice it; what is more, he advocates it only during an aberrant moment of madness. Kurtz, symbolic though he is, is clearly not meant to be understood as embodying the Congo State's post-1894 "method" of murder and pillage. This is also evident in Marlow's comment about the severed heads, to the effect that "there was nothing exactly profitable" in them. It also emerges unmistakably from the Manager's assertion that "Mr. Kurtz has done more harm than good to the Company. He did not see the time was not ripe for vigorous action. Cautiously. Cautiously. That's my principle. We must be cautious yet. The district is closed to us for a time. Deplorable. On the whole, the trade will suffer" (*HD* 57, 61). Moreover, in reply to the Manager's assertion that Kurtz's "method is unsound," Marlow proposes that his method was really "no method at all" (*HD* 61). These words, whatever else they may do, do not describe Leopold's elaborately devised "system."

If, on the one hand, in the context of *Heart of Darkness* the Manager is to be viewed as a representative of the "old gang" of vicious intriguers, it cannot also be that such a person is here advocating Leopold's "system" by paradoxically recommending a policy of cautious "restraint" along with a temporary abandonment of an entire district. Nor, on the other hand, can Kurtz's lack of restraint and lack of "sound" method be understood to be representative of Leopold's "system," for whatever else may be said about that system, in financial terms it undeniably "worked." Kurtz's "method" or lack of "method," then, is unique to Kurtz; it is a policy that is neither advocated by other company agents in the Congo—indeed, it is explicitly condemned by them—nor endorsed by the "gang of virtue" residing in the Whited Sepulchre back home. Moreover, if nothing else, Kurtz's essential irrelevance to Leopold's system of exploitation is apparent in the fact that Conrad has Kurtz concentrate entirely on the collection of ivory, with no concern whatever for rubber. (The word *rubber* is never mentioned in the novel.) By late 1898, however, when Conrad was beginning to write his story, ivory had become strictly a sideline for the Congo State, so that in terms of the impending scandal about "red rubber," Kurtz's abuses in the "heart of darkness," horrifying though they are, make little sense.

Nevertheless, despite its apparent inconsistency, Conrad's indictment of the cruelty of the Congo State is undoubtedly unforgettable—writing to Arthur Conan Doyle in 1909, E.D. Morel called *Heart of Darkness* "the most powerful thing ever written on the subject" (*History* 205)—but Conrad apparently failed to realize, as Glave had also failed to realize before him, the awful extent to which the new role of rubber had completely altered relations between Africans and Europeans in the Congo. Many of the old villages were being abandoned or destroyed, as workers were compelled to neglect their fields and desert their families in order to collect their obligatory quota of rubber. None of this systematic horror appears anywhere in Conrad's story. And yet in some curiously undefinable way, Conrad seems to expect his reader to take the changed conditions in the Congo for granted. This assumption of awareness on Conrad's part is most apparent in something that is absent from the story rather than present in it: namely the Arabs. At the time Conrad visited Stanley Falls (also the time when, in the implicit view of most critics, Marlow visits there),[13] the dominant force was unmistakably Arab. Everywhere, including the Congo State Station, their characteristic white robes and caps were an unavoidable sight. In *Heart of Darkness*, however, they have become completely invisible; they are just as mysteriously absent as the rubber is. Instead there is a despotic, mad, and moribund white man allied with a splendid African Queen and a tribe of fierce warriors. Why this should be is never satisfactorily explained in the novel, nor anywhere else in Conrad's work (or in the criticism for that matter), but it may be that Conrad's surprising omission is due to one of two mutually exclusive factors.

The first is that Conrad knew (and knew that his readers knew) that the Arabs were no longer a force to be reckoned with in the Congo and therefore, given this situation, he did not wish to complicate an already complicated issue by introducing yet another set of characters. Their absence, moreover, cannot be attributed to Conrad's unfamiliarity with Arabs or their customs, for in other contexts, such as *Almayer's Folly* and *An Outcast of the Islands*, he evinces no reluctance to portray Arab characters.[14] The other and, I think, more likely possibility is that Conrad actually does include them in his novel but only, as it were, obliquely and metaphorically. Significantly, both the Amazon and her tribe are, as the Arabs were, too, strangers at the Inner Station, having traveled there from distant settlements near the great lakes of Central Africa. Ethnically, too, the Arabs were, as Lewis Gann and Peter Duignan point out, "Swahili-speaking Muslims (commonly though not usually correctly, described in contemporary literature as Arabs)"[15] (Gann and Duignan 56). In other words, for the most part the Arabs looked like dark-skinned Central Africans rather than light-skinned North Africans. Furthermore, the Amazon and her followers have been led to believe, as were also Tippo Tib and his so-called Arabs, that the white man would keep faith with them, instead of which the Congo State launched all-out war against them and, at the conclusion of the conflict, expelled or exterminated all those who would not submit.

Like Kurtz, Glave was, though he did not know it, dying. At the moment when he reached out his hand to help a starving African somewhere near Matadi, he himself had less than a month to live. Though he had suffered occasional bouts of fever during much of his journey across Africa and had only recently complained of feeling "seedy," he was sure that his health was good enough to manage the long trip back home to England. He was even confident enough to have his baggage put aboard the ship, though, when its departure was delayed, he decided to return to "Underhill," the mission house on the outskirts of Matadi. Even his hosts, Lawson Forfeitt and his wife at the American Baptist Mission, had no inkling that his death was so imminent. It was only when Glave had but a few hours left to live that they and he realized the gravity of the situation. Except for a brief interval of delirium and violence minutes before he died, Glave's death was peaceful. And there must, at least, have been consolation for him in the knowledge that he was dying in the company and care of fellow English people who shared his ideals and who, he genuinely (and rightly) believed, could be relied on to carry out his last wishes for the proper disposal of his effects and papers (Russell, "Last Letter" 798).

For Glave, then, there was no moment of horrifying self-enlighten-ment, as there would be for the fictional Kurtz. For this reason, if for no other, Brian Spittles's contention that "there may be an echo of this case in the way Kurtz dies and Marlow becomes the custodian of his papers and last wishes" seems dead wrong. Noting the fact that on January 3, 1896, the London *Times* published a letter describing Glave's death, Spittles goes on to speculate that "all documents written in the midst of the African experience had potential official, political and commercial significance, and clearly it had been felt that Glave's personal observa-tions may have value in those areas. In any event, if Kurtz is a reference to the Glave case it was a reminder that the British were not entirely absent from the exploitative horrors of the Congo" (79–80). This is, of course, precisely what the "Glave case" did not do, for as must have been clear to all readers of Glave's *Century* essays, Glave not only did not participate in any of the "exploitative horrors of the Congo," but actually did his utmost to expose them.[16] In fact, he was the first to do so systematically and in detail in the pages of a respectable journal possess-ing a wide circulation, long before Conrad sat down to write *Heart of Darkness* or Glave's old friend, Roger Casement, published his celebrated indictment of the atrocities being committed in the Congo.[17] If Conrad did read Glave's *Century* essays—or even if he read only parts of them— he no doubt must have realized that Glave's short life had not been a sham but a genuinely heroic example. In this respect the sonnet "Glave," written by R.W. Gilder shortly after receiving news of Glave's death, reflects, despite its archaic and rather flowery language, what might very well have been Conrad's sentiments—especially in its closing line:

This day I read in the wise scholar's page
    That the old earth is withered and undone;
    That faith and great emprise beneath the sun
    Are vain and empty in our doting age:
'T were best to calm the spirit's noble rage,
    To live in dreams and all high passion shun,
    While round and round the aimless seasons run,—
    Pleasured alone with dead art's heritage.
Then as I read outshone thy face of youth,
    Hero and martyr of humanity,
    Dead yesterday on Afric's shore of doom!
Ah, no; Faith, Courage fail not, while lives Truth,
    While Pity lives, while man for man can die,
    And deeds of glory light the dark world's gloom. (868)

CONCLUSION

EXTERMINATING ALL THE BRUTES

A People, coming into possession of a land by warre, do not alwaies exterminate the ancient Inhabitants.

Thomas Hobbes

Man harbors too much horror; the earth has been a lunatic asylum for too long.

Friedrich Nietzsche

According to Roger Smith, our modern conception of genocide as the most heinous of all imaginable crimes differs fundamentally from the way prior generations viewed it. "While the slaughter of whole groups has occurred throughout history," he writes, "it is only within the past few centuries that this has produced even a sense of moral horror, much less been thought of as 'criminal'" (28). He goes on to refer to the grisly but well-documented records of mass extermination that include the Bible (especially the book of Joshua), Greek and Roman epic poetry, contemporaneous accounts of the Crusades and other religiously inspired massacres, descriptions of horrific Mongol depredations in Asia and Europe, and narratives of the brutal Spanish conquest of South America. Not only were these mass slaughters openly acknowledged by their perpetrators but also, as Smith remarks, they often boasted of the great number of their victims and the immense terror that their actions inspired in subject populations. And, one might add, in some cases they or their admiring heirs even turned these mass slaughters into works of art, as in the case of the destruction of Troy.

By the twentieth century, however, attitudes toward genocide had changed dramatically, and the Fourth Hague Convention of 1907 specifically denounced the murder of civilians in time of war as an international crime (Fein, *Sociological* 2). No longer were mass slaughters of civilian populations the subject of national pride; as Smith points out, no country in this century has ever admitted to committing genocide while actually engaged in the process of doing so. If genocide was acknowledged at all, it was only subsequently—and with great reluctance and shame—as in the case of the Germans after the Holocaust or the Russians during the so-called Thaw following the death of Stalin.[1] Unfortunately, this radical change in attitude toward genocide was not productive of a correspondingly radical reduction in the number of atrocities. On the contrary, when counted in absolute numbers of civilians killed, the twentieth century appears to lead all others by a very considerable margin. In 1994 R.J. Rummel calculated their number at nearly 170 million, whereas the sum total of all recorded genocides in preceding centuries was approximately 133 million (Rummel v).

Striking as these figures are, or as Smith's insight into the change in the moral conception and reception of genocide is, one needs to be cautious in accepting such statistics or conclusions at face value. For in order to be able to determine the relative truth or falsity of these assertions, one first needs to understand what they (and we) mean when we use the word *genocide*. Like *racism* and *imperialism, genocide* is a word (and a concept) whose definition is flexible and various, one that easily lends itself to serious misuse and misunderstanding. Like them, too, it is a word of our time, first devised in 1944 by the American legal historian Raphael Lemkin in the wake of the Holocaust to designate "the destruction of a nation or an ethnic group" (*OED*). The word was explicitly employed by the United Nations in Count 3 of the 1945 indictment brought against the Nazi leaders at the Nuremberg Trials, where they were charged with having "conducted deliberate and systematic genocide—namely, the extermination of racial and national groups" (*OED*). It was not until 1948, however, that the United Nations got around to actually defining what kinds of mass annihilations of civilians were to be included and excluded by its definition. The most significant omissions concerned political groups and social classes that, though mentioned in the original draft of the United Nations Convention on Genocide, were removed especially at the insistence of the Soviets, with the curious result that none of the Soviet murders of millions of people of middle-class origin, kulaks, or political undesirables "officially" counts as genocide (Fein, *Sociological* 10–11; Jonassohn and Chalk 11). Nor, for that matter, do Pol Pot's notorious killing fields with their nearly two million dead.[2]

According to one of the most respected authorities on genocide, Helen Fein, genocide is defined as the "sustained purposeful action by a perpetrator to physically destroy a collectivity or indirectly, through interdiction of the biological and social reproduction of group members, sustained regardless of the surrender or lack of threat offered by the victim" (Fein, *Sociological* 24). In contrast to the United Nations definition, Fein's has the merit of including the extermination of social and political groups, but it deliberately excludes civilian casualties incurred in connection with war. So, for example, the Allied firebombing of Dresden in the winter of 1945 or the atom bombings of Hiroshima and Nagasaki during the following summer are, in her view—and in that of many other authorities, such as Rummel—not to be counted as acts of genocide.[3] Nor, for that matter, are non-"purposeful" deaths, such as those of native Caribbean or Eskimo peoples who were killed "accidentally" by infectious disease introduced by invading or colonizing Europeans. Like Fein, Roger Smith is quite unambiguous and unwavering in his insistence that all genocide must, to qualify as such, be a conscious and even rational activity, although in this last respect Smith differs from most other authorities. A small minority of influential writers on the subject, such as Zygmunt Bauman and Richard Rubinstein, however, tend to agree that there is a strong rational component in the carrying out—if not always in the motivation—of genocide, at least insofar as the twentieth century is concerned.

The first genocides were, according to Kurt Jonassohn and Frank Chalk, retributive; that is, they were intended to permanently eliminate a recurrent threat from what was perceived as a dangerous or potentially dangerous rival group. The best-known instance of this type of genocide is the Roman destruction of Carthage and its inhabitants after the Third Punic War. Arguably, however, other types of genocide also contain a retributive element when viewed from the perspective of the perpetrators.[4] So, for example, the leaders of the Communist Party in the 1920s and 1930s murdered or imprisoned as many members of the aristocracy and the bourgeoisie as they could because they thought they consisted entirely of inveterate and incorrigible enemies of the proletariat. Similarly the Nazis murdered the Jews, denouncing them as congenital and unassimilable enemies of "true" Germanhood. Therefore, although it would seem that the motivation for genocide is often mixed, it is evident that, etiologically speaking, genocide can and should be divided into two distinct categories, one of which, however brutal it may be in actual practice, is characteristically "pragmatic," whereas the other is primarily "ideological." The destruction of the defeated Carthaginians by the Romans, for example, was largely pragmatic. From the point of view of the Romans, it seemed the most effective way of ensuring that they would never pose a threat to Rome again. The destruction of the unarmed Jews by the Nazis, on the other hand, was chiefly ideological; it had no practical end in view—on the contrary, it not only killed many potentially productive German citizens but diverted German military personnel who could have been used on the battlefront.

Ideological genocide always involves a questioning of the fully human status of the victim—in moral and religious, as well as biological terms—whereas pragmatic genocide does not, at least not as a necessary enabling condition. The Romans never doubted the full humanity of the Carthaginians; they merely feared their renewed and all-too-human hostility. The same is true, on the whole, of the Communists: they acknowledged the essential humanity of their class enemies but believed that there was no way of blunting their socially conditioned hostility short of killing them or incarcerating them in concentration camps. The Nazis, though, denied the humanity of the Jews by turning them into biologically determined fiends who could never be redeemed by any kind of social or educational reconditioning. This is what Helen Fein appears to mean when she posits that genocide can only take place when one group places another outside the "universe of moral obligation," or what Richard Rubenstein has in mind when he says that genocide results (or may result) from an exclusionary answer to the question "'Who is to have a voice in the political order?'" (Bauman 26; Rubinstein 289). Persuasive as their arguments are in connection with the Holocaust, however, such categories or questions can have little relevance in the context of purely pragmatic genocide. When the Romans destroyed Carthage or the Mongols devastated Baghdad, there never was any question of the inhabitants of those cities being placed within "the universe of moral obligation" or of achieving "a voice in the political order." Fein's and Rubinstein's strictures belong more to a conceptual framework uniquely characteristic of modern Western democracy than they do to actual events occurring over the long course of a generally undemocratic history.

The really crucial question in cases of ideological genocide does not concern the relative openness of any particular political system but the moral, religious, and biological assumptions underlying that system, namely: *Is a particular group judged to be fully human?* The word *human* here, let me repeat, is to be understood in moral and religious terms and not merely biological ones. As Pat Shipman observes, during the latter half of the nineteenth century the word *human* was generally understood as meaning "'like us' in a class, cultural or ethnic sense [rather] than 'any member of the human species'" (75). Genocide undertaken for religious reasons is customarily justified by diabolizing and thereby dehumanizing its victims. Whenever and wherever the question about a potential victim's full humanity is answered negatively, the targeted group is in great danger of being subjected to genocide. It is also the very question, as we have seen in the foregoing chapters of this book, that lies at the center of *Heart of Darkness*. And it is also the question that Kurtz in his infamous postscript answers succinctly with respect to Africans: "Exterminate all the brutes!" Africans, so Kurtz explicitly concludes, are "brutes," not human beings. Therefore, they may be subjected to "extermination" in the same way that animals that are considered pests or dangerous are routinely exterminated.

Kurtz's genocidal impulse has a precedent in "An Outpost of Progress," when Carlier, enraged at the loss to a nearby village of a hippopotamus that he has shot, talks about "the necessity of exterminating all the niggers before the country could be made habitable" (*Unrest* 108). Such views, as horrible as we find them today, would not have surprised or outraged most of Conrad's first readers, for in terms of late-nineteenth-century thinking about the future of "inferior" races, Kurtz's (or Carlier's) genocidal wishes are reprehensible only for the violence, not for the tendency of their expression. The idea itself had the most respectable scientific support. As George Frederickson points out, Darwin himself maintained in 1881 that natural selection had assisted

> "the progress of civilization." He argued that the Turks had failed to conquer Europe because the "more civilized so-called Caucasian races have beaten the Turkish hollow in the struggle for existence," and he added prophetically: "Looking at the world at no very distant date, what an endless number of lower races will be eliminated by the higher civilized races throughout the world." This final comment echoed a prediction he had made in the *Descent of Man*, in 1871: "At some future period, not very distant as measured by centuries, the civilized races of man will almost certainly exterminate and replace the savage races throughout the world." (230)

The "civilized races," it should have become amply apparent by now, are here conceived of as being—implicitly at least—more fully human (and therefore fitter to survive) than their "savage" and supposedly less fully human counterparts.[5] What was left more or less muted and unsaid by Darwin became unmistakably clear in the work of social Darwinists like Benjamin Kidd. According to Gary Adelman, Kidd "defended the domination and destruction of inferior races as a necessary stage in the evolutionary process. . . . primitive peoples, being so much less evolved, were not many notches above man's animal antecedents" (41). "Primitive" people, in other words, were not quite human.

How tenaciously traces of this attitude survived even in the most advanced and tolerant of twentieth-century European intellectuals is evident from Hannah Arendt's comments while "explaining" the European killing of Africans during the late nineteenth century. "What made them [the Africans] different from other human beings," she argues, "was not at all the color of their skin but the fact that they behaved like a part of nature, that they treated nature as their undisputed master, that they had not created a human world, a human reality, and that therefore nature had remained, in all its majesty, the only overwhelming reality— compared to which they appeared to be phantoms, unreal and ghostlike. They were, as it were, 'natural' human beings who lacked the specifically human character, the specifically human reality, so that when European men massacred them they somehow were not aware that they had committed murder" (192). Here again the principal point to be noted is that Europeans did not recognize the full humanity of the black Africans whom they encountered, and so they killed and hunted them down as if they were mere animals or "brutes."[6]

Despite his genocidal postscript, Kurtz, of course, never actually engages in genocide. He executes six "rebels" and then publicly displays their shriveled heads, he leads his warriors on bloody expeditions to steal ivory, and he engages in unspeakable rites: all of these actions suggest that he is a violent, irresponsible, and immoral person, but his reprehensible behavior is still far from sufficient reason to charge him with committing genocide.[7] Furthermore, though Kurtz undoubtedly does advocate genocide, he does so only in a moment of apparent madness, when he scrawls a brief postscript negating his sometime grandiose beliefs about the suppression of supposedly savage customs. When Marlow subsequently releases the essay for publication after Kurtz's death, he first eliminates the postscript and its infamous exhortation to "[e]xterminate all the brutes!" Whatever Marlow's ultimate motives in doing so may have been, it seems clear that he wishes to perpetuate Kurtz's public memory as that of an emissary of a possibly bogus or sham imperial ideal rather than that of an insanely violent—if perhaps more "real"—impulse of imperial destruction. If, therefore, it were possible to charge Kurtz "posthumously" with genocide and place him before a United Nations tribunal, there can be no doubt that he would be acquitted though he certainly would be found guilty of committing atrocities. No even remotely genocidal action depicted in the novel is committed by Kurtz. The only actions that pertain at all to the subject are those dealing with the industrial development of the Lower Congo—the incipient railway construction and its associated "Grove of Death"—or with the so-called Pilgrims who accompany Marlow on his voyage to the Inner Station and are prepared to fire on the Africans ashore as if they were on a hunting expedition. Given these circumstances, it seems rather odd that Kurtz should be singled out by critics of the novel as exemplifying nineteenth-century imperialist genocide.

To be sure, the fact that one of the two main characters of the novel does advocate genocide, even if only in a brief aside, implies that some part of Conrad's agenda is to focus public attention on the issue. But just why he should wish to do so is not immediately apparent. (The subject of genocide is also raised in *The Inheritors,* but by the time of its publication in 1902 the atrocities in the Congo had already become something of a scandal in Britain.) As a Pole whose nationality, language, and culture were being forcibly absorbed at this time by two of the three powers that had divided up the country among themselves (Russia and Germany, but not Austria), Conrad no doubt felt that this was something that deeply affected his own identity.[8] From his personal perspective, then, the real point of focusing on the maltreatment of Africans in the Congo may be attributable to his desire to imaginatively mirror the suffering of his Polish compatriots in Europe.

It is also possible, though I think less likely, that Conrad may have been alluding, as Sven Lindqvist suggests, to the massacre of the Arab dervishes during and after the battle of Omdurman in late 1898—that is, not long before Conrad started to write *Heart of Darkness.* If that is indeed the case, then the fact that Conrad omits all mention of Arabs in his story becomes doubly strange, especially since the Arabs whom he saw at Stanley Falls were regularly (though in hindsight wrongly) linked with the Mahdi's dervishes in the European press (see Appendix). Even odder is the fact that nowhere in Conrad's correspondence of this period is there the slightest hint of criticism uttered against any official British action in Africa or elsewhere in the vast Empire on which the sun did not set. On the contrary, as we have seen, Marlow explicitly commends what the British are doing in their African colonies as "real work." That Conrad never intended his story to be read as an attack on British imperialism is clear also from the example of E.D. Morel, the fiercest and most unyielding of King Leopold's British critics. As Adam Hochschild points out, Morel was incapable of conceiving a parallel between what Leopold was doing in the Congo and what Britain was doing elsewhere in Africa. For, paradoxically, if he had been able to do so, he could never have enlisted wide public support in Britain to bring about an end to Leopold's atrocities. "If he had believed, as we might conclude today," Hochschild writes, "that Leopold's rape of the Congo was in part a logical consequence of the very idea of colonialism, of the belief that there was nothing wrong with a country being ruled other than by its own inhabitants, Morel would have been written off as being on the fringe. No one in England would have paid much attention to him. But he did not believe this; he believed with all his heart that Leopold's system of rule constituted a unique form of evil. People in England's ruling circles, therefore, could support his crusade without feeling their own interests threatened" (Hochschild, 1998, 212–13). So too with Conrad's first readers when he published "The Heart of Darkness" in *Blackwood's Magazine*. It was the Belgians who were *shams,* not the British.

What is more, as even Lindqvist's ample quotations from Winston Churchill's enthusiastic account of the battle of Omdurman demonstrate, contemporaneous reactions were generally admiring of the fanatical but utterly futile courage of the Arabs. Their suicidal bravery was viewed as a grand, heroic gesture, testifying more to their antiquated martial ideals and methods than to any perceived British brutality in annihilating them virtually to a man, including several thousand of their wounded. It was after all a "fair fight," in which the enemy got what they asked for—and a little more. As Molly Mahood points out, at the close of the last century the British were much more given to glorifying their apparently stupendous imperial achievements—especially their military ones—than to denigrating them. And one should also bear in mind that this was the period not only of the great victory at Omdurman—which most British people in any case viewed as a just vengeance for the wrong done General Gordon at Khartoum—but also of Queen Victoria's Diamond Jubilee, an event that was celebrated with great pomp throughout the Empire (13).

It is therefore difficult to accept Lindqvist's assertion that Conrad is implying in *Heart of Darkness* that the whole of Europe, and particularly Britain, were acting "according to the maxim 'Exterminate all the brutes.'" It is even more difficult to believe him when he concludes that among the British, as among the Germans during the Second World War,

"everyone knew" what horrible atrocities were being committed overseas in their name, or that it was precisely because of this secretly shared
knowledge that "Marlow can tell his story as he does in Conrad's novel.
He has no need to count up the crimes Kurtz committed. He has no need
to describe them. He has no need to produce evidence. For no one doubted
it" (171–72). Not only, however, did many people doubt it, some even
maintained the opposite. Demetrius Boulger, for one, argued in an essay
published in *The Fortnightly Review* not long before Conrad started
writing his novel that the "standard of humanity and progress has been
firmly planted in the midst of a population of thirty millions, the deca-
dence of those millions has been arrested, peace exists where there was
only slaughter and savagery, and prosperity is coming in train of improved communications, and of the development of the natural resources
of a most promising region. In the history of Empires that of the Congo
State is unique" ("Twelve," 565). In point of fact, even an outspoken
Little Englander like E.M. Forster had no worse to say of his archetypal
British Imperialist, Henry Wilcox, than that he, as the head of the thriving Imperial and West African Rubber Company, had "carved money
out of Greece and Africa, and bought forests from the natives for a few
bottles of gin" (Forster 283). This relatively mild criticism, it should be
remembered, dates from about 1910, not long after the peak of the publicity campaign in the English press about Leopold's crimes in the Congo.
Like other sympathizers with oppressed Colonial peoples, such as Conrad
and Morel, Forster tended to exempt the British from more than "normal" criminal offences. This also explains why, after having the German
idealist father of his two anti-imperialist protagonists in *Howards End,*
Margaret and Helen Schlegel, decide to leave Germany because it had
turned materialist and imperialist, Forster can plausibly make him emigrate to a Great British empire much vaster in size and more overtly
committed to commerce than the Wilhemine *Reich.* Such behavior hardly
serves to confirm Lindquist's hypothesis. The real problem with arguments like Lindquist's is that they are just as impossible to refute as they
are to prove because they proceed purely by metonymical innuendo.
Like his hypothesized Marlow, Lindqvist feels no need to produce any
actual evidence. He is able to demonstrate his case by merely juxtapos-
ing a particular historical event with an apparent lacuna in the text of
Heart of Darkness.[9]

The widespread perception that *Heart of Darkness* is a work relevant to the subject of genocide is primarily a result of the Holocaust,

though it is also true that not long after the public emergence of the Congo atrocities at the beginning of this century, Conrad's novel came to be viewed as the most powerful fictional expression of those crimes. Although, as we have seen, the word *genocide* did not yet exist at the time, the atrocities of which Leopold's agents stood accused included not only slave trading (and raiding) and the systematic mutilation of human bodies (especially the cutting off of hands), but also mass extermination. Speaking in this connection in 1907, Sir Gilbert Parker, the Conservative Member of Parliament for Gravesend (the town closest to the spot where the *Nellie* lies moored at the beginning of Conrad's novel), charged that during the preceding quarter-century three million Congolese inhabitants out of a total population of twenty million had simply "disappeared" (qtd. in Castelein 202). His unmistakable implication was that their disappearance was due not to accident or statistical miscalculation but to deliberate murder or, at the very least, to malign neglect on the part of Belgian colonial officials.

That the population of the Congo had decreased dramatically during Leopold's administration was also a contention made by Roger Casement's celebrated 1903 *Report* to the British Foreign Office, though a precise number was never given. However, despite its widely acknowledged role in eventually leading to Leopold's reluctant transfer of the Congo Free State to Belgian parliamentary authority, Casement's *Report* does not directly charge Leopold's agents with practicing genocide.[10] Indeed, except for a listing of a relatively small number of Congolese people killed chiefly by non-Congolese African soldiers (e.g., 106), the two principal factors that Casement cites as responsible for the very discernible population decline are sleeping sickness and emigration to the French territory located on the north side of the Congo River (98, 104). With respect to the latter, Casement provides one example: approximately five thousand Bateke tribespeople abandoned their villages near Stanley Pool (including Kinshasa) for the French Congo. Their principal motive for doing so was, they claimed, Leopold's ruthless "system" of rubber collection that forced them to leave their homes and fields for long periods at a time and rewarded them at most with barely subsistence wages. Inevitably, therefore, those who did not emigrate or die of disease, succumbed to starvation.

That the population decline in the Congo was not, however, merely the result of relatively uncontrollable factors such as disease and economic upheaval is apparent from testimony provided by E.D. Morel's classic exposé of the Congo atrocities, *Red Rubber*. Here, for example, a British missionary with many years of experience in the Congo is quoted to the effect that

> with regard to the causes of depopulation in the Lalonga district where I have lived for fourteen years I emphatically affirm that for one who has died of sleeping sickness there have been twenty deaths due to lung and intestinal diseases; and for one death due to smallpox, there have been forty due to lung and intestinal troubles . . . the lung and intestinal troubles are without doubt due, in a very large proportion of the cases, to exposure involved in collecting the taxes [i.e., forced labor], and in hiding from the soldiers in the forest, as well as the miserable huts the natives now live in, because they have neither time nor heart to build better. (72)

What emerges from this and other related testimony is the unmistakable suggestion of more sinister causes behind the marked population decline in the Congo than those suggested by Casement, namely the deliberate pursuit of a policy leading to large numbers of civilian deaths. Eventually this ended in accusations, such as the one leveled by Chinweizu, that under Leopold's conscious direction the agents of the Congo Free State carried out a genocidal policy with "Nazi-style perfection" culminating in the deaths of over ten million people, or a little more than half the population (59–62). More recently, Adam Hochschild has repeated the same charge in the pages of the *New Yorker* (46).[11] It is a conclusion that Jan Breman arrived at already in 1990 on the basis of archival work carried out by A.M. Delathuy (Jules Marchal) and Daniel Vangroenweghe. What is more, according to Breman, "the whites [in Leopold's Congo State] not only knew about such unpardonable offences against mankind, but . . . they frequently ordered them to be carried out and even committed them" (105).

It is difficult to determine how much truth there is in these numbers because there is no reliable data about the size of the population of the Congo State when Leopold assumed absolute control over it in 1885. According to Lewis Gann and Peter Duignan, "at the end of the nineteenth century Stanley made a purely speculative estimate of the population, placing it at twenty-eight million" (Gann and Duignan 44). Actually, in 1895 Stanley claimed with apparent assurance that the population of the Congo ranged "between 15,000,000 and 18,000,000, according to the most careful estimate" ("Story" 505). In 1897 he gave an even more "precise" figure of 16,300,000 (Stanley, "Twenty-Five," 474). A few years earlier, in 1888, Camille Coquilhat, one of Leopold's ablest and most trusted lieutenants, gauged the population at somewhere between twelve and sixteen million inhabitants (471). In 1910 Sir Harry Johnston thought the population was about twenty-five and a half million (*Grenfell* 539). In the *Cambridge History of Africa*, Jan Vansina—the same authority cited for genocide by Adam Hochschild—refuses to venture any guess at all because he cannot find the empirical evidence on which to base one. "No hard demographic data are extant," he writes, "and the population estimates, which range from 27 million to 12 million, in early years are completely unreliable." Like Casement, Vansina argues that the principal killer was not Belgians but disease, at first smallpox and later sleeping sickness—the latter with a mortality of 80 percent in affected areas (354–55). In point of fact, the first more or less reliable census of the population of the Belgian Congo was carried out in the 1920s and yielded a figure of about ten million.

However, in his introduction to Daniel Vangroenweghe's book about the atrocities committed in the Congo as a result of the rubber regime, Jan Vansina "attributes the halving of the population between 1880 and 1920 to the nature of the colonial regime in combination with the large-scale epidemics that occurred during that period. . . . Vansina considers that there is no longer any good reason for disputing a direct linkage between colonial misrule and population decline in the period" (Breman 107). What Vansina's conclusion, however, does not make clear in terms of its relevance to Conrad's period of service in the Congo is that Vangroenweghe's evidence all postdates 1892, with most of it actually post-dating 1899. Given the additional fact that Vangroenweghe's discoveries regarding King Leopold's "gulag" only became possible after the Belgian archives were made accessible to him (and Jules Marchal) in the 1980s, it seems highly unlikely that Conrad was aware or could have been aware of the terrible ramifications of Leopold's system at the time he wrote *Heart of Darkness*. Nevertheless there is no doubt that, great artist and connoisseur of human nature that he was, he somehow instinctively realized what was going on and presciently described Leopold's crimes in horrifying detail.

How then are we to decide whether genocide was committed in the Congo Free State by Leopold's agents and henchmen? That they perpetrated atrocities on individuals and smaller groups is unquestionable, but the evidence is probably inadequate to reach a definitive decision on the issue of actual genocide.[12] Even in his study of the devastating effects of King Leopold's policy of diabolic greed, *King Leopold's Ghost*, Adam Hochschild concludes that what happened in the Congo under his misrule was "not, strictly speaking, a genocide," even though the killing there "was of genocidal proportions. . . . The Congo State was not deliberately trying to eliminate one particular ethnic group from the face of the Earth" (Hochschild, 1998, 225). Nevertheless, it is clear that many qualified observers thought that genocide had occurred; the same opinion persists today. However, the problem is not simply one of numbers; it is also one of definition. Even if we accept Parker's or Chinweizu's figures of somewhere between three and ten million dead during Leopold's rule, we still need to decide whether the deaths of these millions of people were brought about deliberately or "by accident." For, as Roger Smith points out, at times "genocidal consequences precede any conscious decision to destroy innocent groups to satisfy one's aims. This is most often the case in the early phases of colonial domination, where through violence, disease, and relentless pressure indigenous people are pushed toward extinction. With the recognition of the consequences of one's acts, however, the issue is changed: to persist is to intend the death of a people" (23). In other words, in the case of the Congo Free State we need to determine whether—and if so, when—Leopold and his subordinates became aware that the policies they were instituting and carrying out were in fact leading to the deaths of very large numbers of people and whether, knowing this, they nevertheless continued to pursue those policies. Here again there is a paucity of reliable evidence, which prevents us from answering these questions definitively one way or the other.

In our particular context, we also need to ask what specific relevance this discussion of genocide in the Congo Free State has to a better understanding of *Heart of Darkness*. And we need to determine what knowledge (or suspicions) Conrad may have had that genocide was actually being committed there. As noted in chapter 6, the young Conrad who left the Congo in late 1890, disillusioned and ill though he was, almost certainly had no knowledge and probably little suspicion that officials of the Congo State were carrying out policies leading to the extermination of the native population. What suspicions or certainties subsequent events in the Congo (and reports of those events in the British press) may have later aroused in Conrad is less clear, but there is no evidence in Conrad's letters, essays, or fiction written prior to *Heart of Darkness* that specifically proves that he believed genocide was being committed in the Congo State.

That Conrad did, however, wish to suggest that the absence of any coherent "method" in the administration of the Congo State was leading at the very least to what Roger Casement later called "misgovernment" and "oppression" is evident at several points in *Heart of Darkness*, most notably in the unforgettable description of the so-called Grove of Death. Though the kind of casual neglect described in this scene is not to be equated with actual genocide, the resemblance is certainly close enough to evoke the idea in the minds of present-day, post-Holocaust readers, as it was perhaps also for Conrad's original readers. Significantly, the scene opens with a description of the apparently chaotic and "objectless" work being carried out on the railway line linking the Outer and Central Stations. This would have struck Conrad's first readers as particularly perverse, for by the end of the nineteenth century the railway had become the primary symbol of Western technological progress. It would also have been particularly perverse for such readers as were aware (as presumably Conrad himself was) that the line linking Matadi with Kinshasa had been completed as recently as mid-March 1898—some eight months before Conrad started work on *Heart of Darkness*—and had been greeted with approval not only in Belgium but throughout Europe. Even Roger Casement, who had been in charge of an advance survey party for the railway in 1888, was to write approvingly at the outset of his 1903 *Report* on atrocities in the Congo State: "A railway, excellently constructed in view of the difficulties to be encountered, now connects the ocean ports with Stanley Pool, over a tract of difficult country, which formerly offered to the weary traveller on foot many obstacles to be overcome and many days of great bodily fatigue" (73, 98). As far back as 1892, E.J. Glave had looked forward to the completion of the railway link from Matadi to Kinshasa because then "there will be an uninterrupted service of steam from the civilized world to the heart of Africa" (*Savage* 246).

In fact, as Lewis Gann and Peter Duignan point out, "the railway pioneers had to cope with extraordinary geographic obstacles; they lacked the most rudimentary technical information; they had no reliable charts or maps; they faced tremendous supply problems; they had to labor in an oppressive climate; and they were decimated by sickness. Within four months during 1891–1892, some 900 men—17 percent of the black workmen engaged in railway building—died of disease" (Gann and Duignan 71). The absolutely worst period of death and desertion was the two and a half months at the end of 1891 and the beginning of 1892 (341). Actual construction had begun on March 15, 1890, but preliminary planning and surveying had been going on for the previous two years. By the time Conrad reached Matadi in mid-June 1890, "the work," as Marlow puts it ironically, had been going on for only a little under three months. Whether Conrad's knowledge of machines and construction was good enough for him to be able tell whether what the Belgians were doing at Matadi made any technological sense is difficult to say, but surviving photographs of Matadi from the early stages of construction do not show anything like the kind of senseless chaos described by Marlow (e.g., Cornet 369). It would seem, therefore, that Conrad's aim in depicting Belgian folly and incompetence in this way is to impugn their administrative skills and to contrast them with the supposed "real work" being done in British Africa.

According to Marlow, the chain gang he sees, with their expression of "complete, deathlike indifference" (*HD* 19); the random detritus of rusting machinery and rails; the mysterious sandpit; the broken drainage pipes; the pointless blasting— all of these disjointed impressions are testimony to the sham "work" of the "flabby, pretending, weak-eyed devil of a rapacious and pitiless folly" (*HD* 20).[13] They are results not of deliberate, rational intention or even of a malevolent but *real* method; if they had been, so Marlow remarks, they would have been familiar to him, for he had already experienced the effects elsewhere of the "strong, lusty, red-eyed devils" of violence, greed, and hot desire (*HD* 19–20), but he had never before seen the senseless work of this peculiarly Leopoldian devil. Blinded by the sunshine—and so plunged into a proleptic and symbolic darkness—he foresees, like a kind of latter-day Tiresias, that he will have further dealings with this "insidious" devil: "But as I stood on this hillside I foresaw that in the blinding sunshine of that land I would become acquainted with a flabby, pretending, weak-eyed devil of a rapacious and pitiless folly. How insidious he could be I was only to find out several months later and a thousand miles farther" (*HD* 20). The actual personification of the particular devil whom Marlow *envisions* here is almost certainly not Kurtz—his elongated, bony figure scarcely corresponds to anything that could be considered even remotely flabby; rather, it is more likely to be identified with the plump Manager who villainously (and foolishly) confides to Marlow his view that Kurtz had been pursuing an "unsound" method at the Inner Station. Marlow's reply is that Kurtz has been following "no method at all," an answer that seems to refer back directly to his first vision of the "method" (or, rather, the lack thereof) employed by the company at its Outer Station.

What seems to irritate and even outrage Marlow nearly beyond endurance is not the downright wickedness or even stupidity of what he sees but its pretense, its quintessentially *sham* nature—a fitting counterpart, ironically, for the "whited sepulchre" that is the Belgian capital. It is, to use a word that has become one of the key words for modern critics of the novel, a *lie*. Standing next to the "cautious" Manager and reflecting on the havoc caused by the *hotly* devilish Kurtz, Marlow is filled with revulsion—but not against Kurtz: "It seemed to me I had never breathed an atmosphere so vile, and I turned mentally to Kurtz for relief—positively for relief" (*HD* 61). The vile atmosphere he breathes is the atmosphere of hypocrisy, a peculiarly insidious stench emanating from the great gulf between the stated objectives of the Congo State and its actual practice. As Guy Burrows remarked in 1903, "in no part of the world can be found such painful differences between promise and performance, grandiloquent phrasing and sordid and imperfect achievement" (63). The despairing, moribund blacks in the Grove of Death are doomed not because of any overt desire on the part of Leopold or his agents to exterminate them—no Belgian other than Kurtz ever expresses a wish in the novel to exterminate anybody, though the whites on board Marlow's steamer do try to kill the defenseless mass of people gathered to bid Kurtz farewell at the Inner Station—they are dying, as Marlow recognizes, of quite unplanned "disease and starvation" (*HD* 20). That they are dying nevertheless, though "only" as the result of malicious folly rather than malignant evil, provides them with little consolation.[14]

The utter hypocrisy of the Congo State is most succinctly expressed in the ironic contrast between Kurtz's verbose and grandiose treatise on abolishing so-called savage customs and his curt postscript exhorting his compatriots to "[e]xterminate all the brutes!" This contrast corresponds to the even greater and far more real irony that the État Indépendant du Congo had been originally established by the various powers at the Berlin Conference of 1885 with the express intention of preventing, as one of the original delegates put it, a renewal of "'that policy of extermination of the natives which had formerly been practiced in the two Americas'" (Slade 41). An even further irony is that the powers apparently succeeded in their aim, for there was no "policy" of extermination practiced in the Congo Free State. The natives died—or were exterminated—with no policy at all.

A final irony is that Marlow's contempt for the lying hypocrisy he encounters both in the Whited Sepulchre and in the heart of darkness does not prevent him from engaging in a little lying hypocrisy of his own. Asked by Kurtz's fiancée what Kurtz's last words were, Marlow is understandably reluctant to tell her:

"'Repeat them,' she murmured in a heart-broken tone. 'I want—I want—something—something—to—to live with.'
"I was on the point of crying at her, 'Don't you hear them.' The dusk was repeating them in a persistent whisper all around us, in a whisper that seemed to swell menacingly like the first whisper of a rising wind. 'The horror! The horror!'
"'His last word—to live with,' she insisted. 'Don't you understand I loved him—I loved him—I loved him.'
"I pulled myself together and spoke slowly.
"'The last word he pronounced was—your name.'" (HD 75)

Though he claims to abominate lies, Marlow himself lies here; and yet, as he realizes, to have told the truth in such circumstances would have been "'too dark—too dark altogether'" (HD 76).[15] After all, Kurtz's fiancée desperately needed "something to live with," as desperately, perhaps, as the dying black needed the piece of ship's biscuit Marlow gave him in the Grove of Death. There are lies, so it would appear, and there are lies. Some lies are lies to live with; other lies are lies to die with. How to tell the difference? Perhaps only by the relative goodness or wickedness of the results. Perhaps the lies to live with are like the "life-lies" that Doctor Relling prescribes in Henrik Ibsen's play The Wild Duck, that is, they are lies intended to alleviate the harsh realities that most people cannot face directly, lies that serve to hide the real truth about ourselves. The truth kills, as Relling and, behind him, Ibsen maintain, or at the very least the truth leads to devastation and incurable unhappiness[16] (63–64). "Human kind," as T.S. Eliot remarked with more than a trace of Conradian irony in Burnt Norton, "cannot bear very much reality."

Nor, it would appear, can that subspecies of humankind known as the literary critics, including, as we have seen, some of the most notable recent critics of Heart of Darkness. But unlike Marlow's lie, which is meant to moderate the Intended's grief, some contemporary critics lie about Conrad and his celebrated novel because they find his depiction of the Western imperialist treatment of Africans to be insufficiently "dark" to satisfy their sense of what "really" occurred in the Congo Free State (and in Africa generally) at the close of the last century. They insist, paradoxically, on darkening an already dark Heart of Darkness to the point of finding no redeeming qualities in it whatsoever. In order to bring about this desired result they provide partial or skewed (or both) quotations from the novel along with generally unsubstantiated aspersions of its advocating strong (or "bloody") racism and, to a lesser degree, imperialism. Kurtz's final expression of "horror" becomes for these critics the final verdict to be passed upon the novel itself, thereby making it unfit for the presumably innocent eyes of the young students who are annually exposed to it in innumerable required courses. Unlike Marlow, these critics do not possess the courage to acknowledge their lie for what it is, namely a kind of half-truth (or even less than half) that has been forcefully inflated into a whole truth, made to conform arbitrarily to a set of preconceived notions about how "the" West is said to have traditionally conceived of Africa. Paradoxically, in this way those who object to the stereotyping of Africa on the part of a hypothesized monolithic West have succeeded in stereotyping what was in fact a highly variegated European response to Africa, Africans, and European imperial activity in Africa at the close of the nineteenth century, including *Heart of Darkness*. Like the Intended, their essentially Romantic need for a morally cleansed version of reality has superseded the need for a more complex and more realistic truth that might be difficult to "live with" in the short term but that would in the end produce a deeper understanding, not only of Conrad and Conrad's book, but of life itself. For like Kurtz (but unlike Marlow) they are incapable of dealing with a reality that belongs neither entirely to the realm of the angels nor to that of the fiends.

APPENDIX

Oscar Baumann, "The Stanley Falls Station: Description of the Topography and Inhabitants at the Seventh Cataract of the Stanley Falls of the Congo River," *Mittheilungen der Kaiserlich-Königlichen Geographischen Gesellschaft* 29 (1886): 504–13, 647–56; 30 (1887): 65–69. Translated and updated by Peter Firchow.

Since the Stanley Falls Station has always aroused a great deal of interest in Europe, and since I myself had the opportunity to become acquainted in some detail with conditions obtaining there during a stay of several months, I would like to take the liberty of describing them in what follows.

As is well known, Stanley Falls Station—the name by which it is called on the Congo—is located at the western end of a long, narrow island separated from the mainland by a channel that is approximately twenty meters wide. A footpath leads from the station itself to a maze of huts known as Singi-Singi's Village. Continuing along the shore, one soon reaches a stretch of water that, after forming the channels separating the island, makes a considerable drop before rejoining the Congo. The terrain of the island slopes slightly upward from the main body of the river until it reaches a kind of flat shoulder, and then it drops again more steeply in the direction of the side arm of the river. All of the area of the island not occupied by dwellings or plantations is covered with dense and partly swampy forest, as is also the case with the shore immediately opposite. On the farther side of the above-mentioned stretch of water, navigable for canoes even at normal water levels, there rises a steep wall of rock resembling a fortress, which consists of horizontal layers of red sandstone, the upper parts of which are overgrown with lush, overhanging vegetation and crowned by the huts and banana trees belonging to Nsaki's village.

This hard red sandstone forms the basis of the whole area surrounding the seventh cataract, but despite much searching, we were unable to find any fossils embedded in it. A steep path leads up to the elevated plateau on which Nsaki's village is built; and at its eastern limit the plateau slopes gently downward toward the river. At the extreme end of the island there is a landing from which one can see the two flat, long, drawn-out islands belonging to Tippo Tib. Both of these are covered with well-cared-for plantations, among which are scattered the houses of the Arabs and the low huts of the natives. Near the left bank of the Congo there is also a small island that is almost completely occupied by a village. Located on the slightly ascending shore of the mainland are several villages as well as the homes of the subordinate Arab chiefs, Nasr and Mwana Nsigi; the home of the latter is placed directly opposite the station. Rising up right behind these brown leaf-roofed houses is the tall, dark jungle, a wilderness in which it is said there is no village within three days' march.

As for the river itself, it flows past Tippo Tib's island with deceptive calm but raging speed, only to plunge from an elevation of one and one-half to two meters as it thunders and foams along its whole width. This waterfall is interspersed with numerous rocks and divided into two parts by an uninhabited, wooded island. Below the cataract the river does not become any calmer. Interrupted as it is by rapids and whirlpools, it is navigable for canoes when they are handled by knowledgeable natives, whereas steamers can approach only as far as the western end of the station island. The narrow arm of the river drops at the eastern end of Nsaki's island from a height of about four meters over a stretch of washed-out red sandstone; once over the fall, however, the water is safe, interrupted by rapids only in a few spots that represent no particular danger for canoes. The width of the main body of the river in front of the station flagpole is, according to my measurement, 634 meters, calculated from shore to shore. As for seasonal variations in water level, I am hard put to find any pattern in them, though during my stay these ranged from to three to four meters. From the time of our arrival on February 15 until February 22, the river rose consistently. Thereafter it fell approximately one meter, so that rocky islands became visible in front of the station. From March 5 to 14, the Congo once again began to rise sharply, only to drop again until March 29. After that it rose almost up to the station ramp, so that all the islands and rocks disappeared and even the rapids themselves grew less visible. This lasted until April 12, after which the water fell to something like a medium level, where it stabilized for quite some time. The river continued to drop even further, and then on May 18 it began to rise. On June 1, however, it fell rapidly until my departure on the *Peace* on June 9. In July and August 1885 Mr. Deane found the river so extremely low that the creek between Singi-Singi's and Nsaki's villages could be crossed on foot without getting wet.

The inhabitants of this area must be divided into three distinct groups: the Europeans and the black workers at the station; the native fishermen belonging to the Wagenia tribe; and the Zanzibari Arabs under the leadership of Tippo Tib, along with their followers and slaves. During my stay, two Europeans were stationed at Stanley Falls, Mr. Deane (an Englishman), who acted as chief officer, and Mr. Eyken (a Belgian). The two whites live in two houses located along the shore. Both houses have walls that are whitewashed and roofs made of banana leaves. These dwellings also serve as storehouses. The job of one of the Europeans is to oversee the work of the black employees, and the other is responsible for purchasing food and supervising the stored supplies and the trading goods. These tasks essentially subsume the totality of the whites' activities, for as yet it is hardly possible to speak of their having any sort of influence or authority over the natives. At most one could mention in this connection the tradition at the station of demanding a toll payment for every canoe loaded with bananas or quanga traveling upriver. The food that is acquired in this way is later distributed among the station employees.

These employees are approximately 150 in number; among them are the Haussa, the Bangala, and the women and boys bought from the Arabs. On the Congo the name Haussa refers to a varied collection of people who enlisted on the Guinea coast for three years' service as "soldiers" and who for the most part do not actually come from Haussa territory. There are among them men who come from Futajallon and Accra, from Popo, Lagos, and the Niger estuary; there are even people from Adamaua and Kano. Only a few of them have actually served in the English Army. For the majority of them, their soldierly status extends only to the possession of an old uniform and a Snider rifle that they know how to discharge, if need be. Most of the Haussa are very lax in their practice of Islam. They are pretty trustworthy; thefts are not overly frequent among them. They are fiercely courageous in battle, but in peacetime they also have a tendency to violence. They possess great faith in the white man and, given proper discipline, can be used successfully in agricultural work and other similar tasks. The noncommissioned officers are mostly quite intelligent people, able to speak English;

as for the enlisted men, along with their mother tongue, they are able to make themselves more or less understood in one of the Congo languages.

The Bangala at the station are worthy of note in that for the first time an attempt is being made to hire natives from the Upper Congo as permanent employees. If one bears in mind that even today the Bangala remain a savage, cannibalistic tribe, and that ten years ago they attacked Stanley with mad fury, then it must be accounted greatly to the station's credit that these people now enter into one-year work contracts and are prepared to follow the white man into unknown, distant lands. For the most part the Bangala are slender, powerful fellows whose sole item of clothing is a loin cloth. At first the idea of regular work was evidently foreign to them, since they descend from a line of warlike loafers. When one heard, in the morning, the screams of someone being punished, then it was generally some Bangala who was getting whipped for laziness. In this respect, however, things have improved considerably and the probability is great that the Bangala can be successfully trained to become good workers. In their daily life and in their customs, they still remain complete savages, but this too may change over time as they interact with the whites. As for the aforementioned women, these have either been bought by the Haussa as wives or else they belong, along with the boys, to the station. They come primarily from the northern regions, where Tippo Tib carried out his most recent raids. Female slaves and young boys are to be had very cheap, for twelve to twenty-four colored handkerchiefs (that is, somewhere between fifty crowns and one florin in Austrian money). That the station buys people in this way is anything but inhumane: these homeless slaves are offered for sale by the Zanzibaris when they are in a lean, miserable condition, full of sullen indifference; and it is astonishing to observe how such unhappy people acquire a cheerful, well-fed appearance after only a few weeks. They naturally also receive an allowance for living expenses (four to five brass wires, equivalent to sixteen to twenty Austrian crowns per week), just as every Haussa or Bangala does, along with a salary. This allowance is enough to provide them with good nourishment.

The work of the station employees consists, as far as the Haussa and Bangala are concerned, of felling trees and clearing the forest, as well as of filling up swampy areas with earth; the women and boys are set to work in the fields under the supervision of a Haussa sergeant. The plantations belonging to the station have, to be sure, been established only recently. They consist of bananas, manioc, and maize, as far as native plants are concerned; there are also peanuts and sweet potatoes and papaya and citrus trees, for which the seeds were brought from the lower Congo, as well as rice, which is provided by Tippo Tib. The station livestock consist of three cows and several sheep (gifts from Tippo Tib), numerous goats captured at Monangiri, and chickens, ducks, and doves. The climate at the station can only be described as bad. Dysentery especially is endemic among both whites and blacks and has killed a number of the latter. As evidence I would like to cite the cases of those whites who were stationed here for longer periods and with whose state of health I became familiar. Wester, who spent about twenty months here, suffered many severe attacks of dysentery and one bout of virulent bilious fever; he was forced to leave the station before the expiration of his contractual period for reasons of ill health. Both Gleerup and Harris suffered bad attacks of dysentery. While I was at the station, Mr. Deane also had an attack of dysentery. Mr. Eyken was put to bed twice with dysentery and twice with severe cases of fever, and he could hardly walk because of the sores on his feet; he too had to leave the station on the *Peace* for reasons of ill health. I myself was forced to spend forty-five days in bed, confined to my room, because of dysentery, and I suffered four attacks of fever, whereas elsewhere in Africa I felt quite well. Whether or not draining the swamps will improve the climate of the island is something only the future can tell.

Before passing on to the subject of the natives, I would like to describe a typical day in the life of the station, a routine that varies only on Sundays. Every day at six o'clock in the morning, the bell in the station house rings, a signal that is then amplified by means of the reveille sounded by the trumpeter in the enlisted men's huts as well as by the mad drumbeating of Kassuku, the Manyema drummer. The latter may well be thinking nostalgically of the time when, under the admiring eyes of thousands of onlookers, he beat his wooden drum at the Antwerp Exhibition of 1885. His audience at present, however, must be described as much less appreciative. Soon all the workers are gathered together in a circle in front of the Station House. There the station chief distributes the work assignments and oversees the carrying out of sentences of punishment. The latter consist of beatings with a stick or lashings with a strap made of hippopotamus leather—the "chicotte" of the West Coast. It is necessary to point out that without this kind of punishment—which may strike us as cruel—it would be difficult, perhaps even impossible, to maintain order and discipline among a group of untutored characters such as these. However, punishment must be carried out in moderation and with a strict sense of justice, which unfortunately is not always the case. It is to be hoped that future officials of the Congo State judiciary will develop a more humane but still effective means of disciplining their black enlisted men.

After finishing his breakfast, the station chief busies himself with supervising the blacks, while the other European goes off to the store-room. Usually there are already a number of Tippo Tib's "soldiers" wait-ing in front of the latter, hoping to sell chickens, goats, and so forth, that they have captured on their most recent raids. At noon the bell rings again; this time it is greeted with howls of joy. The workers rush into the shadow of their huts, and the whites gather for "luncheon" in the breezy veranda. At this meal—as with all others in Africa—there is only chicken or goat meat, fish, rice, and sweet potatoes; everything else has to be taken from tins, something that happens only rarely at Stanley Falls, since no one knows when the next steamer will come bringing fresh supplies. For the steamers do not by any means come and go with any frequency; the interval between arrivals varies from three to seven months. At two o'clock work starts again and lasts until six o'clock. At this time any of the canoe levies that have been collected are distributed among the men, along with their weekly living allowance if it is a Saturday. The tropical night sinks rapidly over the station, and the Europeans eat their evening meal. By eight o'clock all has fallen silent. The muted tinkle of the Haussa guard, signaling his state of alertness, and the chirping of the crickets and cicadas are the only noise in the immediate vicinity of the station. But from without one hears the mighty sound of the thunderous seventh cataract, as well as the distant drumming of night-time native fishermen. This is how life passes at the station, a routine disturbed only on Sundays and on those days when a steamer docks at Stanley Falls.

As for the natives of this area, they call themselves Wagenia and belong to the same group of fishing tribes that inhabit the whole region of the cataracts. Because of their usefulness as boatmen, they have been spared Tippo Tib's usual attentions. Consequently, they are also allowed to bear arms and pursue their fishing trade without any hindrance. Most of them are very strong and have massive builds. Especially the upper body area and the arm muscles are powerfully developed, though the legs are in proportion short and weak, so that these people are charac-terized by a somewhat slow and unsteady walk. One wonders if this peculiar body shape may not derive from generations of continuous—almost permanent—residence in canoes.

As for the women, aside from the crust of dirt that covers them, they are rather pretty when quite young. But very soon they put on so much weight that the sight of their fleshly nudity becomes disgusting to a European. To be sure, as they grow old they once again grow thin— even to the point of becoming skeleton-like—but without gaining beauty in consequence.

The attire of the men consists of a loin cloth made of a fiber that is produced by beating a fibrous plant material with a wooden (or, more rarely, with an ivory) mallet. The resulting cloth is reddish-brown in color and has not yet been replaced by European cloth. The women are even more scantily dressed. Both sexes often paint themselves with a red paint that they make by rubbing colored wood on a damp stone plate. The Wagenia are not acquainted with the daring hairstyles that are customary further downriver; they simply shave their hair and beards off completely.

Both sexes wear animal teeth as jewelry in their perforated upper lips; they also wear strings of little glass beads in their earlobes. Sometimes they also perforate their nostrils. On their arms and legs they wear very tight, even constricting, rings made of woven bast fiber, copper, iron, or (imported) brass. They decorate their necks with bands of tin or iron pearls; the latter are also used to cover their loins, but they are gradually being replaced by European glass beads. Cowries are almost never used. The men often wear caps made of monkey fur and a colorful bunch of feathers.

Since, as mentioned above, the Arabs have not completely subjugated the Wagenia, the latter are not prevented from bearing arms. Consequently, every man carries with him a spear about two and one-half meters long with a short broad tip. This tip is protected by a wooden sheath wrapped in bast fiber, so that it always stays clean and razor-sharp. In addition they carry a prettily engraved, pointed dagger in the same wooden sheath. They do not use the bows and poisoned arrows customary among their neighbors, the Bakumu. They also have a few rifles imported by the Arabs, and the latter often sell them captured weapons as well. The blades of the spears and their daggers are likewise not domestically produced but imported from further downriver. The Wagenia are very attached to their weapons and can only very rarely be persuaded to sell them.

The main occupations of the Wagenia consist of catching fish and of going on trading missions either downriver or to tribes living on the Lindi. Their lives are thus bound to the canoe, where they feel very much at home. Their canoes are made by the Wamanga tribe on the Lindi river, and along their sides one can still discern clear traces of the countless strokes of their primitive adzes. In contrast with the lightweight boats of the Bangala, their canoes are made extremely tight but remain easily maneuverable; they seldom leak and probably could withstand the shock of a collision with a rocky reef. There are platforms extending at both ends of the canoes.

For longer trips in their canoes, they set up roofs of banana leaves with bamboo-palm supports; within or in front of the latter they put fireplaces made of clay, around which the women and children huddle. The canoe size ranges from the two-paddle pirogue to giant boats about seventy feet long that are also impressively wide. The paddles are more than man size, with the narrow, pointed blades taking up almost half the total length. The stem is often decorated with iron and copper rings, topped off with an ivory knob, whereas the blade is decorated with carvings. In the use of these paddles the Wagenia are unexcelled masters. In a standing position, with their knees braced firmly against the sides of the boat, they literally spring forward with every stroke of the paddle; in this way they drive the canoe through the river with incredible power and speed. The two men on the forward and rear platforms steer the boat, acting in complete coordination; and it is amazing how easily they steer it through reefs of raging rapids, where the slightest miscalculation could cause the boat to capsize or break up. They paddle tirelessly, day and night, on their trips downriver, until their knees begin to bleed; or, going upriver, they drive their boats against the strong current, keeping close to shore and using long poles. Even small boys have to help with the paddling, and women often as well, though in a seated position and without exerting a great deal of effort.

Catching fish is, as mentioned before, the main occupation of the Wagenia and also their principal source of food; it is an occupation they pursue with untiring zeal. Fishing with a pole is something they leave to children. One can often see the men paddling out amid driving rain into the middle of the swirling rapids, where they anchor their canoes and try, while swimming or clinging to the mighty rocks, to lure the huge silurus fish or the slippery eel into their nets. They work not only during the day; one can see their fires glowing at every hour of the night and hear their shouting and the sound of their drums. But by far the greatest part of their catch is made with the use of fish traps. They have rammed long posts down into the bottom of most of the rapids, as well as into the raging tumult of the cataract, and then tied them together with poles and ropes of bast fiber. This whole structure is then anchored to the shore, and on this structure they fasten their funnel-shaped basket traps, into which the unwitting fish are unfailingly driven by the current and held captive. Every day one sees the reckless natives, bespattered with spray from the falls, clambering about on the poles and ropes in order to empty the traps of their catch. In the rapids along the northern side arm of the Congo, the posts connecting both shorelines are so thickly planted that one has the impression of seeing a forest. When the water level is high, the catch is relatively small, but it rises as the water begins to drop. Some of the fish are smoked and traded downriver. No doubt the drumming that one hears day and night emanating from the villages and canoes is also connected somehow with the fishing. It is said that the Wagenia are able to communicate perfectly by this means. But probably the sounds are only signals concerning the catch, dangers, and so on.

The Wagenia have no tradition of planting crops. There are no plantations surrounding their villages, and the bananas that when seen from a distance lend their villages so lush an appearance have long ago borne fruit and are of no value. For this reason the Wagenia import all their vegetables and fruits from the region lying between the Lindi and Aruwimi Rivers, and especially from the Lomami River. That is the name used for the river, first explored by Grenfell, that flows into the left bank of the Congo about two days' journey downriver from Stanley Falls. On Stanley's new map the river that joins the Congo above the cataracts is still designated as the Lomami. The Arabs, however, along with the slaves who come from this area, claim that the whole region between Grenfell's Lomami and the Congo up near Nyangye is known by this name. There is a quite lively interchange between these regions and the Wagenia, who trade their smoked fish and primitive iron axes for blades, canoes, bananas, manioc, and palm oil. For, oddly enough, the oil palm is not to be found in the Stanley Falls area, but only a number of miles downriver.

The Wagenia villages do not make a particularly favorable impression. Their huts are built low and covered with banana leaves; they are also dirty and kept in a semiruinous state. They are set in rows, forming streets, and are divided up into sections by means of fences. Every house has a small porch that is usually filled with clouds of smoke emanating from the door. Here the women and unoccupied men are seated, pounding manioc with wooden (or, more rarely, ivory) pestles, or making fishing utensils, or doing other such tasks. One almost never sees dogs in the villages, and goats and chickens are also rare. Along the shore there is always a good deal of activity; the loaded canoes dock there, and there is a sort of permanent market going on. The noise produced there is horrendous, with the women especially literally delivering orations accompanied by enraged facial expressions. Most of the women carry babies on their backs, hanging from two straps, with one strap serving as a seat and the other fastened around the mother's red-painted head. Evidently the child is not feeling overly happy about its mother's oratorical accomplishments. As money they use the above-mentioned axe heads and brass wire (*mitako*). The items for sale are fish and the imported fruits and vegetables, above all quanga, the principal source of nourishment on the Congo. As is well known, it is produced from fermented manioc flour and smells a little unpleasant, but after one gets used to it the taste is quite good. At Stanley Falls quanga is sold in square packages wrapped in leaves; two of these are sufficient to feed one Negro. There is a regular kind of stock market in quanga, which is followed by the enlisted men with lively interest. At the beginning of my stay, one could buy five packages for one mitako, later eight packages, and the latest news from the southern shore leads one to expect a drop in price to twelve packages for a mitako, so that experienced hands fear a crash will soon be coming. The Wagenia are not acquainted with tobacco or intoxicating spirits; they are not familiar with any of the wines produced by natives further downstream out of coconuts, bananas, or sugar cane.

As for recreational activities, I have observed only dancing and games. The dancing practiced by this tribe of fishermen is original and unique, for it is carried out exclusively on the open river—in a canoe. Thirty to forty partly painted men, wearing their feather caps and carrying swords, clamber into one of the big canoes and paddle out into the middle of the most violent rapids. At the back part of the boat, two men beat the long wooden boat drums that, along with the long-drawn-out singing of the dancers, form the accompaniment to the rhythm of the paddle strokes. The dance consists only of a much exaggerated version of the paddling movement. The principal dancers stand on the platforms, where they execute daring leaps without in the least losing track of how the boat is being steered through the dangerous waters. In a game I have observed, a number of young people gather together and hunch down in a circle. They then spin black fruit seeds like tops on the ground. As far as rules are concerned, I know only that this game usually ends in quarreling and poking other people in the ribs.

To learn anything about the inner lives of the Wagenia is very difficult, given the absence of direct communication with them, as well as their shyness.

With regard to their treatment of sick people, the little bags of fur with all sorts of appendages that various men wear around their necks suggest that they must be connected with "medicine." A favorite method of treatment seems to be the enema. Using a long-necked gourd in which a hole has been made, water from the Congo is poured into the patient's body. It is unclear whether the Wagenia throw all their dead or only their slaves into the river, though the former is more likely, since I have seen no burial grounds nor heard of any ceremonies for the dead. Similarly, I was unable after much effort to discover any sort of fetish figures or any other evidence of religious ideas.

The villages are under the command of chiefs, whose influence, however, is insignificant, as usual in Central Africa. These chiefs are friends of the station, which gives them gifts and buys banana leaves from them to cover roofs. It is claimed that the Wagenia are cannibals, but this has by no means been proved.

Their language belongs to that group of languages spoken approximately from the territory of the Basokos on the Aruwimi up to the area above the cataracts (according to Stanley). It can be recognized by the traveler who is moving upstream by means of their customary loud greeting, "Sehnehneeeh!" The ease with which natives learn the Zanzibari language indicates that their language belongs to a single language group that includes all other Congo languages. With its broad intonation, the language is also reminiscent of the idiom of the Krumen on the west coast of Africa. The Wagenia resemble the latter in many other respects too, and, who knows, perhaps this tireless and enterprising folk of fishermen may be destined someday to play the same essential role on the Congo that the Krumen have already played for so long for the steamship lines and trading companies along the west coast.

We have now reached that point in our discussion where we should deal with the third group of people living near the cataract, namely those bold Mohammedans who, leaving behind their homes on the Indian Ocean, have penetrated deep into the heart of Africa, as far as distant Kidsingitini, or "roaring waters" as it is called in Swahili. It is of course not our task here to provide a description of the life and doings of the Zanzibari Arabs. But since at the time of my departure, numerous false rumors were circulating about Tippo Tib and his relations with the Congo State, rumors that connected the Arabs in the Congo with the Mahdi, I will herewith take the liberty of discussing the links between the local Zanzibaris and the Stanley Falls Station. Above all I want to emphasize that the peace reigning between the station and the Arabs has never been disturbed. Under the previous commanding officer, Mr. Wester, who spoke fluent Swahili, the relationship was even extraordinarily cordial. Under the present leadership, relations may have cooled off somewhat but without giving the least cause to fear future trouble.

The material advantages for both sides are of course evident. Tippo Tib supplies the whites with rice and seeds for their plantations, gives them livestock and fowl, and even provides them, when the steamer is delayed, with salt, sugar, and coffee. In return he receives not only valuable cloth but also a variety of both useful and luxury items that he otherwise would be able to import only via the time-consuming overland route from Zanzibar. Furthermore, his own people are able to trade captured fowl and surplus vegetables and fruit for cloth at the station.

Visits are exchanged on the best of terms. Tippo Tib—or, in his absence, his representative, Mwana-Nsigi—appears at the station with a large retinue of white-robed Arabs, where they are served sweet preserves, sardines, and tea. The whites at the station return the honor by visiting the various Arab chiefs, who provide them with an orientally ceremonious reception.

If the commanding officer of the station should in any way object to the behavior of any person belonging to the Arab contingent, a single word from him is sufficient to ensure harsh punishment at the hands of their masters. One of Tippo Tib's slaves who had stolen something from a Haussa was immediately brought to the whites with the message that they should cut off his right hand and consider him their slave. (The punishment was commuted to one hundred lashes with the chicotte and work on the chain gang.)

That the Europeans put complete faith in Tippo Tib's sincerity and honesty is evident from the circumstance that already two of the whites stationed here (the Belgian Amelot and the Swede Gleerup) placed their lives in his hands in order to travel to Zanzibar under his protection. Indeed, it would be extremely peculiar if Tippo Tib—to whom, as is well known, so many explorers from Livingstone on down owe a great part of their success—would suddenly of his own accord turn against the Europeans. Although he has claimed sovereignty over the whole of the Stanley Falls region, he nevertheless tacitly acknowledges the whites' possession of the station island, and he in no way interferes with their activities.

But however accommodating and extravagantly polite the Arabs may be toward their white "brothers," and however slight any outward sign of enmity may appear to be, it is unmistakably clear to both sides that this state of harmony depends entirely on fulfilling a single, rather peculiar-sounding condition: namely, that Tippo Tib not be hindered in pursuing his business of stealing ivory and slaves on a large scale.

But before we touch on the recent arrangements that have led to overlooking the continuation of this scandalous activity, I would like to discuss briefly the role the Arabs play at Stanley Falls. As one can see from the foregoing topographical description of the area surrounding the cataract, Tippo Tib has established his own residence on an island located above that cataract, whereas his subordinate chiefs have settled on both sides of the shoreline. Mwana-Nsigi, Tippo Tib's representative, lives opposite the station. The somewhat larger houses of the Arabs are always close to shore; behind them lie the extensive, usually well-managed plantations of rice, maize, manioc, and so forth, among which the huts of the "soldiers" are interspersed. The slave women and the boys belonging to these "soldiers" take care of the work in the fields. These men are known and feared under the name of "Matamatamba"; they are Negroes from previously conquered areas who are either de facto or actual slaves of Tippo Tib. They are commanded by Zanzibari leaders. Some of these troops look quite impressive, dressed in snow-white shirts and caps, wearing European cartridge belts, and carrying rifles on their shoulders; some of the others have not gone much beyond their old national costume, the loin cloth. Their rifles are mostly of an antiquated type (though not muzzle-loaders) and would be no real match for the Snider rifles of the Haussa. The cartridges for the latter, however, suffer from a grave defect about which the officers of the Congo State often complain bitterly. Most of them are duds, for which the blame is partly the manufacturer's and partly the damp storage areas where they are kept for months and even years in the Congo.

It is hardly necessary anymore to describe the system of Arab raiding parties. As is well known, the raiders attack unsuspecting villages at night and kill everyone who offers resistance, taking the remainder prisoner. Many of the latter are able to buy their freedom back with ivory, for it is with this commodity in mind above all else that the Arabs undertake their raids. Only women and young boys are seized as slaves, with the former being distributed among the men as part of the booty and the latter raised to be future porters or Matamatambas.[1]

In each of the villages that has been conquered and, for the most part, disarmed in this way, a few Zanzibaris along with a small number of Matamatambas are left behind. No doubt to begin with, as they gradually return, the natives look askance at their alien oppressors, but soon some of the young villagers begin to take a liking to a life of banditry. Then, after they are given a muzzle-loader, they are completely converted, and a new gang of Matamatambas has come into being. It does not take long for them to raid and pillage their neighbors, joining with the very same people who previously sucked their own village dry and perhaps killed their parents and to whom they now belong body and soul.

And it is here that the greatest strength of the Arabs resides: in their knowledge of how to first plunder the natives and then make them into friends and allies. Only a very few courageous tribes, such as the Basoko on the Aruwimi, have succeeded in expelling the invaders. Religious fanaticism plays virtually no part in these Arab raids; the Matamatambas rarely convert to Islam, and nowhere are the natives influenced to do so. Up to the time when he was driven out by the Basoko, Tippo Tib's furthest encampment was located at the mouth of the Aruwimi river. As we traveled upriver, we noticed that though the natives above the Aruwimi are no doubt subject to Arab rule, since they have been deprived of their weapons and one can see canoes turned upright along the shoreline— they have not yet been blessed with Matamatamba garrisons.

Even the fixed Arab encampment at the mouth of the Lomami has been abandoned; we observed the first Zanzibaris in Sangandia, a village on the left bank about half a day's journey above the juncture of the Lomami and the Congo. From this point onward, however, the countryside is crawling with Zanzibaris, and even the inland Bakumu villages to the north seem to be full of them. The villages on the Lindi and on the Okirro, the Wamarga, the Wabeda, the Wabai, and so forth appear to be completely in Arab hands. Altogether, as far as Stanley Falls is concerned, the north is now the most important area of exploitation, and the gigantic ivory tusks that one sees among the Arabs show that it is not unremunerative. It is difficult to determine how far northward the raids extend, but I have now come pretty much to the conclusion that the horror story told to us by Tippo Tib about the disappearance in the north of Ali ben Mohammed and his troop of several hundred men is pure fabrication. He simply did not want to refuse outright to supply us with porters, because he is much too clever to want to have Europeans observe his heroes in action. That is not to say, however, that the Arabs would necessarily interfere in any way with an individual traveler who had only a small number of porters and who did not threaten to interfere with their business.

It is quite understandable that as soon as the reports of Tippo Tib's raids on the Congo made their way to Europe, leading officials of the Congo State immediately came up with the idea of putting an end to those raids. This was to have been partly brought about by negotiation between the station (and the division) chief at Stanley Falls and partly by other, more enterprising means.

The nature of Tippo Tib's reaction to the idea of negotiations may be determined from two of his replies: the station chief had received orders to demand from him the cessation of any further raids downriver. This was done, and to everyone's surprise, the Arab agreed, though he maintained that he would first have to exact revenge from the Basokos on the Aruwimi, who in any case were also enemies of the Congo State, given the fact that the steamer *Stanley* had burned down their villages. In response to another demand to withdraw his Zanzibaris from the navigable segment of the Congo, he claimed to be astonished that anyone would think such an action desirable, since his men were only stationed there in order to teach the natives how to farm in a systematic way. These negotiations are not leading to any tangible result, as is apparent from the fact that flotillas of canoes continue to come and go as they please and that during my stay two caravans of bound slave women and children passed through the vicinity of the station without anyone bothering to stop them.

Offensive measures on the part of the Congo State have begun with the withdrawal of the Zanzibari employees from the station, since they are countrymen of the Arabs. They have been replaced by a reinforced Haussa garrison. Furthermore, the supply of rifles and ammunition has been increased; the station has been provided with three Krupp cannons, and orders have been given to fortify the station. Hitherto, the priority at the station was planting crops rather than building forts, but now the logs have already been cut and construction will probably begin in a few months. If the purpose of fortifying the station is exclusively to protect it from night attack—against which it has hitherto been virtually defenseless—then that purpose will certainly be achieved. If, however, the aim is to use it to hinder the Arabs from continuing their raids downstream and thereby stop the slave raids on the navigable segment of the Congo, one can only say that this is a pretty hopeless undertaking. My evidence for reaching this conclusion will be provided in what follows.

Above all, one has to bear in mind that all of the boatmen employed by the Arabs at the Falls are natives, that is, Wagenia, who also use their own canoes. If the river were to be blockaded, the Arabs would only have to travel overland to some previously agreed-upon spot while their Wagenia friends paddled their canoes individually downstream past the station. How would it be possible to distinguish such canoes from numerous others that move past the station daily in order to catch fish or to engage in trade? Even assuming that the Arab settlements were destroyed and that it would be feasible to actually close off the Congo to the Arabs, they would still have a number of other possibilities open to them.

They could establish their posts above the cataract and then would only need to avoid it and the station, traveling overland until they reach the subjugated areas downriver, where they would again have access to canoes and paddlers. The same is true of the Lindi and Okioro rivers: the latter can be reached from the Falls in a few days' journey, and from there they can travel by canoe down to the Congo. Fortifying Stanley Falls would still leave the so-called Lomami route completely open, a route that is already being used by the Arabs today. They travel up a river that flows into the Congo in the cataract area until they reach a point where the Lomami River is said to be only a single day's march away. Traveling down the Lomami, they reach the Congo without even touching Stanley Falls. Thus, in order to provide a fort at Stanley Falls with even a semblance of justification, one would also have to establish other forts at the mouths of the Lomami and Mbura Rivers. All of this, of course, is only practicable under the assumption that the Arabs do not offer any kind of real resistance. For if the Arabs were to blockade the Wagenia trading missions downriver and in this way isolate the station completely, and if in addition they were to use their hordes of armed men to attack the station, then the question arises as to whether so utterly remote a fort could manage to hold out for months on end.

Occasionally, a very bold plan is still bruited about that would arm the natives and urge them to revolt against their oppressors. But in view of what has been said already, it seems that the most likely outcome of such a strategy would be that they would sell their rifles to their Arab friends, provided, that is, that they did not prefer to use them themselves while acting as Matamatambas against their benefactors.

Nevertheless, this is not to argue that Tippo Tib will not consider himself injured by such measures. It is even quite possible that he would be led to leave a part of the country that, for the most part, has already been sucked dry and is therefore no longer attractive to him; he might therefore prefer to focus his attentions on other "hunting grounds." This is, as I say, possible, but it depends entirely on Tippo Tib's own choice. For our visit to Stanley Falls did not leave me with the impression that, given its present weak condition, the Congo State would be able to successfully resist an Arab invasion.

There is, however, a circumstance that offers some hope that the noble Mohammedans and their Matamatambas will be departing relatively soon from the navigable segment of the Congo. Namely, that Tippo Tib and his Arabs are clearly subject to the authority of the sultan of Zanzibar. The sultan will order Tippo Tib to present himself in Zanzibar, and the latter will travel thither from the heart of Africa; the sultan will then forbid him to export his ivory via the west coast, and the Arab will therefore forgo using the more convenient route. As Tippo Tib himself says, it is out of regard for the sultan and in order to spare him any unpleasantness that he has sought to maintain good relations with the whites. And what is it that could make this Arab chieftain so fearful of the sultan, when he himself is lord over thousands of slaves and huge territories, when he is the owner himself of immense treasures? Nothing but the knowledge that, if he disobeyed the sultan's orders, the latter could forbid him and his followers ever to return to a homeland where, no doubt, they all hope to spend the remainder of their days.

Some enterprising Power could induce the sultan to exile Tippo Tib and his followers from Zanzibari territory unless he withdraws to a place above Stanley Falls, forfeits all rights to the whole area downriver along the navigable segment of the Congo, and desists from all further raiding in that area. Tippo Tib would surely accede to such a threat and to the assurance that it would be strictly carried out. For as far as he is concerned, the loss of this area is in fact relatively negligible, since—unfortunately—in the interior of Africa there still remain such immeasurably vast tracts of land open to his unhindered marauding.

It is then possible to hope that the plundering hordes will soon cease forever from pursuing their scandalous business along the navigable Congo. But it will probably be many, many years before the last village in the Congo State sinks into smoking ruin after a nocturnal attack by the Matamatambas, before the last slave has been carried off from his home in the new Free State to some unknown and distant destination. May the mature, reinvigorated and well-organized Congo State achieve what as yet has remained beyond its grasp, as a mere infant among states: namely, to put an end to the curse of Arab raids along the Congo and in the rest of this vast territory.

Supplement
Madeira, January 20, 1887

In the foregoing report, I argued that the friendship between the whites and the Arabs at Stanley Falls could endure only so long as the station did not offer any meaningful resistance to the management of the Arab slave trade or to the prosecution of their other activities. Up to now the commanding officers at the station have always lived alongside the Arabs in perfect cordiality, since, bearing in mind their utter helplessness, they were rational enough to ignore the despicable aspects of their friends' enterprises. However, the most recent chief, Mr. Deane, has presumed to defy the Arabs with a degree of self-confidence that borders on megalomania. The inevitable consequence of such behavior soon ensued: last August Stanley Falls was occupied by the Arabs, and the station—the remotest outpost of civilization in the interior of Africa, whose foundation Stanley justifiably deemed to be the crowning achievement of his career—this station no longer exists.

There is no need to spend time describing Mr. Deane's personality; readers of the *Mittheilungen* will be acquainted with him from Professor Lenz's reports, where he figures as the hero who burned down the villages of Busundi, Monageri, and Basoko [260]. His style of command was very much the same at the Falls. For the purpose of characterizing this gentleman, I might cite an incident when he permitted a dog to run free who had severely bitten an innocent worker in the lower part of his body; or I could describe how his men, whom he treated abominably, hated him, though Mr. Deane had blind faith in their reliability; or how he assigned an incompetent boy to care for the Belgian Eyken during the grave illness from which he subsequently died.[2] I could go on to mention numerous other character traits, some bordering on the incredible, which finally made life unbearable for me at the station and led me to take advantage of the hospitality of the Arabs instead. However, I would rather go on immediately in medias res to deal with the origin of the quarrel with the Arabs. When Mr. Deane assumed command of the station in February 1886, the relationship between the two groups was extremely friendly. The former chief, Mr. Wester, who spoke fluent Swahili, had always been on the best of terms with Tippo Tib and his followers. The latter had all the more reason to expect the same treatment from the new leadership, since he had gone out of his way to help the station during a period of scarce supplies, had transported the Swede Gleerup to Zanzibar free of charge, and had done the whites various good services, such as increasing their livestock, and so forth. Some of Deane's impudent actions, however, soon convinced him of his error, so that he sent his secretary over to the station to inform Deane that he (Tippo Tib) feared neither the Krupp cannons nor the Haussa, that he regarded the island as his property by right of conquest, and that if any further untoward incidents occurred he would simply expel the whites. As it turned out, while the great Arab chief remained at the Falls, no serious quarrel took place. His successor, Mwana Nsigi, an old and very pious man, seemed to be a great deal less energetic, preferring to let things run their own course with oriental equanimity. Mr. Deane then brought matters to such a head that practically all communication between the two parties ceased and only Matamatambas and a few individual Zanzibaris visited the station. Among the latter group there was an aged, eternally smiling fellow who belonged to the Arab settlement near the southern shore of the small arm of the Congo next to the Falls. He would bring seeds for sale and attempt to induce the whites to make him small presents by first giving them mats and similar items. When he came he was always accompanied by a female slave, whom Mr. Deane tried several times to buy from him. Then at the end of May 1886, she suddenly appeared at the station without her master. The latter soon arrived, though, with his perpetual smile, and Mr. Deane explained to him that he wanted absolutely to buy this slave from him. At first the old man demanded a ridiculously high price and then he said that she simply was not for sale since he had raised her from childhood. At this point Mr. Deane changed tack completely and explained to the astonished Zanzibari that, as a citizen of the Congo State, this woman had placed herself under the protection of the flag and that he would accordingly afford her his protection, that is, keep her. The old man was dumbfounded and departed, but not without first giving his slave a few fatherly words of warning. These had the effect of causing the woman to escape that night and return to her master. The latter, however, was unable to prevent the head of his settlement from punishing the renegade. Although this punishment cannot have been very severe, since it left no physical marks on her, it was nevertheless sufficient to induce the woman to escape once again to the station. Mr. Deane now exhibited great indignation over the case, even though none other than himself had formerly fired on defenseless refugees at Monagiri, not to mention that he daily meted out punishment to his own people and in other respects was anything but tender-hearted. Of course he kept the slave.

That was the state of things when at the beginning of June Mr. Grenfell arrived with the *Peace*. Mwana Nsigi thought that this would be a good opportunity to negotiate with Mr. Deane in the presence of all the whites and a number of the Arabs. Upon formally being requested to finally hand over the female slave, Deane said that he would never do so. The white-bearded Arab then gazed at him for some time and said, "Give heed that you don't lose your head over this affair." Deane treated these words with contempt, but I was utterly convinced of the gravity of the threat made by this laconic, fanatical old man, and my mind was filled with ominous forebodings as we left the station on June 9.

How well-founded my worries were has been more than confirmed by recent events. The official report on the matter appeared in a document dealing with the events at Stanley Falls written by Captain Coquilhat and published in the *Mouvement Géographique* of December 19, 1886, page 107. This document lists the following occurrences:

> In the middle of August a female slave escaped from the Arab encampment lying opposite the station. Mr. Deane refused to extradite her, but on August 23 made peace with the Arabs while the *Stanley* was at the station. However, no sooner had the steamer departed than the Arabs launched an attack against the station. Deane and his new assistant, the Belgian Dubois, together with their Haussa and Bangala soldiers, succeeded in repelling them four times. On the evening of the twenty-sixth the blacks ran out of ammunition, whereupon they refused to continue fighting and fled in canoes downriver. The two whites remained behind with four Haussa and four boys, doused the buildings with petroleum, and set them on fire. Only after exploding both cannons did they think of retreating themselves. This they then effected by moving along the north edge of the Congo, very close to the river, where the riverbank is very steep. Mr. Deane took a false step and fell into the water but quickly managed to climb out again. A moment later Dubois in turn lost his footing. Deane leapt to his aid and managed to bring him within a meter of the rock, where they would both be safe. Then Dubois let go of Deane's hand, so that both could struggle back to land. After Deane got there, he turned around to look for Dubois. The latter had disappeared forever. Deane found refuge with some natives who fed him and hid him from the Arabs. In the meantime the Haussa and the Bangala had reached the Bangala Station on September 7. Upon hearing their report, Captain Coquilhat immediately set out with the small steamer *A. T. A.* for Stanley Falls, where he managed to find Mr. Deane after an intensive three-day search.

According to this report—whose author, Captain Coquilhat, was surely intent on discovering the truth—the incident with the female slave, which I witnessed in May, has been postdated to August, and she was also made to escape from a different encampment. Either Mr. Deane had his reasons for changing the facts of the case in this way or else he thought it advisable to extend the protection of the Congo State over yet another female slave. As for the peace agreement, the main point is never addressed, namely whether or not the slave had been returned. With regard to the events that occurred after the departure of the *Stanley,* the report does not provide much clarification. To begin with, topographi-

cal details are omitted entirely, so that one does not know whether the
Arabs attacked from the river or from the shore, or whether the attack
occurred in daylight or at night. Altogether puzzling, too, is the circumstance that the two whites did not immediately burn the houses after
they had run out of ammunition and then retreat together with the
Haussas, since there obviously was no hope that they would be able to
resist the Arabs single-handed. One can only explain their behavior if
we assume that the black soldiers secretly abandoned their leaders; but
if so, it is still astonishing that the Arabs should have allowed two defenseless whites to destroy a station that contained what they must have
considered valuable booty.

As for Lieutenant Dubois's death, it would have been helpful if the
precise location of the catastrophe could have been cited, for the north
shore is steep only where the side arm of the river separates the island
from the mainland, dropping off in a wall of red sandstone. But how a
powerful, well-built man like the Lieutenant Dubois whom I met could
have drowned in such a spot is inexplicable to me, since the water there
is only knee-deep. But the description does not fit the right bank, where
the Congo opens up wide at the bottom end of the island, since the
ground there is swampy and by no means steep. Finally, it seems odd
that the natives (of course, it is not specified whether they were Wagenia
or Bakumu) should have concealed Deane so carefully that even his res-
cuers were able to locate him only after an intensive three-day search;
instead, they could simply have provided him with a canoe from their
ample supplies. Then he and his four Haussas would no doubt have
managed to get downriver unaided.

But however little we can determine the actual course of events from
the official report, the indisputable fact of the matter remains that the
station is now in Arab hands. I am utterly convinced that the sole cause
of this result is to be found in Mr. Deane's behavior and is in no way
connected with other, less immediate considerations, as has been argued.
There is no truth whatever in the newspaper reports that the Arabs at
Stanley Falls were acting in concert with the Arabs of the Sudan, since
they have no connection with them at all.

I have no idea whether the Congo State plans to rebuild its station at
Stanley Falls. If that should be the case, though, it is my hope that the
Arabs may be induced to reach a compromise by means of negotiations
carried out at the Falls or in Zanzibar. I hope Mr. Deane will bask in the
laurels of his English homeland, where he will no doubt be feted as the
heroic protector of a—or perhaps several—oppressed female slaves, even

though the price he paid was to forfeit the life of a first-rate officer and lose a station that was the product of ten years' labor, along with excellent prospects for the future. I cannot help being reminded in this connection of Gellert's fable in which a boy pursues a butterfly through a thornbush. He wounded his face, got all dirty, tore his clothes, and afterward had to confront his angry father: "But he managed to catch the beautiful butterfly."

Addendum

Peter Firchow
Stanley Falls Station from August 1886 to September 1890

The Congo State did not rebuild or reoccupy its station at Stanley Falls for nearly two years, and when it finally decided to do so, it was under very different conditions. In December 1886 Leopold signaled his willingness to renogiatiate the Free State's relations with Tippo Tib. These negotiations, initiated by the British Consul in Zanzibar, were concluded by Henry Morgan Stanley on February 24, 1887. According the new agreement, Tippo Tib officially recognized the Congo State's sovereignty over the whole area along the Congo River, agreed to prohibit subject native tribes and Arabs from engaging in the slave trade, and promised to fly the flag of the Congo State at Stanley Falls. To facilitate his intercourse with officials of the Congo State, a permanent secretary was assigned to him. In exchange, he was appointed the Congo State's governor (or *Wali*) at Stanley Falls with a monthly stipend of thirty pounds and given leave to trade without hindrance throughout the area over which he had jurisdiction.

Nevertheless, it was not until June 1888 that new station staff under the provisional command of the Belgian Alphonse Vangele arrived in the Falls, together with Tippo Tib's new liaison officer, Alfred Baert. The station was rebuilt at a spot on the mainland about one kilometer downriver from its previous location. Vangele left behind two officers, Omer Bodson and Edward Hinck, to take charge of the reconstruction pending the arrival of the new station chief, Louis Haneuse, in August 1888 (Flament 32). Work on the new station was completed on November 15, 1888; it had been, so the entry for Haneuse in the *Biographie Coloniale Belge* expressly informs us, rebuilt by the very Arabs who had destroyed the original station (Salmon, *Documents* 10–11). Sometime thereafter, according to the official Belgian history of the *Force Publique*, a subsequent chief resident officer, Nicolas Tobback, moved the Congo

Free State station once again, this time right into the camp of the Arabs on the left bank of the river. Though a map contained in the history gives a date of 1888 for this second removal, it could not have taken place earlier than the end of April 1890, since Tobback supposedly undertook it in order to express his full confidence in the new "Wali," Tippo Tip's nephew, Rashid (Flament 33). Given the additional fact that Dragutin Lerman, who replaced Tobback as chief station officer in May 1890 after the latter had left for Europe the previous month, makes no mention of his house being situated within the Arab encampment, it is probable that this "third" station was not built until after Conrad's brief stay in Stanley Falls later that summer. According to Jules Marchal, Tobback returned to resume his duties in Stanley Falls in January 1891, at which time "Rashid and his Resident lived side by side on the left bank of the river." The probable date, therefore, for the construction of the third station is sometime after January 1891 (Marchal 1:237–38; my translation). According to a map contained in W. Holman Bentley's account of "Progress on the Upper River: 1890-1899," by the end of the century, the State Station was located on the West bank of the river at some distance from the Arab settlements (Bentley 2:283). Relations with Tippo Tib in late 1888 were complicated by the nearby presence of a large armed force consisting of the rear guard of Stanley's Emin Pasha Relief Expedition. These troops were anxiously awaiting Tippo Tib's assistance in providing porters. It soon became clear that the Arabs were not adhering to treaty obligations that required them to desist from slave raids. The Congo State garrison at Stanley Falls, however, was not only too weak to prevent the raiding but also under instructions from Brussels not to do so. Food supplies were at times extremely scarce and became even scarcer as local natives became aware that Congo State forces were either powerless or reluctant to protect them from Arab incursion. The situation grew more precarious when Tippo Tib departed from Stanley Falls for Zanzibar in April 1890, leaving his nephew Rashid in charge.

Despite manifold difficulties, however, by the time Conrad arrived at the Falls on board the *Roi des Belges* for a stay of a week at the beginning of September 1890, the station had become the greatest trading center in Central Africa, largely because the transport of goods (especially ivory) by steamboat up and down the Congo River had rendered the old and very time-consuming caravan routes to and from Zanzibar superfluous (Ceulemans 199). The Congo State was now also profiting from increased trade by imposing new duties on the export of ivory and by restricting commerce as much as possible to agents of the state or to state-owned companies. River traffic on the Congo had increased enormously; by the end of 1889 there were some twenty-three steam-powered vessels of various sizes on the upper reaches of the Congo, with the largest, the *Ville de Bruxelles,* able to transport three hundred people in "comfort," carrying in this way, as Dragutin Lerman put it, with no trace of irony, "the torch of progress into the remotest parts of the Congo and its confluents" (qtd. in Lopasic 199).

Lerman was the resident officer in charge of the Falls Station when Conrad made his brief visit there. In a letter written at the end of May 1890 and later published in his hometown newspaper in Croatia, Lerman describes a scene no doubt very much like the one Conrad actually saw a few months later:

> Stanley Falls station is built near the river surrounded by a dense and large forest[,] in this way giving the station a green belt. The other neighborhood is also nice. Houses are well built and comfortable. The house of the commandant is situated in the middle and has a nice verandah, in the front of which is the flagstaff flying the colours of the Congo State. To the left and the right are the offices and the ware-houses where food, tools, arms and goods are stored. The Northern part of the station is occupied by the barracks and lodgings belonging to the freed slaves. In front of the buildings are banana trees leading to the gardens. The whole station is surrounded by a manioc forest enclosing the station on three sides. On the fourth is the river Congo. In the Western part of the station, in the woods, are gun-powder magazines and further barracks occupied by the Bangala soldiers. Behind the woods are the rice fields. South across the Congo one can see the scattered houses of our Arab neighbors. (qtd. in Lopasic 141)

Conrad's description of the Inner Station in *Heart of Darkness* seems to be an imaginative fusion of the old and new stations. The topography during the final approach to Kurtz's residence resembles that of the old station, as Marlow catches sight of "an islet, a mere grassy hammock of bright green in the middle of the stream." This small island, like the actual Wana Rusari Island, is associated with a sandbank and a series of barely visible shoals, much as Oscar Baumann describes them as existing at low water levels. Even Marlow's having to choose between a channel to the right and to the left of these obstructions suggests a further resemblance to the island location of the earlier station; and both are also flanked by a high riverbank and densely overgrown forest on the mainland side (*HD* 44–45). The dilapidated principal station building, situated in a clearing on the summit of a slope, is probably based on

Conrad's memory of what the ruins of the old station looked like after four years of deterioration: "A long decaying building on the summit was half buried in the high grass; the large holes in the peaked roof gaped black from afar; the jungle and the woods made a background. There was no enclosure or fence of any kind, but there had been one apparently, for near the house half a dozen slim posts remained in a row, roughly trimmed, and with their upper end ornamented with round carved balls. The rails or whatever there had been between had disappeared" (*HD* 52). However, the fact that the station is explicitly located on the mainland rather than on the island is more in line with the appearance of the new station, as is the absence of any reefs or falls on the river. The fact that Marlow is able to turn his boat around easily in the open reaches of the river also suggests that Conrad has the new station in mind, for that is something he would never have been able to do at the old one. To be sure, writing as he was about a place he had seen only once nearly a decade earlier, Conrad may simply have been a little muddled about the exact location of his Inner Station. So, the manuscript version has "east" and "eastern" as cancelled alternative choices for the corresponding "west" and "western" in the published description of Marlow's final approach to the station: "The banks looked pretty well alike, the depth appeared the same, but as I had been informed the station was on the west side I naturally headed for the western passage" (*HD* 45).

Of course, Conrad's depiction of the fictional Inner Station also differs radically in important respects from the reality of both the old and the new stations. Striking, to begin with, is the utter and complete absence of all Arabs or Zanzibaris. And since there are no Arabs, there are naturally no Arab dwellings or plantations either. Nor are there any peaceful native fisher folk or traders. In Conrad's narrative, all or at least most of the Africans resident at the Falls appear to be members of a distant tribe that Kurtz has induced to return with him from the Lake country to the North and East of the Falls. They are led by a powerful female chieftain, who is also Kurtz's consort. In actual fact, however, there was no history whatever of matriarchal rule in the vicinity of the station. Indeed, as Baumann is careful to point out, most of the women there who were not members of the patriarchal Wagenia tribe were slaves. Finally, Kurtz himself and even his position are unique. He is evidently not the commanding officer of the station but only an "agent" (like Kayerts and Carlier in "An Outpost of Progress"), whose main task is simply to secure as much ivory as possible rather than to "show the flag" or, in general, to represent the authority of the State. Also, unlike virtually all other Europeans at the station (old or new), he is and has for some time been the only white agent there, having dismissed his single European subordinate in disgust several months earlier. To be sure, the first resident officer of the station, a Scottish engineer named Adrien Bennie, had been left as the sole white representative there from December 1883 until he was relieved by the Swede Arvid-Mauritz Wester in April 1884 (*BCB* 1:51–52). It would seem, therefore, that the differences between Conrad's Inner Station and the actual historical stations at Stanley Falls loom a good deal larger than the similarities. His Inner Station is more a symbolic station of the psyche and the heart than it is a realistic rendering of the settlement Stanley founded in 1883 at what he then believed to be the furthest navigable point of the Congo.

NOTES

Preface

1. There is as yet no consensus as to what constitutes nationalism, and the development of new jargon has not made the attempt at definition any easier. So Walker Connor complains that substitute terms like *primordialism, tribalism, regionalism, communalism, parochialism,* and *subnationalism* have contributed to "the terminological confusion impeding the study of ethnonationalism" (72, 92). Like many other contemporary writers on nationalism, Connor argues that "the essence of the nation . . . is a matter of *self*-awareness or *self*-consciousness" (104). So, too, Peter Alter sees nations as being "constituted by the social group's (the *people's*) consciousness of being a nation, or of wanting to be one, and by their demand for political self-determination" (17–18). However, George Mosse maintains that nations only started to define themselves in terms of consciousness at the close of the eighteenth century; prior to that time nations were simply conceived of as groups of people who happened to live under a single ruler or inhabited a specific territory. It is especially significant in the present context that the attempt to locate national identity in mental states dovetails neatly with literary studies analyzing ethnic and national stereotypes (Mosse 38).

2. A fairly recent example is Dean Peabody's *National Characteristics* (1985), which asserts the social reality of national characteristics, though without really addressing the question whether these are innate or acquired. For example, he claims that the English are marked by six dominant characteristics: (1) they play "by the rules of the game," (2) they value public over private virtues, (3) they avoid obvious self-assertion, (4) they dislike overt expression of hostility, (5) they are ascetic with respect to food and sex, and (6) they exercise "reserve" (96–99). An earlier study, William Buchanan and Hadley Cantril's *How Nations See Each Other: A Study in Public Opinion* (1953), seeks to define national character on the basis of national autoimages and heteroimages derived from a UNESCO-sponsored survey carried out not long after the Second World War. Manfred Fischer maintains that the "strictly scientific" study of national stereotypes in literary contexts begins only with the abandonment of antiquated nineteenth-century conceptions of the "reality" of national stereotypes (or national character) (29).

3. This is an argument that may be more familiar to readers in terms of shaping class identity, since it is a favorite theoretical hobbyhorse of the well-known Marxist critic Terry Eagleton. More recently, however, it has been adapted to show how national consciousness is in many ways a product of the institutions of high culture, including canonical literature. See Robert Colls and Philip Dodd, eds., *Englishness: Politics and Culture, 1880–1920* (London: Croom Helm, 1986).

4. So Walter Lippmann, usually considered to have been the first to coin the phrase "national stereotypes," believed them to be not only negative but also false. One of the most common areas in which national stereotypes are employed is humor, where such stereotypes are referred to as "slurs," thereby clearly indicating their supposedly false and negative nature (Dundes 102).

5. See also Julia Kristeva, "What of Tomorrow's Nation?" in *Nations without Nationalism* (New York: Columbia Univ. Press, 1993), 17.

6. For the notion of counteridentities, see Ranum 68, 78; Dyserinck 132; and Fischer 20. According to George Mosse (12), stereotypical binarism (as distinguished from relatively random national prejudice) did not develop until the eighteenth century with Winckelmann's notion of an "ideal-type" of Greek beauty, according to which Jewish and black African countertypes of supposed ugliness were established.

7. More recently the word has also turned up as a synonym for marketing through advertising. See Mark C. Taylor and Esa Saarinen, *Imagologies: Media Philosophy* (London: Routledge, 1994).

8. In its own way *Orientalism* suffers from precisely the same kind of debilitating lack of objectivity as the "image/mirage" work of Carré and coworkers. On the one hand Said is outraged that some Europeans (the nefarious orientalists) produced a false stereotype of the "Orient," but on the other hand he can produce with absolute equanimity stereotypical (not to say racist) statements like the following: "It is therefore correct that every European, in what he could say about the Orient, was consequently a racist, an imperialist, and almost totally ethnocentric" (*Orientalism* 204). As John Ellis points out, "[i]n criticizing Europeans for attitudes that were simply those of their time, both [Stephen] Greenblatt and Said miss what was distinctive about them—their ambivalence and the strong signs of their eventual renunciation of those attitudes. And so Greenblatt and Said both preach historicism yet judge ahistorically; they both preach Enlightenment values yet attack the very group that originates and spreads those values" (103).

Introduction

1. Conrad was himself surprised, pleased, and a little puzzled by his early popularity in Sweden. In 1923 he thanked Professor Ernst Bendz of Göteborg for sending him a pamphlet "on myself and my work," noting and objecting to the fact that he was "regarded in that country as literally a sort of Jack London" (quoted in Jean-Aubry, *Life* 2:295).

2. Recently K. Anthony Appiah has revived the word, using it with much the same meaning. Citing Matthew Arnold's "racialism" (Arnold did not use the word),

Appiah claims that "he believed—and in this he was typical of educated people in the English-speaking world of his day—that we could divide human beings into a small number of groups, called 'races,' in such a way that the members of these groups shared certain fundamental, heritable, physical, moral intellectual, and cultural characteristics with one another that they did not share with members of any other race" (Appiah 54). So, on the one hand, "racialists" are people who believe in a necessary link between physical and mental/emotional characteristics in races. Thomas W. Thompson, on the other hand, distinguishes between "racialism," meaning a vaguely Romantic doctrine of racial/ethnic superiority, and "racism," referring to the modern pseudoscientific doctrine of race superiority (3–4).

3. According to Léon Poliakov's *Aryan Myth*, "the idea that Jews were constituted differently from other men, and specifically from Christians" arose in the late nineteenth century as a direct result of far-fetched speculations on the part of anthropologists and biologists (281).

4. In Michael Banton's view, this sort of race-thinking (or, in present-day terms, ethnic-thinking) received a tremendous boost from Sir Walter Scott's novels, especially *Ivanhoe,* where the Saxon "race" is contrasted with the Norman "race." "It is probable," writes Banton, "that no single book or event did more to introduce the word race into popular thought than Scott's historical romance" (13). The definitive substitution of the word (and concept) of *race* with that of *ethnic groups* came relatively late, with the first draft of the UNESCO Statement on Race in 1950. There, the principal author, Ashley Montagu, denied the biological validity of the concept of race, using instead a phrase first proposed by Julian Huxley in 1935, "ethnic groups." Montagu did, however, accept that there were three major "subdivisions" within the species of *homo sapiens*, "the Mongoloid, the Negroid, and the Caucasoid" (qtd. in Shipman 163).

5. That Conrad or his narrators are at times prepared to make blatantly biased generalizations about other ethnic groups is apparent from comments like the one about Schomberg in *Victory*, that "the innkeeper was not mercenary. Teutonic temperament seldom is" (26–27); or about the Spaniards in *Romance* who are described "as a race" that has never been "for all the conquests . . . on intimate terms with the sea." In the latter novel, the sympathetic English protagonist and narrator, John Kemp, contrasts himself with his fanatically Irish rival, Patrick O'Brien, in the following terms: "There we were, Irish and English, face to face, as it had been ever since we had met in the narrow way of the world that had never been big enough for the tribes, the nations, the races of man" (363, 196).

6. To be sure, environment plays a minor role here as well in that higher elevations appear to provide some protection against the "poison." That this involves being almost literally nearer to God, however, is apparent from Challenger's reference to the last survivor's being found again "upon the summit of some Ararat" (Doyle 244).

7. It is also significant that Conrad's ethnic ranking differs in important respects from the standard Victorian conception of the hierarchy of racial and national groups: "The British at the top, followed a few rungs below by the Americans,

and other 'striving, go-ahead' Anglo-Saxons. The Latin peoples were thought to come next, though far behind. Much lower still stood the vast Oriental communities of Asia and North Africa. . . . Lowest of all stood the 'aborigines' whom [sic] it was thought had never learned enough social discipline to pass from the family and tribe to the making of a state" (Robinson, Gallagher, and Denny 2–3). According to Cedric Watts, Conrad ranked the chief imperial nations of his time in the following descending order: Great Britain, France, Spain, Japan, Austria, Holland, the United States, Belgium, Germany, and Russia (*Preface* 58). Here, although Britain retains the top spot, France follows closely behind and one non-European empire (Japan) outranks several European or ethnically European ones.

8. As early as 1784 Johann Gottfried Herder had argued against using the word *race* to designate groups that were biologically cross-fertile (Banton 6).

9. Positive attributes assigned to ethnic or racial groups are never considered racist (at least in anything beyond the "weak" sense), though there is no logical reason why they should not be. Common examples are the "sense of humor" stereotypically associated with the Irish or "athletic ability" with Africans or people of African descent.

10. A striking exception is George Watson, who maintains that "there is no clear evidence that British imperialism and Victorian doctrines of race are linked in any causal way" (215).

11. Some contemporary usage in distinguishing between the terms *imperialism* and *colonialism* varies considerably from Hobson's. According to Pierre van den Berghe, "colonialism" is a specially virulent form of "imperialism," involving domination over "distant peoples who usually live in noncontiguous, overseas territories and who therefore look quite different from their conquerors, speak unrelated languages, and are so culturally alien to their colonial masters as to provide little basis for mutual understanding" (85).

12. According to J.A. Hobson, the main difference between ancient and modern imperialism is that in the case of the latter there is competition among a number of empires, whereas in the former the empire consisted of a single, hegemonic federation of states, as instanced most notably in the Roman Empire and its successor, the Holy Roman Empire (8). Something of the same distinction is made by H.G. Wells when he differentiates between an older imperialism that was "synthetic" and "world-uniting" (i.e., good) and a modern imperialism that is "essentially a *megalomaniac nationalism*, a nationalism made aggressive by prosperity; and always finds its strongest support in the military and official castes; and in the enterprising and acquisitive strata of society, in new money, that is, and big business. . . . Modern imperialism is the natural development of the Great Power system which arose, with the foreign office method of policy, out of the Machiavellian monarchies after the break-up of Christendom" (2:844). Here Wells sees more clearly than other writers on the subject that imperialism is not merely an economic but also a psychological phenomenon that has to do with the need to define one's own collective national importance against rivals by means of "conquests" and "possessions" published in atlases and history books.

1. Envisioning Africa

1. Conrad left Bordeaux on the *Ville de Maceio* on May 10, 1890, and disembarked at Boma, the capital of the Congo Free State, on June 10, 1890. Three days later he traveled by boat to Matadi (the Outer Station of the novel), where he stayed for two weeks before leaving on foot for Kinshasa (the Central Station) on June 28, arriving there on August 2. After ten days' rest, Conrad left for Stanley Falls aboard the steamer *Roi des Belges*, which reached its destination on September 1. After a week's stay in Stanley Falls, the *Roi des Belges*, now under Conrad's temporary command and with the dying Georges Antoine Klein on board, returned downstream. Back in Kinshasa on September 24, Conrad was refused a place in Alexandre Delcommune's Katanga expedition, though this had been promised him in Brussels. Seriously ill, Conrad left Kinshasa on October 23 for the coast, reaching Matadi on December 4 and departing for Europe shortly thereafter (Knowles 13–15).

2. According to Frederick Karl's biography of Conrad, the epigraph from Grimm's *Fairy Tales* is intended by Conrad to refer only to the accompanying dedication of the book to Jessie Conrad (*Joseph Conrad* 539 n). This assertion is doubtful, however, since the fairy tale in question is "Rumpelstiltskin" and the "something human" refers to the miller's daughter's first child. If directed at Jessie, therefore, the allusion might have been understood by her as offensive rather than complimentary. Oddly enough, in his earlier *Reader's Guide* Karl had argued that "the appropriateness of the epigraph to the *Youth* volume . . . is nowhere more apparent than in Conrad's study of the loss of heart and its terrible consequences: specifically, the loss of responsible heart in Kurtz" (134). In R.C. Churchill's view, the epigraph may be usefully applied to the whole body of Conrad's work, pointing to its characteristically broad and generous humanity (980).

3. In old age Conrad remembered how as a boy he had been fascinated by the tragic history of Sir John Franklin, who was lost with all his crew while attempting to find a Northwest Passage through the Canadian Arctic. It was this initial fascination with the frozen North that eventually extended to the explorers of tropical Africa (*Last Essays* 15–22). Significantly, in Conrad's only other novel dealing with Leopold II's imperial adventures, *The Inheritors*, the exploitative "Empire" is located in the Arctic.

4. The terminology is from Wayne Booth, who takes a middle position. Conrad does of course begin by telling the story from the point of view of a nameless, though clearly not omniscient, narrator, a strategy very similar (except for the great difference in length) to that adopted in *Lord Jim* (Booth 152–54).

5. Max Weinrich's way of distinguishing a dialect from a language is to call a language "a dialect with an army and navy" (qtd. in Pinker 28).

6. Notably Watts ("Bloody Racist"), Hawkins ("Racism"), and Sarvan.

7. According to Richard Burton, the effective fighting force of this Amazon unit in 1864 consisted of 1,700 women out of a total population of 150,000 people (263). The entry "Dahomey" in the eleventh edition of the *Encyclopedia Britannica* claims, however, that as much as a quarter of the female population was enrolled in

the army and that they were the best and most courageous warriors, apparently impervious to pain.

8. Thomas Cleary and Terry Sherwood are, to my knowledge, unique among Conrad's critics in making the connection between Dido and the Black Amazon, but they do not take into account that this intertextual relationship reveals Conrad's positive conception of her. Instead, they argue that "Kurtz's surrender to his Dido is the mark of his corruption," citing as evidence for this hypothesis Kurtz's having been compelled by Marlow to leave Africa. Aeneas, on the other hand, being a true hero, departed of his own accord (185–86). For a discussion of other Virgilian elements in *Heart of Darkness*, see Feder.

9. This sense of trying to get at the often contradictory *totality* of a situation is evident also in Conrad's much-censured piling up of adjectives. In Conrad's case, however, this strategy leads to the peculiar result that the more one attempts to pin down the truth of a thing, the more elusive it becomes. Hence, with respect to Erich Auerbach's famous distinction between the hypertactic style (characteristic of the *Odyssey*) and the paratactic style (characteristic of the Bible), Conrad adheres unmistakably to the former, but his actual stylistic effects nevertheless tend to resemble the latter. That is, though he seeks to bring everything he (or Marlow) sees into a brightly illuminated foreground by using a plethora of qualifications and subordinating clauses, he succeeds paradoxically only in pushing everything further into a profoundly obscure and ambiguous background. In this sense, as in so many others, Conrad's fiction is very much a "mixed" thing (Auerbach 3–23).

10. This is not quite so absurd as it may at first appear. After all, Marlow does put forward the very Christian (not to say Catholic) idea that the only important moment of life is the moment of death: "[P]erhaps all the wisdom, and all truth, and all sincerity, are just compressed into that inappreciable moment of time in which we step over the threshold of the invisible" (*HD* 69). If Marlow is right about Kurtz's repentance in the last moments of his life—and there is certainly no trace of obvious irony here to make us doubt it—then Kurtz has been absolved of his sins. In this sense too, of course, Kurtz has preceded Marlow into that ultimate "heart of darkness," which is death, but which for those who possess the "true stuff" is also salvation.

11. There are also (or at least there are intended to be) comic elements in Goethe's *Faust*, especially in the prologue.

12. In these satirical portraits Conrad notoriously wreaked revenge on the brothers Camille and Alexandre Delcommune. In real life, far from possessing no entrails, Camille Delcommune died of hematuria only two years after Conrad had left the Congo (*BCB* 2:184). As for his older brother Alexandre, his expedition to the Katanga region suffered appalling casualties, losing more than 500 of the original contingent of 670 members. Alexandre himself survived, however, and on his return to Belgium in April 1893 was given a triumphal reception. He eventually went on to become one of the principal administrators of the Belgian colonial service, dying in 1922 (*BCB* 2:259–61).

2. A Mere Animal in the Congo

1. In the introduction to his edition of *Letters from Joseph Conrad, 1895–1924,* Edward Garnett remembers Conrad's remark phrased a little differently: "According to his emphatic declaration to me, in his early years at sea he had 'not a thought in his [*sic*] head . . . I was a perfect animal'" (8).

2. According to Jeffrey Meyers, Conrad errs in distinguishing Kinshasa from Léopoldville, since these are simply "African and Belgian names for the same place"(*Conrad* 107). Though this may be the case now, during the late nineteenth century, when Conrad was making his journey downriver, they were two quite distinct places. As is evident on the map reproduced in E.J. Glave's *In Savage Africa* (1892), Kinsassa (Glave's spelling) lies several miles upriver from Léopoldville. In late 1889 it took Dragutin Lerman an hour and a half to walk from Léopoldville to Kinshasa (Lopasic 130). In an essay published in 1890 in the *Century Magazine,* Glave describes the station at Leopoldville as being "built on a hillside . . . on the lower end of Stanley Pool and commands an excellent view of the surrounding country. It is the central dépot of the Congo Free State, whence supplies are forwarded to the stations on the upper river. There is at present a staff of about twenty-five Europeans attached to this station, carpenters, engineers, captains of boats, in addition to administration officials. There are five large river steamers and two small ones." As for Kinshasa (Conrad's Central Station), it is "eight miles above Leopoldville" and "has assumed great importance, as the two largest commercial enterprises, the Dutch and the Belgian, have selected this district as their base of operations for the ivory trade on the upper Congo" ("Congo" 620).

3. "An Image of Africa: Racism in Conrad's *Heart of Darkness*" (first given as a lecture in Amherst, Massachusetts, in 1975). A few years later Achebe made the point even more explicitly, condemning *Heart of Darkness* for showing an Africa that "teems with Africans whose humanity is admitted in theory but totally undermined by the mindlessness of its context and the pretty explicit animal imagery surrounding it" ("Viewpoint" 113). According to Homi K. Bhabha, animality is the prevalent stereotype imposed on blacks by Europeans (77).

4. Even as Conrad finished the story in February 1899, he used animal imagery to describe it to another friend, R.B. Cunninghame Graham: "Somme toute, c'est une bête d'histoire" [In short, it's a beast of a story (my translation)] (qtd. in Jean-Aubry 1:268).

5. For brief discussions, see Fothergill 81–85 and Watt, *Conrad* 155–57.

6. Already in the 1820s the idea had been raised that ontogeny recapitulates phylogeny, though it received a decisive setback when Karl Ernst von Baer "showed that the embryo of a higher animal is never like the adult of a lower animal but only like its embryo" (Banton 18). Ian Watt sees Kurtz as embodying "a monitory variant of the biogenetic law" (*Conrad* 166).

7. Conrad may be singling out Upoto because of its reputation, in Herbert Ward's words, for being inhabited by "the nudest of the Congo tribes" and for the supposedly frequent cannibalism and human sacrifice practiced there (*Five* 155).

Conrad's point may be to suggest that, despite his awareness of the worst that can be said against black Africans, he is still prepared to affirm their humanity.

8. Conrad first met Casement in the Congo in June 1890. See "The Congo Diary" in *Last Essays* 238. In making this remark Conrad was anticipating E.D. Morel's observation in his classic account *History of the Congo Reform Movement* that "barbarism, which is merely a stage in human development, has, in the case of the Congo, been talked and written of as though it were a crime" (11). Unlike Morel, however, Conrad—or Marlow at any rate—does not entirely endorse the idea of a gradual but unequal cultural evolution.

9. "Delayed decoding" in this substantive sense can be said to exist even on the symbolic level of the novel, in terms of both Marlow himself and his readers (or auditors). For not only he and his friends aboard the *Nellie* but also we (including we-the-critics) have experienced a considerable and possibly infinite delay in decoding the significance of *Heart of Darkness*. That Conrad occasionally uses the device (again not merely technically but substantively) in a playful manner is apparent from a scene in *Lord Jim*: Jim is repairing a clock after spending three days in the Rajah's stockade when he suddenly realizes the danger he is in. The clock, of course, reminds him at last that his "readiness" is also in immediate need of repair. On some level, Jim's delay in decoding the "message" here—as on an earlier occasion aboard the *Patna*—may also be Conrad's way of obliquely suggesting Jim's "simplicity."

10. As John Batchelor points out, readers of *Blackwood's Magazine* (in which "The Heart of Darkness" was first published in three installments in 1899) tended to belong to a fairly homogeneous group consisting of "army and navy officers and administrators of the Empire, ex-public school middle-class Englishmen who liked to have their self-esteem reinforced by stories about people like themselves: men of action doing good jobs in hazardous circumstances" (94). Benita Parry is even more explicit when she says that readers of *Blackwood's* constituted "an audience still secure in the conviction that they were members of an invincible imperial power and a superior race" and that "the subversive implications of fictions which disturbed even as they consoled were not apparent to contemporary reviewers" (1). Andrea White also argues that "for many contemporary readers, the familiarity of the discourse masked the subversion" at least partly intended by Conrad (*Adventure* 5). According to Lawrence Graver, however, "when readers picked up the spring issues of *Blackwood's* in 1899, they found the serial called 'The Heart of Darkness' something of a puzzle," primarily because "from first to last the text was filled with unmistakable attacks on colonial barbarism" (77). That Conrad himself was aware of the sort of audience he was reaching (and wanted to reach) is apparent from the following remark he made to his agent James Pinker in 1911: "'One was in decent company there and had a good sort of public. There isn't a single club and messroom and man-of-war in the British Seas and Dominions which hasn't its copy of Maga'" (qtd. in Watt, *Conrad* 131).

11. Similarly, the Intended's arms are "black" as she stretches them "across the fading and narrow sheen of the window," though her clasped hands nevertheless

remain "pale" (*HD* 75). In some editions, to be sure, the word is "back" rather than "black," as for example in Murfin's casebook edition (93). For the source of the sorcerers' red dye, see Appendix.

12. John Crompton concludes that the colloquial English that the young Conrad learned aboard a variety of ships "must have consisted of seaman's technical jargon, some of which is, of course, current idiom . . . and the blaspheming, swearing slang which [J.A.] Cuddon would call 'argot,' that is, basically the kind of language used by social outcasts. Once Conrad became an officer, his spoken language environment would have improved considerably, though he would obviously not have forgotten his earlier one" (213–15). It is perhaps significant, therefore, that in *Nostromo*, which has a social setting that is generally speaking more elevated than that of any of his preceding narratives, blacks are uniformly referred to as Negroes, though their implied status is also uniformly inferior to that of the so-called Creoles.

That a distinction was made during the late Victorian period between a "nigger" and a "Negro" is evident from Joseph Thomson's comparison between the Negroes who "know their place" and the "niggers" who have become Europeanized: "'You discover that the erewhile [*sic*] negro has degenerated into a *nigger*, bids you "Good morning," and wears a lawn-tennis hat with a sunflower embroidered on it—the latest fashion on the river'" (qtd. in Rotberg 314). Conrad, however, does not adhere to this distinction, for the Manager's impudent "boy" is referred to as a Negro, whereas the old chief whom Fresleven beats mercilessly is termed a "nigger." Conrad also uses the more neutral word *black* several times in the story to refer to Africans. As Edward Said remarks, Conrad's use of the English language in general was affected by the fact that he was "a self-conscious foreigner writing of obscure experiences in an alien language, and he was only too aware of this" (*Conrad* 4).

13. Conrad's choice of asses as mounts is an obvious satiric touch, but it should be noted that as a matter of historical fact African explorers used a variety of animals in their expeditions, especially after horses had been found to be unsuitable for tropical conditions. David Livingstone, for example, customarily rode an ox named Sinbad during the early phases of his exploration (Huxley 80).

14. As Conrad's use of the name El Dorado for this expedition suggests, Alexandre Delcommune (the model for the Manager's uncle) was charged with a mission to find gold in the remote eastern Katanga province. As Joseph Moloney notes, "M. Delcommune's instructions were that he should repair to Bunkeia [in Katanga], and, if possible, persuade [King] Msiri to accept the flag; and then advance, without loss of time, to the south, where the gold-fields were reported to lie." The special urgency was due to reports that Cecil Rhodes was about to put in a claim for the area (8).

15. These interracial friendships probably derive, as Martin Green implies, from Cooper's depiction of the friendship between Natty Bumppo and Chingachgook (310). The notable absence of such friendships in the African narratives may be the result of Conrad's conception of Africans as inferior to Asians, for according to Robert F. Lee, Conrad writes about "Africa and the Negroes as he never wrote of the Orient with its advanced cultures and civilizations" (41). Although it is true that Conrad knew Africa much less well than he did the Malay Archipelago—and

that this may also be why his narratives about Africa are shorter than those about the Far East—it is also true that these close interracial relationships tend to have a European element (the exceptions are Dain in *Almayer's Folly* and Aissa in *An Outcast of the Islands*). Significantly, Jim's friend Dain Waris is said by Marlow to fight like a "white man" and to possess a "European mind" (*Lord Jim* 157). It is likely, however, that Conrad's conception of such relationships was influenced by the interracial friendship of the black Mesty and the white Jack in Captain Marryat's *Mr. Midshipman Easy* (1836), since that was one of his favorite books. Although in some ways conforming to stereotypical conceptions of blacks (especially in terms of his supposedly comic language), Mesty is on the whole very much in the tradition of the noble savage, so that when Jack offers him his hand, he is moved so profoundly that if "the feelings which were suffocating the negro [could] but have been laid before sceptics, they must have acknowledged that at that moment they were all and only such as could do honour, not only to the prince [Mesty is of royal lineage], but even to the Christian" (128).

16. As Andrea White points out, the lessons Marlow learns from reading Carlyle's *Sartor Resartus* in "Youth" are applied in *Heart of Darkness*, especially to the notion of "work" (*Adventure* 168). Also the contrasts between the real and the sham, the naked and the clothed—and especially the "cloak of time"—are probably indebted to Carlyle. There is a further possibility that Conrad may have had in mind Max Nordau's essay "Rabies Africana, and the Degeneracy of Europeans in Africa" (1891). There Nordau distinguishes between two opposed European attitudes toward Africa, which he identifies as either that of the "Hypocrites" or the "Cynics:" "The former say: 'We take Africa in order to improve the condition of the natives;' the latter state, 'We pocket Africa for our own profit.' The Cynics have at least the merit of sincerity" (Nordau 70). Nordau's Hypocrites are Conrad's shams; and his cynics are Conrad's madmen.

17. The idea of every "race" of mankind having its appropriate geographical place dates back at least as far as the mid–eighteenth century when it was proposed by Montesquieu in his *Spirit of Laws*. His rationale was that the perceivable differences in color and shape among humans in various parts of the world were due to climatic influence and that they could therefore only function properly if they remained in their original "place" (Banton 8).

18. According to Marianna Torgovnick, Conrad hints only "in the most indirect way" that "Kurtz has apparently mated with the magnificent black woman and thus violated the British code against miscegenation" (146). Though it is true that Conrad does not describe any overt sexual activity between the Black Amazon and Kurtz, only the most naive present-day reader (or Victorian reader, for that matter) would have missed the point. That Conrad was not unique in presenting sexual relations between different races in this way is evident from Robert Louis Stevenson's novel *The Beach of Falesá* and Rudyard Kipling's story "Without Benefit of Clergy."

19. In connection with the nineteenth-century European failure to appreciate African art, it is interesting to note that, according to the generally acknowledged principal progenitor of European racism, Count Josephe Gobineau, "Art is a prod-

uct of the imagination; and imagination is not characteristic of a true Aryan. It is an alien drop of blood in his veins; for it comes from the Negroes" (qtd. in Cassirer 241). That many Europeans—even strongly racist ones—did admire African craftsmanship is evident from comments like that of Herbert Ward about some of the native blacksmiths of the Upper Congo: "The rough iron ore, as provided by nature to man, enters this rough African savage's hands, and leaves it either in the shape of a knife, arrow-head, or spear, so deftly and artistically worked as to be universally admired. Long practice has given them a very wide knowledge of the nature of metals, and they know exactly how to temper them" (Ward, 1890, 145).

20. That language and meaning are (and even must be) separable is suggested by Steven Pinker's Chomskyan analysis of the relation between language and thought in *The Language Instinct*. "People do not think in English or Chinese or Apache," he writes; "they think in a language of thought." Pinker calls this ingrained or instinctive language "mentalese" and argues that "knowing a language . . . is knowing how to translate mentalese into strings of words and vice versa. . . . [I]f babies did not have mentalese to translate to and from English, it is not clear how learning English could take place, or even what learning English would mean" (81–82).

21. This is how Achebe phrases it in the original version of his essay in the *Massachusetts Review*. In the revised version published by Norton, he "softens" or at least Americanizes the charge to "thoroughgoing racist" (*HD* 257).

22. Jonah Raskin argues that Conrad's views on race were influenced by Max Nordau's *Degeneration*, which he was reading in 1898. Nordau's work, however, which focuses on the environmental effects of industrialization and urbanization, is only marginally concerned with race. As for Raskin's hypothesis that in *Heart of Darkness* Conrad is expressing a fear of "re- barbarization," prevalent at the turn of the century, most of the prominent contributors to this debate postdated Conrad's novel. Hence, his conclusion that racism is "critical" in *Heart of Darkness* but only "slight" in his earlier fiction does not seem warranted by the evidence he cites (128–31).

23. In this connection, it is worth recalling that in Wolfram von Eschenbach's great medieval romance *Parzifal*, the titular hero has a brother (his only brother) who is both a great prince and courteous knight, and also half-black. His name is Feirefiz, and he is the son of Gahmuret (also Parzifal's father) and the African Queen Belacane.

24. The same idea—but with a very different emphasis—was put forward in 1973 by Ernest Gellner. He views Western fascination with "primitives" primarily as an attempt to "'catch an innocent glimpse, and see ourselves as we truly are. We also long for the *frisson* of seeing, of seizing conceptually, the wholly Other, the savage. . . . We hope to see what is normally obscured by the decencies, and find out some truth about ourselves in the process'" (qtd. in Cerroni-Long 79). The aim, in other words, is not to reject the "Other" but rather to discover and claim it. In a somewhat different and clearly nonracist sense, Conrad seems to agree with Achebe when he implies in *The Mirror of the Sea* that what people say of others usually reflects morally on themselves. Speaking of the kinds of remarks the Roman com-

mander of a boat moving up the Thames estuary might have heard before undertaking his voyage, Conrad remarks that "the instructive tales about native chiefs dyed more or less blue, whose character for greediness, ferocity, or amiability must have been expounded to him with that capacity for vivid language which seems joined naturally to the shadiness of moral character and recklessness of disposition" (*Mirror* 102).

25. Jacques Berthoud puts forward the thesis that Marlow's robust confidence in his own national and social identity permits him to assert both his own difference from and his similarity to the blacks in the canoe. His "very recognition of difference" is, in Berthoud's view, "an acknowledgment of otherness; the grotesque masks belong to 'these chaps': because he accepts dissimilarity, he is able to affirm a common humanity" (*Major* 47). What Berthoud seems to be saying here is that, paradoxically, Marlow can accept the Africans as "brothers" because he sees them so very clearly as "others." If that is true, then Berthoud's use of the concept "other" would be very different from the one current today. For most critics writing since the eighties, it is understood that the "Other" is that part of ourselves that we either consciously or unconsciously reject and which we therefore attempt to associate exclusively and pejoratively with *other* racial, ethnic, national, religious, or gender groups. The real "Other," in other words, is the unacknowledged self. In this view all human beings are essentially identical and, cultural differences aside, there can be no "other" other than the imagined or mentalistic other. This is the sense in which Achebe uses the word when he claims that Europeans always think of Africans as the "Other."

26. Achebe himself provides no source for the Schweitzer quotation. In the 1977 version of his essay he refers to it as something that he has often quoted, "but must quote one last time" (*Massachusetts Review* 787), whereas in the Norton revision it becomes simply "a comment which has often been quoted" (*HD* 257). As Marianna Torgovnick points out, H.M. Stanley, who is sometimes identified as one of the models for Kurtz, claims near the beginning of his *How I Found Livingstone* (1874) that he is "prepared to admit any black man, possessing the attributes of manhood, or any good qualities, to my friendship, even to a brotherhood with myself; and to respect him for such, as much as if he were of my own colour and race." In Torgovnick's view, however, these are empty words, belied by the events narrated and even the illustrations contained in the same book, which show Stanley threatening a black carrier with a pistol (32–33). She is apparently not aware that George Washington Williams, who was black, was similarly disposed. "I traveled through a country absolutely destitute of food," he writes of his travels through the Congo in 1890. "The courage of my men began to abate and it looked on several occasions as if I would be compelled to execute one or two subordinate fellows who were endeavoring to bring on a mutiny" (qtd. in Franklin 100). In part, however, Torgovnick may be doing Stanley an injustice for a different reason, since he is perhaps thinking of "brotherhood" in terms similar to Schweitzer's junior/senior distinction, as apparently Rider Haggard also was when he created the character of Umslopogaas in *Allen Quatermain*. That is, it may "simply" be

that Stanley's conception of brotherhood with Africans was primarily ceremonial, for, as his protégé E.J. Glave recounts, Stanley arranged for Glave to participate in a ritual of "blood brotherhood" with a nearby chief in order to assure his personal safety. "This custom of blood-brotherhood prevails throughout Central Africa," Glave writes in *In Savage Africa* (1892), "and its observance is the surest way of gaining the confidence of the native chiefs. It has with them a religious significance. The natives who have entered into relations prescribed by this rite invariably respect them, and both Livingstone and Stanley have often owed their safety to the sacredness of the pledges given by chiefs whose favor and protection they gained in this manner. The ceremony took place in Stanley's presence" (46–47).

27. Schweitzer may be consciously echoing here Heine's remark that "it is true that we are all brothers, but I am the big brother, and I am entitled to a more substantial portion" (qtd. in Enright 29). Schweitzer was probably also aware that nineteenth-century abolitionists propagandized for their movement by means of a poster depicting a kneeling, manacled slave, asking the question "Am I not a man and a brother?" (Barker 194).

28. Achebe's contempt for detail becomes apparent when he introduces the long quotation by describing it as "almost a whole page from about the middle of the story when representatives of Europe in a steamer going down the Congo encounter the denizens of Africa" (*HD* 253). It is not altogether irrelevant or unimportant to the meaning of the story that the "representatives of Europe" (substantially assisted by an African crew Achebe has momentarily forgotten) travel not *down* but *up* the Congo River. To be sure, the direction of the river's flow has confused other critics as well. David Thorburn, for example, has Marlow ferrying the dying Kurtz "back up river on his ancient steamer," when it should obviously be back *down*river (143). Also the "ancient" steamer is unlikely to have been more than five years old, and possibly less if it is to be identified with the *Roi des Belges,* on which Conrad traveled upstream to Stanley Falls. The *Roi des Belges* was launched in March 1888, a little more than two years earlier—assuming, of course, that the story is set in 1890, the year Conrad went to the Congo (Liebrechts 208). The first steam-powered vessel on the Upper Congo was brought there by Stanley in 1881.

29. That Conrad is, however, deliberately exaggerating the "primitiveness" of what he saw as he traveled upriver is apparent from Oscar Lenz's detailed account of the same journey five years earlier aboard the *Stanley.* Lenz makes it clear that frequent stops were customary at various well-established native villages along the shore, where, for the most part, the steamer occasioned no surprise and was given a friendly reception. In fact, the only hostile activity Lenz witnessed consisted of several unprovoked attacks launched by the commanding officer, Deane, supposedly in retaliation for native attacks on an earlier occasion. In one instance, Deane's Bangala soldiers actually cut off the head of a dead man, stuck it on a pole, and set it up close to the shore (151–55, 257–64).

30. According to the entry "Africa" in the eleventh edition of the *Encyclopedia Britannica,* "Africa with the exception of the lower Nile Valley and what is known as Roman Africa . . . is, so far as its native inhabitants are concerned, a continent

practically without a history, and possessing no record from which such a history might be reconstructed." This statement reflects the standard historical view during Conrad's lifetime. However, the lack of precolonial historical documentation for Africa (chiefly sub-Saharan Africa) is also acknowledged by the contemporary historian Basil Davidson in a number of his books, including *The Lost Cities of Africa* (128). Achebe censures the well-known Oxford professor of history, Hugh Trevor Roper, for claiming that "African history did not exist" (*HD* 250) but provides no source for the citation. In his 1965 essay "The Novelist as Teacher," Achebe sees his own fiction as fulfilling a historical function: "I would be quite satisfied if my novels (especially the ones I set in the past) did no more than teach my readers that their past—with all its imperfections—was not one long night of savagery from which the first Europeans acting on God's behalf delivered them" (*Hopes* 30).

31. For the concept of historicism in the nineteenth century, see also Culler 15. However, even quite conventional nineteenth-century Christians accepted, according to Philip Curtin, "the idea of stages in human progress. This idea was, in fact, implicit in the Biblical story and in most of the Christian historical traditions" (390).

32. This "scientific" notion has clear links with the traditional stereotype of the African as "child," most notoriously expressed in Rudyard Kipling's description of the African as "half devil and half child." Of this stereotype, V.G. Kiernan remarks that "endorsed at times even by a Livingstone . . . a theory came to be fashionable that mental growth in the African ceased early, that childhood was never left behind" (233). In 1863 James Hunt, president of the Anthropological Society of London, delivered a speech, "The Negro's Place in Nature," to the British Academy. Not only did he maintain that the mental development of Africans stopped at puberty, but he also claimed that they were "nearer to the ape and had a smaller brain than the European" (qtd. in Street 95). That this infantile image of the African has survived well into modern times is evident from Alberto Moravia's observations in 1963 about the "childish character of the African." According to Moravia, the contemporary African is just as fascinated by modern consumer goods as he was earlier "by the brass and copper wire and the Venetian glass beads which the adventurers of a century ago offered them in exchange for gold, ivory and precious woods." Moravia goes on to assert that "there is no difficulty in realizing that Black Africa is at a cultural stage which was precisely that of Europe some thousands of years ago" (5, 7). In his 1974 essay "Colonialist Criticism," Achebe complains about the "latter-day colonialist critic," who, "equally given to big-brother arrogance [as was Albert Schweitzer], sees the African writer as a somewhat unfinished European who with patient guidance will grow up one day and write like every other European" (*Hopes* 46).

33. Rossetti goes on to say that "in contrast to the ethnocentric and racist tradition, Malinowski tried to make his pupils and the general public see that non-European institutions had intrinsic value, that general harm could be done by arbitrarily suppressing them, that they had meaning for the peoples who had evolved them, and that they could be rationally defended against the arguments of the Europeans. . . . He never regarded rural societies as mere primitive and remote provinces

of a vast and superior empire, nor as fossils of past ages of the evolution of man-kind" (486–87). Malinowski himself was very conscious of following in Conrad's footsteps, at least anthropologically speaking (Tiffin 232). According to Adam Kuper, the orthodox contemporary view among anthropologists today is that "there never was such a thing as 'primitive society'" (7).

34. Marlow is not entirely consistent in his position here. A few pages later, while discussing the increasing hunger of the cannibal crew, who have not had a substantial meal for more than a month, he remarks that "they had been engaged for six months (I don't think a single one of them had any clear idea of time as we at the end of countless ages have. They still belonged to the beginnings of time—had no inherited experience to teach them, as it were)" (*HD* 42). Nevertheless, it is clear that even here Marlow views the cannibals' sense of time as strictly a matter of social acculturation.

35. Patrick Brantlinger's assertion that this young woman belongs to a group of "modern-day imperialists, satirically depicted as invaders from a 'spiritualist' alternative world" does not jibe with her adamant opposition to the Duc de Mersch, who, as Brantlinger also recognizes, is undoubtedly based on Leopold II. Perhaps, though he does not say so, the young woman and the other "inheritors" are meant to represent a future counterpart of the "gang of virtue." But then in *Heart of Darkness*, the "virtue" of this gang is personified only by Kurtz, whose fate does not suggest that he will be an inheritor of much of anything (Brantlinger, *Rule* 258). How strongly both Ford and Conrad felt about the odious nature of Leopold may be appreciated from the fictional name they assign to him: Mersch, a combination of the first syllables of the French *Merde* and the German *Scheisse*.

36. It is surely significant that in those sections of the story relating to the Inner Station—the supposed "heart of darkness"—Marlow repeatedly and almost insis-tently refers to the Africans as *humans*. So the cannibal boatmen are described as possessing "one of those human secrets that baffle probability," and when Marlow looks at them, he does so "as you would at any human being" (*HD* 43). The "men on the shore" are, even when hostile and potentially lethal, unquestionably human: they possess "human limbs" (*HD* 46) and are seen indistinctly as "human forms" in the forest (*HD* 52). When he finally sees them up close, Marlow emphasizes their humanity by repeating the word *human*: "streams of human beings—of naked hu-man beings . . . were poured into the clearing" (*HD* 59). Later, together with the Russian he sees "dark human shapes that could be made out in the distance" (*HD* 60); and as the ship departs, he singles out the figure of the helmeted woman among "a mass of human bodies" (*HD* 66).

37. It is possible that Marlow may be referring to the Narrator when, just after he has begun his story, he says, "Light came out of this river since—you say Knights?" (*HD* 9). If so, this would mean that either the Narrator is named "Knights" or else (more probably) that Marlow is referring to the Narrator's earlier remark about the "great knights-errant" (8) who have gone forth from the Thames River. In the latter case, however, this would mean that Marlow has been able to overhear a remark that, so far as it is possible to determine, was meant exclusively for readers of the

story and not for the men aboard the *Nellie*. In other words, a narratologically impossible chronological link would have been established between the time of Marlow's narration and that of the Narrator of the frame story.

38. Herbert Ward, who had paid his last of many visits to Stanley Falls a year before Conrad first came there, took pains to learn three different African languages spoken in the Congo: "the Kikongo, spoken by the lower Congo tribes; the Kibangi, of the Upper Congo; and Kiswahili, the language of Tippo Tib's Arab followers at Stanley Falls" (Ward, *Five* 3). By 1895 forty-two distinct languages had been identified in the Congo Basin alone, only a small number of which had been studied by linguists; for some of the languages of the Upper Congo region, it was only possible to obtain inadequate dictionaries (Wauters 179). It is significant that Conrad nowhere gives any sign of condemning African languages in the way that Christine Bolt says Victorian writers on the subject did, namely "as complex but inferior" because of their supposed "absence of abstract terms, of concepts of a single, beneficient deity in the Christian idiom, and of a recorded literature, except in the Arab-dominated parts of the continent" (149).

39. In Conrad's story "Amy Foster," the English villagers react similarly to Yanko Garool's incomprehensible Polish.

40. Marlow's grunt is not immediately recognizable as such. The sound he makes, "ough," is, however, identical with the sounds made by Baker in *The Nigger of the 'Narcissus,'* sounds that are explicitly identified as grunts. For more on Baker's grunts, see the following note.

41. In *The Nigger of the 'Narcissus,'* which Conrad had completed only a couple of years before starting work on *Heart of Darkness*, one of the main characters, who is clearly intended to be thought of sympathetically, grunts continuously. This is the first mate, Baker, who "had that trick of grunting so [i.e., of making the sound "Ough! Ough! Ough!"] between his words and at the end of sentences. It was a fine effective grunt that went well with his menacing utterance" (12). In contrast, James Wait (the "Nigger" of the title) not only has no grunt at all, but possesses instead a frightful tubercular cough. He speaks and pronounces English better than any other member of the crew: "he enunciated distinctly, with soft precision. The deep rolling tones of his voice filled the deck without effort" (10). In *Romance* (1903), which Conrad was working on with Ford Madox Hueffer not long after finishing *Heart of Darkness*, there is a description of the black commander of a Cuban sugar boat that evokes the cannibal headman: "He was a very good sailor, I believe, taciturn and intelligent. . . . He gave his short orders in low undertones and the others, four stalwart blacks, in the prime of life, executed them in silence" (438).

42. In a letter of December 1903, Conrad says of Carlier that he "took the trouble to make a soldier out of that animal deliberately" (*Letters* 3:94).

43. That Conrad participates in the general "language-crisis" afflicting modernist writers is a point often made by critics. Phil Joffe, for example, remarks that Conrad's supposedly inflationary use of adjectives actually represents "an essential element in the book's meaning. *Heart of Darkness* manifests Conrad's modernist perception of the inadequacies of language" (84).

3. Envisioning Kurtz

1. The first systematic attempt to correlate Conrad's personal experience of the Congo with the account provided in *Heart of Darkness* is Gérard Jean-Aubry's *Joseph Conrad in the Congo* (1926), which makes extensive use of Conrad's "Congo Diary" and his correspondence, as well as contemporaneous Belgian publications. Though Jean-Aubry occasionally takes note of evident differences, such as the absence of any model for the Chief Accountant, he does not ascribe these to any deliberate desire on Conrad's part to effect changes. Instead, they apparently derive, implicitly or explicitly, from inadequate biographical knowledge on our part. So Jean-Aubry is sure Kurtz must have been modeled on someone Conrad knew personally. In his view, this person was Georges Antoine Klein, who died aboard the *Roi des Belges* as it steamed back downriver from Stanley Falls under Conrad's temporary command. (*Congo* 65–66). Jean-Aubry develops this hypothesis more fully in his biography of Conrad, where, even though unable to cite any specific evidence, he affirms his conviction that there is between Klein and Kurtz "much more in common than a mere similarity in names." Of this, he says, "there can be no doubt in the mind of anybody who knows Conrad's psychological method" (*Life* 136). Unlike subsequent biographical critics such as Sherry, Jean-Aubry pretty much takes Conrad's claims regarding the close biographical basis of his story literally.

2. That *Heart of Darkness* does not always reflect Conrad's actual personal experience was suggested as long ago as 1930 by the Danish captain Otto Lütken, who thought that the first part of the novel (up to and including the Central Station) was realistic, whereas the latter part was not based on personal experience. Specifically, he argues that the Inner Station does not resemble the real station as it then existed at Stanley Falls, noting especially the absence of the Arabs. Lütken also suggests that Conrad's depiction of the Belgians in the novel is "less than just" (42). For an account of the Stanley Falls Station, see the Appendix.

3. Marlow explicitly views the meeting with Kurtz at the Inner Station as "the farthest point of navigation and the culminating point of my experience" (*HD* 11). Conrad himself also believed that he had undergone some kind of epiphanic experience on reaching Stanley Falls, one that, like Marlow's, consisted of a profound disillusionment. "A great melancholy descended on me," he writes in "Geography and Some Explorers." "What an end to the idealised realities of a boy's daydreams!" (*Last Essays* 25). From a strictly geographical point of view, there is no doubt that Stanley Falls lies in the "heart" of Africa. As Herbert Ward points out, "It is situated exactly in the middle of central Africa. The distance from the ocean in either direction is about fifteen hundred miles" (Ward, 1890, 155).

4. In November 1888, another central European, Dragutin Lerman, was struck by the generally pleasant and comfortable conditions of Boma, including the hotel (Lopasic 44–45). On the other hand, August Boshart, a German national in the employ of the Congo State, confirms Conrad's impression of the place when he revisited it in November 1890 after an absence of several years. "Over the last twelve years," he writes. "M'Boma has deteriorated progressively. Once in a while a few new wooden shacks spring up in which the blacks lead their disorderly lives,

but the old foreign trading posts that were the real heart of the place are gradually closing down. In reality there is nothing here but a confused conglomerate of hastily constructed wooden and tin shacks covered with tar-paper roofs, with the result that the three or four brick buildings seem ludicrously out of place." Of the celebrated hotel, prefabricated of metal parts in Belgium and assembled on site, Boshart notes that it was infested by insects, including fleas and cockroaches. "The walls," he goes on to observe, "are made of double metal sheets separated by an air space. They are inhabited by legions of rats which during the day shamelessly scurry about the walls and at night noisily and mercilessly gnaw away at everything that isn't locked away securely in steel trunks." Boshart makes similarly deprecating remarks about Matadi, though he excepts the more solid buildings recently put up by the Railway Company. And he has nothing but praise for the establishment and maintenance of the portage road linking Matadi and Stanley Pool: ". . . in the Congo State a five-hundred kilometer long passage has been made that is usable and— given the fact that it is absolutely safe—unique in all of Central Africa" (Boshart 111, 116-17, 130; my translation).

5. Both Sherry and Batchelor were anticipated in 1951 by José Gers, who argued that in *Heart of Darkness* Conrad "massively darkened the oppressive atmosphere which bathes the experience he had lived through, his deception and his disillusions, his quarrels with the 'Manager,' his physical exhaustion" (qtd. in *BCB* 2:551, my translation).

6. In the view at least of the Belgians, Klein's status was so insignificant that he was not provided with an entry in the exhaustive biographical lexicon of Belgian colonial activity, the *Biographie Coloniale Belge*. The *BCB* does, however, have an entry for a Danish national named Hans-Lindholm Kurtzhals, a sometime lieutenant in the Royal Danish Navy, who in June 1892 captained the *Ville de Gand* on its way to Stanley Falls with the notorious Lothaire aboard. After participating in the Arab wars, Kurtzhals completed his service in the Congo in 1900 as captain of the Port of Banana (*BCB* 5:516-17). Why Conrad chose to change the name from Klein to Kurtz is not clear. Ian Watt is apparently indulging his fancy when he remarks that in changing the name from Klein to Kurtz, Conrad was evoking "a much more sonorous and menacing sound" (*Conrad* 137).

7. There is, of course, no doubt that Conrad himself felt a hearty dislike for the two Delcommune brothers and would no doubt have been pleased to find further evidence of their skullduggery. Given the fact, however, that Hodister's position vis-à-vis Alexandre Delcommune was far more secure than that of Kurtz vis-à-vis the Manager, it seems unlikely that he would have been quite so easily outmaneuvered as Kurtz supposedly is. That whites often quarreled among themselves is, of course, something Conrad was fully aware of. Indeed, his other story about Africa, "An Outpost of Progress," is based on that perception. Some thirty years later, Evelyn Waugh's description (174-75) of an absurd misunderstanding between himself and the captain of a Congo paddle-steamer may owe something to Conrad's depiction of the comic aspects of such quarrels.

8. As Jean Stengers points out, the idea that Conrad may have had Hodister in mind when creating Kurtz was suggested as long ago as 1929 by Léon Guébels.

Even so, Stengers finds the identification with Hodister unpersuasive, explicitly agreeing here with the 1971 *TLS* review of Sherry's book ("Leopold's" 752–54, 760). In *Conrad and His World* (1972), however, Sherry makes no mention of Hodister but refers only to Klein as "the model for Kurtz" (62).

9. Achebe is not alone in finding Conrad's association of Africa with "darkness" at least potentially offensive (*HD* 261). Even a defender of Conrad's story such as Frances Singh wonders if Marlow does not push the metaphoric implications of the title too far in a racist direction (271). More generally, Benita Parry writes of the title that it "registers its manifold preoccupations . . . by signifying a geographical location, a metaphysical landscape and a theological category," thereby addressing itself "simultaneously to Europe's exploitation of Africa, the primeval human situation, an archaic aspect of the mind's structure and a condition of moral baseness" (20). Conrad himself may have felt some qualms about the title, for in "Geography and some Explorers" he goes out of his way to say that the atlas that he used as a boy, dating from 1852, "knew nothing, of course, of the Great Lakes. The heart of its African [*sic*] was white and big." A few pages later he tells of being derided by his schoolmates when he put his finger "on a spot in the middle of the then white heart of Africa" (*Last Essays* 20, 24). The equivalent passages in *Heart of Darkness* and *A Personal Record* refer instead to "blank spaces" and make no mention of any "heart." In *Journey without Maps* Graham Greene makes a novel association between "heart" and the map of Africa. He thinks of Africa not as a "particular place, but a shape, a strangeness, a wanting to know . . . the shape, of course, is roughly that of the human heart" (17). Some critics, however, have reacted negatively to Conrad's supposed "blanking" out of Africa. Thus, Christopher Miller notes the "absence" of Africa as a *name* in the story, along with all other African place names (except for quasi-humorous ones like Gran' Bassam and Little Popo). He does not, however, mention the equally absent Belgium or Brussels or, for that matter, the absent London (175). Terry Eagleton, too, hears "at the centre of each of Conrad's works . . . a resonant silence," though it is not specifically a silence associated with the suppression of place names (137). According to Cedric Watts, the absent names have an altogether different significance; they represent Conrad's subtle device for drawing the British reader into an awareness of his complicity with the imperialist abuses in the heart of darkness: "by never actually calling the company Belgian or the region the Congo" and by stressing Kurtz's English and cosmopolitan origins, he "makes it impossible for the British reader to stand smugly aloof from the indictment of imperialism." Suggestive as this argument is, it would follow from the same reasoning that, since the Belgians are also *not* named, their (or their king's) empire is not being specifically impugned (*Preface* 127). Andrea White, however, reaches a conclusion similar to Watts's solely on the basis of Kurtz's partially British origins ("Conrad" 192).

10. Aside from the by now familiar assertion that Kurtz is Marlow's (and perhaps also Conrad's) "double" (Burden, *Heart* 101), various attempts have been made to link Kurtz more or less closely with Conrad's own father (Batchelor 84), with Nietzsche and Schopenhauer (Burden, *Heart* 43), with David Livingstone (Jean-Aubry, *Life* 2:121), and with Cecil Rhodes (Hay 113). Jane Ford proposes Roger

Casement as a possible model, citing a 1923 New York interview with Conrad (129). Molly Mahood suggests J.S. Jameson, another member of Stanley's Emin Pasha relief expedition, as a possibility; she also points to Pierre Mille's story "Le Vieux du Zambèse" as providing a literary parallel (25–26). Yves Hervouet also mentions Rimbaud's *Une Saison en enfer* and Loti's *Le Roman d'un spahi*, as well as echoes of Flaubert and Maupassant (63). Peter Knox-Shaw tries to make a case for identifying Kurtz with the explorer Richard Burton on the basis of the latter's admitted participation in "the dance that initiated the complex rituals of human sacrifice," as well as his great intellect and diabolical reputation (147–48). To this already ample and very mixed bag one might add the name of the Belgian captain Guillaume Van Kerckhoven, who belonged to what might be called the antislavery "gang of virtue" and who apparently was killed accidentally in August 1892 while leading an exploratory mission from the Congo to the Nile. Van Kerckhoven's mother's surname was Miller, possibly indicating English ancestry. In 1891 he became notorious for confiscating ivory worth hundreds of thousands of francs from Arab caravans on the pretext of freeing their slaves. In the process he and his forces killed an estimated eighteen hundred men. In this way Van Kerckhoven helped provoke the outbreak of the so-called Arab Wars, which lasted until 1894 (Ceulemans 326–31). Conrad may have crossed paths with Van Kerckhoven on the latter's arrival in Boma at the beginning of December 1890. According to Albert Chapaux, an early historian of the Congo Free State, Van Kerckhoven deserved to be placed in the first rank of those who contributed to the development of the colony (*BCB* 1:565–73; Bourne 147–64). Jules Marchal also links Kurtz with Van Kerckhoven in his brief discussion of *Heart of Darkness* (Marchal, 1:169). Worth considering too is the possibility that Conrad may have meant his readers to think of Leopold II himself as as a kind of ultimate model for Kurtz. In terms of physique (bald, very tall) Leopold certainly resembled Kurtz, as he did also in personality. Leopold was an immensely energetic and egotistical man, given to vastly ambitious plans and partly deceived by his own hypocrisy but at the same time also motivated by a curious kind of altruism. Like Kurtz, too, "all Europe contributed to the making of" Leopold (*HD* 50). His Cousin Victoria was Queen of England (Kurtz's mother is half-English) and his knowledge of English was nearly as good as his French. Like Kurtz again, Leopold had a German surname (Saxe-Coburg), though his mother was the daughter of the last French king, Louis Phillippe. Also, if we think of the characters of the Amazon and the Intended in allegorical terms as representing, respectively, the Congo and Belgium, Leopold, like Kurtz, has deceived and betrayed—and profoundly touched the lives of—both. Like Kurtz, he was undoubtedly a "remarkable man."

11. This "system" is described in detail by Captain Guillaume Van Kerckhoven in Salmon (*Le Voyage* 76). In his report to the governor-general of the Congo Free State, Van Kerckhoven describes how Arabs habitually attack villages without warning; kill everyone who offers resistance, including women; take the remaining women and children prisoner; and then pillage and lay waste to the buildings. Several days later, they enter into negotiations with the returning male villagers, exchanging prisoners for ivory and leaving behind a garrison to ensure further deliveries. The ac-

tual raiders were not Arabs themselves but mostly members of previously subjugated tribes who were provided with guns and ammunition for the purpose of carrying out these raids under Arab leadership. (See also the Appendix for a more impartial description of this "system" of trade.) As none other than H.M. Stanley himself pointed out, however, this was a "system" (sans the essential ivory component, to be sure) that the Arabs did not invent. It was, in Stanley's view, a system devised and perfected by the British themselves in the seventeenth century: "[T]he system adopted by the British crews in those days was very similar to that employed by the Arabs to-day in inner Africa. They landed at night, surrounded the affected village, and then set fire to the huts, and as the frightened people issued out of the burning houses, they were seized and carried to the ships; or sometimes the skipper, in his hurry for sea, sent his crew to range through the town he was trading with, and, regardless of rank, to seize upon every man, woman, and child they met" ("Slavery" 614). Later in the same essay Stanley describes, in terms similar to those used by Van Kerckhoven, the methods practiced by Tippo Tib and other Arabs to obtain ivory.

12. According to Sir Harry Johnston, as Leopold began to feel more secure in his possession of the Congo, he gradually "de-internationalized" its administration, a process that was complete by about 1890 (*History* 226).

13. In this connection it is relevant to note that Conrad himself was an accomplished draftsman and, while in the Congo, either planned to write or actually wrote reports for an unidentified French-language journal (Mahood 34, 192–93). Examples of his considerable drawing skills may be found in Bernard Meyer 326ff.

14. It seems, however, that Conrad had Stanley in mind in making Kurtz a "journalist." In "Geography and Some Explorers," Conrad strikingly omits Stanley's name from the list of great British explorers, despite the fact that Stanley was the one most closely identified with the exploration of the Congo River and was in fact by this time generally acknowledged to have been the "greatest" of all the British explorers of Africa, including Livingstone and Mungo Park. Conrad does refer to him obliquely, deprecatingly, and unmistakably, however, when, having reached Stanley Falls, his mind is filled with "no great haunting memory, but only the unholy recollection of a prosaic newspaper 'stunt' and the distasteful knowledge of the vilest scramble for loot that ever disfigured the history of human conscience and geographical exploration" (*Last Essays* 25). On the basis of this hostility, it seems possible that Conrad, when planning the story, may originally have thought of Kurtz as a journalist who, like Stanley, first went out to Africa to "explore" and write articles but then (again like Stanley) got caught up in the scramble for loot. That already by 1890 Stanley was viewed by some segments of the British public as a pious hypocrite is evident from a pamphlet like D.J. Nicoll's *Stanley's Exploits; Or, Civilizing Africa* (1890), which features a frontispiece depicting a fully armed Stanley in the foreground standing in prayer while in the background an African, dressed only in a loincloth, is shown hanging dead from a tree. Above Stanley's head a winged John Bull, trumpeting Stanley's name and bearing the inscription "Capital[ism]" on his hat, is about to place a crown of laurels on his head. The reference to "exploits" in the title is clearly two-edged, and indeed on the opening

page Stanley is compared to pirates and Spanish conquistadores rather than to honorable explorers like Livingstone (5).

The word *scramble*, when applied to European imperialist expansion in Africa, refers primarily to the decade following the 1885 Berlin Conference, which sanctioned Leopold's rule in the Congo. Looking back in disgust at the end of this period, Robert Brown writes that it was "distinguished by many of the least dignified features of 'land-grabbing' on a large scale." His description of the results of the scramble reads like a translation into numbers of the map Marlow sees hanging in the company offices in Brussels: "The scramble over, the participants sat down to count their gains. Of the 11,500,000 square miles of continental Africa, 2,300,000 of the Sahara are not coveted by any European Power, though France regards herself as possessing a claim on all between Algeria and Senegal, and Spain a huge tract behind the Rio de Oro. But over 8,000,000 are, more or less directly, attached to some European Power. Of this area France has 2,750,000 square miles, with a population of 24,000,000. Britain comes next with 1,828,000 square miles and 35,000,000 people. Germany asserts her power over 822,000 square miles, with an estimated population of 6,000,000. Italy over 603,000 square miles and 6,3000,000 subjects; Spain over 213,770 square miles and 437,000 people; and the Congo State over 900,000 square miles and 14,000,000 people" (176–78). Of this imperialist land-grabbing rivalry, E.M. Forster has one of his characters remark in *Howards End* (1910) that "it is the vice of the vulgar mind to be thrilled by bigness, to think that a thousand square miles are a thousand times more wonderful than one square mile, and that a million square miles are the same as heaven" (29).

15. Aside from the focus in both characters on their voices, there remains a central and enduring question as to whether they are "real" or "shams." Further points of resemblance are that they both provoke a compelling fascination (or antipathy) on the part of the other characters and that they both must die and be removed from their respective vessels before the voyage can be completed.

16. Conrad himself, however, seems to have believed that *Heart of Darkness* did possess a kernel of meaning. Describing the story to Blackwood, he wrote that "the *idea* in it is not as obvious as in *Youth*—or at least not so obviously presented" (*Letters* 2:139). And writing to Cunninghame Graham, Conrad again refers to "the idea" of the story as being "so wrapped up in secondary notions that You—even You!—may miss it" (*Letters* 2:157). In the letter to Blackwood, Conrad specifies that the "idea" of the story is "the criminality of inefficiency and pure selfishness when tackling the civilizing work in Africa," but in the letter to Cunninghame Graham it seems only vaguely associated with a "right intention" that may refer to its anti-imperialist bias. Whatever it is, however, this "idea" cannot be identical with the "shell" or "husk" of Marlow's tale.

17. Eloise Knapp Hay calls Marlow "a detective of the human soul" (129). The structure of a trial, with the interviewing of relevant witnesses, is also imitated in *Lord Jim*, the composition of which Conrad interrupted to write *Heart of Darkness*.

18. As confirmed by the "special recommendations" that "were turning up again" in the letters that Kurtz receives on board the steamer and which lead him to tell Marlow that he is "glad," presumably because he recognizes in him a fellow

member of the "gang of virtue" (*HD* 60). Marlow's is a very peculiar type of lie: he lies about telling a lie, but lies about it in such a way that we immediately recognize it for what it is, namely a truth. The fact that this "lie" is no lie may also reflect favorably on the later lie that he tells the Intended, a lie that has caused much discussion and dissension among critics of the story. It too is more of a passive than an active lie, told chiefly because Marlow recognizes that it is precisely what his interlocutor wants and expects to hear. Besides, since he had earlier promised the Russian Harlequin to keep Kurtz's reputation safe, Marlow would have been breaking his word if he had told Kurtz's fiancée what his last words actually were (*HD* 62). As Marlow assures his friends aboard the *Nellie*, he has "remained loyal to Kurtz to the last, and even beyond" (*HD* 70). Part of the reason why the rites are unspeakable is apparently because Marlow has made a vow never to speak of them, a vow that he has kept in the letter if not altogether in the spirit.

19. Joseph Dobrinsky speculates that, aside from the possible pun on "curse," Conrad may be referring obliquely to his own surname, Korzeniowski (Kurtz/Korz). Though Dobrinsky does not make the connection with the mysterious phrase "man in the name," it would follow from his argument that Conrad himself is the man in the name (2).

20. J. Hillis Miller resolves the problem by the simple expedient of substituting the preposition *behind* for the preposition *in* (213), whereas for Homi Bhabha, "Kurtz is just a word, not the man with [*sic*] a name" (124).

21. In his letter to Cunninghame Graham of February 8, 1899, Conrad tells him that he "must remember that I don't start with an abstract notion. I start with definite *images* and as their rendering is true some little effect is produced" (*Letters* 2:157–58, my italics). Frederick Karl even goes so far as to argue that the whole of *Heart of Darkness* "is structured like an imagist poem on a series of trenchant images whose cumulative effect is to provide a frame for Kurtz" (*Reader's Guide* 124). According to J. Hillis Miller, "all Conrad's work turns on this double paradox: first the paradox of the two senses of seeing, seeing as physical vision and seeing as seeing through, as penetrating to or unveiling the hidden invisible truth, and second the paradox of seeing the darkness in terms of the light" (210–11). Miller does not "see," however, that for Conrad the concept of *sight* also includes the eidetic imagination, or what I have called "envisioning." H.M. Daleski, who also approaches *Heart of Darkness* in terms of "seeing," equates "penetration" (of people and places) with "insight" (52). The phenomenon is not identical with, but related to, the "visualizing faculty" as described by Sir Francis Galton in his chapter "Mental Imagery" in *Inquiries into Human Faculty and Its Development*, first published in 1883 (57–78).

22. Edward Garnett recounts how, when Conrad first told him the story of *Heart of Darkness*, it was longer by at least a third than the story he got around to writing soon thereafter (14). It also included the above scene from Mungo Park's *Travels*, recounted as if it had been part of Conrad's own experience. It was not until Hay (121) noticed the resemblance between the two episodes that Conrad's confusion of his own experience with that of another person was revealed. That Conrad took care to back up his own experience with extensive reading from geo-

graphical and historical sources is evident from his ironic remarks about supposedly getting the cultural background wrong in his Malaysian stories: "Curiously enough all the details about the little characteristic acts and customs which they hold up as proof [of Conrad's supposed ignorance] I have taken out (to be safe) from undoubted sources—dull, wise books" (*Letters* 2:130). Similarly dull and wise sources clearly supplemented Conrad's own experience in the writing of *Heart of Darkness*.

23. Jacques Darras takes a further and even more ironic step by claiming that in Marlow's quest for Kurtz, Conrad is retelling the story of *How I Found Livingstone*, but with the roles of Stanley and Livingstone reversed. Not that Conrad is doing anything so simple as a simple reversal, however; no, his real aim, according to Darras, is "to prove that a kind of complicity, reproducing the real complicity which existed between Livingstone and Stanley, unites Marlow and Kurtz" (66). The kind of complicity they share is symbolic: they are the "two halves of the West. . . . The other side of Livingstone is Stanley. Angel and beast cannot be separated" (67). Unlike Achebe, Darras manages to discover the "Other" not in Africa generally but in the isolated figure of Kurtz.

24. Some of the contradictory nature of Kurtz is probably also attributable to Conrad's desire to have his readers associate him with Goethe's Faust. For more on Conrad's use of Goethe, see my *Death of the German Cousin* (57–60).

25. Tzvetan Todorov arrives at a roughly similar conclusion about *Heart of Darkness* by a rather different and somewhat more circuitous route. In his view, "the story of Kurtz symbolizes the act of fiction, a construct based on a hollow center . . . Conrad's allegory is intratextual: if the search for Kurtz's identity is an allegory for the act of reading, then reading symbolizes in turn all processes of knowledge, of which the knowledge of Kurtz is but one example. The symbolized tale takes on a symbolizing function of what was previously symbolized; symbolization is thus reciprocal" ("Knowledge" 174).

26. The successive changes in Kurtz's facial expression (pride, power, terror, despair) presumably are meant to correspond with a series of inner changes reflecting a progressive loss of confidence and, perhaps, self-centeredness. Significantly, Marlow's description differs radically from that provided by the standard British work on human emotions at the time, Charles Darwin's *Expression of Emotions in Man and Animals* (1872), where, soliciting responses to a picture showing a man experiencing horror, Darwin notes that thirteen of twenty-three respondents identified it as "horror, great pain, torture, or agony; three answered extreme fright. . . . Six, however, said anger. . . . One said disgust." Darwin also observes that horror is usually accompanied by a series of characteristic body movements, such as the raising of both shoulders, "a shudder, as well as by a deep expiration or inspiration. . . . The sounds thus made are expressed by words like *uh* or *ugh*" (305). Kurtz's "horror," however, is strictly confined to his face, and he remains fully articulate even at this extreme moment. These facts imply that Conrad meant Kurtz to retain his dignity and "remarkability" to the very end. This is also evident in Marlow's habit of usually referring to Kurtz as "Mr. Kurtz" throughout the narrative.

27. Jeffrey Meyers makes the interesting point that Marlow's account of Kurtz's last moments of life is untrustworthy because "like the other white men and the

Africans who have been transformed from vital and energetic coastal men into list-less corpses in the Grove of Death, Marlow has been severely affected by the jungle. . . . Though Marlow does not realize it, he has become unmoored and has lost his precious grip on reality" (*Fiction* 65). If Meyers is right about Marlow's becoming unhinged and lapsing into unreliability at this stage of his journey, then it follows that the older, narrating Marlow must be unreliable too, for it is after all he who is providing us with the unreliable information. If correct, this would help account for his lasting fascination with Kurtz and his continuing, almost supernatural visions of him. It would also, however, throw the *whole* of the older Marlow's narrative into question, not just that part of it concerned with Kurtz's final moments. And that, I think, is a consequence most readers of the story are not prepared to accept.

28. Martin Green suggests that Conrad is the first important novelist to turn his attention away from the successes and toward the failures of empire: "Conrad saw—and this was why subsequent writers chose him as their godfather—that the Empire was a stage strewn with extraordinary failures, as well as with extraordinary successes." Though Green does not make the point, Kurtz would seem to be even more remarkable in this gallery of failures because he is simultaneously a failure and a success, whereas Jim is (apparently) more conventionally first a failure and then a success (307).

4. Imperial Sham and Reality in the Congo

1. A simple (too simple?) way of resolving the disparity between the original and the sham Kurtz is to argue that the original one was sane, the sham one mad. Madness is certainly a component of (and excuse for) the later Kurtz's behavior, though Marlow is careful to point out that while the soul is mad, his mind remains lucid. In a letter to Blackwood written more than two years later (May 31, 1902), Conrad stresses the crucial importance of the "last pages" of the story, that is "the interview of the man and the girl." This section provides a "suggestive view of a whole phase of life [presumably of the "original" Kurtz] and makes of that story something quite on another plane than an anecdote of a man of a man who went *mad* in the Centre of Africa" (*HD* 210, my italics).

2. In the 1917 "Author's Note" Conrad says that "it is well known that curious men go prying into all sorts of places (where they have no business) and come out of them with all kinds of spoil. This story, and one other ["An Outpost of Progress"], not in this volume, are all the spoil I brought out from the centre of Africa, where, really, I had no sort of business" (*HD* 4). The equation here between the business of the writer and that of the imperialist (and the further redefinition of that "business" as *spoil*) lies only just beneath the surface. Paradoxically, there would be no "ivory" (art) without the exploitations of a Kurtz (imperialism). This is, as Stein says of Jim's romanticism, "'very bad—very bad. . . . Very good, too'" (*Lord Jim* 132).

3. This idea that Africans show unusual restraint in resisting temptation eventually became a kind of commonplace among subsequent literary voyagers in Africa. André Gide remarks that his carriers and servants were "scrupulously honest"

and that no theft occurred although he left valuable objects lying about in the open—"a thing we should never dare do in France" (94). Similarly, it astonished Graham Greene that he was "able to travel through an unpoliced country with twenty-five men who knew that my money-box contained what to them was a fortune in silver" (87).

4. There is some question as to Conrad's supposed failure to grasp the essentially ritual aspects of cannibalism. According to Patrick Brantlinger, the notion of so-called food cannibalism is purely "mythical" ("Victorians" 184). There is, however, plentiful contemporaneous evidence testifying to its existence. Emil Torday, for example, describes it as an "everyday occurrence" for which "he has never been able to trace any magical or religious basis" (83–84). The entry "Cannibalism" in the eleventh edition of the *Encyclopedia Britannica* distinguishes among various types of cannibalism in different parts of the world but adds that "simple food cannibalism is common in Africa." Ian Watt even goes so far as to claim as an "incontrovertible fact" that "there really was a great deal of cannibalism in this part of the Congo" ("Critics" 7). Regardless of the actual historical facts, however, it is important to remember that at the time Conrad wrote *Heart of Darkness* it was generally believed that food cannibalism did exist in sub-Saharan Africa and that Conrad was merely reflecting this general view.

5. The word *detribalization* did not exist at the time Conrad wrote, but some part of its meaning is captured in his notion of being out of place, as expressed in the 1917 "Author's Note." Suggestively, Hugh Clifford uses the word *denationalization* for Kurtz in his 1902 *Spectator* review of *Heart of Darkness* but fails to elaborate more fully on the idea (*Conrad* 144). Harold Collins first applied the concept systematically more than forty years ago, but his analysis is largely limited to the Africans in the story (299–310). Avrom Fleishman also recognizes the process at work among whites but applies the word itself only to blacks (82, 91).

6. That Conrad identified with the Roman commander is apparent from his more extended re-creation of the latter's situation in the autobiographical *Mirror of the Sea*, where, just after finishing his account of the Romans' first cautious voyage up into the Thames estuary, he describes his own reactions on first viewing this "historic spot" (101–3).

7. This idea of the "dumb" capables may derive from Carlyle, especially as it is developed in *Past and Present*. Benjamin Kidd applies the idea to British imperial expansion by arguing that individual intellectual ability is not necessary and may even be an impediment to "social efficiency" (94). A character like Singleton in *The Nigger of the 'Narcissus'* exemplifies this type of admirable but purely intuitive person. However, a real hero in Conrad's world must possess brains as well as brawn, as is the case with Stein or Marlow or even Kurtz.

8. In "Geography and Some Explorers," Conrad distinguishes between an ethic of the sea and an ethic of the land, remarking that he had never felt lonely in the vastness of the sea, whereas he had undergone an epiphany of solipsism one night while his boat lay moored just below Stanley Falls (*Last Essays* 24–26).

9. It is important to remember that, despite the fact that Kurtz has been in Africa for only a year when Marlow first meets him, he is not a raw beginner but

has behind him something of a career in journalism, politics, painting, and perhaps administration. In this respect he differs not only from the "young chap in a toga" but also from those young Congo State officials who quickly lost their moral bearings after arriving in Africa. Of this latter group Alfred Parminter, a friend of E.J. Glave's who came to the Congo in the early eighties, remarks that they are responsible for much of the misery of the native population because of "(1) the absolute inexperience of most of the officers; (2) the impossibility of checking their actions from headquarters. For the most part the officers arrive straight from a Belgian town. They have probably never been outside their own country before, and on suddenly being thrust, with almost unlimited power, among conditions that are strange, dangerous, unhealthy and depressing, it is no wonder that they lose their heads, and adopt their own means to obtain rapid promotion and wealth, in order the sooner to return to Europe. Hence the endless cases of brutality that occur" ("Belgian" 2).

10. Though of course Conrad does tell the "Manager's" story, from a profoundly satirical point of view, in "An Outpost of Progress."

11. In this phrase lies part of the explanation for the presence of the blindfolded woman in the picture that Kurtz had left behind and which Marlow happens see in the Central Station. The other part—presumably the part intended by Kurtz—is that the goddess of justice is usually depicted with her eyes blindfolded.

12. The notion of "efficiency" has been much discussed by Conrad's critics, especially with reference to Benjamin Kidd's use of the term in *Social Evolution* (1894). For a general discussion of Kidd, "efficiency," and imperialism, see Semmel 34–75. For the ways in which these ideas are relevant to Conrad, see Watt, *Conrad* 157; and Hawkins, "Critique" 288–90. According to Avrom Fleishman, Conrad cannot be endorsing Marlow's enthusiasm for "efficiency" and Carlyle's work ethic because that would mean he "would have had to acknowledge the value of German ventures in Africa" (94). Hawkins agrees with this view, citing Conrad's 1915 denunciation of Germany as "'that promised land . . . of efficiency'" ("Critique" 295). Aside from the fact that there is a considerable gap in time between 1899 and 1915, both Fleishman and Hawkins seem to forget that, even before he had finished writing his story, Conrad famously described it to his publisher William Blackwood as dealing with the "criminality of inefficiency and pure selfishness . . . in Africa" (*Letters* 2:139–40). Furthermore, Marlow specifically and ironically identifies the German presence in Africa with the purple patch on the map where the "jolly pioneers of progress drink the jolly lager beer" (*HD* 13)—hardly indications of their devotion to efficiency. In fact, Germans in Conrad's fiction (with the notable exception of Stein) are generally represented as lazy, shiftless, and rather cowardly braggarts. The German captain of the *Patna* and the villainous Schomberg are examples. It would seem more likely that we are intended to equate "efficiency" with the "real work" that Marlow claims is being performed in the "vast amounts of red" on the map (*HD* 13), especially since the contrast between what is "real" and what is "sham" is an important recurrent theme in the novel. H.M. Daleski, who also thinks Conrad is using the concept of efficiency ironically, bases his conclusion on the fact that the "first-class" agent Kurtz is reputed to be very efficient. This line of argu-

ment ignores the fact that Kurtz would not be of any real interest to Marlow (or to us) if he did not possess at least some "redeeming" virtues; moreover, it should be clear that his reputation for efficiency among the Pilgrims is not based on an accurate assessment on their part of the real nature of the "methods" employed by him. Also, as Jan Verleun points out, the book on shipbuilding by Towser/Towson, aside from representing English skill and efficiency, is associated by the Russian, who is thereby also made to seem a favorable figure, with the neat pile of wood left behind (197). It should also be noted that elsewhere in Conrad's fiction of about this time, efficiency tends to be thought of positively. Thus, the youthful Nostromo is described as being "a prodigy of efficiency in his own sphere of life" (*Nostromo* 48). Finally, if it is indeed true, as Sven Lindqvist argues, that Conrad was to some degree inspired to write *Heart of Darkness* because of the discussion of Congo State atrocities published in the *Saturday Review* on December 17, 1898, then one should also take into account the view expressed there that the "true moral" to be extracted from those atrocities is simply that, unlike the British Royal Niger Company, the "company chartered by Europe with King Leopold as chairman" has failed to make "the most of its opportunities." Britain, in other words, has shown itself to be an efficient imperial power, whereas Belgium has not ("Courtney" 802).

13. Sir Harry Johnston seems almost to have this passage of *Heart of Darkness* in mind when he remarks, "[A]s regards the Negro or any other backward race, I am not a sentimentalist. I have no pity in retrospect for the sufferings of the Celtic and Iberian inhabitants of Great Britain during their conquest by the Romans, I do not regret the Norman remodelling of England. These movements have done much to make the United Kingdom one of the foremost among the civilized free nations. The greater part of Africa has got to submit to a similar discipline. There are many tribes of Negroes at the present day who are leading lives not much superior in intellectual advancement to those of brutes; *but there is not an existing race of man in Africa that is not emphatically human and capable of improvement*" ("Introductory" xii–xiii).

14. Something very much like this indignation is expressed by Conrad himself in a letter dated July 22, 1896, written while he was working on "An Outpost of Progress": "All the bitterness of those days, all my puzzled wonder as to the meaning of all I saw—all my indignation at masquerading philanthropy—have been with me again, while I wrote" (*HD* 199).

15. This ironically intended oxymoronic designation is further defined as "the new gang" (*HD* 28) by the Mephistophelean Brickmaker, a name that suggests that an important change of policy had occurred back in Belgium, one that presumably was meant to take the high ideals of a "civilizing mission" more seriously than had been the case with the old gang of vice. This hypothesis is apparently confirmed by the Manager's subsequent report to his uncle that, during his brief stay at the Central Station, Kurtz had harangued him about how "each station should be a beacon on the road towards better things, a centre for trade of course but also for humanising, improving, instructing" (*HD* 34). Significantly, Marlow is himself surprised to discover that he is perceived as being a member of this "new gang." Aside from Kurtz, he encounters no other members, a circumstance that indicates either that there is

no such progressive group among the colonial officials or that its numbers are minimal. In terms of Leopold's actual policy toward the Congo, there is no evidence that such a change was in fact being introduced, though Conrad may have been under the impression that it was, given the international antislavery meeting that was taking place in Brussels from November 1889 to July 1890, at the very time he was hired (Emerson 151). In actual fact, it was at approximately this time that Leopold issued secret orders regarding state monopolization of the ivory trade and the payment of illegal premiums for agents recruiting native labor. By dividing in this way the whites in the Congo into bad and (possibly) good ones, Conrad may also have been attempting to provide a more "balanced" view of what was happening there. It is true that, historically, there were two often overlapping groups of colonial officials in the Congo: those who were directly employed by the Free State and those who were employed by closely linked trading companies, such as the Sanford Exploring Expedition (later to become the Societé Anonyme pour le Commerce du Haut-Congo). Arthur Hodister, for example, worked for the Free State during his first three-year tour of duty and then shifted to Sanford for the second. At the time he was killed in May 1892, he was serving as director of the Syndicat·Commercial du Katanga (*BCB* 1:515).

16. Conrad's account of the used-up people, the random blasting, and the rusting machinery makes it seem as if all this "sham" work had been going on for some time. In fact, however, actual work on the railway bed at Matadi began only a little more than two months before Conrad arrived on the scene, and the first rails and sleepers shipped there were actually part of the cargo of the *Ville de Maceio* on the same voyage that Conrad took (*BCB* 2:549; Wauters xxxiii).

17. Aside from the June 1896 account mentioned in the *Spectator* of his experiences as an officer of Leopold's *Force Publique* in 1894 and 1895, Salusbury published two more essays about the Congo State in the *United Service Magazine*. The first responded to a letter and an interview published in the British press, respectively by his sometime commanding officer in the Congo, Francqui, and by Sir Hugh Gilzean Reid ("Defenders"); and the second was an account of the so-called Stokes affair ("Murder"). Replying to Salusbury's several attacks on the Congo State activities, Henry Morgan Stanley, M.P., published his own refutation in the *United Service Magazine,* citing as evidence official records and correspondence from Salusbury both to him personally and to other representatives of the Congo State. Stanley's apparent intention in this essay was to make Salusbury out to be a greedy, lying, and backstabbing malcontent ("Captain").

18. According to Christopher Gogwilt, Homi Bhabha "suggestively replaces the 'white thread' with 'white writing' to show how the metonym for narrative draws attention of [*sic*] colonialist discourse" (124). Less abstractly, Brian Spittles points out that since this thread is not only white but also made of worsted, that could only have meant "English manufacture." The conclusion to be drawn from this fact—a conclusion, according to Spittles, apparently intended by Conrad—is that British imperialism is complicit with Belgian imperialism in the Congo (76–77). More likely, however, is the possibility that the dying African is actually a British subject, since most of the African workers on the railway were in fact re-

cruited in the British colonies. During the initial stages of construction there were virtually no Congolese blacks employed.

19. This is not, I think, a reference to Kurtz but either to one of the Pilgrims on board Marlow's steamer, "a little fat man with sandy hair and red whiskers, who wore side-spring boots, and pink pyjamas tucked into his socks" (*HD* 41) or, more likely, to the Manager himself, who shortly before reaching the Inner Station, hypocritically (in order "to preserve appearances") informs Marlow that he would be "desolated" if anything were to happen to Kurtz. Even if we do not accept Cedric Watts's suggestive theory (*Deceptive* 120) that *Heart of Darkness* is actually a "murder story," with the Manager deliberately delaying the expedition to relieve a gravely ill Kurtz, still the Machiavellian Manager and his butcherlike uncle are fitting manifestations of malicious folly. The same theory was put forward by Alan Hunter (15–16) at about the same time as Watts but with less detail, and both Watts and Hunter may be indebted to Ian Watt's raising the possibility in the first place (*Conrad* 140).

20. This figure is probably meant to be read as a satirical sketch of Henry Morgan Stanley, though Stanley himself had grave reservations about the kind of agents the company in Brussels sent out to him. One of his books contains a whole chapter on the miserable failures that all but four percent of those agents were. He even provides an account of "one, who has loudly professed himself to be heroic," who shows himself utterly incapable of even keeping the station under his charge in some semblance of order. Returning to this "hero's" station some months later, Stanley finds that "the wild grass has overrun our native village, so that it is scarcely visible. Not one house has been added to the structures we had raised for him. The station is also in a state of siege; a palisaded circle shows that once an alarm had bestirred him to spasmodic action; famine beleaguers the garrison; four days searching far and wide only brings enough to last a few hours; the stores are empty; there are only enough brass rods to last three days. The natives leave him and his station so severely alone that he is in actual risk of starvation" (*Congo* 2:244–45). The first stations on the Kasai River (the setting for "An Outpost of Progress") were established in late 1884 at Luluabourg and Luebo by the German explorer Wissmann. They were staffed by Captain de Macar and Lt. Paul Lemarinel, respectively, neither of whom suffered anything like the fate described by Conrad in his story (Liebrechts 133; Dupont 205).

21. The theme of progress, usually treated ironically, is prominent in Conrad's early work. The folly of *Almayer's Folly* is primarily Almayer's foolish sense of his supposed white superiority over his Malaysian wife and prospective son-in-law, Dain, but the title itself specifically refers to the large, uncompleted house he built when it seemed as if the British Empire was about to expand into his part of northern Borneo; here, too, the apparent prospect of progress leads to actual regression, as it does also, even though in different ways and for quite different reasons, in Jim's Patusan. Moreover, the modernization described by the narrator as having taken place in Singapore between the middle and the end of the nineteenth century in "The End of the Tether" (*Youth* 54–64) is by no means wholly favorable; and the debate on the subject of progress between the optimistic Whalley and the pessimistic Van Wyck is clearly won by the latter when the former reaches the real and

symbolic end of his "tether." In "The Outpost of Progress," Conrad almost seems to be elaborating on Baudelaire's acid remark that "belief in Progress is a doctrine of idlers and Belgians. It is the individual relying upon his neighbours to do his work" (61). How consciously or deliberately Conrad may have been echoing Baudelaire in *Heart of Darkness* is uncertain, though Patricia Clements (along with Ian Watt) sees Baudelaire's poem "Le Voyage" as a probable influence. She even goes so far as to argue that Conrad "plays throughout with Baudelairean sources"—the overturned railway car at the Outer Station, for example, supposedly evokes "Une Charogne" (7, 389). The influence, to be sure, has not gone all one way, for as Christopher Miller remarks in connection with French writings about Africa, *Heart of Darkness* is "the strongest of all Africanist texts" (170, 182 n).

22. One of the members of Alexandre Delcommune's Katanga expedition (the "Eldorado Expedition" of the novel) was a Russian count named Soustchof, whom Conrad may have met or at least heard of (*BCB* 2:260).

5. Unspeakable Rites and Speakable Rights

1. This character especially seems emblematic of the "sham" enterprise associated with the "gang of vice." Instead of doing "real work," such as making bricks, he spends his time intriguing for petty perks like candles or doing small-time spying on behalf of the Manager. Here again, however, Conrad may be deliberately attempting to make the practical achievements of Leopold's agents seem more futile than they actually were. According to Lieut. Theodore Masui, bricks (both red and white) were in fact successfully produced for the first time on the Upper Congo in 1887 in Bangala, a port halfway between Kinshasa (the Central Station) and Stanley Falls (the Inner Station). Conrad and the *Roi des Belges* stopped there in August 1890; thus he would have had an opportunity to observe their manufacture and view at least one extant brick structure. Stopping in Bangala in 1888, Herbert Ward admired the nearly completed "new brick house, intended for a mess room and a provision store," whose construction featured "a double arch at the top in alternate red and white bricks" (Werner 197). Also, as early as 1889 some of the buildings at the English Baptist Mission in Kinshasa were made of brick (Lopasic 130). According to Masui, the long-range goal of the Congo Free State was to produce brick housing not only for its white agents but also for its black employees. He envisioned a time twenty years further on—he was writing in 1897—when the interior of Africa would boast brick homes "similar to the villas of our suburbs" (Masui 229–30, my translation).

2. Of the "wonderful fascination" of craniometry, the Cambridge anthropologist Alfred Haddon remarks in 1898—the same year Conrad began writing *Heart of Darkness*—that he had succumbed to its charms after a period of initial skepticism. It was put on a pseudoscientific footing by the French anatomist Paul Broca in the 1860s; and Darwin's so-called bulldog, T.H. Huxley, was the acknowledged leading practitioner of the "science" in Britain. The great anthropologist Edward Taylor applied craniometrical techniques to the comparative study of races, an enterprise that eventually led him to believe in "the general inferiority of all non-

Caucasian races" (Thompson 30). Alfred Wallace (whose book on Malaysia was a favorite of Conrad's) published in 1898 an essay on the "Neglect of Phrenology" (as the study of the relation of skull shape to psyche was called), in which he lamented the formation of "enormous collections of skulls" by British scientists who, aside from measuring and cataloging them, reached no meaningful conclusions. "Never perhaps," writes Wallace, "was so much scientific work productive of so inadequate a result" (183). Craniology is mocked in one of Conrad's favorite books of the sea, Captain Marryat's *Mr. Midshipman Easy,* where the hero Jack's eccentric, republican father is satirized for his passion for measuring skulls (368). It is these associations that perhaps account for Conrad's ironic sketch of the company doctor, though in symbolic terms a link is also apparently intended between the Belgian preoccupation with skulls in the sepulchral city and Kurtz's grisly collection of "decorative" skulls in the heart of Africa.

    3. This character too seems to have had an actual real-life original. Asked by a Polish acquaintance in 1914 what had most impressed him of all the sights he had ever seen in his life, Conrad replied (perhaps ironically) that it was "'a certain woman, a Negress. That was in Africa. Hung with bracelets and necklaces, she was walking in front of a railway station'" (qtd. in Watt, *Conrad* 138). As Watt sensibly points out, Conrad's memory must be playing tricks on him here, since no railway line (much less a station) was in existence in the Congo at the time Conrad went there. Indeed, Marlow witnesses what appear to be its pathetically inadequate beginnings in the Outer Station. What Watt fails to grasp, however—not that he is to blame, since he is relying on an original misapprehension of Conrad's interlocutor, Angela Zagórska, further compounded by an inadequate translation—is that Conrad was referring here not to a railway station but to a company station, like the one he stayed in at Kinshasa (the Central Station of the story). Zagórska evidently misunderstood Conrad's Polish answer, for she goes on to fantasize about seeing a small railway station "like (for instance) Wolomin, transported into the depths of Africa" (Najder, *Joseph Conrad* 218). But Conrad was not talking about that kind of station at all, as his remark in French to Zagórska's mother (also quoted by Zagórska) makes obvious: "'C'était la maitresse du chef de la station.'" In French, the word for railway station is *gare,* not *station.* It would seem to follow, therefore, that Conrad *did* base his portrait of the Black Amazon on a woman he had actually seen and was very likely acquainted with, given the fact that she was the mistress of the station manager and Conrad's immediate superior, presumably Camille Delcommune (though, as explained below, in his conversation with Zagórska he may actually have been referring to Alexandre Delcommune). If this woman is indeed the original of the Black Amazon, it is now at least (and at last) possible to conclude definitively what the relationship is between her and Kurtz—they are lovers. Nevertheless, whatever immense impression the very impressive black woman at the station made on Conrad, she seems to have had nothing of the warrior queen about her, so that some of her most memorable characteristics must be sought for elsewhere, possibly in fictional sources. According to Bernard Pinian, the sources of this "hieratic goddess of inaccessible beauty" are to be sought in Flaubert's *Salammbô,* Mallarmé's *Herodiade,* and Oscar Wilde and Richard Strauss's opera *Salomé.* "The domain to

which *Heart of Darkness* refers," Pinian concludes, "belongs less to the equator than to the stage of the Théâtre des Champs-Elysées, namely among Serge Diaghilev's ballets and Igor Stravinsky's *Rite of Spring*" (51, my translation). According to Hugo Ridley, late-nineteenth-century French colonialist fiction at times dealt explicitly with white European male/black African female relationships, notably in Pierre Loti's *Le Roman d'un spahi* (1881) and Vigné d'Octon's *Chaire noire* (1889), though in virtually all of these cases the relation is shown to be flawed because of the women's excessive sexual demands (81). British novelists tended to avoid depicting interracial sexual relationships or marriages (or when they did, as in Rider Haggard's *She*, the principal white male characters married *white* African princesses). Nevertheless, it should be kept in mind that most works of exploration and travel dealing with Africa showed nude or seminude African women either in photographs or drawings, thereby drawing their predominantly male, white European readers' attention to female African sexuality. Conrad's extremely positive and relatively asexual description of the Black Amazon is, to the best of my knowledge, unique in an interracial context, made even more unusual in that there were relatively few accounts for him to draw on of contemporaneous women in the Congo who either occupied leading roles in the social structure of their tribes or led them into battle. Two of these isolated instances occur in a text possibly known to Conrad, Winwood Reade's popular *Savage Africa* (1864), where the seventeenth-century Queen Shinga of the Kingdom of the Congo (located in what is now Angola) is said to have fought many successful wars, or the even more formidable Tebandumba, queen of the Jagas, who was a celebrated warrior given to killing her lovers after sex and then feasting on their remains (289–95). Dr. L. Wolf, who accompanied Hermann von Wissmann in his exploration of the Kasai River, gives an account of how, when he approached a group of hostile warriors lining the shore of the river, "suddenly the chief's daughter rushed to the water's edge, commanded the sullen crowd to drop their weapons, and invited the white man ashore" (Adams 39). Conrad may also have been aware that Alexandre Delcommune, under whose command he had originally hoped to undertake an exploratory voyage, was married to an African "princess of royal blood" (Slade 82).

4. William Golding is probably alluding to this passage when, in *Lord of the Flies,* he describes the grinning head of a pig killed by a group of marooned boys. The identification rises even closer to the surface when Golding's protagonist, Ralph, is threatened with a stick that has been sharpened at both ends, suggesting that his head, once severed, is to be impaled on it.

5. See chapter 6 for a more detailed discussion of the links between Rom and Kurtz and, more generally, between Glave and Conrad.

6. Of Torday, Basil Davidson, the well-known progressive historian of Africa, remarks that despite being an "enthusiast," "his thoughts on the past of central Africa, even if they stray a little to the side of romantic idealism, are none the less nearer to the truth than the miseries of savage chaos that others have presented as a description of that past" (19–20).

7. That the display of skulls could also serve a cautionary function in Congolese villages (not just for Kurtz's "rebels") is apparent in H.H. Johnston's account

of a village near Bólóbó where "many skulls were stuck on the top of the houses. They were those of mis-doers, we were told, who had been slain by the fetish-man for their crimes, and their skulls were then exposed for the admiration of others" (*River* 249). That Marlow (and evidently Conrad, too) is so obviously ironic about Kurtz's "rebels" is interesting in light of the repeated revolts on the part of various Congo tribes to overthrow Belgian rule. These followed the successful prosecution of the so-called Arab War in 1892 and were not entirely put down until 1900. The report in the eleventh edition of the *Encyclopedia Britannica* specifically uses the word "rebellion" to describe these uprisings. Marlow's (and/or Conrad's) ironic response to the Russian's claim that these heads belonged to "rebels" ("I shocked him excessively by laughing. Rebels! What would be the next definition I was to hear. There had been enemies, criminals, workers—and these were—rebels") supports the idea, put forward by Norman Sherry and John Batchelor, that Marlow, or Conrad and Marlow, are seeking to denigrate Belgian rule in the Congo (*HD* 58).

8. The significance of the skulls is, from the point of view of Conrad's contemporary critics, similar to that of the significance of cannibalism in the story. On the one hand, Conrad (or Conrad and Marlow) is censured for suggesting that cannibalism existed in Africa in anything but ritual form, despite the fact that virtually all contemporaneous authorities were convinced that it was more or less widespread in the Upper Congo region. In other words, regardless of whether so-called food cannibalism was a historical truth or a historical fiction, in the view of contemporary anachronists Conrad/Marlow should have known what the "real" facts were. Even so, since Marlow and Conrad were ("strong" or "bloody"?) racists, they went ahead anyway and committed slurs against Africans. These very same critics nonetheless accept and propagate without a murmur the notion that Kurtz was acting like a brutal white imperialist in displaying the skulls of decapitated black "rebels," without taking into consideration that this kind of display was a recognized part of tribal tradition in the Congo. Contemporary critics of Conrad, it would appear, like to have it both ways.

9. Brantlinger relies here principally on Sidney Langford Hinde's account in *The Fall of the Congo Arabs* (1897). What Brantlinger does not mention, however, is that in Hinde's view "the question of cannibalism in Africa has been very little discussed. . . . So far as I have been able to discover, nearly all the tribes in the Congo Basin are, or have been, cannibals; and among some of them the practice is on the increase" (65–66). In James Jameson's *Story of the Rear Column of the Emin Pasha Relief Expedition* (1890), there is a gruesome account of how the unwitting Jameson paid to have a seventeen-year-old girl killed and cut up for food. "Until the last moment," he says, "I could not believe that they were in earnest. I have heard many stories of this kind since I have been in this country, but never could believe them, and I never would have been such a beast as to witness this, but I could not bring myself to believe that it was anything save a ruse to get money out of me, until the last moment" (291). For Belgian accounts of cannibalism in the Congo, see Massoz 166–71.

10. What Brantlinger presents as factual is for Watt primarily a "myth" about white men "going native" that was "already a commonplace in popular stories"

(*Conrad* 144). Significantly, though Brantlinger accepts Johnston's testimony in this connection, he fails take account of Johnston's assertion that the Congo Basin west of the longitude of Stanley Pool was a region "almost the whole of which, except in the south" was populated by "confirmed cannibals" ("Introductory" x).

11. That Conrad means us to understand fetishism as something that affects both blacks and whites—in both Africa and Europe—seems apparent from his description of Brussels as an "unreal" and even cursed city. As Christopher Miller observes with respect to Marlow's African engineer, "what Conrad is actually describing is *mutual fetishism*: for the African, the machines of Europe are animated by gods; for the European, everything African is moved by the troublesome darkness at its heart" (180).

12. Here Conrad resembles one of his favorite authors, Mary Kingsley, whose efforts to secure humane treatment for black Africans were an inspiration for E.D. Morel. "Let him," she writes, referring to black Africans, "have gin if he wants it, he is no drunkard. We are in West Africa to trade not to preach. I am absolutely for Secret Societies. Witch doctors, on the whole, do more good than harm. The cannibal tribes are the finest in West Africa. Domestic slavery should not be condemned off-hand. Polygamy is a necessary institution and its chief supporters are women" (qtd. in Cline 17). Kingsley's culturally relativistic outlook, though unusual, was by no means unprecedented. As early as the sixteenth century, Montaigne had argued, on hearing about a tribe of cannibals in Brazil, that "there was no more barbarism in their eating men alive than in some of the things he and his readers had lately seen in France" (qtd. in Banton 7). Similarly, Richard Burton, after describing in detail what he thought were the "purely religious" rites of human sacrifice in the Kingdom of Dahomey, relativizes the practice by arguing that a "Dahoman visiting England but a few years ago would have witnessed customs almost quite as curious as those which raise our bile now . . . the executions are, I believe, performed without cruelty; these Negroes have not invented breaking on the wheel or tearing to pieces their victims" (232).

13. Other admirers of Conrad's fiction share Leavis's frustration with Conrad's penchant for overwriting in *Heart of Darkness*. Jocelyn Baines remarks that in this novel, as in much of his early work, Conrad bombards the reader's emotions to excess: "There are too often those extra salvoes that Conrad cannot refrain from firing even though the defences are already flattened. The pages are spattered with such epithets and phrases as 'inconceivable,' 'incomprehensible,' 'implacable,' 'inscrutable,' 'inexplicable,' 'irresistible,' 'impenetrable,' 'impalpable,' 'unfathomable enigma,' 'indefinable meaning.' These words become debased by their constant use, while a sentence like 'the cry of inconceivable triumph and of unspeakable pain' is almost devoid of meaning' (225). Although agreeing that "portentousness is throughout the main danger hovering over the story," J.I.M. Stewart contends that *Heart of Darkness* is "one of Conrad's greatest things" (78). And Frederick Karl remarks that the substance of the story "is too close to the political and cultural crises of the twentieth century to warrant dismissal for over-statement, although these allegations can perhaps in part be justified by the text" (*Reader's Guide* 136). Only H.L. Mencken seems to appreciate fully Conrad's meticulous attention to style and struc-

ture in this story: "There is in 'Heart of Darkness' a perfection of design which one encounters only rarely and miraculously in prose fiction: it belongs rather to music. I can't imagine taking a single sentence out of that stupendous tale without leaving a visible gap. . . . As it stands it is austerely and beautifully perfect, just as the slow movement of the Unfinished Symphony is perfect" (520).

14. The name of this fictional society alludes unmistakably to King Leopold's International Association for the Exploration and Civilization of Africa, founded in 1876. Kurtz's (and Marlow's) membership in the new "gang of virtue" may also be linked to the reinvigoration of the antislavery movement at the time Conrad was seeking employment in the Congo. In the words of the official history of the *Force Publique:* "In response to the pathetic appeals of Cardinal Lavigerie, anti-slavery societies were founded in Brussels, Paris, Rome, Madrid, Cologne, in Portugal, Austria, Sweden. . . . In November 1889 an international conference met whose labours culminated in 1890 with an agreement establishing measures to be taken for the suppression of the slave trade, on land and at sea" (Flament 200; my translation).

15. Marlow's choice of words in this scene recalls his earlier description of traveling upriver and penetrating ever further into "the heart of darkness" (*HD* 37). There he had compared his boat (and by association, its passengers) to a beetle *crawling*—using for emphasis some form of the word *crawl* four times in one paragraph—toward its destination. His Kafkaesque sense of having become beetle-like eventually culminates in a feeling of disorientation: "The earth seemed unearthly." In its own way, and admittedly in a minor key, Marlow's experience at this point prefigures Kurtz's later crawling and kicking free of the earth, his metamorphosis into a being that has become both less and more than human but is nevertheless neither angel nor fiend.

16. Marlow's celebrated definition of crime in *Lord Jim* is relevant here as well: "The real significance of crime is in its being a breach of faith with the community of mankind" (96). Jim's crime, like Kurtz's, is against *humanity* in general even though, like Kurtz's again, it is committed against a supposedly inferior people who, in the words of the odious German captain, are mere "cattle"—animals, that is, rather than humans. Failing to take full recognition of another's humanity is to break faith with the community of mankind.

17. Conrad first met Casement in the Congo in June 1890. See "The Congo Diary" (*Last Essays* 238). In making this remark Conrad was anticipating E.D. Morel's observation in his classic account *History of the Congo Reform Movement* that "barbarism, which is merely a stage in human development, has, in the case of the Congo, been talked and written of as though it were a crime" (11). Unlike Morel, however, Conrad does not entirely endorse the idea of a gradual but unequal cultural evolution.

18. Just how unlikely Reid's "dying-god" hypothesis is may be inferred from the Russian's remarks that he had been "'risking my life every day for the last fortnight to keep her out of the house'" (*HD* 61). To be sure, since he also admits to not understanding "'the dialect of this tribe,'" it is possible that he too has not grasped the Black Amazon's intentions with respect to his future demigodly role at the Inner Station. If we accept this view, however, the complications, not realized apparently

by two of the main characters in the narrative, Marlow and the Russian, become so convoluted that one may venture to say that only Reid himself can read or has read them aright. Significantly, Molly Mahood contends (without reference to Reid's theory) that the Black Amazon's intention is not to sacrifice Kurtz for the Russian's sake, but rather to do the opposite. In Mahood's view the whole situation here is reminiscent of an absurd H. Rider Haggard plot in which the Black Amazon plans "to sacrifice, quite literally, the Harlequin as a way of retaining Kurtz—a fate that Marlow in his turn narrowly avoids" (29).

19. Conrad no doubt also counted on his readers' associating these "unspeakable rites" with the rituals of human sacrifice described by Burton in *A Mission to Gelele* (1864) as taking place in Dahomey. These associations would have been refreshed by the publicity connected with the 1897 British punitive expedition against the Kingdom of Benin. See also Ryder 248–50, 290.

20. Reid quotes Frazer to the effect that in Central Africa "'the man-god must be killed as soon as he shows symptoms that his powers are beginning to fail.'" Frazer then goes on to state, specifically in connection with the Congo, that the dying man-god's chosen successor must enter the latter's tent and club or strangle him to death (Reid 46). From this it follows, according to Reid, that Kurtz's indecision about whether to leave with Marlow or to stay for the impending midnight dances has to do with his greater or lesser willingness or unwillingness to suffer the doom of the man-god. Aside from the unanswered question (a question not asked by Reid) as to what knowledge Conrad might have had of Frazer or of Frazer's sources, what this theory assumes, of course, is that (1) Kurtz's Lake tribe conforms precisely to the Frazerian pattern, which is based on a very small body of evidence relating to the Upper Congo region at this time; (2) Marlow's understanding of the "unspeakable rites" is radically different from Kurtz's, in that the former has no idea of what ominous last "rite" the latter is apparently facing; (3) the Black Amazon, rather than being Kurtz's mistress, consumed with grief at the prospect of his departure, is in fact a cold-blooded ritualist urging him to submit to the fatal ceremonial formalities of his chosen tribe. Her outstretched arms, in other words, are not so much a sign of a lover's grief as of a female "facilitator"'s frustration at having been cheated out of her prey; (4) Kurtz's instructions to his followers to frighten away the steamer become part of a complex, hermetic plan rather than simply the attempt on his part to continue his unspeakable activities undisturbed; and (5) Kurtz himself believes that he is dying, something that in the text remains very much in doubt until he is actually at the point of death. It should also be noted that Reid's claim that past rituals involved cannibalism and that the heads on Kurtz's poles are the remaining evidence of such indulgence lacks textual or other support.

21. When Marlow visits Kurtz's fiancée and has a vision of them together, he feels as if he "had blundered into a place of cruel and absurd mysteries not for a human being to behold" (*HD* 73). Here again Marlow finds himself "out of place," a reluctant witness to rites that, even if they are "speakable," are nevertheless cruel and absurd. What Marlow means his listeners to perceive here, I think, is that the Intended is in fact the last and perhaps most gruesome of Kurtz's human sacrifices—an execution all the more cruel for being slow and nonviolent.

22. Torgovnick's reading (along with Humphries's) is indebted to Frederick Crews's classic—and now also self-abjured—Freudian interpretation of the story, according to which, among other things, the blank spaces of Africa represent the female genitalia; the severed heads, castration; Marlow's trip upriver, the return to the womb; Kurtz, the Oedipal father; and the "unspeakable rites," the primal scene (Crews 56). In this connection, it is interesting to note that, according to Iris Murdoch (50), Freud considered severed heads (e.g., the severed head of the Medusa) to be symbolic representations of the female genitalia, feared and not desired.

23. Conrad may be basing his description of the Africans' reaction to the blowing of the steam whistle on an analogous account in Hermann von Wissmann's *My Second Journey through Equatorial Africa* (1891). Traveling up the Kassai River (where "An Outpost of Progress" is set) in 1886 with George Grenfell, Wissmann observed what happened when the former blew the whistle in order to break up a quarrel between the crew and some villagers: "The impression was again so overpowering that all the natives took to their heels in wild fear, disappearing in the thickets and rushing towards the village. Only one old white-haired Herculean chief, who was standing close to the river, felt ashamed to run, but was terrified to such a degree that he staggered backward, and only kept his footing by catching hold of a tree" (20).

24. How fearful Conrad was of offending his readers' sensibilities in this area is apparent from Thomas Moser's (77-79) and Ian Watt's argument that Conrad was unable to complete work on *The Rescue* (his main project at the time he diverted his energies to write *Heart of Darkness* and *Lord Jim*) because he could not face describing the adulterous relationship between Tom Lingard and Edith Travers (Watt, *Conrad* 129). That sexual relationships between black women and white males were very "speakable" in the Congo in the late nineteenth century is evident from the fact that the missionary George Grenfell was married to a black West Indian woman, with whom he had several children. Writing in 1887, James Jameson noticed "that one of the chief occupations of the Belgian officers at the different stations is to civilize the country by adding to the population specimens of half-breeds, as they are all more or less married to native women" (50). In this respect, however, the Belgians (along with the Dutch, Portuguese, and French) also differed from their British imperialist counterparts, for as Harry Johnston remarks, the latter group's "lapses from continence in Africa, if they occurred, were furtive. If they became the fathers of children, one was told that they tendered shame-facedly some sort of 'compensation' to the mother and then tried to ignore the matter as much as possible. Whereas the Dutch, French, Portuguese father brought up his own half-caste child with care and kindness, and if it were a boy sent it either to some superior mission school for an education, or even to Europe" (*Story* 95).

6. E.J. Glave, Captain Rom, and the Making of Heart of Darkness

1. Rom's twenty-one heads did not, of course, *stand* but were set, as Glave's description makes clear, in the ground along the edge of a flower bed. This is a not unimportant difference, especially since, as Lester also notes, Kurtz confines his

grisly display to six heads mounted on what appear to Marlow to be fence posts. If anything, Glave's account of Rom's use of skulls as horticultural ornaments seems closer to Stanley's description in 1878 of the skulls he saw displayed in the village of Kampunzu, to the southeast of Stanley Falls: "The most singular feature of Kampunzu village were two rows of skulls, ten feet apart, running along the entire length of the village, imbedded about two inches deep in the ground, the 'cerebral hemispheres' uppermost, bleached, and glistening white from weather. The skulls were 186 in number in this one village" (*Dark Continent* 111).

2. Even for us this is difficult, since Forbath unfortunately does not name the American missionary or cite the source of his information. It is, however, possible that this account is somehow connected with Lawson Forfeitt, who was in fact British rather than American and who wrote a letter about Glave's death that was published in the *Times* on January 3, 1896 (Spittles 79).

3. The link with Glave was also made by Henryk Zins in 1982, though he too was seemingly unaware that *Century Magazine* was an American publication (38).

4. Conrad could not have met Rom at Stanley Falls, for Rom served as commanding officer there only from April 26, 1894, to November 1, 1895 (*BCB* 2:825).

5. The reference to the North Pole by Marlow may be a proleptic allusion to *The Inheritors*, where the Duc de Mersch's brutal empire is said to be located in the Arctic regions. It may, however, also be linked to Glave, who in the early nineties spent several months exploring remote regions in Alaska.

6. On May 7, 1890, Conrad signed a contract in Brussels to serve as captain of a steamer for a term of three years. His monthly salary was 250 Belgian francs (Gers 437).

7. Conrad himself had no such difficulties, leaving Kinshasa as he did on the *Roi des Belges* within a few days of his arrival there in early August 1890. Marlow, however, waits for nearly three months before he gets the rivets necessary to repair the vessel that the rescue party will then use to steam up the Congo (*HD* 32). Though Glave's account of his difficulties may be relevant here, Conrad may actually have based his account primarily on what he probably heard while aboard the *Roi des Belges* about its extremely difficult assembly two years earlier. Some of the long delay was caused by the fact that porters had abandoned various essential pieces along the way from Matadi to Kinshasa, so that Alexandre Delcommune was forced to personally search the route for the missing pieces. Once they were found, the ship was assembled using Bangala labor for the riveting of the plates, but on launching it turned out that the boat leaked. One of the rivet holes had been left without a rivet and was therefore letting in dangerous amounts of water. The whites at this point were at a loss as to how to proceed until one of the Bangala workers offered to dive under the boat and insert the rivet—a simple but very dangerous procedure that solved the problem (Liebrechts 208–10).

8. During his first tour of duty in the Congo Free State, E.J. Glave met his boyhood hero Stanley while going upriver and heard him tell how in 1877 he had been attacked "by those barbarous cannibals, the Bangala" but had managed to escape "through an atmosphere darkened by the flight of arrows and gleaming spears hurled by the man-eating hordes, whose significant war-cry of 'Niama!

Niama!' (Meat! Meat!) warned their enemies of the fate in store for prisoners" (Glave, *Savage* 39). The general resemblance between this episode and the attack on Marlow's steamer is a further piece of evidence that Conrad may have had Glave's book in mind while writing *Heart of Darkness*.

9. Herbert Ward, a close friend of Glave's who had known him since his arrival in Africa in 1883, describes Glave as "quick to learn the native language, and so remarkable was his sense of sound that it was difficult to distinguish his voice from that of the natives. This quality, combined with his apt gestures and natural sympathy, made him unusually popular among natives" (*Voice* 246).

10. This procedure is reminiscent of the one described by Hilaire Belloc in his account of an exploring expedition in Africa: "We shot and hanged a few, and then / The rest became devoted men" (42).

11. Vansina also points out that up to the very end of its existence in 1908, the Congo Free State refused to allow the introduction of money. The aim was to prevent Africans from avoiding forced labor by paying taxes in cash. Like the "company store" policy in effect in the United States at this time, it also made it difficult for consumers to buy their goods from anyone but the "King, Incorporated" ("King" 394).

12. According to Jean Stengers, this reputation was largely undeserved since Leopold was interested only in the "principles" of administering his overseas possessions, not the details ("Leopold's" 320–21). This claim, however, does not conform easily to Stengers's earlier claim that Leopold insisted on micromanaging the Congo: "The master he was, not only theoretically, but also in practice. He never delegated power, he exercised it personally" (317). Stengers's explanations for Leopold's behavior sound suspiciously like rationalizations. It is, in fact, partly with Stengers in mind that Jan Breman writes that it "is an astounding fact that the majority of Belgian historians have persistently managed to distort the nature and scale of these inhuman practices for so long, notwithstanding the lively debate on the subject held abroad in the early years of the twentieth century" (108).

13. That Conrad was thinking of his own experience is unmistakable from his description of the chaotic railway construction going on at the Outer Station. Though plans for a railway linking Matadi with Kinshasa were finalized as early as 1888, actual construction did not begin until March 1890. In fact, the first rails were contained in the hold of the *Ville de Maceio* when Conrad boarded the ship in Bordeaux on May 10, 1890. Part of Conrad's overt hostility against this project may be due to the fact that it was initially meant to be undertaken by a British syndicate whose contract was abruptly terminated and then reassigned to a Belgian company headed by Albert Thys (Cornet 367, 369–70).

14. In *Lord Jim*—the novel on which Conrad interrupted work to write *Heart of Darkness*—Jim "redeems" himself for his cowardice by leading a daring attack on the Arab encampment of Sherif Ali, which has been terrorising the native inhabitants. This exploit is actually more reminiscent of what Belgian officers like Francis Dhanis did in in the Congolese Arab Wars than of anything Conrad ever experienced himself while in Malaysia.

15. In 1890, not long before Conrad arrived at Stanley Falls, Dragutin Lerman

drew up a list of the Arab chiefs who were either living at the Falls or nearby, with notations regarding their respective skin color. Some he described as "white" or even "very white," others as "dark" or "very dark," with Tippo Tib included in the last group (Lopasic 145).

16. Significantly, M. Coosemans's account in the *Biographie Coloniale Belge* of Glave's life omits specific reference to Glave's *Century* essays or to his exposure of the brutal "methods" of rubber collection as practiced by the Congo State. These essays are only alluded to as a "diary" in which Glave is said to have reached "a generally favorable verdict about the State's attempts to put an end to slavery." The only hint that Glave might have been critical of the Congo State is contained in the remark that Glave "put himself on the side of those who claimed that the State sometimes made use of black forced labor, without, however, ever falling into the error made by many others who saw in this practice nothing but a disguised form of slavery" (*BCB* 2:414–15, my translation).

17. There were, of course, earlier reports concerning atrocities in the Congo, notably George Washington Williams's "Report upon the Congo State" (1890), but none received wide publicity or appeared in an English-language newspaper or magazine except for Salusbury's "The Congo State: A Revelation," published in the *United Service Magzine* in 1896. This report was picked up by the *Spectator* at the end of May of the same year and helped bring about the Parliamentary debate on the issue that summer. According to Adam Hochschild, for a few years after 1897 (and, ironically, at the very time when Conrad was writing *Heart of Darkness*) "attacks on Leopold almost completely disappeared from the European Press. The King's critics kept up sporadic fire, but no one seemed to heed them" (*King Leopold's Ghost* 175). One person, however, who did heed them—other than Conrad, that is—was Demetrius Boulger, who in an essay on "The Congo State and Its Critics," published in 1899 in the *Fortnightly Review* "attempted to vindicate the Government of the Congo State against the *violent critricisms* to which it has been subjected of late" ("Critics" 442, my italics).

Conclusion

1. Smith sees a connection in this modern revulsion against genocide with Nietzsche's contention (as expressed most notably in *The Genealogy of Morals*) that cruelty and suffering were valued positively during the age of pagan, "heroic" Greece, whereas the triumph of Christianity brought about a radical transvaluation of these earlier values. In a later and very different context, George Orwell remarks that dictators like Stalin and Hitler (and their henchmen), though indirectly responsible for murder, never used plain or direct words to describe what they were doing; instead, they euphemistically "liquidated" their victims or found a "final solution" for them (516). Here Orwell essentially anticipates Smith's argument about the characteristically modern attitude of shame toward mass murder. But Smith's argument, though certainly worthy of serious consideration, is not completely persuasive. Significantly, he does not refer to the fact that the American use of atom bombs on essentially civilian targets was openly and proudly proclaimed at the time (and some-

times still is), though it was never officially classified as genocide. Furthermore, at least in fictional contexts (both literary and cinematic), mass destruction is still a very popular commodity, as for example in the James Bond and the Rambo films, or in the apparently more respectable context of J.R.R. Tolkien's fantasies.

2. Nor does Rummel include in his survey of twentieth-century genocide any of the mass killings committed in Africa either by the colonial powers, such as King Leopold's Belgium, or by the Africans themselves, such as Idi Amin.

3. Leo Kuper, however, is adamant in his insistence that these actions fall unmistakably within the terms of the United Nations definition of genocide. See L. Kuper 33–35. For a counterargument, see Fein, "Genocide" 95–108.

4. For surveys of the various categories of genocide, see Jonassohn and Chalk 3–20, Chalk 47–63, and Charny 64–94. For the full text of the 1948 UN Convention of Genocide see Andreopoulos 229–33.

5. As Pat Shipman points out, the young Darwin found it hard to believe that the indigenous people he encountered in South America "were human in the same sense that he was" (75). Sven Lindqvist discusses in some detail the widely accepted assumption during the latter half of the nineteenth century that more "primitive" peoples would gradually become extinct after extended contact with the more "vital" and aggressive Europeans (84–107). Lindqvist's discussion needs to be supplemented, however, with the caveat that such projected "extinction" usually does not qualify as genocide as the United Nations or most contemporary authorities define it. Even British critics of imperialism, such as Gilbert Murray, did not claim that the British were actually massacring their subject peoples. "If we hear of a race like the Tasmanians or the Red Indians disappearing quietly," he writes without apparent irony in 1900, "under no stress of persecution, no massacres or poisonings, we are perhaps inclined to look upon the process as a harmless and painless one. It is not so. Those men and women who look broken down by the time they are thirty, who leave no children behind them, who have forgotten their fishing and their hunting and their old rude forms of art, who sit (as I have seen one or two) with heads bowed, doing nothing, saying nothing, in a world in which there is no longer anything they can call their own—those men and women are, I think, engaged in a process that we sometimes read about but do not often see: they are dying of despair" (149). Even supporters of British colonial expansion such as Havelock Ellis did not envision violence being used to gain their ends. "If we English are certain to make little progress where, as in Asia, the great task is conciliation," he writes in 1890, "when it is a question of stamping out a lower race—then is our time! It has to be done; it is quite clear that the fragile Red men of America and the strange wild men of Australia must perish at the touch of the White man. On the whole we stamp them out as mercifully as may be, supplying our victim liberally with missionaries and blankets" (21). It is perhaps significant that African blacks are not specifically named as candidates for racial elimination. Indeed, according to Peter Bowler, Robert Knox specifically excludes them in *The Races of Man* (1850): "The vast majority of non-white races lacked all capacity for civilization and were doomed to extinction. Only the true Negroes stood a chance of resisting the Saxon on his own territory" (110).

6. Arendt's analysis probably owes something to the German existentialist philosopher Martin Heidegger's distinction between *foreground* and *background*, with the consequent idea that "primitive" humanity lived wholly in the latter whereas "civilized" humanity dwells in both. In this connection, however, it needs to be stressed that the failure to recognize others' full humanity was not confined to modern Europe. During Stanley's voyage across Africa he stopped at a village not far from Stanley Falls where he found 186 "'cerebral hemispheres'" "imbedded about two inches in the ground . . . bleached and glistening white from weather." When he asked whether the skulls belonged to humans, as he thought they did, he received the reply that they were the skulls of "Sokos," a term that Stanley did not recognize but thought referred to some hitherto unknown species of ape. The chief of the village then went on to describe these creatures as "Nyama [meat] of the forest," able to walk like a man, nearly five feet tall, using a stick "with which he beats the trees in the forest, and makes hideous noises. The Nyama eat our bananas, and we hunt them, kill them, and eat them." Two of these skulls were eventually brought back to London by Stanley, where T.H. Huxley examined them and found them to be human (Stanley, *Dark Continent* 111–12).

7. Despite Marlow's observations to the contrary, Kurtz is evidently also capable of exercising some degree of restraint. So, for example, he tries at first to frighten away the steamer sent to "rescue" him, and only when this strategy fails does he permit his warriors to launch a half-hearted attack.

8. The term *ethnocide* is used to describe the cultural but not physical extermination of a people (Jonassohn and Chalk 7).

9. If, as Lindqvist maintains, the British were just as guilty of atrocities in their colonies as the Belgians were in the Congo, it seems difficult to explain why neither H.R. Fox Bourne's Aborigines Protection Society nor E.D. Morel's Congo Reform Association ever pointed this out to the members of their apparently philanthropic organizations or to the British public at large. Are we to believe, then, that they were merely dupes of a British imperialist strategy bent on depriving Leopold of his profitable colonial possession—the only European colony in Africa that actually was profitable? Or, worse, did they really "know" just like "everyone" else supposedly "knew," and did they therefore act out of a purely cynical desire for profit and publicity? Even Sir Harry Johnston, who had a lifetime of experience in African colonies (British and otherwise) and who therefore should have "known" if anyone did, was convinced that, "thanks to Exeter Hall and the Exeter Hall spirit, Great Britain had strayed less frequently from the right path" than other colonial powers (Johnston, *Grenfell* 475).

10. In a telegram to Lord Lansdowne of the Foreign Office, dated September 15, 1903, Casement charged the Congo Free State with "'wholesale oppression and shocking misgovernment.'" When Casement submitted the actual report early the following December, however, he surprised more conciliatory members of the Foreign Office with its subdued tone. As William Louis concludes, "it was not a verbally scathing denunciation of the Congo administration; it was, above all, understated" (99, 109).

11. Anthony Fothergill gives a figure for the so-called "decline" of between three and six million but provides no supporting evidence (39).

12. It is undoubtedly significant that Leopold ordered most of the Congo State records destroyed when Belgium assumed control of the colony in 1908 (Gann and Duignan 237).

13. That the stack of rails should be described as "rusty" is particularly odd, since the first rails were actually brought to the Congo in the hold of the very ship Conrad himself had arrived in.

14. According to H.R. Fox Bourne, in 1896 Houston Chamberlain, then secretary of state for the colonies, forbade further recruitment of British colonial subjects by the Congo State as a result of complaints about their mistreatment there. Hitherto the great majority of African employees of the Congo Railway had been recruited from Liberia, Sierra Leone, and other British African colonies (125).

15. Though Marlow openly admits to lying to the Intended, it has been suggested (only half-humorously) that he may, without knowing it, actually be telling the truth—that is, if we assume (1) that Kurtz's last words are spoken in English and (2) that Marlow mishears them as "The horror! The horror!" when what Kurtz was actually saying was: "The whore! The whore!"

16. Ian Watt points out the parallel between the treatment of lying in *The Wild Duck* and in *Heart of Darkness* but without suggesting that Conrad is in any way indebted to Ibsen. That Conrad was aware of Ibsen's work emerges from a letter he wrote referring to *Ghosts* on January 7, 1899, while occupied in writing *Heart of Darkness* (*Letters* 2:149). There was a notable production of *The Wild Duck* in London in 1897, reviewed by George Bernard Shaw in the *Saturday Review* (M. Meyer 563).

Appendix

1. *Baumann's note*: "However, I want to make it absolutely clear that I am speaking here only of the region downriver from the cataract which is perhaps too remote a location for practicable export of slaves to the east coast."

2. For a very different account of Deane's career, see Glave, *Savage* 222–27. Glave refers to him as "one of the bravest" white officers he knew in the Congo and provides a detailed description of the attack on him and his men that provoked him to take revenge.

WORKS CITED

Achebe, Chinua. *Hopes and Impediments: Selected Essays, 1965–1987*. London: Heinemann, 1988.

———. "An Image of Africa: Racism in Conrad's *Heart of Darkness*." In Joseph Conrad, *Heart of Darkness*, 3d ed., ed. Robert Kimbrough, 251-62. New York: Norton, [1988].

———. "An Image of Africa: Racism in Conrad's *Heart of Darkness*," *Massachusetts Review* 18 (1977): 782-94.

———. *Things Fall Apart*. New York: Fawcett Crest, 1991.

———. "Viewpoint." (London) *Times Literary Supplement*, Feb. 1, 1980, 113.

Adams, Charles C. "Recent Discoveries in the Congo Basin." *Harper's Weekly* 34 (1890), 37–40, 47.

Adelman, Gary. *Heart of Darkness: Search for the Unconscious*. Boston: Twayne, 1987.

Alter, Peter. *Nationalism*. London: Edward Arnold, 1989.

Andreopoulos, George J., ed. *Genocide: Conceptual and Historical Dimensions*. Philadelphia: Univ. of Pennsylvania Press, 1994.

Angell, Norman. *The Public Mind: Its Disorder, Its Exploitation*. New York: Dutton, 1927.

Anstey, Roger. *Britain and the Congo in the Nineteenth Century*. Oxford: Clarendon Press, 1962.

Appiah, K. Anthony, and Amy Gutmann. *Color Conscious: The Political Morality of Race*. Princeton, N.J.: Princeton Univ. Press, 1996.

Arendt, Hannah. *The Origins of Totalitarianism*. New York: Harcourt, Brace, Jovanovich, 1973.

Auerbach, Erich. *Mimesis: The Representation of Reality in Western Literature*. Princeton, N.J.: Princeton Univ. Press, 1953.

Baines, Jocelyn. *Joseph Conrad: A Critical Biography*. New York: McGraw-Hill, 1960.

Bannister, Robert C. *Social Darwinism: Science and Myth in Anglo-American Social Thought*. Philadelphia: Temple Univ. Press, 1979.

Banton, Michael. *Racial Theories*. Cambridge: Cambridge Univ. Press, 1987.

Barker, Anthony J. *The African Link: British Attitudes to the Negro in the Era of the Atlantic Slave Trade, 1550–1807*. London: Frank Cass, 1978.

Batchelor, John. *The Life of Joseph Conrad: A Critical Biography.* Oxford: Blackwell, 1994.

Baudelaire, Charles. *Intimate Journals.* Trans. Christopher Isherwood. San Francisco: City Lights Books, 1983.

Bauman, Zygmunt. *Modernity and the Holocaust.* Ithaca, N.Y.: Cornell Univ. Press, 1989.

Baumann, Oscar. "Die Station der Stanley-Fälle: Beschreibung des Landes und der Bewohner am siebenten Katarakte der Stanley-Fälle des Congo." *Mittheilungen der Kaiserlich-Königlichen Geographischen Gesellschaft* 29 (1886): 504–13, 647–56; 30 (1887): 65–69.

Beachey, Raymond Wendell. "The East African Ivory Trade in the Nineteenth Century." *Journal of African History* 8, no. 2 (1967): 269–91.

"The Belgian Advance on the Nile." *Standard,* Sept. 8, 1896, 2.

Belloc, Hilaire. *Cautionary Tales.* London: Duckworth, 1939.

Bentley, W. Hilman. *Pioneering on the Congo.* 2 vols. 1900. Reprint, New York: Johnson Reprint Corporation, 1970.

Berthoud, Jacques. "Joseph Conrad." In *Early 20th Century Britain: The Cambridge Cultural History,* vol. 8, ed. Boris Ford, pp. 55-60. Cambridge: Cambridge Univ. Press, 1992.

———. *Joseph Conrad: The Major Phase.* Cambridge: Cambridge Univ. Press, 1978.

Bhabha, Homi K. *The Location of Culture.* London: Routledge, 1994.

Biographie Coloniale Belge (BCB). Brussels: Institut Royal Colonial Belge, 1948–.

"The Black Question." *Spectator* 76 (October 19, 1895), 511–12.

Bolt, Christine. *Victorian Attitudes to Race.* London: Routledge and Kegan Paul, 1971.

Bontinck, François, ed. and trans. *L'Autobiographie de Hamed ben Mohammed el-Murjebi Tippo Tip (ca. 1840–1905).* Brussels: Academie Royale des Sciences d'Outre-Mer, 1974.

Booth, Wayne. *A Rhetoric of Fiction.* 2d ed. Chicago: Univ. of Chicago Press, 1983.

Boshart, August. *Zehn Jahre afrikanischen Lebens.* Leipzig: Otto Wigand, 1898

Boulger, Demetrius C. "The Congo State and Its Critics." *Fortnightly Review,* n.s. 65 (January-June 1899): 434–44.

———. "Twelve Years' Work on the Congo." *Fortnightly Review,* n.s., 64 (July-December 1898): 565–74.

———. *The Congo State, or the Growth of Civilisation in Central Africa.* London: Thacker, 1898.

Bourne, H.R. Fox. *Civilisation in Congoland.* London: P.S. King and Son, 1903.

Bowler, Peter J. *The Invention of Progress: The Victorians and the Past.* Oxford: Blackwell, 1989.

Brantlinger, Patrick. *Rule of Darkness: British Literature and Imperialism, 1830–1914.* Ithaca, N.Y.: Cornell Univ. Press, 1988.

———. "Victorians and Africans: The Genealogy of the Myth of the Dark Continent." *Critical Inquiry* 12 (autumn 1985): 166–203.

Breman, Jan, ed. *Imperial Monkey Business: Racial Supremacy in Social Darwinist Theory and Colonial Practice.* Amsterdam: Vrije Universiteit Press, 1990.

Brown, Robert. *The Story of Africa and Its Explorers*. Vol. 4. London: Cassell, 1895.

Buchanan, William, and Hadley Cantril. *How Nations See Each Other: A Study in Public Opinion*. Urbana: Univ. of Illinois Press, 1953.

Burden, Robert. "Conrad's Heart of Darkness: The Critique of Imperialism and the Post-Colonial Reader." *L'Epoque Conradienne* 18 (1988): 63–83.

———. *Heart of Darkness*. Houndmills, Eng.: Macmillan, 1991.

Burrows, Guy. *The Curse of Central Africa*. London: Everett, 1903.

Burton, Richard. *A Mission to Gelele, King of Dahome*. London: Routledge and Kegan Paul, 1966.

———. *Two Trips to Gorilla Land and the Cataracts of the Congo*. 2 vols. London: Sampson Low, 1876. Reprint: New York: Johnson Reprint Corporation, 1967.

Casement, Roger. *The Black Diaries*. Ed. Peter Singleton-Gates and Maurice Girodias. London: Sidgwick and Jackson, 1959.

Cassirer, Ernst. *The Myth of the State*. New Haven, Conn.: Yale Univ. Press, 1946.

Castelein, Auguste. *The Congo State; Its Origin, Rights, and Duties; The Charges of Its Accusers*. 1907; reprint, New York: Negro Universities Press, 1969.

Cerroni-Long, E.L. "Child of Colonialism: The Primitivist Premises of Western Anthropology." *North Dakota Quarterly* 57, no. 3 (summer 1989): 76–98.

Ceulemans, P. *La Question Arabe et le Congo (1883–1892)*. New Series. Vol. 22. Brussels: Academie des Sciences Coloniales, 1959.

Chalk, Frank. "Redefining Genocide." In Andreopoulos, 47-63.

Charny, Israel W. "Toward a Generic Definition of Genocide." In Andreopoulos, 64-94.

Chinweizu. *The West and the Rest of Us*. New York: Random House, 1975.

Churchill, Reginald Charles. "The Age of Eliot." In *The Concise Cambridge History of English Literature*, 2d ed., ed. George Sampson, 944–1030. Cambridge: Cambridge Univ. Press, 1965.

Cleary, Thomas R., and Terry G. Sherwood. "Women in Conrad's Ironical Epic: Virgil, Dante and *Heart of Darkness*." *Conradiana* 16 (1984): 183–93.

Clements, Patricia. *Baudelaire and the English Tradition*. Princeton, N.J.: Princeton Univ. Press, 1985.

Cline, Catherine Ann. *E. D. Morel, 1873–1924: The Strategies of Protest*. Belfast: Blackstaff Press, 1980.

Cohen, Robin. *Frontiers of Identity: The British and the Others*. London: Longman, 1994.

Collins, Harold. "Kurtz, the Cannibals, and the Second-rate Helmsman." *Western Humanities Review* 8 (autumn 1954): 299–310.

"La compagnie du Congo pour le commerce et l'industrie, 1886–1948." *Revue Coloniale Belge* 66 (July 1, 1948): 405–36.

"The Congo State and the English Government." *Spectator* 76 (May 30 1896), 766–67.

Connor, Walker. *Ethnonationalism: The Quest for Understanding*. Princeton, N.J.: Princeton Univ. Press, 1994.

Conrad, Joseph. *Almayer's Folly*. Garden City, N.Y.: Doubleday, 1926.

———. *The Collected Letters*. Ed. Frederick R. Karl and Laurence Davies. Cambridge: Cambridge Univ. Press, 1988.

———. *Heart of Darkness* (*HD*). 3d ed. Ed. Robert Kimbrough. New York: Norton, [1988].

———. *Heart of Darkness*. 2d ed. Ed. Ross C. Murfin. Boston: Bedford Books, 1996.

———. *Last Essays*. London: Dent, 1926.

———. *Lord Jim*. Ed. Thomas Moser. New York: Norton, 1996.

———. *The Mirror of the Sea*. New York: Doubleday, 1928.

———. *The Nigger of the 'Narcissus.'* Ed. Robert Kimbrough. New York: Norton, 1979.

———. *Nostromo*. London: Penguin Books, 1978.

———. *Notes on Life and Letters*. New York: Doubleday, 1925.

———. *A Personal Record*. Garden City, N.Y.: Doubleday, 1925.

———. *Tales of Unrest*. New York: Doubleday, 1923.

———. *Victory, an Island Tale*. New York: Doubleday, 1927.

———. *Youth* and *The End of the Tether*. London: Penguin Books, 1975.

Conrad, Joseph, and Ford Madox Hueffer. *The Inheritors: An Extravagant Story*. Garden City, N.Y.: Doubleday, 1923.

———. *Romance, A Novel*. New York: Doubleday, 1924.

Cookey, Sylvanus John Sodienye. *Britain and the Congo Question, 1885–1913*. Ibadan History Series. London: Longmans, 1968.

Coquilhat, Camille. *Sur le Haut-Congo*. Paris: J. Lebèque, 1888.

Cornet, René-Jules. "Cinquantième anniversaire de l'achêvement du chemin de fer de Matadi au Stanley-Pool (1898–1948)." *Revue Coloniale Belge* 66 (July 1, 1948): 367–73.

["Courtney"]. *Saturday Review*, Dec. 17, 1898, 802–3.

Crews, Frederick. "Conrad's Uneasiness and Ours." In *Out of My System*, 41-62. New York: Oxford, 1975.

Cromer, Earl of [Evelyn Baring]. *Ancient and Modern Imperialism*. New York: Longmans, Green, 1910.

Crompton, John. "Conrad and Colloquialism." In *Conrad: Eastern and Western Perspectives*, vol. 1, *Conrad's Literary Career*, ed. Keith Carabine, Owen Knowles, and Wieslaw Krajka, 211–24. Boulder: East European Monographs, 1992.

Culler, A. Dwight. *The Victorian Mirror of History*. New Haven, Conn.: Yale Univ. Press, 1985.

Curtin, Philip D. *The Image of Africa: British Ideas and Action, 1780–1850*. Madison: Univ. of Wisconsin Press, 1964.

Daleski, Herman Matthew. *Joseph Conrad: The Way of Dispossession*. New York: Holmes and Meier, 1977.

Darras, Jacques. *Joseph Conrad and the West: Signs of Empire*. Totowa, N.J.: Barnes and Noble, 1982.

Darwin, Charles. *The Expression of the Emotions in Man and Animals*. Chicago: Univ. of Chicago Press, 1969.

Davidson, Basil. *The Lost Cities of Africa.* Boston: Little, Brown, 1970.

Deane, Seamus. "Imperialism/Nationalism." In *Critical Terms for Literary Study,* 2d ed., ed. Frank Lentricchia and Thomas McLaughlin, 354-68. Chicago: Univ. of Chicago Press, 1995.

Denby, David. "Jungle Fever." *New Yorker,* Nov. 6, 1995, 118–29.

Dobrinsky, Joseph. *The Artist in Conrad's Fiction: A Psychocritical Study.* Ann Arbor, Mich.: UMI Research Press, 1989.

Doyle, Arthur Conan. *The Professor Challenger Stories.* London: John Murray, 1952.

Dundes, Alan. *Cracking Jokes: Studies of Sick Humor Cycles and Stereotypes.* Berkeley, Calif.: Ten Speed Press, 1987.

Dupont, Édouard François. *Lettres sur le Congo.* Paris: C. Reinwald, 1889.

Dyserinck, Hugo. *Komparatistik: Eine Einführung.* Bonn: Bouvier, 1981.

Eagleton, Terry. *Criticism and Ideology: A Study in Marxist Literary Theory.* London: NLB, 1976.

Ellis, Havelock. *The New Spirit.* New York: Boni and Liveright, [1890].

Ellis, John M. *Literature Lost: Social Agendas and the Corruption of the Humanities.* New Haven, Conn.: Yale Univ. Press, 1997.

Emerson, Barbara. *Leopold II of the Belgians.* Ed. Paul Edwards. New York: St. Martin's Press, 1979.

The Encyclopedia of Philosophy. Ed. Paul Edwards. Vol. 3. New York: Macmillan, 1972.

Enright, Dennis J. "Meant for Mankind: Review of Gordon A Craig, *The Politics of the Unpolitical.*" *TLS,* April 26, 1996, 29.

Feder, Lillian. "Marlow's Descent into Hell." *Nineteenth Century Fiction* 9 (March 1955): 280–92.

Fein, Helen. *Genocide: A Sociological Perspective.* London: Sage, 1993.

———. "Genocide, Terror, Life Integrity, and War Crimes: The Case for Discrimination." In Andreopoulos, 95-108.

Firchow, Peter. *The Death of the German Cousin: Variations on a National Stereotype, 1890–1920.* Lewisburg, Pa.: Bucknell Univ. Press, 1986.

———. "National Stereotypes in Literary Contexts." In *L'imagine dell'altro e l'identità nazionale,* ed. Manfred Beller, supplement to vol. 24 of *Il confronto letterario,* 33–40. Bergamo, Italy: Schena, 1996.

Fischer, Manfred. *Nationale Images als Gegenstand Vergleichender Literaturgeschichte.* Bonn: Bouvier, 1981.

Flament, F. et al, *La Force Publique de sa naissance à 1914: Participation des militaires à l'histoire des premières années du Congo.* Brussels: Institut Royal Belge, 1952.

Fleishman, Avrom. *Conrad's Politics: Community and Anarchy in the Fiction of Joseph Conrad,* Baltimore: Johns Hopkins Univ. Press, 1967.

Forbath, Peter. *The River Congo.* New York: Harper and Row, 1977.

Ford, Ford Madox. *Joseph Conrad: A Personal Remembrance.* Boston, 1924.

Ford, Jane. "An African Encounter, a British Traitor and *Heart of Darkness.*" *Conradiana* 27 (1995): 123–34.

Forster, E.M. *Howards End*. New York: Vintage, n.d.

Fothergill, Anthony. *Heart of Darkness*. Milton Keynes, England: Open Univ. Press, 1989.

Franklin, John Hope. [Williams's "Open Letter to Leopold and the 'Railway Report'"]. In Conrad, *Heart of Darkness,* ed. Kimbrough, 100–103.

Frederickson, George. *The Black Image in the White Mind: The Debate on Afro-American Character and Destiny, 1817–1914*. New York: Harper and Row, 1971.

Galton, Sir Francis. *Inquiries into Human Faculty and Its Development*. 1883; reprint, London: Dent, 1908.

Gann, Lewis H., and Peter Duignan, *The Rulers of Belgian Africa*. Princeton: Princeton Univ. Press, 1979.

Garnett, Edward. Introduction to *Letters from Joseph Conrad, 1895–1924,* ed. Edward Garnett, 1-28. Indianapolis: Bobbs-Merrill, 1928.

Gates, Henry Louis. "Writing 'Race' and the Difference It Makes." *Critical Inquiry* 12 (autumn 1985): 1–20.

Gers, José. "En Marge de 'coeur de ténèbres.'" *Revue Coloniale Belge* 66 (July 1948): 437–38.

Gide, André. *Travels in the Congo*. Trans. Dorothy Bussy. Hopewell: N.J. Ecco Press, 1994.

Gilder, Richard Watson. "Glave." *Century Magazine* 50 (May-Oct. 1895): 868.

Glave, Edward James. "The Congo River To-day." *Century Magazine* 39 (November 1889–April 1890), 618–20.

———. "Cruelty in the Congo Free State." *Century Magazine* 54 (May–Oct. 1897): 699–715.

———. "Glave in the Heart of Africa: Peace and War between Lakes Bangweolo and Tanganyika." *Century Magazine* 52 (May–Oct. 1896): 918–33.

———. "Glave in Nyasaland: British Raids on the Slave-Traders." *Century Magazine* 52 (May–Oct. 1896): 589–606.

———. *In Savage Africa, Or Six Years of Adventure in Congo-Land*. New York: Russell, 1892.

———. "New Conditions in Central Africa: The Dawn of Civilization between Lake Tanganyika and the Congo." *Century Magazine* 53 (Nov. 1896–April 1897): 900–915.

Gogwilt, Christopher. *The Invention of the West: Joseph Conrad and the Double-Mapping of Europe and Empire*. Stanford, Calif.: Stanford Univ. Press, 1995.

Graff, Gerald. *Beyond the Culture Wars*. New York: Norton, 1992.

Graham, R.B. Cunninghame. *Selected Writings*. Ed. Cedric Watts. Rutherford, N.J.: Farleigh Dickinson Univ. Press, 1981.

Graver, Lawrence. *Conrad's Short Fiction*. Berkeley: Univ. of California Press, 1969.

Green, Martin. *Dreams of Adventure, Deeds of Empire*. New York: Basic Books, 1979.

Greene, Graham. *Journey without Maps*. Harmondsworth, Eng.: Penguin, 1978.

Guerard, Albert J. *Conrad the Novelist*. Cambridge, Mass.: Harvard Univ. Press, 1966.

Guiness, H. Grattan. *The Congo Crisis, 1908.* London: R.B.M.U. Publication Department, [1908].

Haddon, Alfred C. *The Study of Man.* New York: Putnam's, 1898.

Hall, Edith. *Inventing the Barbarian: Greek Self-Definition through Tragedy.* Oxford: Clarendon Press, 1989.

Hawkins, Hunt. "Conrad's Critique of Imperialism in *Heart of Darkness.*" *PMLA* 94 (March 1979): 286–99.

———. "The Issue of Racism in *Heart of Darkness.*" *Conradiana* 14 (1982): 162–69.

Hawthorn, Jeremy. *Joseph Conrad: Narrative Technique and Ideological Commitment.* London: Edward Arnold, 1990.

Hay, Eloise Knapp. *The Political Novels of Joseph Conrad.* Chicago: Univ. of Chicago Press, 1963.

Hervouet, Yves. *The French Face of Joseph Conrad.* Cambridge: Cambridge Univ. Press, 1990.

Hinde, Sidney Langford. *The Fall of the Congo Arabs.* 1897; reprint, New York: Negro Universities Press, 1969.

Hobson, John Atkinson. *Imperialism: A Study.* 3d ed. London: Unwin Hyman, 1988.

Hochschild, Adam. *King Leopold's Ghost.* Boston: Houghton Mifflin, 1998.

———. "Mr. Kurtz, I Presume." *New Yorker,* April 14, 1997, 40–47.

Housman, A.E. *A Shropshire Lad.* Boston: International Pocket Library, 1919.

Humphries, Reynold. "The Discourse of Colonialism: Its Meaning and Relevance for Conrad's Fiction." *Conradiana* 21 (summer 1989): 107–33.

———. "Restraint, Cannibalism and the 'Unspeakable Rites' in *Heart of Darkness.*" *L'Epoque Conradienne* (Limoges) (1990): 51–78.

Hunter, Allan. *Joseph Conrad and the Ethics of Darwinism.* London: Croom Helm, 1983.

Huxley, Elspeth. *Livingstone and His African Journeys.* New York: Saturday Review Press, 1974.

Hyam, Ronald. *Britain's Imperial Century, 1815–1915: A Study of Empire and Expansion.* London: B.T. Batsford, 1976.

Ibsen, Henrik. *The Wild Duck.* In *Modern Drama,* ed. Anthony Caputi, 1-74. New York: Norton, 1966.

Jameson, James S. *The Story of the Rear Column of the Emin Pasha Relief Expedition.* New York: Negro Universities Press, 1969.

JanMohamed, Abdul R. "The Economy of Manichean Allegory: The Function of Racial Difference in Colonialist Literature." In *"Race," Writing, and Difference,* ed. Henry Louis Gates, 78-106. Chicago: Chicago Univ. Press, 1986.

Jean-Aubry, Gérard. *Joseph Conrad: Life and Letters.* 2 vols. Garden City, N.Y.: Doubleday, Page, 1927.

———. *Joseph Conrad in the Congo.* London: *Bookman's Journal* Office, 1926.

Joffe, Phil. "Africa and Joseph Conrad's *Heart of Darkness*: The 'bloody racist'(?) as Demystifier of Imperialism." In *Conrad: Eastern and Western Perspectives,* vol. 1, *Conrad's Literary Career,* ed. Keith Carabine, Owen Knowles, and Wieslaw Krajka. 75–90. Boulder: East European Monographs, 1992.

Johnston, Sir Harry Hamilton. *George Grenfell and the Congo*. 2 vols. New York: D. Appleton, 1910.

————. *A History of the Colonization of Africa by Alien Races*. Cambridge: Cambridge Univ. Press, 1899.

————. "Introductory." In Morel, *Red Rubber*.

————. *The River Congo: From the Mouth to Bólóbó*. 3d ed. London: Sampson, Low, Marston, Searle, and Rivington, 1884.

————. *The Story of My Life*. Indianapolis: Bobbs-Merrill, 1923.

Jonassohn, Kurt, and Frank Chalk. "A Typology of Genocide and Some Implications for the Human Rights Agenda." In *Genocide and the Modern Age*, ed. Isidor Wallimann and Michael Dobkowski, 3-20. New York: Greenwood Press, 1987.

Karl, Frederick R. *Joseph Conrad: The Three Lives*. New York: Farrar, Straus, and Giroux, 1979.

————. *A Reader's Guide to Joseph Conrad*. New York: Noonday Press, 1965.

Kidd, Benjamin. *The Control of the Tropics*. New York: Macmillan, 1898.

Kiernan, Victor Gordon. *The Lords of Human Kind: European Attitudes towards the Outside World in the Imperial Age*. London: Weidenfeld and Nicolson, 1969.

Knowles, Owen. *A Conrad Chronology*. Boston: G.K. Hall, 1990.

Knox-Shaw, Peter. *The Explorer in English Fiction*. New York: St. Martin's Press, 1986.

Kuesgen, Reinhard. "Conrad and Achebe: Aspects of the Novel." *World Literature Written in English* 24 (summer 1984): 27–33.

Kuper, Adam. *The Invention of Primitive Society: Transformations of an Illusion*. London: Routledge, 1988.

Kuper, Leo. "Theoretical Issues Relating to Genocide: Uses and Abuses." In Andreopoulos, 31-46.

Lagercrantz, Olof. *Färd med Mörkrets Hjärta*. Helsingborg, Sweden: Wahlström & Widstrand, 1987.

Leavis, F.R. *The Great Tradition*. London: Chatto and Windus, 1962.

Lee, Robert F. *Conrad's Colonialism*. The Hague: Mouton, 1969.

Lenz, Oscar. "Oesterreichische Congo-Expedition." *Mittheilungen der Kaiserlich-Königlichen Geographischen Gesellschaft* 29 (1886): 26–41, 102–9, 141–55, 257–67, 337–52, 417–24.

Lester, John. "Captain Rom: Another Source for Kurtz." *Conradiana* 14 (1982): 112.

Levenson, Michael. "The Value of Facts in the *Heart of Darkness*." In *Heart of Darkness*, ed. Robert Kimbrough, 391-405. New York: Norton, 1988.

Lévy-Bruhl, Lucien. *How Natives Think*. New York: Washington Square Press, 1966.

Liebrechts, Charles. *Souvenirs de l'Afrique: Congo, Bolobo, Léopoldville, Equateur (1883–1889)*. Brussels: J. Lebèque, [1909].

Lindquist, Sven. *"Exterminate All the Brutes."* Trans. by Jean Tate. New York: New Press, 1996.

London, Bette. "Reading Race and Gender in Conrad's Dark Continent." *Criticism* 31 (summer 1989): 235–52.

Lopasic, Aleksander. *Commissaire General Dragutin Lerman, 1863–1918*. Tervuren: Musée Royal de l'Afrique Centrale, 1971.

Louis, William Roger. "Roger Casement and the Congo." *Journal of African History* 5 (1964): 99–120.

Lütken, Otto. "Joseph Conrad in the Congo." *London Mercury* 22 (May–Oct. 1930): 40–43.

Mahood, Molly M. *The Colonial Encounter: A Reading of Six Novels*. Totowa, N.J.: Rowman and Littlefield, 1977.

Marchal, Jules. *L'Etat Libre du Congo: Paradis Perdu. L'Histoire du Congo, 1876–1900*. 2 vols. Borgloon, Belgium: Editions Paula Bellings, 1996.

Marryat, Frederick. *Mr. Midshipman Easy*. Vol. 6 of *The Novels of Captain Marryat*. London: Phoenix Book Co., n.d.

Mason, David. *Race and Ethnicity in Modern Britain*. Oxford: Oxford Univ. Press, 1995.

Massoz, Michel. *Le Congo de Léopold II (1878–1908)*. Liège: Michel Massoz, [1989].

Masui, Theodore. *Guide de la section de L'Etat Indépendant du Congo à la Exposition de Bruxelles-Terveuren en 1897*. Brussels: Imprimerie Veuve Monnom, 1897.

McLynn, Frank. *Hearts of Darkness: The European Exploration of Africa*. London: Hutchinson, 1992.

Mencken, H.L. *A Mencken Chrestomachy*. New York: Knopf, 1949.

Metchnikoff, Léon. *La Civilisation et les grands fleuves historiques*. Paris: Hachette, 1889.

Meyer, Bernard C. *Joseph Conrad: A Psychoanalytic Biography*. Princeton, N.J.: Princeton Univ. Press, 1967.

Meyer, Michael. *Ibsen*. Harmondsworth, Eng.: Penguin, 1971.

Meyers, Jeffrey. *Fiction and the Colonial Experience*. Totowa, N.J.: Rowman and Littlefield, [1973].

———. *Joseph Conrad*. New York: Scribner's, 1991.

Miller, Christopher. *Blank Darkness: Africanist Discourse in French*. Chicago: Univ. of Chicago Press, 1985.

Miller, J. Hillis. "*Heart of Darkness* Revisited." In Conrad, *Heart of Darkness*, ed. Ross C. Murfin, 206-20.

Moloney, Joseph A. *With Captain Stairs to Katanga*. London: Sampson, 1893.

Moravia, Alberto. *Which Tribe Do You Belong To?* London: Secker and Warburg, 1974.

Morel, Edmund D. *History of the Congo Reform Movement*. Ed. Roger Louis and Jean Stengers. Oxford: Clarendon Press, 1968.

———. *King Leopold's Rule in Africa*. London: Heinemann, 1904.

———. *Red Rubber*. London: T. Fisher Unwin, 1906.

Moser, Thomas. *Joseph Conrad: Achievement and Decline*. 1957. Reprint. Hamden: Archon Books, 1966.

Mosse, George. *Toward the Final Solution: A History of European Racism*. New York: Howard Fertig, 1978.

Murdoch, Iris. *A Severed Head*. New York: Viking Press, 1963.

Murray, Gilbert. "The Exploitation of Inferior Races in Ancient and Modern Times." In *Liberalism and the Empire*, au. Francis Wrigley Hirst, Gilbert Murray, and John Laurence Hammonds, 118-57. London: R. Brimley Johnson, 1900.

Najder, Zdzislaw. *Joseph Conrad*. New Brunswick, N.J.: Rutgers Univ. Press, 1983.

————, ed. *Conrad under Familial Eyes*. Cambridge: Cambridge Univ. Press, 1983.

Nelson, Samuel H. *Colonialism in the Congo Basin, 1880–1940*. Africa Series 64. Athens: Ohio Univ. Center for International Studies, 1994.

Nicoll, David J. *Stanley's Exploits; Or, Civilizing Africa*. Aberdeen, Scotland: James Leatham, 1890.

Nietzsche, Friedrich. *The Birth of Tragedy* and *The Genealogy of Morals*. Garden City, N.Y.: Doubleday, 1956.

Nordau, Max. "Rabies Africana, and the Degeneracy of Europeans in Africa." *The Asiatic Quarterly Review*, n.s., 2 (July-October 1891): 68–77.

North, Michael. *The Dialect of Modernism: Race, Language, and Twentieth-Century Literature*. New York: Oxford, 1994.

O'Brien, Conor Cruise. *To Katanga and Back: A U. N. Case History*. London: Hutchinson, 1962.

Oliver, Roland, and George Neville Sanderson, eds. *The Cambridge History of Africa*. Vol. 6. Cambridge: Cambridge Univ. Press, 1985.

Orwell, George. *The Collected Essays, Journalism, and Letters*. Vol. 1. San Diego: Harcourt Brace Jovanovich, 1968.

Park, Mungo. *Travels*. Ed. Ronald Miller. London: J.M. Dent, 1960.

Parry, Benita. *Conrad and Imperialism: Ideological Boundaries and Visionary Frontiers*. London: Macmillan, 1983.

Peabody, Dean. *National Characteristics*. Cambridge: Cambridge Univ. Press, 1985.

Pinian, Bernard. *Congo-Zaire, 1874–1981: La perception du lointain*. Paris: Editions l'Harmattan, 1992.

Pinker, Steve. *The Language Instinct: How the Mind Creates Language*. New York: Harper Perennial, 1995.

Poliakov, Léon. *The Aryan Myth: A History of Racist and Nationalist Ideas in Europe*. New York: NAL, 1977.

Ranum, Orest. "Counter-Identities of Western European Nations in the Early- Modern Period: Definitions and Points of Departure." In *Concepts of National Identity: An Interdisciplinary Dialogue*, ed. Peter Boerner, 63-78. Baden-Baden: Nomos, 1986.

Raskin, Jonah. "Imperialism: Conrad's *Heart of Darkness*." *Journal of Contemporary History* 2 (April 1967): 113–31.

Reade, W. Winwood. *Savage Africa*. New York: Harper, 1864.

Reeves, Frank. *British Racial Discourse*. Cambridge: Cambridge Univ. Press, 1983.

Reid, Stephen A., "The 'Unspeakable Rites' in *Heart of Darkness*." In *Conrad: A Collection of Critical Essays*, ed. Marvin Mudrick, 45-54. Englewood Cliffs, N.J.: Prentice Hall, 1966.

Ridley, Hugh. *Images of Imperial Rule*. London: Croom Helm, 1983.

Robertson, Peter John M. "*Things Fall Apart* and *Heart of Darkness*: A Creative Dialogue." *International Fiction Review* 7 (1980): 106–11.

Robinson, Ronald, John Gallagher, and Alice Denny. *Africa and the Victorians: The Official Mind of Imperialism.* 2d ed. London: Macmillan, 1983.

Ross, Robert, ed. *Racism and Colonialism.* The Hague: Martinus Nijhoff Publishers, 1982.

Rossetti, Carlo. "B. Malinowski, the Sociology of 'Modern Problems' in Africa and the 'Colonial Situation.'" *Cahiers d'Etudes Africaines* 100 (1985): 477-503.

Rotberg, Robert I. "Joseph Thomson: Energy, Humanism, and Imperialism." In *Africa and Its Explorers: Motives, Methods, and Impact,* ed. Robert I. Rotberg., 295-320. Cambridge, Mass.: Harvard Univ. Press, 1970.

Rubenstein, Richard. "Afterword: Genocide and Civilization." In *Genocide and the Modern Age,* ed. Isidor Wallimann and Michael Dobkowski, 283-98. New York: Greenwood Press, 1987.

Rummel, Rudolph Johnson. *Death by Government.* New Brunswick, N.J.: Transaction, 1994.

Russell, Robert Howard. "Glave's Last Letter and His Death" *Century Magazine* 54 (May–Oct. 1897): 796–98.

[Russell, Robert Howard]. "Glave's Career." *Century Magazine* 50 (May–Oct. 1895): 865–68.

Ryder, Alan Frederick Charles. *Benin and the Europeans, 1485–1897.* New York: Humanities Press, 1969.

Said, Edward. *Culture and Imperialism.* London: Chatto and Windus, 1993.

——. *Joseph Conrad and the Fiction of Autobiography.* Cambridge, Mass.: Harvard Univ. Press, 1966.

——. *Orientalism.* New York: Pantheon Books, 1978.

Salmon, Pierre, ed. *Le Voyage de Van Kerckhoven aux Stanley Falls et au Camp de Yambuya (1888).* Brussels: Académie Royale des Sciences d'Outre-Mer, 1978.

——. ed. *Documents inédits de Louis Haneuse, resident aux Stanley Falls (décembre 1888–février 1889).* Brussels: Académie Royale des Sciences d'Outre-Mer, 1988.

Salusbury, Philip H.B. "The Congo State: A Revelation." *United Service Magazine,* New Series 13 (1896), 314-30.

——. "Defenders of the Congo State." *United Service Magazine,* New Series 13 (1896), 420-48.

——. "The Murder of Mr. Stokes." *United Service Magazine,* New Series 13 (1896), 449-60.

Sarvan, C.P. "Racism and the *Heart of Darkness.*" In Conrad, *Heart of Darkness,* ed. Kimbrough 280–85.

Schweitzer, Albert. *On the Edge of the Primeval Forest.* Trans. C.T. Campion. London: A. and C. Black, 1924.

Semmel, Bernard. *Imperialism and Social Reform: English Social-Imperial Thought, 1895–1914.* Cambridge, Mass.: Harvard Univ. Press, 1960.

Sherry, Norman. *Conrad and His World.* London: Thames and Hudson, 1972.

——. *Conrad's Western World.* Cambridge: Cambridge Univ. Press, 1971.

Shipman, Pat. *The Evolution of Racism.* New York: Simon and Schuster, 1994.

Singh, Frances B. "The Colonialistic Bias of *Heart of Darkness*." In Conrad, *Heart of Darkness,* ed. Kimbrough 268–80.

Slade, Ruth. *King Leopold's Congo: Aspects of the Development of Race Relations in the Congo Independent State.* London: Oxford Univ. Press, 1962.

Smith, Roger W., "Human Destructiveness and Politics: The Twentieth Century as an Age of Genocide." In *Genocide and the Modern Age,* ed. Isidor Wallimann and Michael Dobkowski, 21-40. New York: Greenwood Press, 1987.

Spiering, M[enno]. *Englishness: Foreigners and Images of National Identity in Post-war Literature.* Amsterdam: Rodopi, 1992.

Spittles, Brian. *Joseph Conrad: Text and Context.* New York: St. Martin's Press, 1992.

Stanley, Henry Morgan. "Captain Salusbury's Congo 'Revelations.'" *United Service Magazine,* New Series 13 (1896), 645-52.

———. *The Congo and the Founding of Its Free State.* 2 vols. New York: Harper and Brothers, 1885.

———. "Slavery and the Slave Trade in Africa," *Harper's Magazine,* March 1893, 613–32.

———. "The Story of the Development of Africa," *Century Magazine* 29 (1895): 500–509.

———. *Through the Dark Continent.* New York: Dover, 1988.

———. "Twenty-Five Years' Progress in Equatorial Africa." *Atlantic Monthly* 80 (1897), 470–84.

Stengers, Jean. "King Leopold's Congo, 1886–1908: In Europe." In *The Cambridge History of Africa,* vol. 6, ed. Roland Oliver and George Neville Sanderson, 315-27. Cambridge: Cambridge Univ. Press, 1985.

———. "Sur l'Aventure congolaise de Joseph Conrad." *Bulletin des Séances de l'Academie des Sciences d'Outre-Mer* (1971): 74–61.

Stewart, John Innis Mackintosh. *Joseph Conrad.* London: Longmans, 1968.

Stokes, Eric. "Late Nineteenth-Century Colonial Expansion and the Attack on the Theory of Economic Imperialism: A Case of Mistaken Identity?" *Historical Journal* 12, no. 2 (1969): 285–301.

Street, Brian V. *The Savage in Literature.* London: Routledge and Kegan Paul, 1975.

Tennant, Roger. *Joseph Conrad.* New York: Athenaeum, 1981.

Thompson, Thomas W., *James Anthony Froude on Nation and Empire: A Study in Victorian Racism.* New York: Garland, 1987.

Thorburn, David. *Conrad's Romanticism.* New Haven, Conn.: Yale Univ. Press, 1974.

Tiffin, Helen. "Colonialist Pretexts and Rites of Reply." *Yearbook of English Studies* 27 (1997): 219–33.

Tisdel, W.P. "'The Realm of Congo.'" *Century Magazine* 39 (November 1889–April 1890), 609–18.

Todorov, Tzvetan. "Knowledge in the Void: *Heart of Darkness.*" *Conradiana* 21 (autumn 1989): 161–72.

———. "'Race,' Writing, and Culture." In *'Race,' Writing, and Difference,* ed. Henry Louis Gates, 370-80. Chicago: Univ. of Chicago Press, 1986.

Torday, Emil. *Camp and Tramp in African Wilds*. London: Seeley, Service, and Co., 1913.

Torgovnick, Marianna. *Gone Primitive: Savage Intellects, Modern Lives*. Chicago: University of Chicago Press, 1991.

Trilling, Lionel. *Beyond Culture*. New York: Viking Press, 1965.

van den Berghe, Pierre L. *The Ethnic Phenomenon*. London: Praeger, 1987.

Vangroenweghe, Daniel. *Du Sang sur les lianes*. Brussels: Didier-Hatier, 1986.

Vansina, Jan. "King Leopold's Congo, 1886–1908: Occupation and Administration of the State." In *The Cambridge History of Africa*, vol. 6, ed. Roland Oliver and George Neville Sanderson, 327-58. Cambridge: Cambridge Univ. Press, 1985.

———. *The Tio Kingdom of the Middle Congo, 1880-1892*. London: Oxford Univ. Press, 1973.

Verleun, Jan. "Marlow and the Harlequin." *Conradiana* 13 (1981): 195–220.

Wallace, Alfred Russel. *The Wonderful Century: Its Successes and Failures*. London: Swan, Sonneschein, and Co., 1898.

Ward, Herbert. *Five Years with the Congo Cannibals*. 3d ed. 1891; reprint, New York: Negro Universities Press, 1961.

———. "Life Among the Congo Savages." *Scribner's Magazine* 7 (February 1890), 135–56.

———. *A Voice from the Congo*. New York: Scribner's, 1910.

Watson, George. *The English Ideology: Studies in the Language of Victorian Politics*. London: Allen Lane, 1973.

Watt, Ian. *Conrad in the Nineteenth Century*. Berkeley: Univ. of California Press, 1979.

———. "Conrad's *Heart of Darkness* and the Critics." *North Dakota Quarterly* 57 (summer 1989): 5–15

Watts, Cedric. "'A Bloody Racist': About Achebe's View of Conrad." *Yearbook of English Studies* 13 (1983): 196–209.

———. *The Deceptive Text: An Introduction to Covert Plots*. Brighton, Great Britain: Harvester Press, 1984.

———. *A Preface to Conrad*. London: Longmans, 1982.

Waugh, Evelyn. *Remote People*. London: Duckworth, 1985.

Wauters, Alphonse Jules. *Bibliographie du Congo, 1880–1895*. Brussels: Administration du Mouvement Géographique, 1895.

Wells, H.G. *The Outline of History*. 2 vols. Garden City, N.Y.: Garden City Books, 1961.

Werner, John Reinhardt. *A Visit to Stanley's Rear-Guard*. Edinburgh: William Blackwood and Sons, 1889.

White, Andrea. "Conrad and Imperialism." In *The Cambridge Companion to Joseph Conrad,* ed. John Henry Stape, 179–202. Cambridge: Cambridge Univ. Press, 1996.

———. *Joseph Conrad and the Adventure Tradition: Constructing and Deconstructing the Imperial Subject*. Cambridge: Cambridge Univ. Press, 1993.

Williams, George Washington. "A Report upon the Congo-State and Country to the President of the Republic of the United States of America." In Conrad, *Heart of Darkness*, ed. Kimbrough, 84–97.

Wissmann, Hermann von. *Im Innern Afrikas*. Leipzig: Brockhaus, 1891.

———. *My Second Journey through Equatorial Africa from the Congo to the Zambesi*. London: Chatto and Windus, 1891.

Zins, Henryk. *Joseph Conrad and Africa*. Nairobi: Kenya Literature Bureau, 1982.

INDEX

Achebe, Chinua: on Africa as Other,
23, 24, 44, 203 n 25, 205 n 32; on
Africa in *HD,* 20–25, 44, 204 n
28; and Africa's lack of history,
204–5 n 30; and Amazon figure,
114; on cannibalism in *HD, 59;*
on Congo vs Thames rivers 45,
46; on Conrad's dehumanizing
Africans, 34, 110, 198 n 3; on
Conrad's denial of language to
Africans, 41, 57, 58, 59; on
Conrad's lack of sympathy for
African suffering, 46; on Conrad's
neglect of Fang art, 42, 43; on
Conrad's obsession with blackness
and "niggers," 37, 210 n 9; on
Conrad's refusal to recognize
brotherhood of Africans, 43, 45,
48, 49, 52; and inattention to text
of *HD,* 204 n 28; and incomplete
quotations from *HD,* 44, 49, 50;
on Kurtz, 23, 119; on racism in
HD, 3, 4, 37, 44, 45, 202 n 21;
and responses to his critique of
Conrad, 24, 43; on Schweitzer, 24,
46, 47, 52, 203 n 26; on skulls in
African rituals, 113; and *Things
Fall Apart* and *HD,* 51, 54, 55,
113. *See also* racism
Adelman, Gary: on Kidd and genocide,
152, 153
Africa: animality of, 33; benefits of
imperialism in, 219 n 13; cannibalism in, 217 n 4; as Other, 44;
symbolic function of, 20; traditional display of skulls in, 224–25
n 7. *See also* Africans
Africans: aesthetic gifts of, 201 n 19;
and Belgians, 116; and blood-
brotherhood, 203–4 n 26; history
of, 204 n 30; humanity of, 34, 35,
39, 40, 45, 113, 114, 138, 153,
198 n 3; 203 n 26; 219 n 13; 234
n 6; languages of, 41; negative
depiction of, in *HD,* 113, 114,
115, 116, 225 n 8; as "niggers,"
37; nineteenth century scientific
conceptions of, 33; place of, 119,
120; restraint of, 216 n 3;
sexuality of, 223–24 n 3; stereotypical conceptions of, 205 n 32;
and "unspeakable rites," 117–21
Almayer's Folly: Arabs in, 146; Dain
in, 201 n 15; ethic of sacrifice in,
102; and Kurtz, 84, 85; near loss
of manuscript of, 32; progress in,
221 n 21; races present in, 6;
sexuality in, 125
Amazon character: as aristocrat, 124;
and Dido, 25, 197 n 8; and female
armed force in Dahomey, 25, 196
n 7; and Haggard's fiction, 228 n
18; image of in *HD,* 25, 124;
JanMohamed on, 116; literary
models for, 223 n 3; as mistress of
Kurtz, 41, 114, 223 n 3; and

and detribalization, 85, 86, 117, 119, 120; different manifestations of, 20, 72, 73, 81–90, 108, 216 n 1; ethnicity of, 68, 82, 107, 110; as failure, 216 n 28; as Faust, 26, 215 n 24; and "gang of virtue," 206 n 35, 219 n 15, 227 n 14; and genocide, 83–84, 111, 114, 152–54; and Glave, 136–47; and Hodister, 66, 67, 209 nn 7, 8; and homosexuality, 126; and "horror," 79, 215 n 26; and Intended, 228 n 21; as journalist, 69; as kinetic character, 77, 78; literary sources for, 69; and Livingstone, 77, 215 n 23; and Marlow, 74, 76, 80, 210 n 10; "method" of, 144–45; models for, 65–69, 209 nn 6, 8, 210 n 10, 211 n 11; and restraint, 84, 120, 234, n 7; salvation of, 197 n 10; sanity of, 88, 89, 216 n 1; and significance of name, 75, 107, 209 n 6, 214 nn 19, 20; and Stanley, 212 n 14, 215 n 23; status of, 77–78, 108, 110, 119; as symbolic, 67, 68, 110 215 n 25, 215 n 25; as unrepresentative, 9, 62, 190–91, 218 n 9; villainy of, 130

language: and Conrad, 200 n 12; in "Amy Foster," 207 n 39; and exploration, 56, 57, 207 n 38; in HD, 41, 56, 207 n 38; vs. meaning, 56, 58, 59, 202 n 20; and modernism, 207 n 43; in "Outpost," 56, 60
Leavis, F.R., 31, 117
Lemkin, Raphael, 149
Leopold II, King of the Belgians: achievements of, 81; and atrocities, 81, 98, 100, 116, 143, 156–60; British protests against, 143; and destruction of Congo Free State records, 235 n 12; and

finances of Congo Free State, 142, 144; in Inheritors, 196 n 3, 206 n 35; "system" in Congo Free State, 141–45, 157, 159, 231 n 12
Leopoldville, 198 n 2
Levenson, Michael, 69
Lévy-Bruhl, Lucien, 51, 52
Lindqvist, Sven: and genocide, 13, 155–56; on atrocities in Congo Free State, 128, 129, 131; on HD, 128, 130, 154
Lindsay, Vachel, 81
Livingstone, David, 57, 77, 200 n 13, 215 n 23
Lord Jim: and Arabs, 231 n 14; Dain Waris in, 201 n 15; definition of crime in, 227 n 16; delayed decoding in, 199 n 9; German characters in, 7, 56; imperialism in, 92, 93; and Kurtz, 84, 85; sacrifice in, 102, 103; sexuality in, 125; and tourism, 7
Lubbock, Sir John, 252

Mahood, Molly, 115, 130, 131, 155
Maine, Sir Henry, 51
Malinowski, Bronislaw, 52–54, 109
Marchal, Jules, 97, 158, 159
Marlow: and Buddhism, 36; and Conrad, 79, 113; and cultural relativism, 117, 206 n 34; different manifestations of, 20, 36; and Faust, 27; and "gang of virtue," 219 n 15, 227 n 14; and genocide, 156; and Glave, 133–36, 138–40; and imperialism, 95, 99–101; and Kurtz, 76–82, 86, 163, 201 n 18, 214 n 18, 227 n 15; lies of, 74, 75, 163–65, 235 n 15; narrative function of, 22, 23, 72, 73, 215 n 27; and psychology, 57; and seeing vs. hearing, 78, 79
Marryat, Captain Frederick, 201 n 15
Mason, David, 8, 12

DATE DUE

GAYLORD   #3523PI   Printed in USA